Praise for
American Negotiating Beh

"American Negotiating Behavior *is a truly unique study of the American negotiator because it explores the foreign perception of American negotiators."*
—**Zbigniew Brzezinski,** Counselor and Trustee, Center for Strategic and International Studies

"Diplomacy has never been more vital for Americans than in our increasingly globalized twenty-first century. Richard Solomon and Nigel Quinney have written a fascinating and perceptive book on how American diplomats have succeeded, and sometimes failed, to advance our national interests at the international negotiating table. This timely study provides important lessons and insights into how Americans might wrangle, barter, deal, and ultimately negotiate more effectively with friends and foes alike in the future."
—**Nicholas Burns,** professor of the practice of diplomacy and international politics, Harvard University and former U.S. Under Secretary of State

"This book is a gold mine for anyone interested in American negotiation styles and methods, analyzed by two perceptive co-authors and several experienced international practitioners of diplomacy. One of the many merits of the book is that it sets out the parameters for future diplomacy, adapted to a world where dialogue and negotiations will, one hopes, be the primary tools for solving conflicts and global problems."
—**Jan Eliasson,** former Minister for Foreign Affairs of Sweden and former President of the United Nations General Assembly

"Of great importance, this book hammers home a central point little understood outside the diplomatic profession: critical negotiations actually take place more inside nations than between them. The narrative and analyses presented by Richard Solomon and Nigel Quinney are rich in previously untold stories."
—**Leslie H. Gelb,** former *New York Times* columnist and former president of the Council on Foreign Relations

"American Negotiating Behavior *may well become the definitive primer on the art of effective cross-cultural negotiating. It should be an important part of the education of U.S. diplomats, as well as anyone engaged in international transactions."*
—**Henry A. Kissinger,** U.S. Secretary of State, 1973–1977

"A gold mine of useful information and ideas that can help make American negotiators—and their counterparts—more effective and the process of negotiations better understood."
—**George P. Shultz,** U.S. Secretary of State, 1982–1989

American Negotiating Behavior

"Know your adversary, know yourself;
in a hundred battles, a hundred victories."
—Sun Tzu

American Negotiating Behavior

*Wheeler-Dealers, Legal Eagles,
Bullies, and Preachers*

Richard H. Solomon *and* Nigel Quinney

UNITED STATES INSTITUTE OF PEACE
WASHINGTON, D.C.

The views expressed in this book are those of the authors alone. They do not necessarily reflect views of the United States Institute of Peace.

UNITED STATES INSTITUTE OF PEACE
2301 Constitution Avenue, NW
Washington, DC 20037
www.usip.org

First published 2010. Second printing 2011.

Printed in the United States of America

The paper used in this publication meets the minimum requirements of American National Standards for Information Science—Permanence of Paper for Printed Library Materials, ANSI Z39.48-1984.

Library of Congress Cataloging-in-Publication Data

American negotiating behavior : wheeler-dealers, legal eagles, bullies, and preachers / [edited by] Richard H. Solomon and Nigel Quinney.
    p. cm.
    Includes bibliographical references and index.
    ISBN 978-1-60127-047-4 (pbk.: alk. paper)—ISBN 978-1-60127-048-1 (cloth) eISBN 978-1-60127-094-8
    1. Diplomatic negotiations in international disputes—Case studies.
2. Negotiation—United States.   3. United States—Foreign relations.
I. Solomon, Richard H., 1937–   II. Quinney, Nigel.
    JZ6045.A44 2009
    327.73—dc22

2009039068

Contents

Foreword

Madeleine K. Albright
U.S. Secretary of State, 1997–2001

This timely volume about the negotiating behavior of U.S. diplomats brings to mind a story about one archetypical American—Ulysses S. Grant. When still a boy of eight, Grant was sent by his father to buy a horse from a neighbor. Upon reaching the neighbor's house, Grant burst out: "Papa says I may offer you twenty dollars for the colt, but if you don't take that, I am to offer you twenty-two-and-a-half, and if you don't take that, to give you twenty-five." Grant notes, in his autobiography, that the story "caused me great heart-burning [when it] . . . got out among the boys in the village and it was a long time before I heard the last of it."

This tale, simple as it may be, incorporates several useful lessons about bargaining—including the value of patience, the importance of leverage, and the wisdom of concealing one's bottom line.

Like diplomacy, of which it is a core element, negotiation is an art. As such, it demands both careful preparation and a certain measure of inherent skill. In the context of American foreign policy, negotiation is among the essential tools used to advance the interests of the United States. Its purpose is to persuade foreign governments to act in a manner that is helpful to us, or at least acceptable, and to do so in a binding and enforceable way.

Men and women negotiating on behalf of the United States enjoy certain built-in advantages, including the power of our military, the size of our economy, and the historic political influence of our nation. However, they also have to navigate the minefields of our democratic system, which exposes them to intense pressure from Congress and private interest groups, as well as nonstop scrutiny from the media. At every turn, they are asked to explain their strategy, disclose the status of talks, speculate about the outcome, and characterize the attitude of their negotiating partners. The day has long since passed when major international agreements could be reached behind closed doors and then remain secret for years.

Preparatory to any bargaining, U.S. diplomats must negotiate with competing power centers within our own government. The diplomats' purpose will be to secure as many chips and as much independent authority as possible. At the same time, they will try to determine the strategy of each of the foreign parties involved in the negotiation in order to discern the line between what those parties are certain to demand and what they can be made to accept. When discussions begin, our diplomats will often try to take charge of the process by defining the terms, outlining the issues, and proposing a timeline for making decisions. In so doing, they may adopt the tactful approach favored by one early ambassador, Benjamin Franklin, who was careful not to contradict anyone but instead quietly asked questions and raised doubts; or they might prefer a more dramatic style—storming around, threatening to call in the press, assigning blame for failure. In either case, they would be well advised to seek an outcome that will enable all participants to claim at least partial victory. This will inevitably involve the creative use of words, but an agreement that can be welcomed by all sides is more likely to endure than a settlement that is transparently a triumph for one and a defeat for the other.

To some Americans, negotiating is inherently a sign of weakness. The truly strong, it is thought, do not need to talk; they just flex their muscles and impose their will. In rare cases, this may indeed be our country's only alternative; after all, not every issue has two sides, not every adversary is reasonable, and not every problem is best dealt with through discussion. More often, however, diplomacy will prove a valuable instrument for creating change in the existing order, whether by formalizing new friendships, creating a consensus on matters that have been in dispute, or originating rules to keep pace with the rush of events.

Given this reality, it is in America's best interest to ensure that its negotiators have the fullest possible backing when they sit down at the bargaining table, whether the issue at hand involves nuclear security, economic fairness, energy, the environment, or modifications in international law. We may all be thankful that far more issues of public policy are settled peacefully than through force of arms. We should be concerned, however, that the amount of resources available for what might generally be described as international diplomatic purposes is only about 1 percent of our federal budget. If we want those who represent and defend our interests to succeed, we should do a far better job of equipping them to do so.

In *American Negotiating Behavior*, Richard H. Solomon and Nigel Quinney provide a wealth of information about the art of negotiation and about its application in the world today. Their focus on how America's diplomatic style is viewed by those with whom we deal around the globe is particularly valuable for scholars, foreign policy analysts, and prospective U.S. negotiators. The United States cannot influence a world that we do not understand, nor can we understand the world if we fail to listen to what our friends, our critics, and—perhaps especially—those who are both our friends *and* our critics have to say.

Foreword

Condoleezza Rice
U.S. Secretary of State, 2005–2009

Transformational Diplomacy

In his memoir *Present at the Creation*, former Secretary of State Dean Acheson portrayed the world confronting the United States at the dawn of the Cold War "as just a bit less formidable than that described in the first chapter of Genesis." In 1946, as more than two million Europeans found themselves starving in the aftermath of World War II, the concern was not whether Eastern Europe would fall to communism; it was whether Western Europe would succumb. In 1946, the communists won a significant number of legislative seats during national elections in France and Italy. In 1947, civil conflicts broke out in Greece and Turkey. The following year, war erupted in the Middle East, and Czechoslovakia fell to a communist coup. And in 1949, roughly five years earlier than anticipated, the Soviet Union detonated a nuclear weapon—just one month before Mao Zedong's Communist Party declared victory in China. In the face of such seemingly insurmountable odds, few might fault Acheson for suggesting that, just as the world had been born from chaos at Creation, the United States was tasked "to create half a world, a free half, out of the same material without blowing the whole to pieces in the process."

Sixty years later, after a nearly bloodless reunification of Germany and the collapse of the Soviet Union, we remember Acheson for his efforts to transform old diplomatic institutions to serve new diplomatic purposes in a struggle that was driven as much by ideology as it was by traditional great power competition. As the Cold War hardened into place, we focused our diplomacy on Europe and parts of Asia. We hired new people. We taught them new languages and gave them new training. We partnered with old adversaries in Germany and Japan and helped them to rebuild their countries. We created new institutions such as NATO and leveraged innovative diplomatic tools such as the Marshall Plan to rebuild a more democratic Europe. Our diplomacy proved instrumental in transforming devastated countries into thriving democratic allies who joined with us for decades in the struggle to defend freedom from the Soviet challenge.

With the end of the Cold War, America again rose to new challenges. In the 1990s, we opened fourteen new embassies in the countries of Central and Eastern Europe, and we repositioned over one hundred of our diplomats to staff them. Our outreach helped newly liberated peoples transform the character of their countries, opening the door to greater freedom and transparency that facilitated their integration into the larger international community. Few observers in the 1950s would have imagined that former members of the Warsaw Pact would attain membership in NATO and an organization like the European Union.

In the aftermath of the September 11, 2001, terrorist attacks, America was confronted with a world challenged by a different kind of threat, one posed by violent extremists seeking to destroy the very ideals and institutions that form the foundation of democracy. The primacy of sovereignty in the modern state system is now challenged by a variety of non-state actors—from transnational corporations to terrorist networks—that have proved capable of exerting influence in ways once thought to be the exclusive domain of the state. The greatest threats to peace today seem to emerge from within states rather than from conflict between them. The fundamental character of regimes now matters more than the international distribution of power.

In this new century, it is impossible to draw neat, clear lines between our security interests, our development efforts, and our democratic ideals—yet that is precisely what the current structure of our foreign policy institutions would have us do. America's diplomacy must instead integrate and advance all of these goals together. That is why in 2006 I directed our diplomats to pursue "transformational diplomacy," with the objective of working with our partners around the world to build and sustain democratic, well-governed states that can respond to the needs of their people and conduct themselves responsibly in the international system. This initiative is rooted in partnership, not paternalism; in doing things *with* these states—not *for* them.

To advance transformational diplomacy, I built on the work of my predecessors to modernize the State Department so that our diplomatic posture would better reflect the realities of the international system in the early twenty-first century. As of 2006, we had nearly the same number of State Department personnel in Germany, a country of 82 million people, as we had in India, a country of 1 billion people. With the support of Congress, President Bush created 2,000 new State Department positions. Over four years, under Secretary Powell and during my tenure, I requested annual budget increases for our international operations totaling $8 billion, a 25 percent increase. I also worked to dramatically increase the number of diplomats we deploy overseas. In President Bush's 2009 budget request we asked Congress to fund 1,100 new positions for the State Department and 300 new positions for USAID. Finally, we worked to shift about one-tenth of our political, economic, and public diplomacy officers to new emerging centers of international power such as China, Brazil, and India.

Simply reallocating our resources, however, will not be enough; our transformational vision requires America's diplomats to localize our presence and be active in new places far beyond the walls of foreign chancelleries and our embassies. It will require them to work with new partners, not just with a nation's government but also with its local leaders, its entrepreneurs, and its NGOs. This effort to modernize our diplomacy will demand much from our foreign service officers and AID workers, who will have to manage greater amounts of risk while serving in some of the most challenging—yet most essential—diplomatic posts in countries such as Iraq, Afghanistan, Sudan, and Angola. These are countries where we are working with foreign citizens in difficult conditions to maintain security, fight poverty, and promote democratic reforms. To succeed in these challenging assignments, our diplomats must be trained not only as experts of policy but also as first-rate administrators of programs, capable of helping foreign citizens strengthen the rule of law, start businesses, improve health, and reform education.

Decades of experience have shown that foreign assistance is most effective when paired with plans for good governance, sustainable growth, and investments in people and institutions that help countries lift themselves permanently out of poverty. It was this logic that spurred the creation of the Millennium Challenge Corporation, which has devoted at least $5.5 billion in development grants to sixteen partner countries. America will also need to forge a stronger partnership between our diplomats and our military. Our goal of fostering country progress will not always be pursued in peaceful places. Without security there can be no development, and without development there can be no democracy. Leading security experts are increasingly thinking about our fight against terrorism as a kind of global counterinsurgency campaign in which the center of gravity of conflict is not just the terrorists themselves, but the populations they seek to influence and radicalize. Our success will depend upon unity of effort between our civilian and military agencies. Our fighting men and women can create opportunities for progress and buy time and space. But it is our diplomats and development professionals who must seize this opportunity to support communities that are striving for democratic values, economic advancement, social justice, and educational opportunity.

Transforming our diplomacy to meet the challenges of the twenty-first century will not be the work of a single secretary of state or presidential administration. It will require the work of a generation. To move beyond the diplomacy of the past, we need to cultivate diplomats of the future. This new cohort of foreign service professionals needs to reflect the rich diversity of America. The past three secretaries of state—the daughter of European immigrants, the son of Jamaican immigrants, and a daughter of the segregated American South—should not be more diverse than the Foreign Service that supported their efforts.

These men and women will not be managing problems; they will be working with partners to solve problems. To enable them to do so, we need to give our diplomats the best technology to liberate them from embassies and offices and let them work anytime, anywhere. We will need to be better at fostering and rewarding creativity, innovation, and independent thinking, especially among our youngest professionals. And we must not only continue to recruit America's best and brightest to our ranks—we must make them even better and even brighter. That means training in languages such as Chinese, Urdu, Arabic, and Farsi, and honing their skills as negotiators in unfamiliar cultures.

In this volume, Richard Solomon and Nigel Quinney tackle a key component of this transformational vision by critically examining American negotiating practices. This work builds on broader efforts by the United States Institute of Peace to enhance the negotiating skills of military and diplomatic personnel through its Cross-Cultural Negotiation project, described in part I of this book. By analyzing how America's diplomats engage with their counterparts across the world, Solomon and Quinney give us valuable insights into the process of negotiation as we seek to transform our diplomatic practice to meet the demands of twenty-first-century foreign policy.

Preface

The Cross-Cultural Negotiation Project and the Origins of This Book

T his study of American negotiating behavior can be seen as the culmina-
tion—but not the conclusion—of a series of assessments of how different
governments manage international negotiations, and of how culture and
institutions influence negotiating practice.

These studies had their origin in the early 1980s. After five years of working
in the U.S. government on the process of normalizing relations with the People's
Republic of China, Richard Solomon undertook an analysis of Chinese negotiating behavior.[1] He was motivated by his experiences supporting National Security
Adviser Henry Kissinger in his negotiations with Chinese officials. Kissinger, a
scholar-official steeped in European history, was impressed by the differences between Chinese diplomatic practices and those of European diplomats and officials
from the Soviet Union. The Chinese cultivated a positive personal relationship
with Kissinger, whom they came to characterize as an "old friend." In China's cultural context, "friendship" implies obligation as much as personal intimacy, and
over time Chinese officials pressured their "old friend" Kissinger to accommodate
to their policy objectives.

Drawing on the China study, in the early 1990s the United States Institute of
Peace initiated a series of both conceptual and country-specific assessments on the
theme of cross-cultural negotiating (CCN) behavior. In addition to the present
volume, twelve book-length studies have since been published. Three of these are
conceptual studies: *Negotiating across Cultures* by Raymond Cohen; *Culture and*

---

1. The declassified portions of the study were published in 1995: Richard H. Solomon, *Chinese Negotiating Behavior: Pursuing Interests through "Old Friends"* (Santa Monica, Calif.: RAND, 1995). A new edition was published
in 1999 by the United States Institute of Peace Press.

Conflict Resolution by Kevin Avruch; and *Arts of Power* by Chas. W. Freeman, Jr.[2] Of the other nine, seven focus on individual countries (China, Russia, North Korea, Japan, France, Germany, and Iran), particularly their behavior in negotiations with the United States, while two explore specific bilateral negotiating relationships (the Israeli-Palestinian and the Indian-Pakistani relationships).[3] Forthcoming books will examine the cases of Pakistan and Egypt, among others. All the country-specific studies have been informed by a set of analytical categories (reproduced in the appendix to this book) intended to facilitate cross-cultural comparisons.[4] A subsequent phase of the CCN project will analyze the significance of cultural differences in specific negotiating behaviors—pressure tactics, incentives, use of language, sense of time, and so forth.

The basic assumptions that underlie the studies in the CCN series are that negotiating is the usual, if not always the preferred, technique of international problem solving, and that greater understanding of the dynamics of negotiating, greater appreciation of the cultural and institutional influences of a counterpart's behavior, and greater self-awareness will help make specific negotiating encounters more productive. This objective of making negotiations more fruitful—and thus preventing, reducing, or eliminating the use of violence to settle political disputes—conforms with the Institute's congressional mandate to promote the peaceful management and resolution of international conflicts.

One finding of the cross-cultural negotiating project is that few governments give their diplomats *explicit* training in negotiating skills. The U.S. Department of State has only recently begun to give Foreign Service officers such training. Interestingly, a significant feature of this training is instruction in the skills needed to negotiate *within* the U.S. bureaucratic system, in the interagency environment

---

2. The first edition of Raymond Cohen's book *Negotiating across Cultures* was written while he was a Jennings Randolph fellow at the United States Institute of Peace. The volume predated the advent of the Institute's CCN project.

3. In addition to Richard Solomon's assessment of China, the country-specific and conceptual studies include the following, all of which have been published by the United States Institute of Peace Press: Kevin Avruch, *Culture and Conflict Resolution* (1998); Michael Blaker, Paul Giarra, and Ezra Vogel, *Case Studies in Japanese Negotiating Behavior* (2005); Charles Cogan, *French Negotiating Behavior: Dealing with La Grande Nation* (2003); Raymond Cohen, *Negotiating across Cultures: International Communication in an Interdependent World* (revised edition, 1997); Chas. W. Freeman, Jr., *Arts of Power: Statecraft and Diplomacy* (1997); Daniel C. Kurtzer and Scott B. Lasensky, *Negotiating Arab-Israeli Peace: American Leadership in the Middle East* (2008); Dennis Kux, ed., *India-Pakistan Negotiations: Is Past Still Prologue?* (2006); John W. Limbert, *Negotiating with Iran: Wrestling the Ghosts of History* (2009); Jerrold L. Schecter, *Russian Negotiating Behavior: Continuity and Transition* (1998); W. R. Smyser, *How Germans Negotiate: Logical Goals, Practical Solutions* (2003); Scott Snyder, *Negotiating on the Edge: North Korean Negotiating Behavior* (1999); and Tamara Cofman Wittes, ed., *How Israelis and Palestinians Negotiate: A Cross-Cultural Analysis of the Oslo Peace Process* (2005).

4. These assessments also assume that a country's negotiating culture, as a reflection of its broader culture, has a measure of internal coherence or thematic organization, especially in fairly homogenous societies. Thus, in the case of China, the management of interpersonal relationships—the cultivation of "old friends"—is an integrating concept that gives coherence to many aspects of negotiating behavior. See Solomon, *Chinese Negotiating Behavior*, esp. 31–44.

that shapes the policy goals pursued in specific negotiating assignments. Indeed, a dominant aspect of American negotiating practice is the preoccupation of individual U.S. officials with building an interagency consensus in support of their own negotiating objectives. If the Chinese official seeks to cultivate a "friendship" with his foreign counterpart to help attain his negotiating objectives, the American official, in the context of his culture and institutions, seeks to impress his counterpart with the need to accommodate to the interagency consensus behind his negotiating brief.

These volumes of the CCN project are used in the Institute's professional training programs. Designed to promote skills in international conflict management for American and non-American officials, both civilian and military, representatives of international organizations, academics, and practitioners from nongovernmental organizations, such training is a major component of Institute work. The volumes have also attracted the interest of foreign audiences (the study of French negotiating behavior, for example, earned its author a prestigious prize from the Institut de France), and this portrait of American negotiators will doubtless be studied by foreign officials as they prepare to negotiate with American counterparts. If enhanced mutual understanding as well as greater self-awareness lead to mutually beneficial negotiated outcomes, then the purposes of the CCN project will be realized.

The Approach of This Book

There is a natural tendency to assume that one's own culture and behavior are "normal" and that foreigners are the ones who are "different." Yet negotiating—bilateral negotiating—is a dyadic process. Each side brings to the table its own conception of how to negotiate, its own cultural biases, behavioral patterns, and institutional imperatives. The ability of American diplomats to recognize these characteristics for what they are, whether to harness their strengths or to avoid their pitfalls, is critical to the continued success of American diplomacy, which is why the Institute initiated this exploration of American negotiating behavior.

The CCN project first turned its spotlight on U.S. negotiating behavior with a workshop held in July 2000, several months before the election of George W. Bush (by chance, the workshop coincided with the Camp David II negotiations) and more than a year before the attacks on the Pentagon and World Trade Center. A second workshop was held in July 2007. Together, the two workshops brought together more than forty seasoned foreign and American diplomats, senior policymakers, and eminent scholars to discuss how American officials negotiate. Another dozen senior practitioners of international negotiating have offered comments on various documents and drafts of this volume.

Most of these individuals are not American. A basic analytic assumption of the CCN project is that it takes the cultural "distance" of a foreign observer to perceive that which is distinctive about a given culture or negotiating style. For this reason, the Institute invited foreign officials who have negotiated directly with American counterparts to describe what American negotiating behavior looks like from their side of the table. These individuals—most of them former ambassadors, foreign ministers, UN envoys, and other high-ranking officials—come from more than thirty different countries and six continents. Some have represented countries that are close allies of the United States, others have served countries whose relationship with the United States has waxed and waned, and still others are from states regarded at one time or another as rivals or even adversaries of the United States. A number have negotiated with the United States on behalf of multilateral organizations, such as the United Nations and the European Union.

One might anticipate this varied cast of foreign officials having equally varied views of American negotiating behavior—after all, the same behavior can be interpreted very differently by different observers from different cultures. In fact, however, something close to consensus prevailed on almost all aspects of American behavior. Different officials sometimes emphasized different traits, but few if any officials disagreed that this or that characteristic existed.

The starting point in drafting this book—which greatly expands upon a report issued after the first workshop[5]—has been to present the collective insights of these foreign officials as they were expressed at one or both workshops. In other words (and this is crucial to understanding this project's methodology), *the view of American negotiating behavior offered in the following chapters is, essentially, the view from the other side of the bargaining table.* This perspective is explicit in part IV of this five-part volume, which consists of chapters written by foreign officials drawing on their firsthand experience negotiating with Americans. In part II, Richard Solomon and Nigel Quinney offer a composite portrait of the American negotiator that, while it incorporates the views of American officials, is essentially a picture painted by foreign officials.

In writing part II, Solomon and Quinney have taken the opinions and experiences expressed in the workshops and arranged them within an overarching analytical framework. The workshops were conducted according to the Chatham House Rule which stipulates that no comments be reported verbatim or attributed to particular individuals. As a consequence, part II contains no direct quotations from the workshops. However, part II does quote from the contributions in part IV, which gives a very good idea of the flavor and content of the two meetings and which underlines the source of the opinions expressed in part II.

Solomon and Quinney have also tested the observations, characterizations, and accounts provided by non-American officials against the experiences and insights

---

5. Nigel Quinney, *U.S. Negotiating Behavior*, Special Report no. 94 (Washington, D.C.: United States Institute of Peace Press, October 2002).

of a dozen U.S. diplomats and policymakers, both serving and retired. Through interviews, meetings, and reviews of earlier drafts of this volume, these American officials were invited to comment on the non-American assessments of how U.S. negotiators behave. Significantly, they agreed with those assessments in almost all respects. Where differences of opinion emerged, they usually involved differences of degree or emphasis, not of substance. (The most marked difference concerns the extent to which American negotiators were characterized as domineering, or "hegemonic"; perhaps not surprisingly, the Americans saw American behavior as more cooperative, less imperious than did the non-Americans.) The American diplomats and policymakers also supplied firsthand examples and behind-the-scenes accounts of particular negotiations.

Several eminent scholars of negotiation practice and history have shared their insights and helped to refine the project's analytical framework. Solomon and Quinney have also mined published accounts by former U.S. officials for insights and examples, as well as other books generated by the CCN project. The latter constitute a substantial database of comparative information about cross-cultural negotiating behavior and provide, among other things, numerous examples of how other countries tackle the challenges of diplomatic negotiation. The typical approach of American officials to some of those challenges might seem unremarkable (at least to American readers) until it is set alongside the very different approaches favored by negotiators from other countries.

This study looks at those officials who set policies and *design* negotiating strategies as well as those who actually conduct negotiations. In any given negotiation, these individuals might include the president and his key foreign policy and national security advisers; the secretary of state and the heads of other interested government agencies; ambassadors posted to foreign capitals and some members of their embassy staffs; ambassadors and other representatives to intergovernmental organizations, such as the United Nations and the North Atlantic Treaty Organization; bureau secretaries, desk officers, and other staff within the State Department; and members of specific negotiating teams, who are likely to be drawn from not only the State Department but also other agencies involved in international affairs, such as the Department of Defense and the Treasury.

One more clarification is in order: this book focuses on *negotiation*, not on *mediation*. Mediation is a form of negotiation—or, to quote Charles Moore, "an extension and elaboration of the negotiation process"[6]—but it is distinct insofar as it involves a third party that seeks to help the parties directly involved in a conflict change their behaviors or perceptions and voluntarily move toward a settlement

---

6. Charles Moore, *The Mediation Process* (San Francisco: Jossey-Bass, 1986), 6. The definition of mediation used here draws on that provided by Jacob Bercovitch in "Mediation in the Most Resistant Cases," in *Grasping the Nettle: Analyzing Cases of Intractable Conflict*, eds. Chester A. Crocker, Fen Osler Hampson, and Pamela Aall (Washington, D.C.: United States Institute of Peace Press, 2005), 107.

or resolution. Rarely does the United States solicit or consent to mediation of disputes to which it is itself a party. By contrast, U.S. officials regularly play the role of mediator in other countries' disputes. When they mediate between others, inevitably they carry over many of the same traits and tactics they use when they negotiate on behalf of their own country. However, mediators need a different skill set than do negotiators, and if U.S. officials are to mediate effectively, they often have to deemphasize some of their usual traits (impatience, pushiness, and insufficient attention to culture and context, for instance) while significantly accentuating others (such as the ability to empathize and creativity in framing questions and issues).

When a mediated conflict affects vital U.S. national interests, American officials are more inclined to mediate like they negotiate; when few U.S. interests are at stake, American officials are more likely to display patience and cultural sensitivity. To avoid conflating mediating behavior with negotiating behavior, this book discusses only those instances of U.S. mediation in which significant U.S. national interests were at stake—for instance, the U.S. initiative in bringing to an end the war in Bosnia in the 1990s. The forward-looking conclusion to this book, however, contends that, whether negotiating or mediating, American officials will find increasing opportunities and increasing reason in coming decades to take the time and the pains to build relationships and find win-win solutions rather than to push hard for quick settlements on purely American terms.

Acknowledgments

The organization and drafting of this volume is substantially the work of Nigel Quinney. Dr. Quinney has long been associated with the cross-cultural negotiating project, having edited almost all the volumes in the CCN series. He was the author of an Institute Special Report that summarized the discussion of a workshop on American negotiating behavior convened in the summer of 2000. He also was the organizer and moving force behind a second workshop that convened international diplomats in the summer of 2007 in support of this project. Dr. Quinney and I have collaborated closely in developing the interpretations and exposition in this volume of American negotiating behavior.

As coauthors, we are especially indebted to the critical inputs and research support to this project provided by Heather Sensibaugh, my special assistant. We also want to acknowledge the contributions from many other staff members of the United States Institute of Peace, past and present, including Pamela Aall, Jon Alterman, Judy Barsalou, Patrick Cronin, April Hall, Kay Hechler, Steven Heydemann, Mike Lekson, Emily Metzgar, Charles Nelson, Valerie Norville, Deepa Ollapally, Steve Riskin, and Taylor Seybolt. Maureen Sullivan deserves our considerable gratitude for her tireless, inventive, and good-humored support, not least in helping to orchestrate the two workshops. The Institute's Publications department provided highly professional and invaluable support throughout the editing, design, and production of this book. Our sincere thanks also go to the president of the Alliance for Peacebuilding, Charles Dambach, who participated in the second workshop, and to his assistants Rachel Okun and Christy Slice for their administrative support. James Gibney was of valuable service in helping us polish the final text.

The two workshops provided the foundations on which this volume is built, and thus we are indebted to the following individuals for attending one or both workshops and sharing with us their considerable expertise, insights, and illuminating experiences: Anatoly Adamishin, Gilles Andreani, L. Paul Bremer, Chan Heng Chee, Tae-Yul Cho, Raymond Cohen, Chester A. Crocker, John de Chastelain,

Alvaro de Soto, Osama El Baz, Abdel Raouf El Reedy, Sa'eb Erekat, Gareth Evans, Yoichi Funabashi, Charles Gillespie, Dore Gold, Jerrold Green, Richard Haass, Lord David Hannay, Karl Kaiser, Masood Khan, Samuel W. Lewis, Faruk Logoglu, John McDonald, Donald McHenry, Lalit Mansingh, Edward Marks, Jagat Mehta, Langhorne Motley, Ahmedou Ould-Abdallah, Steve Pieczenik, Andrew Pierre, Itamar Rabinovich, J. Stapleton Roy, Mohamed Sahnoun, Robert Schulzinger, W. Richard Smyser, Helmut Sonnenfeldt, Marjorie Sonnenfeldt, Serge Sur, Willem van Eekelen, Ezra Vogel, Koji Watanabe, Robin West, Frank G. Wisner, John Wood, Casimir Yost, and Katrine Wong.

In April 2009, we convened a small group of highly experienced American officials to discuss what steps might be taken to enhance the future effectiveness of American negotiators. For their stimulating suggestions (several of which feature in the final chapter in this book), we are indebted to Morton Abramowitz, Chester A. Crocker, Samuel W. Lewis, Ronald Neumann, and W. Richard Smyser.

Several serving and retired American officials graciously consented to be interviewed for this project. They include Charles W. Freeman, Max Kampelman, Patrick Kennedy, Ronald Neumann, Phyllis Oakley, Thomas Pickering, Patrick Spaulding, J. Stapleton Roy, and Ruth Whiteside.

The authors are indebted to the staff members of the U.S. State Department's Ralph J. Bunche Library, including Chief Librarian C. Elaine Cline, for their expert assistance in tracking down various statistics and other data, and to Judes E. Stellingwerf, special assistant to the State Department's under secretary for management, for other research material.

Last but not least, we are grateful for critiques of various drafts of this book by a wide variety of people, many of whom participated in other aspects of this project. They include Pamela Aall, Morton Abramowitz, Peter Ackerman, Chester A. Crocker, James Gibney, Stephen Hadley, Patrick Kennedy, Samuel W. Lewis, Ronald Neumann, Valerie Norville, Norman Ornstein, Steve Pieczenik, W. Richard Smyser, and Anthony Wanis-St. John, as well as three anonymous reviewers.

Richard H. Solomon

Contributors

Nigel Quinney, president of The Editorial Group, is a consultant to European and American think tanks, academic institutions, publishers, and multinational corporations. He has more than twenty years' experience as an editor, writer, and researcher in the fields of international relations and conflict resolution.

Richard H. Solomon, president of the United States Institute of Peace, formerly served in the U.S. government on the National Security Staff, directed the State Department's Policy Planning Staff, and was assistant secretary of state for East Asian and Pacific Affairs and ambassador to the Philippines. He also headed the political science department of the RAND Corporation and was professor of political science at the University of Michigan.

* * *

Gilles Andreani, conseiller maître at the Cour des Comptes, is the former head of the Centre d'analyse et de prévision in the French Foreign Ministry and a former deputy head of the French mission to NATO. Since 2001, he has also taught international relations at Panthéon-Assas Paris II University.

Chan Heng Chee has been ambassador of Singapore to the United States since 1996. She has also served as permanent representative of Singapore to the United Nations and concurrently as high commissioner to Canada and ambassador to Mexico. She was founding director of the Institute of Policy Studies and director of the Institute of Southeast Asian Studies in Singapore.

David Hannay was British ambassador and permanent representative to the European Union from 1985 to 1990 and then to the United Nations from 1990 to 1995. He subsequently served as the British government's special representative for Cyprus and was a member of the UN Secretary-General's High-level Panel on Threats, Challenges and Change in 2003–4.

Faruk Logoglu spent thirty-five years in the Turkish Ministry of Foreign Affairs. He served as the ambassador of Turkey to Denmark, Azerbaijan, and, from 2001 to 2005, the United States. He is also a former undersecretary of the Turkish Foreign Ministry and a former president of the Eurasian Studies Center in Ankara.

Lalit Mansingh has served as India's foreign secretary, ambassador to the United States, and high commissioner to the United Kingdom. In recent years, he has been professor emeritus at the Foreign Service Institute of India and a member of the Executive Committee of the Institute of Peace and Conflict Studies, New Delhi.

Yuri Nazarkin represented the USSR to the Conference on Disarmament, headed the Soviet Union's delegation to the Soviet-American negotiations on strategic weapons that resulted in concluding START-1 (1991), and served as ambassador-at-large for the Soviet Union and the Russian Federation and as deputy secretary of the Security Council of the Russian Federation. He is a professor at the Geneva School (University) of Diplomacy and International Relations.

Robert Schulzinger is College Professor of Distinction of history and international affairs at the University of Colorado, Boulder, and has written widely on the history of U.S. foreign relations. He chaired the U.S. State Department's Advisory Committee on Historical Diplomatic Documentation from 2001 to 2003 and has been a member of the Central Intelligence Agency's Historical Review Panel since 2006.

Koji Watanabe, senior fellow at the Japan Center for International Exchange, served as Japan's deputy minister for foreign affairs, as sherpa for the G-7 summits in 1990 and 1991, and as Japanese cochairman of the U.S.-Japan Structural Impediments Initiative. He has also served as Japan's ambassador to Russia, Italy, and Saudi Arabia.

John Wood, a former deputy secretary of foreign affairs and trade in New Zealand, served two separate terms as ambassador of New Zealand to the United States. He was also New Zealand's ambassador to Iran, Pakistan, and Turkey. He is now pro chancellor of the University of Canterbury.

Part I

Introduction

1

Introduction

How do American officials negotiate? Few writers have previously attempted to explore this question.[1] To be sure, many authors have asked how *specific individuals* have negotiated or how the United States has handled *specific negotiations*, but few have explored how American officials—*as a general proposition*—negotiate.

Such reticence on the part of scholars and diplomats—two groups not famed for their bashfulness—seems curious at first consideration. After all, the United States has been a major world power for more than a century and thus a country of significant, often compelling, interest to most other countries. Moreover, despite loud complaints in recent years that America—as the world's sole superpower—has all but eliminated negotiation from its diplomatic repertoire and relies excessively on its political, economic, and military power to gain its ends by pressure and intimidation, the United States negotiates not just frequently but continually. The global breadth of U.S. interests ensures that its negotiators are always engaged in a multitude of bilateral and multilateral settings.

How, then, to explain the fact that this book, if not blazing a new trail, is certainly exploring a path seldom traveled? The answer has much to do with the deceptively straightforward nature of that succinct question, "How do American officials negotiate?" For all its apparent simplicity, that question is laden with assumptions and riddled with complications. One major assumption is that one can actually discern behavioral and stylistic patterns in an activity as complex and context-dependent as negotiation—a claim that must always be armored in caveats about exceptions if it is not to be immediately shot down with a quiverful of counterexamples. A second and perhaps more forbidding assumption is that Americans negotiate differently than officials from other countries—a notion that goes against the grain in a world conscious of global interconnectedness and sensitive to the dangers

---

1.   See the bibliography toward the end of this book for a list of other literature relevant to American negotiating behavior. See also the helpful annotated bibliography in Michelle LeBaron, "Culture-Based Negotiation Styles," in *Beyond Intractability*, eds. Guy Burgess and Heidi Burgess (Conflict Research Consortium, University of Colorado, Boulder, July 2003), http://www.beyondintractability.org/essay/culture_negotiation/?nid=1187.

of ascribing particular traits to particular peoples. As for the complications, consider the difficulties of trying to identify and tease out a single thread—officials' behavioral patterns—from a negotiating fabric made up of numerous, closely interwoven strands that include the subject of a given negotiation, the personalities of individual negotiators, and the policies and decision-making procedures of the governments involved.

The analytic challenges are, indeed, real and substantial. But so, too, are the potential benefits of acquiring a better understanding of how U.S. policymakers and diplomats manage and conduct negotiations. For American policymakers, a keener understanding of the stylistic traits of U.S. negotiators can be useful because those traits help shape how foreign policies are formulated, implemented, and perceived. Moreover, American officials can use better self-knowledge to hone their craft and effectiveness. To quote the ancient Chinese military strategist Sun Tzu: "Know your adversary, know yourself; in a hundred battles, a hundred victories." Remarkably, American diplomats, until recently, received virtually no formal training in negotiation from the U.S. State Department. Those diplomats who did not acquire negotiating skills in the private sector before they joined the Foreign Service had to rely on observation and mentoring to develop a fundamental skill of their profession.[2] This book may provide another resource to assist in that process. For officials from other countries, a better knowledge of U.S. negotiating behavior can help to avoid misunderstanding and misreading the American side, thereby enhancing the prospects for mutually beneficial outcomes to negotiations.

We wrote this book with these objectives and benefits in mind. Like the other contributors, we recognize the difficulties of grasping so elusive a subject as negotiating behavior, but we also see the *possibility* as well as the advantages of trying to do so. Some academics may raise an eyebrow at the very notion of national negotiating styles, but few seasoned practitioners would share their skepticism. Certainly, the contributors to this volume, like dozens of other experienced diplomats and scholars who participated in the multiyear project from which this book has emerged, believe that American officials bring with them to the negotiating table a set of distinctly American attitudes and behaviors.

The portrait of American negotiating practice that emerges from this volume is a complex one, more complex than one might expect of a preeminent power with a reputation for throwing its weight around in the international arena. That

---

2.   For instance, Ambassador Stapleton Roy, who served as ambassador to three different countries, including China, recalls that he received absolutely no training in negotiation. "You learn from experience," he notes. Stapleton Roy, interview, Washington, D.C., August 11, 2008. Similarly, when asked if he ever had received training in how to negotiate, Ambassador Charles W. Freeman replied: "Formal training, absolutely not." Freeman points out that the United States, unlike many countries, has no diplomatic academy that offers an extensive grounding in a wide range of topics; instead, the State Department offers its diplomats "short courses in things like negotiation, but whether you actually get to take those or not is hit and miss." Charles W. Freeman, interview, Washington, D.C., September 10, 2008.

reputation may be deserved, but it is only part of the story, a story of sometimes conflicting, sometimes complementary American impulses interacting in a world of cultural diversity, varied political influences, and competing national interests.

This volume argues that four distinctive mind-sets or professional perspectives have combined to shape U.S. negotiating behavior: a businessperson's pragmatism and interest in securing concrete results from a negotiation; a lawyer's concern with careful preparation, precision, and binding commitments; a superpower's inclination to dictate terms, adopt take-it-or-leave-it attitudes, and flex its muscle in pursuit of national interests; and a moralizer's sense of mission, self-worth, and inclination to sermonize.

At the heart of American negotiating behavior, ironically, lies a deep ambivalence about negotiation itself. On the one hand, businesslike and legalistic impulses combine to make American officials inclined to sit down and solve problems, reach deals, and negotiate with confidence that both sides can reap concrete and mutual benefits from an agreement. On the other hand, moralistic and hegemonic impulses make U.S. officials reluctant to negotiate with foreigners whose beliefs and behavior go against American mores. Indeed, they may be skeptical of the need to do so given America's substantial economic, political, and military resources.

The relative weight of these four mind-sets varies from negotiation to negotiation and administration to administration. Journalists and historians have often associated specific impulses with specific presidents (and sometimes even with specific political parties). President Jimmy Carter, for instance, has been portrayed as the archetypal moralist, while President George W. Bush has been characterized as exemplifying a unilateralist or hegemonic outlook. Yet, this quartet of impulses transcends political ideology and personal predilection. Foreign diplomats struggling to make headway in negotiations with the United States have been known to look forward to a change in administration, anticipating that a new president and a new political agenda will transform the approach of American negotiators. Their hopes are usually misplaced. They discover that the attitudes, behavior, and temperament of the new team of negotiators are not so dissimilar to those of the old guard. Policies may change abruptly but negotiating behavior usually changes less dramatically, and even when it does shift markedly to give greater prominence to one of the four mind-sets, the change is usually temporary, as the other mind-sets gradually reassert their influence. (For instance, by the his second term in the White House, President George W. Bush's negotiating behavior vis-à-vis North Korea was not so different from that of President Bill Clinton's, which Bush had entered office determined to change.) In short, sometimes one or another tendency predominates; more often, they coexist. The result is a negotiating style that is highly professional but also pushy, informal but also urgent, cordial but also blunt, calculating but also given to sermonizing.

The American negotiating process is also strongly shaped by the nature of the government's political and bureaucratic system, with intense interagency rivalries waged to win the ear of the president—whose authority is considerable yet circumscribed by congressional pressure, which in turn is shaped by public opinion and the influence of private-sector interest groups. The president and Congress are also keenly aware of the electoral cycles that not only usher them into office but also threaten to remove them before they have left their imprint on the nation and its foreign relations. Such a system limits U.S. negotiators' room for maneuver, places them under considerable time pressure, makes them highly dependent on presidential support for high-profile negotiations, and leaves them vulnerable to domestic political criticism. It also gives them, however, leverage with their counterparts, who recognize that when an American negotiator says, "This is the deal that Washington is prepared to offer you—I can't offer any more," the American official is probably telling it like it is.

Shifts in the fluid constellation of bureaucratic or political forces within Washington can swiftly undermine an interagency consensus on the goals of an ongoing negotiation or thrust a recently concluded agreement into the congressional spotlight. As a consequence, American negotiators often find themselves pressured to increase their demands or to call for the renegotiation of a deal already reached with their foreign counterpart. This phenomenon of "moving the goalposts" is not unique to U.S. officials, but it is certainly highly characteristic of American diplomacy.

Another dynamic form of tension also underlies much of the negotiating behavior and institutional context that this book describes, a tension—so fundamental to American culture—between an emphasis on individualism and a paradoxical capacity for team effort. Even as different agencies and lead negotiating officials vie to persuade the president to adopt a particular strategy, members of different agencies often, but not always, come together to implement a negotiating strategy that the president or one of his senior lieutenants ultimately decides to support.

At the risk of offending those foreign diplomats who complain, not without reason, about the American obsession with sporting terminology, one can draw an analogy between this individual-team tension and the sport that seems to embody the cultural dynamic of American society—football. On the sidelines stand the coaches/agencies arguing over the best plays to call and acutely conscious of the clock; on the field is a team of competitive individuals, each determined to outshine other team members. But when a play is finally chosen, the president, the quarterback, directs the rest of the team, which, at his signal, executes a variety of carefully choreographed moves that together advance the entire team toward the designated goal before the time available runs out. The analogy might be extended even further, for as the following chapters show, American negotiators evince a businesslike preoccupation with advancing toward their goal, a legalistic preoccupation with complex rules and precise measurements, an imperialistic readiness to charge through or steamroll over obstacles in their way, and sometimes even a moralistic tendency to attribute their successes to divine dispensation.

Culture and Negotiation

As is detailed in the preface, this volume is part of the United States Institute of Peace's ongoing Cross-Cultural Negotiation (CCN) project, a major endeavor to assess and compare the negotiating behaviors of different countries and governments. The rationale for comparing negotiating behaviors across cultures is straightforward: negotiating is a preferred method of international problem solving; governments manage and conduct negotiations in different ways; and knowledge of those differences will allow officials to better prepare for and manage negotiating encounters.

The CCN project assumes that at least five factors influence the conduct of any given international negotiation:

- the issues at stake;
- the personalities of the negotiators;
- structural factors such as the institutional process for decision making, negotiating, and policy implementation;
- the geopolitical context, including the relationship of the parties to a negotiation; and
- the cultures involved.

The first of these factors changes from negotiation to negotiation and the second from negotiator to negotiator, thus precluding efforts to relate either factor to enduring patterns or generally shared behaviors in national negotiating styles. In contrast, the third, fourth, and fifth factors typically change slowly and incrementally, and thus it is possible to gauge their longer-term influences. The influence exerted by structural and geopolitical factors on negotiations has occupied the attention of more than a few historians and political scientists. In the case of the United States, for instance, they have devoted much thought and ink to determining how various kinds of power—geopolitical, military, and economic power, as well as "soft power" (cultural influence)—have shaped various diplomatic encounters between the United States and its less powerful negotiating counterparts.[3] But the fifth factor—culture—has received comparatively little attention.[4]

---

3. Among the many studies that explore the influence of power on negotiation, particularly well-known titles include Henry Kissinger, *Diplomacy* (New York: Simon and Schuster, 1994); and Joseph Nye, *Soft Power: The Means to Success in World Politics* (New York: Public Affairs, 2004).

4. The literature on the role of culture in *business* negotiations involving Americans is more voluminous, but the differences between the corporate world and the diplomatic world are so numerous and pronounced that any attempt to view both through the same analytical lens would be problematic, to say the least.

No doubt part of the reason for this lack of attention is that culture is such an elusive and amorphous concept. With this in mind, contributors to the CCN project have gone to great efforts to define the term, and have built upon the definitions and usages of "culture" developed in the twentieth century by anthropologists and political scientists such as Franz Boas, Margaret Mead, Ruth Benedict, and Clyde Kluckhohn.[5] In this book, as in Raymond Cohen's *Negotiating across Cultures*, we regard culture as "human software . . . made up of ideas, meanings, conventions, and assumptions," as well as behavioral patterns, shared by a particular group—as "a grammar for organizing reality, for imparting meaning to the world."[6] More precisely, in the definition employed by Tamara Cofman Wittes in *How Israelis and Palestinians Negotiate*, culture is "the product of the experiences of individuals within a given social group, including its representations in images, narratives, myths and patterns of behavior (traditions), and the meanings of those representations as transmitted among the group's members over time and through experience."[7]

Another author of a book from the CCN series, Kevin Avruch, points out that there are multiple, overlapping subcultures, "generic" and "local," national and ethnic, social and political, and so forth. Any given negotiator will be influenced by his or her distinctive set of cultures; thus, no two negotiators are culturally identical.[8] This distinctiveness, however, does not make cultural analysis impossible or irrelevant—just harder, as well as potentially more useful in disentangling the various strands that shape negotiating behavior and negotiating outcomes.

Some observers claim that within the arena of international diplomacy, culture is an irrelevant influence.[9] Others contend that diplomats have long shared

---

Within the field of diplomacy, one book that does link culture and the conduct of American foreign policy is Walter Russell Mead's *Special Providence: American Foreign Policy and How It Changed the World* (New York: Knopf, 2001). Mead's study is concerned with the making and implementation of foreign policy, rather than negotiation, but it certainly argues that broad cultural patterns within American society affect the conduct of diplomacy. Mead's approach is discussed later in this chapter; see 11.

5. Kluckhohn, for instance, wrote that "culture consists of patterned ways of thinking, feeling and reaction, acquired and transmitted mainly by symbols, constituting the distinctive achievements of human groups, including their embodiments in artifacts; the essential core of culture consists of traditional (i.e., historically derived and selected) ideas and especially their attached values." Clyde Kluckhohn, "The Study of Culture," in *The Policy Sciences*, eds. D. Lerner and H. D. Lasswell (Stanford, Calif.: Stanford University Press, 1951), 86.

6. Cohen, *Negotiating across Cultures*, 12.

7. Wittes, *How Israelis and Palestinians Negotiate*, 4.

8. See Avruch, *Culture and Conflict Resolution*, part II, 23–55. In a similar vein, Wittes emphasizes that the definition of culture she presents "allows, importantly, for individuals within a group to be differently situated by class, race, or other social attributes, such that identifiable subcultures can exist within a broader recognized culture." Wittes, *How Israelis and Palestinians Negotiate*, 4–5.

9. See, for instance, I. William Zartman, "A Skeptic's View," in *Culture and Negotiation*, eds. G. Faure and J. Rubin (Newbury Park, Calif.: Sage, 1993), 17–21. Zartman claims that culture is "every bit as relevant as breakfast [for negotiators] and to much the same extent." Avruch, however, sees significant flaws in the arguments advanced by Zartman and others; see Avruch, *Culture and Conflict Resolution*, 42–48.

a professional and international culture that trumps national cultures.[10] In seventeenth- and eighteenth-century Europe, a shared culture of diplomacy was French-speaking and defined by elaborate forms of conduct and attire. In our globalized age, cultural conformity among diplomats is claimed by some to span the entire world—wherever one goes, one encounters a professional culture that is English-speaking, Western-educated, suit-wearing, and soft-spoken. Many seasoned negotiators, however, disagree: cultural differences among negotiators may not be as pronounced as in earlier decades and centuries, but those differences still exist and can exert a palpable influence on the conduct and outcome of negotiations. Their influence can be felt in such numerous and diverse areas as patterns of interpersonal interactions, styles of both verbal and nonverbal communication, attitudes toward time, the use of enticements and pressure tactics, attitudes toward compromise, and the use of hospitality. This diversity of cultures in the world of diplomacy is maintained, in part, by the lack of formal training in negotiating practice in almost all foreign ministries. National cultures prevail.

One could argue that the degree of cultural difference among diplomats—at least European diplomats—has actually increased over the past century. As the retired American career diplomat Monteagle Stearns notes, "The practitioners of modern diplomacy until the end of the First World War tended, in the words of British diplomat and author Harold Nicolson, to be men who 'possessed similar standards of education, similar experience and a similar aim'—men who 'desired the same sort of world.'" The Russian Revolution of October 1917 disrupted this conformity, with the young Soviet Union initially rejecting established diplomatic conventions—just as the United States disdained diplomatic and consular uniforms and the title of "ambassador" between the Civil War and 1893.[11]

The chapters that form part IV of this volume testify eloquently to the profound belief that many non-American diplomats have in the influence of culture on negotiating behavior. Several of those chapters also investigate the circumstances under which cultural differences become more or less pronounced and influential.

This book is particularly interested in the intersection of two kinds of cultures: national (i.e., American) and institutional (i.e., the structures, norms, and behavioral predispositions of U.S. government agencies such as the State Department,

---

10.   For instance, in his seminal work *The Anarchical Society*, Hedley Bull defines diplomatic culture as "the common stock of ideas and values possessed by the official representatives of states," which was developed over the course of centuries and which is an integral part of the "society of states." See Hedley Bull, *The Anarchical Society: A Study of Order in World Politics*, 3rd ed. (New York: Columbia University Press, 1977), 316.
    An interesting review of the idea of diplomatic culture, and an argument for its continuing relevance, is offered by Geoffrey Wiseman, "Pax Americana: Bumping into Diplomatic Culture," *International Studies Perspectives* 6 (2005): 409–430.

11.   See Monteagle Stearns, *Talking to Strangers: Improving American Diplomacy at Home and Abroad* (Princeton, N.J.: Princeton University Press, 1996), 13, 21.

especially the Foreign Service).[12] The following chapters do not assume that all U.S. negotiators are acculturated similarly in these two cultures; as Jeswald Salacuse rightly notes, "No negotiator is a cultural robot."[13] Nor does this volume disregard the influential roles that other kinds of cultures play in shaping outlook and conduct; indeed, U.S. negotiators come from a variety of professional backgrounds, and thus bring to their official duties a variety of negotiating styles. This book does contend, however, that the shared national background and institutional context of U.S. negotiators exert a significant and recognizable impact on many facets of negotiating encounters.

Whether that impact makes American officials better or worse negotiators is a very good question, but it is a question to which this book offers no definitive answer. Our aim in this volume is to assess *how* American officials negotiate, not *how well* they do so. If this seems like a disappointing lack of ambition on the authors' part, we would point out that disentangling behavioral patterns from a tangled knot of personalities, issues, institutions, and interests seems to us an adequately Herculean task. Trying to gauge with any precision the degree to which those patterns of behavior *typically* affect negotiating outcomes seems, if not a Sisyphean occupation, then a task for another, far bigger research project, one able to squeeze a multitude of variables through a statistical meat grinder and produce something intellectually digestible at the other end.[14] This is not to say that we are silent on the subject of the effectiveness of American negotiators. What we can—and do—point out are instances in which particular behaviors and stylistic traits had a clear effect on a specific negotiation. Evidence of such an impact is also to be found in part IV of this book, in which those who have sat across the bargaining table from American officials recall how various characteristic American traits and tactics made a specific negotiation more or less productive.

The contributors to part IV have no doubt that the behavior of American negotiators reflects to some degree American cultural influences. The precise degree is—for the reasons just noted—impossible to determine, but clearly the impact is both positive and negative. Impatience, for instance, is something of a hallmark of U.S.

---

12.   The Austrian diplomat Winfried Lang contends that "national cultures compete with professional cultures." Among the latter is what Lang terms a "negotiation culture," which features, among other elements, a sense of accommodation, a high regard for flexibility, and an awareness of the need for efficient communication. However, Lang recognizes that "this negotiation culture is constrained . . . by national interests imposed by the respective government on its negotiators by means of more or less stringent instructions." Winfried Lang, "A Professional's View," in *Culture and Negotiation*, eds. Faure and Rubin, 44–45, 46.

13.   Jeswald W. Salacuse, "Implications for Practitioners," in *Culture and Negotiation*, eds. Faure and Rubin, 201.

14.   The kinds of variables that would have to be considered include the relative power and resources of the parties to the negotiation; the history of their relationship; each party's intentions and perceptions; domestic political, economic, and other pressures and constraints; the personalities of the negotiators involved and their personal and professional relationships with their own side and with their negotiating counterparts; the main issues under discussion, together with secondary and linked issues; the influence, interests, and actions of third parties, including not only other governments but also intergovernmental organizations and nongovernmental organizations; and media coverage—not to mention behavioral patterns.

diplomacy, but it often leads American negotiators to focus on short-term gains at the expense of long-term interests. On the other side of the coin, many American officials have a reputation for saying what they mean and meaning what they say, which typically reduces the danger of ambiguities and misunderstandings but also upon occasion complicates or even poisons the negotiating atmosphere.

In his book *Special Providence*, the historian Walter Russell Mead argues that certain American mind-sets, each with strong cultural roots, have helped shape American foreign policy over the course of the country's history. From Mead's perspective, the net effect has been overwhelmingly beneficial, for "American foreign policy . . . has done a remarkably good job of enabling the United States to flourish as history goes on."[15] Insofar as we would venture an overall assessment of the impact of culture on American negotiating behavior (not, of course, the same thing as American foreign policy), we would offer a less emphatic and more mixed judgment. The impact of culture can both help and hinder American negotiators. Moreover, as we discuss in the concluding chapter of this book, any given cultural trait can be a boon *or* a handicap, or even a boon *and* a handicap, depending on the context of a specific negotiation.

The Organization of This Book

This book is organized into five parts. The first part consists of this introductory chapter, which lays out the objectives, themes, and contents of the volume. The second part, consisting of chapters 2 through 5, may be regarded as the analytical distillation of the material gathered together for this project. As described in the preface, we have fashioned an interpretative framework around the assessments offered by non-American officials during two CCN workshops while also incorporating the viewpoints and experiences of American diplomats, policymakers, and scholars. Our goal in this section is to provide an integrated portrait of the primary characteristics of U.S. negotiating behavior.

Chapter 2, "The Four-Faceted Negotiator," seeks to capture the essence of the American approach by exploring the businesslike, legalistic, superpower, and moralistic mind-sets that combine to shape the behavior of U.S. officials at the negotiating table.

The next chapter, "At the Bargaining Table," dissects the tactics and behaviors that U.S. diplomats typically employ within the formal negotiating arena. The chapter begins by examining the positive incentives deployed by American negotiators. These include efforts to engage the other side and build institutional and personal ties, and a variety of inducements such as providing economic compensation and offering political recognition or security guarantees. The chapter then assesses

---

15.   Mead, *Special Providence*, xviii.

U.S. pressure tactics, which range from creating linkages between issues to the use of pressures, leaks, ultimatums, and outright coercion.

In chapter 3, we devote significant attention to the uses made of language and of time. Americans—whose conceptual vocabularies suggest that they view negotiation as part science, part sport—often use English as a blunt instrument but can also exhibit great dexterity in crafting the wording of agreements. When it comes to time, however, U.S. negotiators are less flexible. They have a short-term perspective and are usually driven by domestic considerations to press ahead rapidly before perceived windows of opportunity close; their sense of urgency manifests itself in numerous self-imposed deadlines. Chapter 3 also examines how tactics vary according to the identity of the negotiating counterpart, the subject being negotiated, and the forum (bilateral or multilateral) within which negotiations are conducted.

The focus shifts in chapter 4 to how the United States conducts negotiations *away from* the formal bargaining table. It looks in particular at how American officials use three techniques in support of the formal negotiating process: back-channel communications, hospitality, and the media. Far from being a relic of the Cold War, the use of back channels to explore positions and issues remains a distinctive feature of American negotiating behavior. With their extensive network of diplomatic and political contacts, and their readiness to do what it takes to secure concrete results, American officials are well equipped to navigate in treacherous bureaucratic and political waters through the use of back-channel, or off-line, communications. In the case of hospitality, however, Americans are comparatively disadvantaged by a political disinclination to lavish attention upon their counterparts. To be sure, there are exceptions to this lack of interest in impressing, intimidating, or rewarding counterparts with pomp and protocol, but as a general rule American diplomatic hospitality is modest, if not upon occasion miserly.

The possibilities presented to American negotiators by adroit use of the media are less neglected, with U.S. officials sometimes feeding stories to journalists and "spinning" coverage in efforts to shape perceptions of U.S. ambitions and of the process of ongoing negotiations. Yet such efforts are sporadic and rarely amount to media campaigns, in part because the media are independent actors ("the fourth estate") and are seen as unpredictable and unreliable, and in part because the U.S. side expects to succeed at the bargaining table regardless of media coverage.

Americans and foreigners alike often remark that the most difficult and important negotiations Americans undertake are with other Americans, thrashing out negotiating strategies and defending negotiating gambits in Washington's interagency arena. Chapter 5, "Americans Negotiating with Americans," tackles this distinctive aspect of U.S. negotiating behavior, exploring how the structure, culture, and internal dynamics of the U.S. government and bureaucracy influence the conduct of negotiations with foreign counterparts. The chapter covers a variety of subjects: the role of Congress, which is probably more influential than any other legislature in the world in shaping the conduct of foreign policy; America's electoral calendar, which accentuates negotiators' sense of time urgency and short-term outlook; changeovers in administration, which can retard the progress of ongoing talks, oblige negotiators to raise their demands ("move the goalposts"), and cause the loss of institutional memory; the fierce and sometimes destructive rivalries among different agencies and officials for the ear of the president and control of the negotiating agenda; and the political vulnerability of individual diplomats, who may be accused of giving away too much at the bargaining table if not—on rare occasions—disloyalty.

Although most of this volume centers on negotiations conducted during and, more especially, since the Cold War, part III traces the evolution of the relationship between American presidents and their negotiators since the founding of the republic. Written by Robert Schulzinger, one of America's leading diplomatic historians, this historical overview examines the development of the U.S. government's negotiating machinery and management style, from the lone emissaries of the nineteenth century to today's elaborate bureaucratic structures. Schulzinger emphasizes the central role played by the president in the conduct of diplomatic negotiations. His chapter begins with the Revolutionary War but focuses chiefly on the period after 1919, when the United States—as a newly emerged major world power—institutionalized the management of its foreign relations. As he charts the major developments in U.S. diplomatic practice, he touches on several themes that resonate throughout subsequent chapters, including the conviction that America has a special role to play in world affairs, the use of back channels, the influence of political and interagency rivalries within the Washington establishment, and the domestic political vulnerability of individual diplomats.

Part IV consists of a series of foreign perspectives on different facets and aspects of U.S. negotiating behavior, written by senior non-American diplomats or officials who, with one exception, participated in the 2007 workshop. These accounts are not meant to be a tour d'horizon of the most pressing events, relationships, or issues in American diplomacy; nor are they comprehensive, systematic, or exhaustive in their treatment of their respective subjects. Instead, each is intended to throw a personal light on one or more of the topics discussed in part II, offering firsthand experiences and insights acquired by foreign officials on the other side of the negotiating table.

The selection of foreign contributors was not entirely within our hands. Some officials who were invited to contribute chapters declined to do so, some for personal reasons, others for more diplomatic ones. Future editions of this book will, we trust, feature a wider range of foreign perspectives, including the views of officials (and nongovernmental representatives) involved in negotiations over subjects such as climate change, nuclear nonproliferation, and economic regimes. Even so, as the reader will discover, the chapters that form part IV of this book do not lack for variety—nor for insight and candor.

Chan Heng Chee, Singapore's ambassador to Washington since 1996, examines U.S. behavior in three types of fora—bilateral encounters, negotiations with regional intergovernmental organizations, and negotiations within the context of global multilateral organizations. She sees American negotiators as empowered by their country's superpower status but constrained by its political system and interagency wrangling over negotiating positions.

As Japan's deputy minister for foreign affairs, Koji Watanabe was deeply involved in trade negotiations with the United States in the late 1980s and early 1990s. In his chapter, he dissects those negotiations, contrasting what he characterizes as the bitterness of that experience with the less adversarial and more constructive talks of later years, when Japan became more of an economic partner and less of an economic threat to the United States.

Faruk Logoglu, a former Turkish ambassador to Washington, focuses on the high-powered and ultimately unsuccessful U.S. effort to persuade Turkey to let U.S. troops invade Iraq through its territory, and examines how the U.S. tendency to throw its weight around in security negotiations increased dramatically in the immediate aftermath of 9/11.

John Wood, who served two terms as New Zealand's ambassador to the United States in the 1990s and 2000s, recounts his experience of protracted negotiations within Washington in the mid-1980s, when New Zealand and the United States wrestled over New Zealand's antinuclear stance, which barred U.S. warships from New Zealand's waters.

Yuri Nazarkin, who headed several of the Soviet Union's delegations in arms control negotiations and who served as the Russian Federation's ambassador at large for international security and disarmament, offers a candid account of what it is like to negotiate with American officials when one's country is regarded as an adversary of the United States.

Lalit Mansingh, a former foreign secretary of India, portrays the bilateral relationship between his country and the United States since the 1960s, charting what he characterizes as an evolution of U.S. negotiating behavior from coercive to persuasive diplomacy.

Britain's former permanent representative to the United Nations, David Hannay, looks at how America's exceptionalist instincts, the often-skeptical or idiosyncratic approach of political appointees, congressional interference, interdepartmental feuding, and an overloaded policymaking machinery have conspired to make the United States less influential in the United Nations than its international position would justify.

In the last chapter in part IV, Gilles Andreani, former head of the Centre d'analyse et de prévision in the French Foreign Ministry (the equivalent of the U.S. State Department's Policy Planning Staff), offers a dozen managerial "rules" drawn from his personal experience of how to minimize obstacles and maximize outcomes of negotiations with U.S. officials.

Informed by the observations of these foreign contributors, the final chapter asks how well equipped American negotiators are for the challenges presented by a changing global landscape. Collectively, the four defining facets of American negotiating behavior seem to have served American diplomacy well in the past. But will they continue to do so in the future? Negotiation is becoming more, not less, important as a tool of American foreign policy, and the nature of international negotiation is rapidly shifting in response to globalization, the emergence of problems that demand a collective response, and the weakening of the nation-state system and collective organizations of international action.

The second half of the concluding chapter proposes a series of reforms designed to allow American negotiators to function as effectively as possible in this new international environment. Not much can be done to change behavior rooted in national and institutional cultures, but the negotiating skills of negotiators can be enhanced in other ways. The conclusion recommends a variety of practicable measures, ranging from better training of career diplomats in the arts of negotiation, to improvements in the U.S. government's institutional memory and assessments of past negotiating records, to more supportive congressional funding of diplomacy.

Attitudinal changes are no less important than concrete ones. If U.S. officials are to perform effectively in the coming decades, American negotiating behavior may have to acquire a fifth facet: the mind-set of a "politician" with a capacity for empathy, an ability to nurture and sustain useful relationships, and a sensitivity to the fact that all parties need to leave a negotiation with something to give their constituents. Negotiators from all levels of government need to supplement their use of political, economic, and military resources with greater attention to building relationships and greater self-awareness of American negotiating characteristics. The conclusion of this volume thus ends where the rationale for this book begins, with Sun Tzu's admonition to "know yourself."

Part II

A Portrait of the American Negotiator

2

The Four-Faceted Negotiator

merican negotiators tend to think of themselves—and American governments tend to present themselves—as pragmatic and fair-minded, ready to listen to the other side's point of view and to reach a fair compromise that conveys mutual benefits.[1] Yet Americans—and American administrations of all stripes—are no less inclined to see the United States as the embodiment of a unique and uniquely virtuous set of values, values that must never be compromised and must instead be steadfastly defended at home and championed abroad.[2]

Neither of these two contrasting images tends to obscure the other; instead, they usually coexist, producing an ambivalence about negotiating with foreign governments noted by Americans and non-Americans alike. For instance, Dennis Ross, Middle East envoy for three U.S. presidents, observes:

> While Americans like to think of themselves as always willing to negotiate, a closer look at our self-image and ethos suggests that our attitudes toward negotiations have often been ambivalent.... Because of our self-image, we have often been attracted to concepts that seem to require minimal negotiation.[3]

Gilles Andreani, who served in France's Ministry of Foreign Affairs under two presidents, paints a similar picture in his chapter in this volume. On the one hand, recalls Andreani of his negotiating experiences, American officials "sought to understand our positions and genuinely tried to explore possibilities for compromise." But, on the other hand:

> Negotiation is not, in the United States, what it is for most people in other parts of the world, that is, a sensible thing to do to obtain something from another country. Rather, it

---

1. Ambassador Charles W. Freeman contends that one element of the "distinctive American approach" to negotiation is that "we have in our minds a model of negotiation where there's a 50-50 split implicit." Freeman, interview, 10.

2. The exact composition of this set of values is, inevitably, a matter of dispute and, almost certainly, varies over time. Seymour Martin Lipset, for instance, discerns five strands in what he calls "the American Creed": liberty, egalitarianism, individualism, populism, and laissez-faire. See Seymour Martin Lipset, *American Exceptionalism: A Double-Edged Sword* (New York: W. W. Norton, 1996), 19.

3. Dennis Ross, *Statecraft and How to Restore America's Standing in the World* (New York: Farrar, Straus, and Giroux, 2007), 175.

is a privilege bestowed on deserving foreigners, an exception to the normal course of affairs for Americans, which is to decide by themselves on issues of interest to them, including international ones.[4]

This disinclination to negotiate with other countries is pronounced in the case of countries that seem to threaten U.S. values or interests. In February 2007, former secretary of state James Baker, responding to the resistance of the George W. Bush administration to negotiating with North Korea and Iran, felt it necessary to tell an audience at the Library of Congress: "We must be prepared to talk with our enemies. . . . it is in our interest to do so. . . . Talking to a hostile government, whether it was Moscow during the Cold War or Damascus today, is not appeasement."[5] In few other countries would it be necessary to defend the idea of negotiating with hostile governments. (Winston Churchill was not courting controversy in Britain when he remarked, "It is better to jaw-jaw than to war-war.") But in the United States, talking to "bad guys" has a bad name. Indeed, sixteen months after Baker made his remarks, President Bush told the Israeli Knesset that negotiating with "terrorists and radicals" (a phrase widely interpreted to mean the governments of Iran and Syria, among others) amounted to "the false comfort of appeasement."[6] And in the 2008 presidential election, Republicans hammered candidate Barack Obama for his stated willingness to talk with Iran. In the words of Chester A. Crocker, assistant secretary of state for African Affairs in the Reagan administration, "the concept of negotiated outcomes and diplomatic engagement with troublesome or nasty regimes remains neuralgic in the U.S. body politic."[7]

And yet, despite this reluctance to talk with other countries, especially troublesome ones, the United States does precisely this to a prodigious extent. As of the summer of 2008, the U.S. government had diplomatic relations with 191 of the world's 194 countries.[8] It maintained 268 embassies, consulates, and missions abroad.[9] And it participated in at least 127 regional and international organizations.[10] Such an elaborate and extensive diplomatic apparatus exists to facilitate communication, not to foreclose it.

---

4. See Gilles Andreani, "Negotiating with Savoir Faire: Twelve Rules for Negotiating with the United States," 287.

5. Baker reiterated the point in an article later in that year; see James A. Baker III, "The Big Ten: The Case for Pragmatic Idealism," *National Interest*, August 29, 2007, http://www.nationalinterest.org/Article.aspx?id=15370.

6. See Sheryl Gay Stolberg and Jim Rutenberg, "Bush Assails 'Appeasement,' Touching Off Storm," *New York Times*, May 16, 2008, http://www.nytimes.com/2008/05/16/us/politics/16obama.html?hp.

7. Crocker, "The Art of Peace: Bringing Diplomacy Back to Washington," *Foreign Affairs* (July–August 2007), http://www.foreignaffairs.org/20070701fareviewessay86414/chester-a-crocker/the-art-of-peace-bringing-diplomacy-back-to-washington.html.

8. See U.S. Department of State, Bureau of Intelligence and Research, "Independent States in the World," Fact Sheet (Washington, D.C., August 19, 2008), http://www.state.gov/s/inr/rls/4250.htm.

9. Tallied from the "Geographic Index" on the Web site of the U.S. Department of State, http://www.state.gov/documents/organization/109693.pdf.

10. U.S. Office of Personnel Management, "Detail and Transfer of Federal Employees to International Organizations," http://www.opm.gov/emploe/internat/index.asp.

This "talk/don't talk" ambivalence points to the larger complexity of the American approach to negotiation. Drawing on opinions and evidence gathered during the comparative negotiating behavior project, we find that contemporary U.S. negotiating practice is shaped by four mind-sets, each one representing a bundle of associated assumptions and preferences. These four mind-sets (each one of which corresponds, albeit imprecisely, to a major facet of American life) include a *businesslike* outlook, which is results-oriented, straightforward, and pragmatic; a *legalistic* mind-set, which values process, precision, facts, and professionalism; a *moralistic* disposition, marked by idealism, self-righteousness, and an evangelical zeal; and the mind-set of a global *superpower*—often characterized by foreign diplomats as the mind-set of a "hegemon"—reflecting a readiness to use exceptional resources to dictate terms in pursuit of its own interests.

These four mind-sets sometimes function in harmony, especially the first two and the last two. For instance, the legalistic and the businesslike approaches both emphasize rational argumentation and are open to compromises and trade-offs, while the moralistic and hegemonic mind-sets both tend to reinforce U.S. exceptionalism and unilateralist tendencies. Sometimes, however, the different mind-sets are discordant, generating mixed messages and abrupt tactical switches.

In any given negotiation, the influence of the different mind-sets will vary, their relative proportions determined by factors such as the issue under negotiation, the temperaments of the individual negotiators and of the reigning administration in Washington, and the wider relationship between the parties to the negotiation. What this chapter aims to provide is not a snapshot of U.S. negotiating behavior at a given moment, but a portrait that captures its different modes and instincts.

The Businesslike Negotiator

For an American diplomat, the term "businesslike" is always positive, connoting a purposeful encounter, one typically featuring frank but unimpassioned discussion in pursuit of a productive and mutually beneficial outcome. To take a few examples: Christopher Hill, the senior U.S. negotiator in talks with North Korea about shutting down its nuclear program, publicly applauded his discussions as "good, comprehensive, and businesslike."[11] Allen Johnson, the chief U.S. negotiator in discussions at the World Trade Organization on agriculture, issued an upbeat report: "There is a good atmosphere. People are working in a business-like way to reach a consensus."[12] Admiral Michael Mullen, chairman of the Joint Chiefs of Staff, reported in October 2008 that he had had "a productive, businesslike conversation" with his Russian

---

11.   See Judy Aita, "North Korea Talks on Track, U.S. Negotiator Says," *USINFO*, March 7, 2007, http://www.globalsecurity.org/wmd/library/news/dprk/2007/dprk-070307-usia01.htm.

12.   See "Negotiators Upbeat after WTO Talks," *Goliath*, June 14, 2004, http://goliath.ecnext.com/coms2/summary_0199-450808_ITM. America, it should be noted, is not the only country to applaud "businesslike" diplomacy.

counterpart during a meeting intended to rebuild fences in the aftermath of the Russian intervention in Georgia.[13] A senior official in the Obama administration characterized the president's first meeting with the Russian president as "Let's get down to business"; and asked about Obama's conversation with the Chinese president at the same time, another senior official said, "I would describe the meeting as business-like."[14]

The notion of being "businesslike" is central not only to the American conception of a productive negotiation but also to many Americans' conception of their own professional dealings. Of course, for some U.S. negotiators the description "businesslike" is a literal one: many have been drawn from the ranks of the American corporate world, to which they have tended to return once they have completed their diplomatic service. Edward Stettinius, Jr., who became secretary of state in 1944, was perhaps the epitome of the businesslike negotiator. Stettinius had been vice president of General Motors and chairman of the board of United States Steel. As veteran diplomat Charles Bohlen observed, President Franklin D. Roosevelt looked to him "for the execution of practical tasks, such as working out problems with other Foreign Ministers. Stettinius was typically American in his desire to get on with the business and sometimes was unaware of political nuances."[15] General Motors furnished another high-ranking official, Charles Wilson, who left his job as president of the giant automaker to become Dwight D. Eisenhower's secretary of defense. A blunt, outspoken man, Wilson was asked by the Senate Armed Services Committee if he could imagine a situation in which he, as secretary of defense, would make a decision adverse to General Motors' interests. He responded, "I cannot conceive of one, because for years I thought what was good for the country was good for General Motors and vice versa."[16] Among today's "noncareer ambassadors" (i.e., ambassadors recruited from outside the Foreign Service), observes Ruth Whiteside, director of the State Department's Foreign Service Institute, the most common background is business.[17]

Even negotiators who have spent their entire careers in the Foreign Service, or who have been drafted from the groves of academe, would be unlikely to protest a characterization of their behavior as "businesslike." The term, rooted in that most quintessential of American activities—as President Calvin Coolidge famously observed, "The business of America is business"—connotes above all a preoccupation with achieving concrete results. Even when "businesslike" is used in diplomatic

---

13.   Matti Huuhtanen, "U.S., Russia Military Chiefs Talk," *Seattle Post-Intelligencer*, October 21, 2008.

14.   The off-the-record comments were reported by Jonathan Martin, "Obama: Bush-Era Diplomacy Is Over," *Politico*, April 1, 2009, http://www.politico.com/news/stories/0409/20765.html.

15.   Charles Bohlen, *Witness to History, 1929–1969* (New York: Harper, 1973), 179.

16.   Justin Hyde, "GM's 'Engine Charlie' Wilson Learned to Live with a Misquote," *Detroit Free Press*, September 14, 2008.

17.   Ruth Whiteside, interview, Arlington, Virginia, September 19, 2008, 49.

fashion to describe a frank but unfriendly exchange, a candid but hardly cordial encounter, that usage still testifies to the association of "businesslike" with purposeful and relatively productive activity, and thus resonates with the American ambition to achieve concrete and beneficial outcomes in a negotiation.

U.S. negotiators certainly do appeal to ties of friendship with their counterparts, but unlike negotiators from certain relationship oriented countries—China and Japan, for instance[18]—they do not regard such ties as one of the most powerful weapons in their diplomatic arsenal, and they do not regard negotiating as primarily an exercise in establishing and building relationships. Several chapters in part IV of this book (most notably, Koji Watanabe's account of U.S.-Japanese trade negotiations in the late 1980s and early 1990s) make plain that American officials tend not to be highly sensitive to their counterparts' feelings—for instance, a lingering sense of historical grievance or humiliation at being pushed around by the world's superpower. This is not to say that personal relationships do not matter or are not cultivated and exploited (as is discussed at the outset of the next chapter), only that they are not usually seen by American officials as central to the management of a negotiation or as ends in themselves.

The United States also rarely engages in process for the sake of process, or in talk for the sake of talk.[19] While Asian diplomats, for example, readily see the worth of group gatherings like the Association of Southeast Asian Nations (ASEAN) Regional Forum (ARF) that have focused more on relationship building than concrete results, American officials sometimes dismiss them as irrelevant "talk shops." Not all U.S. officials feel this way. Colin Powell attended the ARF every year during his tenure as secretary of state and described the gatherings as "very, very useful" both for promoting regional cooperation and for the side meetings (at which he accomplished some concrete goals, such as getting all ten ASEAN foreign ministers to sign a joint declaration promising support in the war against terrorism).[20] Powell's successor, Condoleezza Rice, had a different view, however. She skipped two of the four meetings of the ARF on her watch, which some in Asia took as a signal that the United States was assigning a lower priority to their region, but

---

18.   Richard H. Solomon emphasizes the importance to the Chinese of developing and manipulating relationships, especially interpersonal relationships, in his study *Chinese Negotiating Behavior*, the subtitle of which, appropriately enough, is *Pursuing Interests through "Old Friends."* Raymond Cohen makes a similar point in *Negotiating across Cultures*, chapter 3, especially 36–38, where he discusses "high-context" cultures such as Japan and the primacy they accord interpersonal relationships.

19.   Americans do sometimes negotiate for the sake of negotiating, however. For instance, the Nixon administration pursued the Mutual and Balanced Force Reduction (MBFR) negotiations between NATO and the Warsaw Pact in large part so as "to open the prospect of troop cuts negotiated with the Soviet Union and thereby thwart the passage by the US Congress of Senator Mansfield's proposal for a substantial unilateral reduction of the US military presence in Europe." The MBFR talks ran from 1973 until 1989. Jozef Goldblat, *Arms Control: The New Guide to Negotiations and Agreements*, 2nd ed. (Thousand Oaks, Calif.: Sage, 2002), 220.

20.   Quoted in Ralph Cossa, "Rice's Unfortunate Choice," *Asia Times*, July 28, 2005, http://www.atimes.com/atimes/Southeast_Asia/GG28Ae03.html.

which may have merely reflected her sense that her time could be better spent doing something rather than talking about doing something.[21] As Tommy Koh, Singapore's ambassador-at-large, speculated in 2008: "A number of U.S. officials regard ASEAN as a talk shop and an ineffectual regional organization. This dismissive attitude is shared by a number of American think tanks and scholars. . . . For American officials, a meeting may not be worth attending unless it has a concrete deliverable. This could explain the absence of senior U.S. officials from some important ASEAN meetings over the past four years."[22]

American negotiators, though hardly famed for their readiness to sit quietly while others take the lead, are also less given than some of their counterparts to making opening statements with rhetorical fireworks. One French diplomat, for instance, has averred that "the one who wins is he who speaks first," and French diplomats are renowned for their tendency to launch negotiations with verbally and intellectually dazzling displays of Cartesian logic. "The French," comments Gérard Araud, who has served as director of strategic affairs and security at the Quai d'Orsay and as France's deputy ambassador to NATO, "are victims of their combined love of concept and brio, which, in a negotiation, leads them into long and brilliant digressions to explain the luminous logic of their position rather than to concrete propositions of amendments or of texts which are without glory but much more effective."[23]

Americans often forgo such opportunities for semantic showmanship because what matters to them in a negotiation is not flamboyant rhetoric or brilliant argumentation but substance: *how* something is said and *in what order* it is said matters less than *what* is said and with *what results*.

For Americans, substance and results are paramount; the *process* by which results are achieved is important, but less so. In a memoir recounting his indefatigable efforts to broker a deal between the Serbs, Bosnians, and Croats in the mid-1990s, Richard Holbrooke observes that "in diplomacy process can often be as important as substance,"[24] yet throughout the book the author portrays himself forcing the belligerents to look beyond diplomatic niceties and toward the concrete benefits each side could gain from a negotiated end to hostilities. Holbrooke even displays impatience with his European allies and their "minidramas" over issues such as where meetings should be held and who should host them. "If we consulted the [five-nation] Contact Group prior to each action," Holbrooke told his boss, Secretary of State Warren Christopher, "it would be impossible for the negotiations to proceed,

---

21.   See, for example, ibid; and Yoichi Funabashi, "Keeping Up with Asia," *Foreign Affairs* (September–October 2008).

22.   Tommy Koh, "The United States and Southeast Asia," in *America's Role in Asia: Asian and American Views, 2008*, Asia Foundation (San Francisco: Asia Foundation, 2008), 42–43.

23.   Quoted in Cogan, *French Negotiating Behavior*, 122.

24.   Richard Holbrooke, *To End a War* (New York: Random House, 1998; Modern Library edition, 1999), 178.

let alone succeed. Now that the United States was finally engaged in Bosnia, we could not allow internal Contact Group squabbles to deflect us."[25]

Holbrooke's determination to stay on track and reach a peace agreement led him, with Christopher's support, to orchestrate a short but highly intense diplomatic campaign marked by innumerable shuttle flights between Balkan capitals, nonstop talks, and last-minute crises. A similar readiness to pull out all the stops in pursuit of an outcome can be found in many other chapters of the diplomatic history of the United States, including the Herculean efforts by President George H. W. Bush and Secretary of State James Baker to win support for their policy of German unification.[26]

The aim of such intensive efforts is to convince the other side not of the logical rigor or philosophical integrity of the U.S. position but of its practical, concrete advantages for both sides.[27] As Henry Kissinger declares at the outset of his historical tour d'horizon, *Diplomacy*, published in 1994, "No nation has been more pragmatic in the day-to-day conduct of its diplomacy [than the United States]."[28] He had observed much the same as a much younger man, when, back in 1956, he wrote, "American leadership is better prepared to deal with technical than with conceptual problems, with economic than with political issues." Without a conceptual framework, he noted, problems are dealt with in their own merits, which emphasizes the particular at the expense of the general.[29] Fifty-one years later, Dennis Ross asserted as one of his cardinal rules for mediation, "Set Aside Each Side's Principles and Focus on Practicalities."[30] Whether this is actually sage advice for mediators is questionable, but it is quintessentially pragmatic American *businesslike* advice.[31]

---

25.   Ibid., 117.

26.   Ross, for instance, describes Bush and Baker's diplomatic efforts over German unification, efforts that he characterizes as "remarkable for their extensive, intensive, and time-consuming nature." Ross, *Statecraft*, 39.

27.   Again, French diplomats offer a marked contrast. "The French," says Araud, "are prisoners of their Cartesian obsession. They believe, in the religious sense of the term, in reason." Cogan, *French Negotiating Behavior*, 11.

28.   Henry Kissinger, *Diplomacy* (New York: Simon and Schuster, 1994; Touchstone edition, 1995), 18. The sentence concludes thus: "or more ideological in the pursuit of its historic moral convictions." American negotiators may not worry much about displaying conceptual rigor but, as discussed later in this chapter, they certainly can be determined moralizers.

29.   Henry Kissinger, "Reflections on American Diplomacy," *Foreign Affairs* (October 1956): 54–55. For Kissinger, whose early schooling had taken place in Germany, this American trait was nothing to celebrate: "Foremost among the attitudes affecting our foreign policy is American empiricism and its quest for methodological certainty" (p. 38). He complained that "our empiricism dooms us to an essentially reactive policy" when confronted by the Soviets and their faith in the doctrines of Marxism-Leninism (p. 40).

30.   Ross, *Statecraft*, 250.

31.   According to a study of mediation in cases of intractable conflict, "core political issues that define the identities and key interests of the parties cannot be shunted aside (or fudged indefinitely); they must be included in the terms of a settlement if there is to be any hope of reaching a meaningful deal." For instance, "the right of return has been elevated to a core principle by the Palestinian side, to the point that the Israelis or the mediator cannot simply say 'forget about it.'" Chester A. Crocker, Fen Osler Hampson, and Pamela Aall, eds., *Taming Intractable Conflicts: Mediation in the Hardest Cases* (Washington, D.C.: United States Institute of Peace Press, 2005), 155–156.

As businesslike negotiators, American officials see themselves not only empha-sizing concrete results but also achieving those results through plain dealing—through straightforward dialogue and a readiness to give and take. They regard negotiating as an opportunity to explain differences and to search for acceptable compromises, a process of exchanges that competing parties enter to find a mutu-ally beneficial outcome, a win-win solution rather than a zero-sum result. This at-titude mirrors and is shaped by numerous domestic influences, including the field of industrial relations, which strives to professionalize and take the heat out of labor-management disputes—indeed, the word "dispute," with its connotations of limited and resolvable disagreements, is employed instead of "conflict." It is no co-incidence that such distinguished American diplomats as Cyrus Vance and George Shultz acquired their negotiating skills in labor disputes. Leonard Woodcock, who became the first U.S. ambassador to the People's Republic of China, had previously been a union leader. He was, says Ambassador Charles Freeman, "the most effective American negotiator I ever observed. . . . His experience was of a negotiation where there was no higher harbinger. It was not a litigation. It was a union confronting management. It was a union concerned about cultivating relationships and not breaking them because if you broke the relationship, you broke the company."[32]

Other popular terminology in the American diplomatic lexicon highlights the conception of a negotiation as a *straightforward* interchange in a very literal sense: that is, as something that proceeds in more or less a *straight* line, and moves *for-ward*, toward a defined goal. Americans are not the only ones to use metaphors of forward movement to describe negotiations, but they use them far more frequently than most. Witness the resort to train metaphors by American officials, for exam-ple, in the run-up to the Madrid conference on the Middle East in 1991 and dur-ing the Angola-Namibia negotiations in the 1980s.[33] The train metaphor is popular because it suggests not only movement but irresistible movement—except in cases of catastrophic "derailment" or "wreck."[34] Christopher Hill, in his comments on the North Korean talks quoted earlier, was pleased to report that "we feel we are still on track." As metaphorical locomotives of history, trains represent a chance for the parties to a negotiation to climb on board and move ahead. But that opportu-

32.   Freeman, interview, 91–92. Stapleton Roy also esteems Woodcock, describing him as "a very skilled negotia-tor" who "represents the epitome of a good negotiating style. . . . Mastery of the substance, acute understanding of the political factors in the United States, a deadpan negotiating style that totally concealed his reactions to things taking place." Roy, interview, 8.

33.   These examples and the phrase "metaphors of movement" are borrowed from G. R. Berridge, *Diplomacy: Theory and Practice*, 3rd ed. (Basingstoke, England, and New York: Palgrave Macmillan, 2005), 64–65.

34.   Hill quoted in Aita, "North Korea Talks on Track." Allen Johnson, the other official quoted at the start of this section, is no less fond of metaphors of movement, applauding the WTO talks for creating "a lot of momen-tum" but worrying that a change in U.S. administrations might mean that "a lot of these issues will be hitting the road." Johnson quoted in Doug Palmer, "WTO: Ag Deal Possible by Dec 2005," Reuters, October 21, 2004.

nity is fleeting, and negotiating counterparts who are reluctant to "get on board" an American proposal are warned of the dangers of "missing the train." In 1998, for instance, as talks to avert military action against a recalcitrant Iraq faltered, Pentagon spokesman Kenneth Bacon ominously declared, "The train is leaving the station. If diplomacy fails here, we will have to look at different options."[35]

Trains also do not lose their way, which may be why they feature more often in U.S. communiqués and policy statements than another common metaphorical device: automobiles. When cars and driving do feature rhetorically, they often do so in the context of staying on course. For instance, lest there be any doubt as to which direction America wanted the negotiations over the normalization of relations with Vietnam in the early 1990s to take, or over a two-state solution to the Israeli-Palestinian conflict in 2003, the United States issued a "road map."

For the businesslike American, negotiation is often seen as a linear sequence of stages or phases. The process begins with prenegotiation and assessments, advances to the opening moves of formal exchanges, continues through a probing middle phase, and leads to an endgame and a (supposedly) binding agreement. This conception calls to mind the technical and engineering worlds—and, more broadly, the scientific, rationalist, Enlightenment outlook that animated many of America's founding fathers and has dominated America's educational system and basic social outlook. Even the vocabulary employed to describe the course of a negotiation echoes the argot of the engineer: a *problem* is identified, a *process* to resolve it is implemented, and a *solution* is found.

This attitude, it may be noted, is inherently optimistic. Some nations—Japan, for instance—may approach the bargaining table reluctantly, even with trepidation, looking to minimize the scope of negotiations and expecting any agreement to favor the other side.[36] In contrast, American officials usually enter negotiations energetically and in anticipation of a productive outcome. In June 1987, just before President Ronald Reagan was to deliver a forceful speech about tearing down the Berlin Wall, he was asked about the prospects for a summit meeting that fall. His years in sports and as a sports announcer, Reagan replied, had made him "very superstitious about calling the pitcher as doing a no-hitter before the game was over." But Reagan added: "I hesitate to make optimistic statements, always have, but at the same time, I can't deny that I believe there is an increased opportunity for a summit conference and an increased opportunity for actual reductions of armaments,

---

35.   Quoted in CNN, "Diplomacy over Iraq Reaches 11th-Hour Urgency," January 27, 1998, http://www.cnn.com/WORLD/9801/27/un.iraq/index.html.

36.   This is Michael Blaker's assessment of how the Japanese approach negotiations with the United States. See Blaker, Giarra, and Vogel, *Case Studies in Japanese Negotiating Behavior*, 6, and much of the discussion throughout chapters 1, 2, and 3.

particularly of the nuclear kind."[37] This upbeat approach, of course, owes something to the belief that the United States has the power and resources to prevail, but it also reflects a historically grounded optimism and the fact that the United States— unlike most countries of the world—has not been the scene of large-scale violent conflict for more than 150 years. As Kissinger has noted, "our lack of tragic experience" helps shape "our attitude toward foreign affairs"; Americans are accustomed domestically to seeing "great daring rewarded" and "great obstacles overcome." This attitude also colors U.S. behavior on the international stage.[38] Perhaps no president has said it better than Gerald Ford in 1975, speaking in Helsinki before the opening of the Conference on Security and Cooperation in Europe:

> I have come to Helsinki as a spokesman for a nation whose vision has always been forward, whose people have always demanded that the future be brighter than the past, and whose united will and purpose at this hour is to work diligently to promote peace and progress not only for ourselves but for all mankind.[39]

The will to find a solution can indeed be critical to resolving disputes or ending conflicts. Optimism, however, can sometimes have the quality of naïveté. As Chester A. Crocker has commented:

> Our optimistic goal orientation, our results-oriented drive to "get to a deal," also reflects a naïveté and provincialism among Americans who imagine that everyone else in the world enters negotiations because they want to get a deal, end a war, or whatever. Many nations negotiate for quite different reasons—to please their domestic audience, to buy time, to fend off U.S. pressure, to get ready for their next move, to learn more about us and our priorities, and so forth. If we go about our diplomatic business with this "can do" mind-set assuming that "they are like us," it is no wonder that we spin our wheels or that the Chinese sometimes run diplomatic circles around us while the Pakistanis listen intently [to us] and go on destabilizing Afghanistan.[40]

Speaking to a British audience in 1982, Henry Kissinger similarly drew a connection between optimism and naïveté:

> American attitudes until quite literally the recent decade have embodied a faith that historical experience can be transcended, that problems can be solved permanently, that harmony can be the natural state of mankind. Thus our diplomacy has often stressed the concepts of international law, with its procedures of arbitration and peaceful settlement, as if all political disputes were legal issues, on the premise that reasonable men and women could always find agreement on some equitable basis.[41]

---

37. Quoted in Gerald M. Boyd, "Reagan Optimistic on Soviet Summit," *New York Times*, June 12, 1987.

38. Kissinger, "Reflections," 41.

39. The text of President Ford's speech can be found at http://www.ford.utexas.edu/LIBRARY/speeches/750459.htm.

40. E-mail from Chester A. Crocker to Richard H. Solomon and Nigel Quinney, July 13, 2008.

41. From a speech delivered to the Royal Institute of International Affairs on May 10, 1982. Reprinted as "Kissinger's Public Confession as an Agent of British Influence," *Executive Intelligence Review*, January 11, 2002, http://www.larouchepub.com/other/2002/2901_kissinger.html.

The Legalistic Negotiator

The businesslike and the legalistic mind-sets reinforce each other in several ways: a preference for concrete details over abstract principles, for example, and for cool heads over fiery rhetoric. But optimism (at least about the intentions of one's negotiating counterpart) is not usually one of them. By temperament and training, legalistic negotiators reject the first but embrace the second half of President Reagan's favorite arms control dictum: "Trust, but verify."

The Anglo-Saxon tradition of case law, with its emphasis on inductive reasoning and pragmatism rather than on deductive reasoning and abstract principles, comports with the typical approach of U.S. negotiators, which is to focus on the problem at hand and to emphasize the practical advantages of resolving it along the lines proposed by the American side. U.S. negotiators marshal facts and arguments to build an overwhelming case for their position. They are often prepared to countenance compromise on subsidiary issues provided that their primary objective is not sacrificed. They typically take careful notes of the exchanges in the course of each negotiating session and record any progress achieved or areas of disagreement. An agreement, if reached, is supported by the official record and is drafted in precise, binding, and enforceable language. As Chan Heng Chee, Singapore's ambassador to Washington, notes in her chapter in this volume, U.S. negotiators in talks over intellectual property rights "were very legalistic and could tolerate no ambiguity in language in the agreement. They wanted everything explicit."[42]

Many U.S. negotiators have law degrees—as of June 2008, 869 serving Foreign Service officers had graduate-level degrees in law[43]—and many of these have practiced law, including some very prominent figures. President George H. W. Bush's first secretary of state, James Baker, followed his grandfather's advice to "work hard, study, and keep out of politics" for the first forty years of life, concentrating instead on his legal career. But when he succumbed to the lure of politics, he found that his professional background was decidedly helpful. "My study of the law," he wrote, "probably reinforced my emphasis on action over contemplation, and that's how it's been ever since. My legal training left me in good standing when I entered the world of politics and public policy."[44] Warren Christopher, who headed the law firm of O'Melveny & Myers (one of the world's largest), was deputy secretary of state during the Carter administration (when he negotiated for the release of the U.S. hostages from Iran) and secretary of state during President Clinton's first term. The

---

42.   Chan Heng Chee, "Different Forums, Different Styles," 191.

43.   Figure provided by the U.S. State Department; correspondence in authors' files. The total number of Foreign Service officers in the State Department in June 2008 was about 6,500; the number of Foreign Service specialists (who provide technical, administrative, or support services) was around 5,000.

44.   James A. Baker, III, *The Politics of Diplomacy: Revolution, War, and Peace, 1989–1992* (New York: G. P. Putnam's Sons, 1995), 40.

habits acquired during a successful legal career were much in evidence during those years. As Richard Holbrooke commented of his former boss:

> Although the State Department's unique bureaucratic culture has survived every one of its leaders (and defeated some), the personal style of each secretary deeply affects the way the Department reacts to events. Warren Christopher's style was methodical and cautious. He was, as the press often said, a lawyer's lawyer. . . . Unfailingly polite, adept at concealing any annoyance or impatience that he might be feeling, Christopher preferred to let others take the lead in recommending a course of action, while he focused on the risks it entailed. . . . Christopher formed his positions only after careful deliberations.[45]

Relatively few U.S. negotiators are as self-restrained as Christopher, but almost all share his desire to conduct a negotiation in a dignified, undemonstrative fashion. Rather than trying to intimidate interlocutors by shouting or gesticulating, or trying to deceive them by bluffing or presenting inaccurate information, they typically play to their professional strengths and cultivate a reputation for analytical rigor and personal integrity.[46] (There are exceptions to this undemonstrative style, of course—as is discussed in the next chapter.) Discourse tends to be straightforward; lying, bluster, and bluffing are discouraged. David Hannay, Britain's former permanent representative to the United Nations, remarks in his chapter in this volume that the United States "benefit[s] . . . from the professionalism and integrity of its diplomats. You are a good deal less likely to be told an outright lie by a U.S. diplomat than by many others." Such honesty inspires the "degree of trust and confidence between . . . practitioners" that is essential to "the art of negotiation."[47] Thomas Pickering, who served as U.S. ambassador to six different countries as well as to the United Nations, echoes Hannay's assessment that American diplomats seldom dissemble:

> Put it this way: I think that there's a tendency among American negotiators to believe that what they have to say represents the truth. . . . Now, rarely have I heard an American negotiator use what I consider to be a deliberate, entirely false misrepresentation. . . . However, Americans, like any other negotiators, are inclined to embellish their arguments and some for reasons that may be an absence of familiarity with the facts.[48]

Another senior U.S. diplomat, Stapleton Roy, admitted that "Americans lie like everybody else, but in negotiating situations, I do not think it is a characteristic of American negotiating behavior."[49] According to former assistant secretary of state

---

45. Holbrooke, *To End a War*, 79–80.

46. This American style can be disoriented by highly emotional, bombastic, and threatening behavior in a negotiating counterpart. Consider, as a dramatic example, Soviet premier Nikita Khrushchev's inflammatory effort to intimidate President John F. Kennedy at their first summit encounter in Vienna in 1961. See W. Richard Smyser, *Kennedy and the Berlin Wall* (Lanham, Md.: Rowman and Littlefield, 2009), chapter 5, "I Never Met a Man Like That."

47. David Hannay, "Negotiating Multilaterally: The Advantages and Disadvantages of the U.S. Approach," 274.

48. Thomas Pickering, interview, Washington, D.C., July 16, 2008, 39–40.

49. Roy, interview, 45.

Phyllis Oakley and former deputy assistant secretary of state Michael Lekson, Americans rarely lie in negotiations, but they tend not to tell the whole truth.[50]

Facts, figures, and signed documents—not emotions, traditions, and aspirations—carry weight in the legalistic world, which makes it essential to do meticulous homework and to enter into negotiations well prepared and armed with appropriately crafted talking points and supporting data. As many foreign diplomats attest, U.S. officials usually begin a negotiation well briefed in both the substance and details of the issue at hand; and even top-level officials are usually very well informed in their negotiating encounters (although there have been some conspicuous contrasts among presidents).

American negotiators can draw not only on published or otherwise publicly available sources for background material, but also on reports and data generated by America's various intelligence agencies. Good intelligence is of course particularly valuable in negotiations where the subject under discussion is shrouded in secrecy or clouded in uncertainty—for instance, negotiations on arms control, whether with the Soviet Union or Iraq or North Korea—but even in seemingly less politically sensitive and more transparent cases, the data and assessments prepared by the Central Intelligence Agency, National Security Agency, and other bodies can give American diplomats a significant advantage. According to the Commission on the Roles and Capabilities of the United States Intelligence Community, in the first half of the 1990s, "U.S. intelligence provided key support to the U.S. side in numerous bilateral and multilateral negotiations," ranging from nuclear nonproliferation talks to discussions of unfair trading practices and human rights abuses.[51]

Careful preparation has been a hallmark of U.S. negotiating behavior for a long time. When President Woodrow Wilson went to the Paris Peace Conference after the end of World War I, he was accompanied—as Robert Schulzinger notes in his chapter in this volume—by a staff of hundreds that included numerous academic experts.[52] Twenty-five years later, President Roosevelt traveled to Yalta with a series of "black books" that had been prepared for him, in which every problem likely to be discussed at the conference was thoroughly analyzed and recommendations offered for U.S. positions.[53]

---

50. Phyllis Oakley, interview, Washington, D.C., August 8, 2008; and Michael Lekson, interview, Washington, D.C., July 28, 2008.

51. Commission on the Roles and Capabilities of the United States Intelligence Community, *Preparing for the Twenty-First Century: An Appraisal of U.S. Intelligence* (Washington, D.C.: Government Printing Office, 1996), 12–13. There are, of course, dramatic intelligence failures that have significantly undermined or weakened U.S. diplomacy and national security, ranging from the failure to anticipate the Japanese attack on Pearl Harbor in 1941 to the misreading of the status of Saddam Hussein's nuclear program in 2002–3.

52. Robert Schulzinger, "American Presidents and Negotiators," 167.

53. Bohlen, *Witness to History*, 171. Charles Bohlen served as an interpreter at both the Yalta and the Potsdam conferences in 1945; he later became U.S. ambassador to the Soviet Union.

The U.S. record of attention to detail is by no means unblemished. For instance, when negotiating a joint British-Soviet-American statement on Poland in 1945, neither the Americans nor the British focused on the Soviet insertion of the phrase "in the first instance in Moscow" in the text describing who would be authorized to negotiate for the Polish Provisional Government.[54] Such mistakes, however, were not often repeated, especially not with the Soviets once World War II gave way to the Cold War. Surveying U.S. diplomacy in 1956, when the Cold War was still in its formative years, Kissinger observed that "our positions have usually been worked out with great attention to their legal content."[55] A quarter of a century later, when Kissinger was national security adviser, he lavished a similar attention to detail on preparations for President Richard Nixon's visit to China. Kissinger spent no fewer than eighteen months preparing for his own—secret—visit to Beijing, and subsequently spent several more months drafting the communiqué that was issued when Nixon and Mao Zedong (Mao Tse-tung) finally announced that their countries had embarked on a new relationship.[56]

In multilateral negotiations, American officials will sometimes even try to help allied governments do their preparatory homework. In the negotiations over German reunification in 1990, for example, the George H. W. Bush administration briefed the West German leader, Helmut Kohl, on what Secretary of State Baker had recently discussed with Soviet foreign minister Eduard Shevardnadze, and gave Kohl suggestions on how he should handle the tone and substance of his forthcoming meeting with Soviet leader Mikhail Gorbachev.[57]

Such conduct does not go unnoticed by foreign counterparts. A former Turkish ambassador to Washington, Faruk Logoglu, notes that Americans "were generally well prepared for their meetings. They had clear goals and objectives and their 'talking points' were concise and targeted. As long as negotiations stayed smooth and remained within the margins of the agreed interagency positions, American officials performed with skill and efficacy."[58] The veteran Russian diplomat Yuri Nazarkin, an arms control specialist, encountered many lawyers on the American side, because legal experts tended to feature prominently in U.S. negotiating teams for arms control talks with the Soviets.[59] "Our American counterparts," he recollects, "were very good professionals." Except for one political appointee, who

54. Ibid., 192.

55. Kissinger, "Reflections," 46.

56. See Henry Kissinger, *The White House Years* (Boston: Little, Brown, 1979).

57. See Ross, *Statecraft*, 41.

58. Faruk Logoglu, "Negotiating Security: The Pushy Superpower," 212.

59. See, for instance, John H. McNeill, "U.S.-USSR Nuclear Arms Negotiations: The Process and the Lawyer," *American Journal of International Law* 79, no. 1 (January 1985): 52–67.

"was completely lost," all his American interlocutors, "from ambassadors to junior diplomats—were competent, well prepared, and highly qualified.[60]

The Moralistic Negotiator

The moralistic negotiator sits in awkward contrast to the businesslike official. Whereas the latter prefers practicalities to principles and regards emotional out-bursts as distractions from reaching deals, the moralistic negotiator is fired with idealism and sees nothing wrong in passionately expressing those beliefs. The mor-alist has more in common with his legalistic colleague. While the latter may look skeptically at the moralist who brings emotions and ideals to the bargaining table, both are concerned with rules: the legalist wants to ensure that all sides play by the same rules, while the moralist (with a dim view of the morality of problematic countries) anticipates that others will try to flout the rules. George Kennan, the iconic diplomat famous as the architect of the Cold War doctrine of containment, saw a clear connection between the two mind-sets. He denounced in 1951 what he called the "legalistic-moralistic approach to international problems"[61] as "utopian in its expectations, legalistic in its concept of methodology, moralistic in the high demands it seemed to place on others, and self-righteous in the degree of high-mindedness and rectitude it imparted to ourselves."[62]

Kennan, one of the earliest exponents of the realist school of diplomacy, fretted that "idealism" had dominated American foreign policymaking from the Civil War to World War II. And for realists like Kennan, there was no greater embodiment of the flaws of idealism than its greatest presidential exponent, Woodrow Wilson—so much so that "Wilsonianism" now serves as a shorthand for American idealism in international affairs. Another eminent realist, Henry Kissinger, has pointed an ac-cusing finger at the ghost of Woodrow Wilson:

> For Wilson, the justification of America's international role was messianic: America had an obligation, not to the balance of power, but to spread its principles throughout the world. . . . For three generations, critics have savaged Wilson's analysis and conclusions; and yet, in all this time, Wilson's principles have remained the bedrock of American foreign policy thinking.[63]

Thus, when Richard Nixon—"the first president since Theodore Roosevelt to con-duct American foreign policy largely in the name of the national interest"—sought not to excoriate but to negotiate with Brezhnev's Soviet Union and Mao's China, he faced bitter opposition within Washington and discovered that his approach

---

60. Yuri Nazarkin, "Negotiating as a Rival," 239.

61. George Kennan, *American Diplomacy, 1900–1950* (Chicago: University of Chicago Press, 1951), 93.

62. George Kennan, *Memoirs, 1950–1963* (Boston: Little Brown, 1967), 71.

63. Kissinger, *Diplomacy*, 30, 52.

produced "a dearth of emotional resonance among the American people."[64] Nixon's successors in the White House—whether liberals such as Jimmy Carter or conservatives such as Ronald Reagan and George W. Bush—have reasserted the primacy of idealism insofar as their foreign policies, in their public justifications, have emphasized the promotion of U.S. values abroad as opposed to a more power-oriented pursuit of the national interest.

In this volume, we favor the term "moralistic" rather than "idealistic" in part because in the ears of those listening to American negotiators on the other side of the bargaining table, the rhetoric sounds a lot more like moralizing than philosophizing. For instance, Secretary of State John Foster Dulles did not endear himself to his Indian interlocutors when, as Lalit Mansingh, a former foreign minister of India, notes in this volume, "Dulles declared nonalignment 'immoral' and incompatible with friendship with the United States."[65] He adds that "American officials were seen as arrogant, self-righteous, condescending, and culturally insensitive."[66]

Another reason for the choice of "moralistic" over "idealistic" or "Wilsonian" is that this tendency well predates the presidency that gave it its most powerful expression. Indeed, American idealism in the country's formative years was strongly tied to isolationism—that very un-evangelical, un-Wilsonian aversion to involvement in the complex challenges of international affairs lest the necessary contact corrupt or otherwise endanger America's values and security. The leaders of America's fight for independence were in no doubt of the moral worth of their cause: "We are fighting for the dignity and happiness of human nature," Benjamin Franklin declared in 1777.[67] But George Washington in his farewell address and Thomas Jefferson in his inaugural address made clear that the young United States should "steer clear of permanent alliances" or "entangling alliances." Throughout the nineteenth century, the United States often adopted a morally superior tone toward weaker nations in the Western Hemisphere or Asia. When, in World War I, America led by Wilson abandoned isolationism, it did not abandon the urge to moralize. To the contrary, Wilson raised it to new heights, asserting that the fate of the United States depended on it fulfilling its God-given duty to spread the ideal of freedom to other countries:

> We set this Nation up to make men free, and we did not confine our conception and purpose to America, and now we will make [all] men free. If we did not do that, all the fame of America would be gone, and all her power would be dissipated.[68]

---

64. Ibid., 731.

65. Lalit Mansingh, "Negotiating Bilaterally: India's Evolving Experience with the United States," 254.

66. Ibid., 257.

67. Quoted in H.W. Brands, *The First American: The Life and Times of Benjamin Franklin* (New York: Doubleday, 2000), 532.

68. From a speech given in 1919, quoted in Kissinger, *Diplomacy*, 50.

Many U.S. presidents have echoed that call. Jimmy Carter, for instance, in a commencement speech at the University of Notre Dame in June 1977, declared, "It is a new world, and we should help to shape it. It is a new world that calls for a new American foreign policy—a policy based on constant decency in its values and on optimism in our historical vision." He "reaffirmed America's commitment to human rights as a fundamental tenet of our foreign policy," and went on to summarize that policy as follows:

> Our policy is based on an historical vision of America's role. Our policy is derived from a larger view of global change. Our policy is rooted in our moral values, which never change. Our policy is reinforced by our material wealth and by our military power. Our policy is designed to serve mankind. And it is a policy that I hope will make you proud to be Americans.[69]

Among recent presidents, perhaps George W. Bush voiced the greatest crusading zeal, unequivocally expressing his determination to use American power to give other nations the opportunity to embrace values that he saw as God-given and universal yet embodied in the American experience. In his second inaugural address, he declared:

> America's vital interests and our deepest beliefs are now one. From the day of our founding, we have proclaimed that every man and woman on this earth has rights, and dignity, and matchless value, because they bear the image of the Maker of Heaven and earth. Across the generations we have proclaimed the imperative of self-government, because no one is fit to be a master, and no one deserves to be a slave. Advancing these ideals is the mission that created our Nation. It is the honorable achievement of our fathers. Now it is the urgent requirement of our nation's security, and the calling of our time.
>
> So it is the policy of the United States to seek and support the growth of democratic movements and institutions in every nation and culture, with the ultimate goal of ending tyranny in our world. . . .
>
> Americans, of all people, should never be surprised by the power of our ideals. Eventually, the call of freedom comes to every mind and every soul. We do not accept the existence of permanent tyranny because we do not accept the possibility of permanent slavery. Liberty will come to those who love it.[70]

The confidence and willingness to moralize stems in large part from the sense of American "exceptionalism"—the belief that the United States is uniquely blessed in its global mission by God or Providence; by its history, founding principles, political system, or political economy; or by its geography, demography, natural resources, or other physical attributes.[71] According to historian Richard Hofstadter, "It has been our fate as a nation not to have ideologies, but to be one."[72] Exceptionalism

---

69.   Jimmy Carter, "Human Rights and Foreign Policy," http://www.teachingamericanhistory.org/library/index.asp?document=727.

70.   White House press release, "President Sworn-In to Second Term," January 20, 2005, http://www.whitehouse.gov/news/releases/2005/01/20050120-1.html.

71.   Exceptionalism might have first been identified by Alexis de Tocqueville in 1831, but the concept is still hotly debated by the public and scholars. See, for instance, Lipset, *American Exceptionalism*.

72.   Quoted in Michael Kazin, "The Right's Unsung Prophet," *Nation*, no. 248 (February 20, 1989), 242.

has manifested itself throughout U.S. history, from John Winthrop's seventeenth-century notion that the New England Puritans had built "a shining city upon a hill" to stand as a moral exemplar to the rest of the world; to the eighteenth-century assertions that the Revolutionary War had ushered in an entirely new philosophy and system of governance; to the nineteenth-century credo of Manifest Destiny that justified territorial expansion on the American continent; to the twentieth-century Cold War determination with which America spearheaded the crusade against godless and tyrannical Communism.

That said, exceptionalism has had its domestic agnostics, critics, and dissenters. Writing in the mid-1960s, as U.S. involvement in the Vietnam War escalated, Senator William Fulbright cautioned Americans that

> power tends to confuse itself with virtue and a great nation is particularly susceptible to the idea that its power is a sign of God's favor, conferring upon it a special responsibility for other nations—to make them richer and happier and wiser, to remake them, that is, in its own shining image. Power confuses itself with virtue and tends also to take itself for omnipotence.[73]

From the vantage point of the 1990s, Henry Kissinger offered a more ambivalent view, arguing that while "exceptionalism inspired America's foreign policy and gave the United States the fortitude to prevail in the Cold War," it also risks "two [contrasting] temptations": "the notion that America must remedy every wrong and stabilize every dislocation, and the latent [and contradictory] instinct to withdraw into itself." Exceptionalism, argues Kissinger, will not serve America well "in the multipolar world of the twenty-first century."[74] Others have echoed this latter view, arguing that exceptionalism fosters a self-image that makes it hard for Americans to compromise.[75] On a more operational level, Strobe Talbott, when deputy secretary of state under President Clinton, made the case for America abiding "by the common rules of the road" rather than taking an exceptionalist stance: "Well-crafted international commitments and a comprehensive strategy of engagement enhance rather than dilute our mastery of our own fate as a nation. . . . They help the United States to channel the forces of interdependence, bending them to the advantage of our own citizens and of other nations that share our interests and values."[76] Early in her tenure as President George W. Bush's secretary of state, Con-

---

73. William Fulbright, *The Arrogance of Power* (New York: Random House, 1966). Fulbright also contends that while "reason and moderation" prevail in American foreign policy "as long as things are going tolerably well or as long as our problems seem clear and finite and manageable . . . when some event or leader of opinion has aroused the people to a state of high emotion, our puritan spirit has tended to break through, leading us to look at the world through the distorting prism of a harsh and angry moralism."

74. Kissinger, *Diplomacy*, 802–803.

75. See, for instance, Ross, *Statecraft*, 175.

76. Strobe Talbott, "Globalization and Diplomacy: A Practitioner's Perspective," *Foreign Policy*, no. 108 (Fall 1997): 82. Even so, Talbott still emphasized "the United States has a central role to play in that new struggle [between the forces of stability and instability], just as it did in the old one [between East and West]," and argued that by obliging other nations to adhere to "a system of equity and openness," the United States would promote

doleezza Rice advocated bridging the divide between "principles and values" and "policy outcomes" with "practical idealism," which would form "the day-to-day operational policy connection" between ideals and outcomes.[77]

Such arguments and proposals, however, have rarely or only temporarily tempered exceptionalist attitudes. Many Americans believe that the presumed "special status" of the United States renders it exempt from the same limitations on the behavior of other states and deserving of special consideration. Many foreign governments see such an outlook at work, for example, in the American disinclination to ratify the Convention on the Rights of the Child (now ratified by 192 countries, but not by the United States, largely because of domestic political disputes) and the Kyoto Protocol on greenhouse gases (the United States is one of only two of the protocol's 184 signatories not to have ratified the agreement). Likewise, when President Clinton opted not to refer the Rome Treaty creating the International Criminal Court (ICC) to the Senate for its advice and consent (Clinton knew that such consent would not be forthcoming), he raised more than a few eyebrows abroad. After all, the United States had been negotiating to create the ICC for half a century, since the UN General Assembly passed a resolution inviting the creation of such an entity in 1948.

While idealistic rhetoric is more commonly heard at presidential summits than in the trenches of everyday diplomacy, exceptionalist attitudes do percolate down from high-level policymakers to mid- and low-level negotiators and can influence negotiations on almost any subject, from nuclear nonproliferation to trade, from international law to the environment. For diplomats accustomed to negotiating with exceptionalist-minded American officials, the experience can be wearing. Just two examples, both from contributors to this volume, capture the essence of the complaint. Reflecting on bilateral trade negotiations between the United States and Japan, Koji Watanabe observes:

> Exhibiting high-handedness, self-centeredness, and impatience, American negotiators cite their own domestic constraints while ignoring the domestic difficulties of their negotiating counterparts. U.S. officials often refer repeatedly to congressional pressure for import restrictions or antidumping measures, citing various pieces of new trade legislation. At the same time, Americans seem to be almost indifferent to established multilateral norms such as those embodied in the GATT, as if unapologetically taking the approach that "we are the only superpower, so we can break the rules if we want to."[78]

David Hannay, commenting on the U.S. approach to multilateral diplomacy, displays a similar irritation and frustration. The United States, notes Hannay, "was

---

a wide range of noble causes, including "equitable economic development" and "the spread and consolidation of democracy" (pp. 82–83).

77.   See the interview with Condoleezza Rice in the *Washington Post*, July 31, 2005, http://www.washingtonpost.com/wp-dyn/content/article/2005/07/29/AR2005072901435.html.

78.   Koji Watanabe, "Negotiating Trade: A Bitter Experience for Japanese Negotiators," 205.

certainly not dragged unwillingly into [the] massive expansion of multilateral diplomacy and negotiation" that occurred in the aftermath of World War II, but

> gradually a pattern of U.S. exceptionalism took shape, often driven by congressional acts and pressure, under which the United States held other members of these many organizations to tighter disciplines than they were prepared to submit to themselves. . . . Presidents Ronald Reagan and George W. Bush regarded [multilateral diplomacy] as, at best, an optional extra, and they frequently used organizations such as the United Nations as a whipping boy for their frustration when they encountered resistance to U.S. policy choices.[79]

The Superpower Negotiator

The moralistic mind-set predates the rise of the United States to global power, and its prevalence continues to vary according to the personalities of different administrations and officials, and the wider relationship between the parties to a specific negotiation. By contrast, the mind-set of a superpower is now always present; it is the elephant in the negotiating room, an intimidating presence that sometimes charges through discussions, sometimes stands quietly in a corner, but always demands to be acknowledged. In essence, the superpower mind-set is conscious of America's preeminent power and focuses on using or threatening to use that power in pursuit of national interests.

We use the term "superpower," but the term most frequently invoked by the foreign officials who took part in the CCN project was "hegemonic."[80] Some American negotiators accept the description;[81] many, if not most, balk at it, not only because they see it as pejorative but also because they simply do not believe that they are inclined to, or capable of, imposing their will on others. This marked difference in perceptions between American negotiators and their foreign counterparts obviously says a good deal about contrasting self-images and asymmetries of power. It may also indicate some overlap between the moralistic and superpower/hegemonic

---

79.   Hannay, "Negotiating Multilaterally," 272.

80.   Such usage, it may be noted, is common. Robert Kagan, for instance, uses the term several times when characterizing—or quoting—foreign perceptions of the United States. He notes, for example, "The United States, which in the 1990s was already seen by many as a bullying hegemon, came to be viewed after September 11 as a self-absorbed, bullying hegemon." See Kagan, "The September 12 Paradigm," *Foreign Affairs* (September–October 2008): 33.

   Some scholars, however, have argued that "hegemonic" implies omnipotence, something that the United States does not possess. See, for instance, John Mearsheimer, *The Tragedy of Great Power Politics* (New York: W. W. Norton, 2001), 40. The label "hegemonic" can also provoke semantic and political controversy, especially among Americans discussing the United States' position in today's globalized world; see, for example, the discussion involving (among others) Zbigniew Brzezinski and Richard Haass, advisers to Presidents Carter and Bush, respectively, on the BBC program *Analysis*, on July 4, 2004, http://news.bbc.co.uk/nol/shared/spl/hi/programmes/analysis/transcripts/07_04_05.txt.

   In an article titled "Hegemon and Proud of It" and published in 1998, Deputy Secretary of State Strobe Talbott saw "no need to apologize for our leadership role." See "Hegemon and Proud of It," *Slate*, June 27, 1998, http://www.slate.com/id/2509.

81.   Phyllis Oakley, recalling her work in the mid-1990s on humanitarian crises, comments, "Well, there is no doubt that we were hegemonic in dealing with a lot of these international organizations." Oakley, interview, 27.

mind-sets insofar as American officials see themselves as promoting universally beneficial values rather than using their unmatched power to force others to accept U.S. demands. (A somewhat similar readiness to conflate self-interest and universal truths has been noted in the case of French negotiators, who, says Gérard Araud, "do not see in their [negotiating] position the defense of interests but [rather] the expression of a transcendent reason of which they have the monopoly. They sincerely do not see that, as if by chance, this reason justifies their interests precisely.")[82]

During the Cold War, the United States set itself the goal of becoming preponderant in its confrontation with the Soviet Union. A State Department memo of 1952 baldly stated: "Given the polarization of power around the U.S.S.R. and U.S., to seek less than preponderant power would be to opt for defeat. Preponderant power must be the objective of U.S. policy."[83] Forty years later, with the Soviet Union having recently dissolved, an internal Pentagon document, the "Defense Planning Guidance" (drafted under the supervision of Paul Wolfowitz, the undersecretary for policy, and approved by Secretary of Defense Richard Cheney), urged the United States to focus on preserving its status as the world's sole superpower. The document laid out two major policy goals. One was to "address sources of regional conflict and instability" that could "unsettle international relations" by threatening the interests of the United States or its allies. The other goal was "to prevent the reemergence of a new rival" for world power and deter potential competitors for military predominance.[84]

Today, the United States is still the most potent power on the global stage, but it is far from omnipotent. As the currently uncertain outcomes of battles within the "global war on terrorism" demonstrate, translating seemingly preponderant power into solid victories is difficult: efforts to use seemingly overwhelming military force encounter effective counterstrategies and provoke unwanted political repercussions, or "blowback." Moreover, U.S. influence and power may well be declining, at least relatively, as other states rise to contest its political authority, challenge its economic preeminence, and develop effective military countermeasures. The global financial crisis that erupted in 2008 showed that, despite the ability of the American economy to generate tremendous wealth, it remains vulnerable to severe shocks—jolts that in the case of the financial crisis eradicated hundreds of billions of dollars in wealth and added similar amounts of debt to the U.S. fiscal balance sheet as the federal government pursued economic revival. Nonetheless, the U.S.

---

82.   Quoted in Cogan, *French Negotiating Behavior*, 11.

83.   The paper is reproduced in FRUS, 1952–54, 2:64. For Nitze's authorship, see Christopher Layne, *The Peace of Illusions: American Grand Strategy from 1940 to the Present* (Ithaca: Cornell University Press, 2006), 229n79.

84.   Quoted from "'Prevent the Reemergence of a New Rival': The Making of the Cheney Regional Defense Strategy, 1991–1992," Nuclear Vault, part of George Washington University's National Security Archive, http://www.gwu.edu/~nsarchiv/nukevault/ebb245/index.htm.

economy remains the largest and most adaptable in the world. Similarly, while the need to fight two asymmetric wars—in Iraq and Afghanistan—has severely tested the limits of U.S. military capabilities, the U.S. military continues to have no peers in terms of global reach, conventional weaponry and tactics, and logistical capacity. This economic and military superiority continues to underwrite political and diplomatic preponderance.

Inevitably, this preponderant status casts a long shadow over negotiations. The chill of that shadow, however, is felt only on one side of the table—the other side. American officials are conscious, of course, of their country's unparalleled power and the leverage it gives them in almost any negotiating encounter, but most nonetheless tend to see themselves not as bullies but as businesslike negotiators operating from a position of strength—tough but fair. The impression on the other side of the table, however, is often very different: U.S. officials might be courteous and professional, but they are seen as representatives of a hegemonic superpower that is often less inclined to negotiate than it is to overwhelm or intimidate negotiating counterparts into acceding to American positions. Richard Smyser, the U.S. assistant secretary for refugee programs in the early 1980s, has observed that in many multilateral organizations, "Americans had the reputation of thinking that since they made the largest contributions, they could tell everyone how to do things."[85] In this volume, Turkish ambassador Faruk Logoglu recounts the American effort "to overwhelm the Turkish side with a staged show of political power" during negotiations over whether U.S. troops could enter Iraq through Turkish territory. In meeting after meeting, Turkish officials, accustomed to dealing with significantly lower-level American officials, were surprised to find Washington's big guns arrayed against them: first, not one but a group of deputy secretaries of several departments; then, the secretaries themselves; and finally the president himself, who invited the visiting Turkish foreign minister and state minister for the economy to the Oval Office.[86]

The superpower mind-set is naturally associated with realism, which regards power as the primary consideration motivating the behavior of states in the international arena. Even so, many U.S. officials see no contradiction in marrying cold calculations of national interests with assertions of American moral leadership. Some foreign counterparts (especially those from countries unaccustomed to exercising significant power internationally) might see this admixture as peculiar or unseemly, but for Americans steeped in their country's exceptionalism, it comes naturally. Kissinger, citing a speech that Secretary of State George Shultz gave in 1985 about the Reagan administration's policy of supporting anticommunist insurgencies, has observed: "[Shultz's] high-flying Wilsonian language in support of freedom and de-

---

85. Smyser made the comment during a meeting about enhancing American negotiating capacities, United States Institute of Peace, April 17, 2009, Washington, D.C.

86. Logoglu, "Negotiating Security," 216.

mocracy globally was leavened by an almost Machiavellian realism. . . . The Reagan administration dispensed aid not only to genuine democrats . . . but also to Islamic fundamentalists . . . to rightists . . . and to tribal warlords."[87]

At times, however, power is wielded in raw form, ungloved with Wilsonian moralism. Perhaps the most famous—alleged—instance in recent years occurred in the aftermath of 9/11, when, according to President Pervez Musharraf of Pakistan, Deputy Secretary of State Richard Armitage threatened Pakistan's intelligence director that the United States would bomb Pakistan "back to the stone age" unless it cooperated in the fight against al Qaeda.[88] Armitage immediately denied the allegation that he had threatened military action against Pakistan. But two things are worth noting. First, Musharraf's claim was given credence throughout the world, suggesting that though it may well have been inaccurate, it was seen as in keeping with the character of American diplomacy—at least of that time. Second, Armitage's own recollection of the conversation, as quoted in media reports, reveals an American official prepared to brook no hint of compromise or delay as he pressed for acceptance of U.S. demands:

> "I told him [recounted Armitage] in a very straightforward way this was a black-and-white issue for Americans. You were either for us or against us.
>
> He started to tell me about Pakistan's history. . . . I said, 'You should communicate with your president and see if you are willing to cooperate with us.'"
>
> He said he told Gen. M that if the answer was yes, they could meet the next day and Armitage would tell him the U.S. requirements. "They will be onerous," he said he told the Pakistani.
>
> "The general came back the next day and said they were willing to go along with us. And I presented to him a list of items Secretary Powell and I had jotted down the night before."[89]

Clearly, America's sense of its preponderant power—and other countries' awareness of that power—has its advantages for U.S. negotiators. Flexing American muscle worked for Armitage (in whichever version of the conversation one accepts). Other, more subtle benefits also flow from that status. For instance, as Gilles Andreani notes: "The virtue of being the only remaining superpower is to put on others the burden of the proof: unless it is grossly manipulative, or deeply offensive to somebody, the American characterization of the issue will normally carry a great weight."[90]

Global preponderance, however, can also bring its own problems. David Hannay, for instance, remarks that with the end of the Cold War, a wide range of previously taboo subjects "forced their way onto the agenda of international organizations. The

---

87. Kissinger, *Diplomacy*, 774.

88. See, for example, the BBC report, "U.S. 'Threatened to Bomb' Pakistan," September 22, 2006, http://news.bbc.co.uk/2/hi/south_asia/5369198.stm.

89. "Armitage Refutes Musharraf's Claims," CBS News, September 22, 2006, http://www.cbsnews.com/stories/2006/09/22/terror/main2035633.shtml.

90. Andreani, "Negotiating with Savior Faire," 283–84.

United States alone had to decide on pretty well every one of them whether to back collective action or to prevent any collective response or to see it fail through neglect. . . . These demands led to the overloading of the policymaking machine in Washington and also to the overload on the U.S. ambassador at the United Nations."[91] Taking a broader view, Yuri Nazarkin sees America's "hegemonic approach" as threatening the country's negotiating skills. If U.S. policymakers and diplomats calculate that if they can dictate terms, then they do not need to negotiate and compromise, he argues. In the event that U.S. foreign policy returns "to the spirit of balanced negotiation and showing willingness to compromise . . . the professionalism and skills of the negotiators of the 1970s and 1980s will again be in demand."[92]

Nazarkin—not surprisingly, perhaps, for a former Soviet negotiator—dates a growing U.S. reliance "on pressure and arm twisting" to the demise of the Soviet Union. Other observers point to other turning points, most commonly 9/11. Logoglu, for instance, comments:

> While generally imperial in essence, American negotiating style in the pre-9/11 period was not necessarily overbearing or pushy. The United States knew it could afford to be generous, flexible, patient, and accommodating. Many of the abrasive features of American behavior did not have to rise to the fore.
>
> This all came to an abrupt and violent end on September 11. That day America forever lost its insular innocence. Permanently scarred, feeling vulnerable and less safe, America was never again to be the same.[93]

Certainly, the terrorist attacks on the Pentagon and World Trade Center made U.S. officials more inclined to cross the always hazy line between, on the one side, an exceptionalist self-image and a superpower's self-confidence and, on the other side, the uncompromising behavior of a nation under threat. The very real sense of national vulnerability made American negotiators both reluctant to scale down U.S. demands and impatient with time-consuming deal making and consensus building; it also fostered a readiness—even an eagerness—to go it alone. As President George W. Bush famously put it in his September 20, 2001, speech to Congress, "Every nation, in every region, now has a decision to make. Either you are with us, or you are with the terrorists."[94]

The most evident recent instance of this inclination, of course, was the Bush administration's determination to press ahead with an invasion of Iraq despite failing to secure the support of the UN Security Council in early 2003 for a resolution unambiguously authorizing military action. (This episode is discussed in chapter 3,

---

91.   Hannay, "Negotiating Multilaterally," 273.

92.   Nazarkin, "Negotiating as a Rival," 238.

93.   Logoglu, "Negotiating Security," 211.

94.   George W. Bush, "Address to a Joint Session of Congress and the American People," United States Capitol, September 20, 2001, http://www.whitehouse.gov/news/releases/2001/09/20010920-8.html.

pp. 86–88.) Foreign leaders have also taken many other American moves, both before and after the invasion of Iraq, as evidence of unilateralism, among them the U.S. withdrawal from the Anti-Ballistic Missile Treaty, rejection of the Kyoto Protocol on global warming, and opposition to the creation of an International Criminal Court. French prime minister Lionel Jospin declared in July 2001, "The United States often behaves in a unilateral manner and has difficulty in assuming the role it aspires to as organizer of the international community." Six weeks earlier, the French foreign minister, Hubert Védrine, had described "the predominant weight of the United States and the absence for the moment of a counterweight" as "the major fact of the global world today." The United States' weight, he said, "leads it to hegemony, and the idea it has of its mission to unilateralism. And that's inadmissible"[95] Six years later, in February 2007, the *Washington Post* reported that Russian president Vladimir Putin "said that Washington's unilateral, militaristic approach had made the world a more dangerous place than at any time during the Cold War. 'The United States has overstepped its national borders in every way,' he said in an address at an annual international security conference here. 'Nobody feels secure anymore, because nobody can take safety behind the stone wall of international law.'"[96]

Each of these claims is debatable—and each of these claimants is hardly a disinterested observer—but at a minimum it seems accurate to say that in the early years of the twenty-first century the United States adopted a policy described by Richard Haass (head of Policy Planning in Colin Powell's State Department) as "multilateralism à la carte."[97] And as Clyde Prestowitz, a trade negotiator during the Reagan administration, pointed out in 2002, "Often the form matters as much as the substance. As an editor in Tokyo noted, 'Imagine how different the reaction to U.S. rejection of the Kyoto treaty would have been if the U.S. had explained the treaty's flaws publicly and made a counterproposal, rather than just saying the treaty wasn't good for the American economy.'"[98]

The superpower mind-set is by no means necessarily unilateralist. The United States was *a* predominant power when President George H. W. Bush and his secretary of state, James Baker, sought support for the first Gulf War, and it was *the* predominant power for most of the 1990s, when the United States sought out multilateral solutions to many issues confronting it. The administration of George W. Bush secured the military support of almost three dozen countries for the Iraq campaign, and of more than three dozen countries in the NATO-led operation

---

95.   Quoted in John Vincour, "Going It Alone: U.S. Upsets France," *International Herald Tribune*, August 18, 2001.

96.   Thomas E. Ricks and Craig Whitlock, "Putin Hits U.S. over Unilateral Approach," *Washington Post*, February 11, 2007.

97.   Quoted in Henry C. K. Liu, "US Unilateralism: Nonproliferation and Unilateral Proliferation," *Global Research*, August 29, 2006, http://www.globalresearch.ca/index.php?context=viewArticle&code=LIU20060701&articleId=3089.

98.   Clyde Prestowitz, "America the Arrogant: Why Don't We Listen Anymore?" *Washington Post*, July 7, 2002.

in Afghanistan.[99] To some extent, indeed, collective action affords greater opportunities than unilateralism for the expression of predominant power; after all, unilateralism often entails ignoring other states, whereas predominance typically entails employing one's power to impress, overawe, intimidate, cajole, and co-opt other states, as well as to assemble coalitions and create diplomatic and political momentum.

But if, like an actor, the superpower mind-set likes an audience, it does not necessarily like to trade lines with other actors, preferring instead to direct the action and determine the denouement. Seen from the other side of the bargaining table, American negotiators can sometimes seem domineering, insistent, and uncompromising. They can be less concerned to negotiate, in the sense of exchanging views and trading concessions, than to dictate terms or to persuade their counterparts of the rightness or potency of the U.S. position. Even cordial and conspicuously polite U.S. representatives will sometimes adopt take-it-or-leave-it positions or assert the primacy of the American role in world affairs in unvarnished form. Secretary of State Madeleine Albright provoked a good deal of critical comment abroad when, during a television interview in 1998, she asserted that as "the only superpower" the United States has unique responsibilities but also unique abilities. "We stand tall," she told ABC-TV's Ted Koppel, "and therefore we can see further."[100]

U.S. negotiators do not consistently behave in high-handed fashion. Especially when Americans undertake third-party mediation, they are often evenhanded, patient, and ready to listen. In some bilateral and multilateral encounters, especially in a time of national security crisis, however, U.S. negotiators display limited grace and humility as they seek to impose—at the direction of their superiors—inflexible terms. In such situations, American negotiators tend to subscribe to Armitage's definition: "Diplomacy is the art of letting the other guy have our way."[101]

* * *

The mind-set of a superpower, it must be remembered, is just one of four mind-sets that shape U.S. negotiating behavior. While some American officials may—in certain circumstances—be inclined to steamroller their counterparts, others will seek out win-win solutions that involve compromises on both sides. Furthermore,

---

99.   In March 2004, soldiers from thirty-three countries other than the United States were in Iraq; see http:// pwhce.org/willing.html#troops. By August 2006, the figure was down to between twenty-one and twenty-seven (the latter figure was the State Department's); see http://www.globalsecurity.org/military/ops/iraq_orbat_coalition. htm. In March 2008, NATO listed thirty-nine troop-contributing countries (one of which was the United States) to the International Security Assistance Force in Afghanistan; see http://www.nato.int/isaf/structure/nations/ index.html.

100.   From an interview with Ted Koppel on ABC's *Nightline* program, February 20, 1998. A transcript is at http://www.fas.org/news/iraq/1998/02/20/98022004_tpo.html.

101.   Quoted in Barbara Slavin, *Bitter Friends, Bosom Enemies: Iran, the U.S., and the Twisted Path to Confrontation* (New York: St. Martin's Press, 2007), 223.

in most circumstances, foreign officials will encounter not the pure form of a single mind-set but a blend of all four.

The composition of a specific blend will depend on a wide range of factors, making reliable predictions of U.S. negotiating behavior in any given situation impossible. Some general patterns are discernible, however. For instance, the superpower mind-set is likely to be more pronounced when vital interests, especially matters of national security, are on the line; the moralistic approach will be more evident when American values seem to be at stake and when a negotiation takes place in the spotlight of public or congressional attention (see chapter 5); the businesslike and legalistic mind-sets are more pronounced when economic issues are involved and congressional or media interest in a negotiation is low, when negotiations have become protracted and routine, and when the negotiating partner is an ally.

Although the admixture of the four mind-sets can produce a wide variety of behaviors, that range still has its limits. Indeed, one way to grasp the essential character of American negotiating behavior is to define what it is not. For instance, rarely, if ever, will an American negotiator adopt a submissive or subordinate posture, display indifference to the passage of time, let the other side dictate the wording of an agreement, or talk for the sake of talking.

But if these specific behavioral activities are, within the world of diplomatic negotiation, un-American, what types of behavior are quintessentially American? What particular negotiating activities, traits, and characteristics do the four mind-sets engender? We take up these questions in the next three chapters.

3

At the Bargaining Table

Whereas the previous chapter presented a composite portrait of the American negotiator, this chapter assesses the dynamic elements in American negotiating behavior: how American negotiators typically build relationships, deploy inducements, exert pressure, manage their time, and communicate with their interlocutors. The chapter also highlights some differences between the American approaches to bilateral as opposed to multilateral negotiations.

While the chapter covers a range of subjects, it focuses only on "track-one" negotiations (i.e., direct negotiations between official representatives from two or more states) and only on U.S. behavior *within the formal negotiating environment*. To be sure, the notion of such an environment is imprecise, temporally, physically, and conceptually. Diplomatic negotiations range over time and space. They begin long before two negotiating teams take their seats around a green baize table festooned with flags and supplied with bottled water. They may proceed along two or more tracks simultaneously—sometimes with one track a secret, more authoritative venue for exchanges[1]—and they almost always involve people far away from the formal venue. And they conclude—if, in fact, they do come to agreement—at not one but several different points in time: when the U.S. negotiating team concludes the elements of a deal; when the U.S. president or secretary of state signs the formal statement of that agreement; when the Senate ratifies the agreement (if a treaty is part of the deal); when the agreement begins to be implemented; and when—if ever—implementation is completed.

Yet, for all this complexity, it is both analytically and operationally useful to distinguish between negotiations that involve designated officials from the respective governments bargaining directly with one another, and negotiations conducted indirectly (e.g., through the media or in back channels) or negotiations conducted internally (i.e., negotiations among U.S. officials). As chapter 4 discusses, Americans are often so confident that they will prevail in formal, direct negotiations that

---

1. The American use of secret, or "back channel," diplomacy is discussed in chapter 4.

they devote relatively little effort to bolstering their position away from the negotiating table by, for example, creating public expectations via the press or bringing third parties into play. And as chapter 2 suggests and chapter 5 confirms, American officials tend to behave differently when they negotiate among themselves than when they deal with foreign counterparts. This is hardly surprising: different players are involved and different rules obtained. To take just one example: the superpower mind-set identified in chapter 2 might see negotiations between states as a contest in which power is both the primary weapon and the primary goal, but when American officials negotiate among themselves, they are competing not for power per se but for the ear of an acknowledged arbiter and authority, the president.

Building Relationships

Officials from some nations value negotiations as an opportunity to foster, cement, or exploit relationships. They will cultivate and leverage personal and national associations during a negotiation to secure a favorable deal for their government. Chinese negotiators, for example, will nurture "friendships" with foreign counterparts—develop *guanxi*—to "enmesh the foreign negotiator in a position they can manage to their own advantage."[2] By contrast, Japanese officials, despite their country's economic success, will often adopt a supplicant posture, rooted in the Japanese concept and practice of *amae*—"the inferior partner's expectation of the stronger party's benevolence in a hierarchical relationship."[3] Other East Asian negotiators carefully calibrate their bargaining stance according to their nation's status within the wider context of regional power relationships.

U.S. officials, by contrast, take a less personalized approach. From a businesslike perspective, negotiations are first and foremost about securing a concrete outcome. Building relationships per se is not the point of a negotiation, nor do relationships predetermine the U.S. posture toward a negotiating counterpart. Raised in a society characterized by high social mobility and relatively modest cultural markers of social stratification, American officials accord their interlocutors the courtesy and respect of equals. They may not regard the other country as the equal of their own; the enduring influence of exceptionalist ideas and the reality of post–Cold War predominance do not encourage notions of national equivalence. But at the negotiating table, American officials prefer to be treated and to treat others as equals, not as supplicants or superiors within the context of the wider bilateral relationship. Nor does that wider relationship necessarily dictate the terms of any agreement reached; indeed, as John Wood's chapter on U.S. negotiations with New Zealand

---

2. See Solomon, *Chinese Negotiating Behavior*, 31.

3. Cohen, *Negotiating across Cultures*, 89. Cohen discusses the application of *amae* not only by Japan but also by several other countries.

demonstrates, a long-term relationship may be sacrificed if it stands in the way of securing a highly significant shorter-term goal.

Yet Americans are hardly indifferent to relationships or oblivious to the advantages a positive personal association can impart to a negotiation. "Empathy for the other side is the normal basis of negotiations," declares Charles Freeman, who served as deputy chief of mission in Bangkok and Beijing and ambassador to Riyadh. "If people regard you as an interesting person, a bright person, a discerning person and you then turn around and show that you respect their intellect, you have high regard for their character, you think they're interesting, then you have a basis for discussion that facilitates solutions."[4] Stapleton Roy concurs, noting that "if the other side doesn't like or respect your negotiator, they will be reluctant to give that negotiator an agreement.... Whereas, if they respect your negotiator, the other side will give weight to the negotiator's judgment."[5]

While American officials do not cultivate relationships as assiduously as do some of their foreign counterparts and do not take pains to nurture relationships with lavish and carefully choreographed hospitality (see chapter 4), they nonetheless strive to develop positive associations with their opposite numbers. This is equally true of the topmost ranks of the U.S. policymaking system as well as of lower-level diplomats.

Relationship building at the highest levels

American presidents and their most senior lieutenants have long recognized the benefits of building personal relationships with their opposite numbers. During the prelude to German reunification, for instance, President George H. W. Bush and Secretary of State James Baker launched a highly intensive campaign of personal diplomacy designed to win the confidence of their counterparts in Germany, Britain, France, and Russia for Washington's policy toward German reunification. Over the course of twelve months, Bush held eleven bilateral meetings with those leaders and met several of them five or six more times in multilateral gatherings.[6] Baker was even more active, meeting his counterparts on almost thirty separate occasions, most of which lasted several hours and several of which spanned more than a single day. As Baker recalls in his memoir, *The Politics of Diplomacy*, these encounters were not purely businesslike. Interpersonal bonds were forged not only during substantive discussions but also in more relaxed social settings. Soviet foreign minister Eduard Shevardnadze, for instance, took Baker on a visit to a Russian Orthodox seminary outside of Russia, prompting the secretary of state to wonder,

---

4. Freeman, interview, 9, 53.

5. Roy, interview, 9.

6. Bush was equally energetic in his use of telephone diplomacy. Between the start of the Gulf crisis in August 1990 and the end of that year, for instance, he exchanged no fewer than forty telephone calls with his Turkish counterpart. See Stearns, *Talking to Strangers*, 14.

as the two men lit candles together, "if these exhibitions of faith, like the religious icon he gave me in Wyoming, weren't his way of showing me that we had more in common than politics." A couple of weeks later, the two men and their presidents were at Camp David, discussing regional affairs "in a very relaxed way and in causal attire," with Gorbachev reeling off "hilariously funny" one-liners. As Baker notes, Gorbachev's risqué jokes were "more appropriate to the relaxed conversation the six men were having than to publication in a book with 'Diplomacy' in its title."[7]

In fact, mutual enjoyment of spicey one-liners facilitated the kind of diplomacy that Bush and Baker were conducting, a diplomacy that depended on creating relationships of mutual respect and trust. Such relationships were nurtured not only by jokes and frequent meetings but also by the ability to empathize, to offer advice, and to make the counterparts' political lives a little easier. Bush, recalls Dennis Ross, explained to the Soviet leader at a summit in Malta "how he had deliberately understated the U.S. response to the fall of the Berlin wall—drawing some domestic U.S. criticism for it—so as not to 'complicate your life.' And Gorbachev said he had noted that and appreciated it." Ross goes on to note that "Gorbachev's whole demeanor changed as Bush presented his initiative and they had this exchange."[8]

Bush's and Baker's predecessors—Ronald Reagan and George Shultz—were equally cognizant of the value of personal relationships in winning foreign support for U.S. policy. Indeed, the nature of that policy, as well as its diplomatic projection, was shaped by personal relationships. Richard Schifter, assistant secretary of state for human rights and humanitarian affairs from the mid-1980s to the early 1990s, remembers:

> Margaret Thatcher was the first prominent Western leader to make the point that Gorbachev "was a man that one can do business with." At the outset there was skepticism on that subject in U.S. government circles. Change came about as a result of the development of a close personal relationship between Secretary Shultz and Foreign Minister Shevardnadze. As Shultz describes his first meeting with Shevardnadze in August 1985: "Overall, the substance of the Soviet position was unchanged. But I was struck by Shevardnadze's tone: it was far less polemical. This might just be a different style, but it might also indicate that the Soviets were taking a new look at themselves."
>
> It did not take long for the personal relationship between Shevardnadze and Shultz to become increasingly friendly. To Shultz it became clear that the Soviets were indeed "taking a new look at themselves" and that the person who was responsible for the changes that were taking place was Gorbachev. In November 1985 Gorbachev had his first meeting with Ronald Reagan. It took place in Geneva. As Shultz describes the concluding press conference of the two leaders: "The personal chemistry was apparent. The easy and relaxed attitude toward each other, the smiles, the sense of purpose, all showed through."[9]

---

7. Baker, *The Politics of Diplomacy*, 248, 254.

8. Ross, *Statecraft*, 42, 345n25. This discussion of German unification draws from chapter 2 of Ross, *Statecraft*.

9. Anatoly Adamishin and Richard Schifter, *Human Rights, Perestroika, and the End of the Cold War* (Washington, D.C.: United States Institute of Peace Press, 2009), 234–235. The quotations are from George Shultz, *Turmoil and Triumph*, 574, 606.

Such camaraderie and sense of partnership between a U.S. official and his or her foreign counterpart is not unusual; many examples can be found of American negotiators reaching out to build or preserve a relationship of trust and easy communication. Numerous observers have commented on President Bill Clinton's reputation for empathizing, pointing to his success in persuading large sections of both the Protestant and Catholic communities in Northern Ireland that he understood their predicament and cared about their future. On Clinton's first visit to Belfast in November 1994, he famously shook hands with Sinn Fein's Gerry Adams. To overcome British hesitation at the idea of direct U.S. involvement in the Northern Ireland peace process, Clinton decided to appoint an "economic envoy," former senator George Mitchell, who eventually helped broker the Good Friday Accord. In a speech in 1998 following a car bombing in Omagh by Republican terrorists that killed twenty-nine people, Clinton said, "We came here knowing that words are not very good at a time like this, simply to express our sympathy and to support your determined refusal to let a cowardly crime rob you of the future." Clinton was also able to convince Syrian president Hafez al Asad, a statesman long recognized for his shrewd and calculating style, that the United States was sensitive to Syria's attachment to the Golan Heights.[10] In an earlier administration, James Baker had used flattery rather than empathy to make a positive impression on Asad in a personal meeting, during which the Syrian leader confirmed his commitment to attend the Madrid Peace Conference in 1991.[11]

All the above examples are of U.S. presidents and secretaries of state cultivating *personal* relationships, rather than *national* relationships, although the line between the two is usually very fuzzy. Like many of his peers, President Franklin D. Roosevelt believed that a good personal relationship could overcome considerations of national interest—and thus he cultivated a personal association with Stalin in the expectation that it could lead to better deals with "Uncle Joe."[12] More than fifty years later, President George W. Bush came to a similar conclusion about another Russian leader, Vladimir Putin. Speaking at a press conference following a meeting with Putin, Bush was asked if he felt America could trust Russia and Putin. Bush famously responded:

> I looked the man in the eye. I found him to be very straightforward and trustworthy. We had a very good dialogue. I was able to get a sense of his soul; a man deeply committed to

---

10.   Ross recollects Asad grabbing him by the arm and declaring, "President Clinton is a real person. He speaks to you with awareness and understanding. He knows our problems better, and is committed to solving them. I haven't felt this from an American president before." Ross, *Statecraft*, 200.

11.   "In negotiations, flattery is almost always useful, and I wanted to appeal to Asad's considerable ego," notes Baker; *The Politics of Diplomacy*, 489.

12.   See, for example, Bohlen, *Witness to History*, 134–154 and 173–201, on FDR's approach to Stalin during his first meeting at Tehran and during the Potsdam Conference.

his country and the best interests of his country. And I appreciated so very much the frank dialogue.

There was no kind of diplomatic chit-chat, trying to throw each other off balance. There was a straightforward dialogue. And that's the beginning of a very constructive relationship. I wouldn't have invited him to my ranch if I didn't trust him. (Laughter.)

Secondly, I appreciate the opportunity to be able to talk about a new relationship, and we will continue these dialogues. . . .

Friends don't destroy each other. People who cooperate do not have a basis of peace on destruction. Our nations are confronted with new threats in the 21st century. Terror in the hands of what we call rogue nations is a threat. I expressed my concern, and so did the President, very openly, about nations on his border and nations that can't stand America's freedoms developing the capacity to hold each of us hostage. And he agreed.[13]

As it turned out, neither Roosevelt nor Bush was able to turn personal rapport into political advantage. If anything, the two Americans found themselves taken advantage of by the Soviet and Russian leaders, who were happy to smile and laugh with the U.S. presidents but who thereafter pursued policies hostile or contrary to U.S. interests. Conscious that his predecessor had received a lot of criticism for his misplaced trust in the Russian leader, President Barack Obama adopted a much more businesslike approach when he first met his Russian counterpart during the G-20 economic crisis summit in London in March 2009.

In Obama's first face-to-face meeting with Russian President Dmitry Medvedev, there were smiles and handshakes but none of the backslapping that characterized the relationship between their predecessors, George W. Bush and Vladimir Putin.

Aides said it was a conscious effort by the U.S. president, known for his "no-drama Obama" style, to strike up a more formal relationship with his Russian counterpart when they met on the sidelines of a G20 economic crisis summit in London.

"Our strategy is to develop an agenda based on interests, also accentuating where we disagree, but not to make the goal of these meetings to establish some buddy-buddy relationship," one U.S. official said after the talks.[14]

Even when personal relationships between national leaders (and other very senior political figures) spur the development of closer national relationships—the example of Reagan and Gorbachev (and Shultz and Shevardnadze) springs readily to mind—their impact is often evanescent. Furthermore, when it comes to specific negotiations, personal relationships—whether between presidents, ministers, team leaders, or lower-level officials—rarely if ever determine the outcome, which is usually dictated by sober, hard-headed assessments of national interest.

The readiness of U.S. presidents and secretaries of state to go to the trouble of nurturing relationships also depends on the complex interplay of factors ranging from ideologies and political processes to personalities. Administrations with a unilateralist bent might pay scant attention to relationship building, whereas

---

13.   White House, Office of the Press Secretary, "Press Conference by President Bush and Russian Federation President Putin, Brdo Castle, Brdo Pri Kranju, Slovenia," June 16, 2001, http://www.whitehouse.gov/news/releases/2001/06/20010618.html.

14.   Matt Spetalnick and Caren Bohan, "No Soul-searching, No Colgate in Obama's G20 Diplomacy," Reuters, April 1, 2009, http://www.reuters.com/article/politicsNews/idUSTRE5305N420090401.

presidents with an outgoing personality might be more likely to try to form close ties. But what happens when a president has both a unilateral-minded administration and an outgoing personality? Such was the case with George W. Bush, whose administration was repeatedly characterized as unilateralist, but who famously formed close relationships with foreign leaders such as Britain's Tony Blair and Mexico's Vincente Fox. Clearly, contending impulses can pull in different directions simultaneously.

If there seems to be one more or less reliable predictor of when top-level American officials will give especially high priority to relationships, it is when the prospective foreign partner not only has shown a willingness to forge a closer relationship but also controls something of considerable potential value to the United States. Once President Reagan decided that Gorbachev was in earnest with his overtures, the president embraced him, because Gorbachev possessed the power and the readiness to bring the Cold War to an end. In other words, U.S. negotiators have a fundamentally instrumentalist approach to developing relationships: good relationships with a negotiating counterpart are valuable insofar as they can help U.S. negotiators achieve concrete results.

Relationship building by lower-level U.S. negotiators

Almost all of what has been said above about the relationship-building propensities of presidents and their secretaries of state can also be said of lower-level officials.

For instance, the chemistry that developed between Reagan and Gorbachev, and between Shultz and Shevardnadze, was reinforced a little lower down the diplomatic ladder. Richard Schifter formed a remarkably close and productive relationship with Anatoly Adamishin as the two negotiated human rights issues from 1987 through 1991. Working together, the two pushed successfully for Soviet reform on human rights issues such as emigration and the abuse of psychiatry for political purposes. "We had agreed not to deal with each other, as Anatoly put it, as if we were in a bazaar," observes Schifter, who for his part "presented specific cases and expressed concern regarding the underlying policies to Anatoly in an informal . . . unpublicized, non-threatening fashion." Schifter attributes the progress they made chiefly to the fact that "we had the confidence of our immediate superiors," but also to the fact that "we had become personal friends and had come to trust each other. Each of us knew that both of us were trying to attain the same result."[15]

Not surprisingly, the relative importance of relationship building to the negotiating counterpart plays a role in the American readiness to develop relationships. Faced with counterparts who "do not expect to develop a continuing relationship," U.S. negotiators do not waste energy trying to do so, but they may be more inclined

---

15.   Adamishin and Schifter, *Human Rights, Perestroika, and the End of the Cold War*, 242–243.

to nurture such ties when the counterparts prize and pursue long-term relationships.[16] The counterpart's cultural norms also have an influence. For instance, U.S. diplomats tend to find it easier to form personal ties with Chinese than with Japanese officials, the latter generally displaying much greater formality and reserve.

The lack of such ties can complicate a negotiator's job. Ronald Neumann, who served as U.S. ambassador to Afghanistan in 2005–07 and had previously been ambassador to Bahrain and Algeria, observes that negotiations are more challenging without a personal connection because it is harder "to understand for sure what the other party's bottom line is where they can't go further. And it may make it harder for them to accept that your bottom line is really your bottom line."[17]

The U.S. Foreign Service's policy of moving its diplomats to a new post every three or four years exacerbates the challenge of building useful relationships. Such mobility, of course, means that even when U.S. diplomats do develop good relationships with officials from other countries, they are denied the time necessary to deepen those relationships to the point that they can provide a revealing and reliable window into the other side's thinking and a valuable resource for preventing or managing misunderstandings. The Japanese diplomatic system stands in marked contrast. Many Japanese diplomats seek to cultivate personal ties with foreign counterparts over an entire career—a pattern facilitated by *gaimusho* (Ministry of Foreign Affairs) posting patterns, which make sure an official has assignments that put him in contact with the same foreign official over the span of a career. The U.S. policy of rotating diplomats has exasperated Chinese Foreign Ministry officials, who invest considerable energy in cultivating relationships and then have to start afresh when an "old friend" is replaced by a new and unfamiliar American official.

This policy of rotating assignments owes much to administrative reforms introduced in the first half of the 1950s, against the backdrop of attacks on the loyalty of State Department personnel orchestrated by Senator Joseph McCarthy. "The Foreign Service Act of 1946, as well as the reforms proposed by the Commission on the Organization of the Executive Branch of Government (Hoover Commission) in 1949 and by a committee formed under President Henry M. Wriston of Brown University in 1954 . . . [recommended reforms] aimed partly at familiarizing the domestically based civil service with the world and partly at preventing the foreign service from losing contact with American life."[18] The effort was known as "Wristonization" and brought about a threefold increase in the number of Foreign Service officers through the integration of many civil servants into the Foreign

16.   Nancy Adler, *International Dimensions of Organizational Behavior*, 4th ed. (Cincinnati: South-Western College Publishing, 2002), 209.

17.   Ronald Neumann, interview, Washington, D.C., July 17, 2008, 15–16.

18.   Alan K. Henrikson, "Elitism," *Encyclopedia of American Foreign Policy*, http://www.americanforeignrelations. com/E-N/Elitism.html.

Service. Henceforth, Foreign Service officers would spend more time in Washington and civil servants would serve overseas.

Among other things, Wristonization and the "consequent frequent rotation of policy personnel" have been blamed for "the loss of a backlog of experience concerning long-run policy problems."[19] Former career diplomat Monteagle Stearns contends:

> On the constant shuffling of officers from one assignment to another in the modern Foreign Service, however, few stay long enough to risk contagion. As a result, few become real experts. Franklin's more than eight years in France and Jefferson's five contrast with the average tenure of three years to which contemporary American ambassadors are limited. The loss to American foreign policy in depth of knowledge and continuity is incalculable.[20]

However, the Wriston reforms have had positive effects, including giving diplomats more experience in the interagency contests conducted within the Washington Beltway to establish the goals and strategies for forthcoming negotiations with foreign powers. And while the lack of continuity in personnel can certainly affect the pace of a negotiation, the lack of a personal relationship has rarely, by itself, caused a negotiation to fail.

Deploying Inducements

The instrumental, unsentimental view that U.S. negotiators have of relationships is mirrored in their approach to the use of inducements. Generally unconcerned (unlike their French counterparts, for instance) with the philosophical consistency of their positions, American negotiators have few inhibitions about offering the other side incentives to reach agreement on American terms, particularly when the inducements pose no inherent domestic political or economic costs and offer some strategic benefit.

Indeed, U.S. negotiators are more likely to offer inducements than to compromise—and for good reasons. In the first place, to compromise is to give up something one's own side values, whereas to offer an inducement is to present the other side with something it values but which one's own side might not value, or might possess in abundance. In the second place, the idea of compromise can make moralists profoundly uneasy and evoke domestic political opposition. By contrast, the notion of providing compensatory payments or side deals and other sweeteners to secure a deal sits comfortably with the results-oriented, businesslike mindset; and the notion of a contractually enshrined quid pro quo is part and parcel of the legalistic outlook. In the third place, a readiness to compromise can be seen as a sign of weakness (as a form of appeasement, which gained such a bad reputation in the

---

19.   Richard Bilder, "The Office of the Legal Advisor," *American Journal of International Law* 54 (1962): 641.

20.   Stearns, *Talking to Strangers*, 26.

prelude to World War II), whereas the ability to provide inducements testifies to wealth or power. Fourth, with its unmatched resources—military capacity, political influence, and economic strength—the United States can induce agreement from its negotiating partners with a wide and generous array of incentives. And fifth, research suggests that inducements can be more persuasive to a foreign negotiator than punitive measures, particularly when the foreign counterpart is in a vulnerable domestic position.[21]

Sometimes, the incentives are distinctly palpable, as in the case of the Geneva Agreed Framework, a complex agreement negotiated with North Korea and signed in 1994. Under the agreement, the Pyongyang government would freeze and eventually dismantle its nuclear facilities that could be used to produce fuel for nuclear weapons; in return, the United States and its coalition partners would provide proliferation-resistant light-water reactors and half a million gallons of heavy fuel oil per year.[22]

Other inducements are a good deal less tangible, though no less tempting, such as offering political recognition to a rogue government, dealing directly with a rebel group (thus giving it a measure of legitimacy), or promising to support a state in its efforts to secure membership in a trade or security organization. After the 1967 Six Day War, the United States terminated diplomatic relations with Iraq. However, in the 1980s President Reagan nonetheless sought to engage Saddam Hussein's regime so as to make Iraq a stronger counterweight to Iran, as well as to

> pry it from the Soviet embrace, and to encourage its restraint on weapons of mass destruction. Iraq was removed from the list of terrorist sponsors, diplomatic relations were reestablished, while Washington furnished Baghdad with military intelligence on Iran and provided economic assistance in the form of credit guarantees for the purchase of U.S. agricultural products.... The [George H. W.] Bush administration reaffirmed, in National Security Directive (NDS) 26, a policy of engagement and expanded "political and economic incentives."[23]

The promise of American pomp and publicity can also be enticing. Very few world leaders can resist the lure of a high-profile trip to Washington, especially if it includes a presidential state dinner or a visit to Camp David. Sometimes even the promise of photo ops with high-ranking U.S. officials can help clinch a deal. Visits by U.S. officials to foreign capitals are also highly prized—though some are valued more highly than others. When James Baker met the Chinese foreign minister, Qian Qichen, in 1990 to ask for China's support of a Security Council resolution regarding Kuwait, the Chinese official asked for something in return:

---

21.   See Kenneth N. Waltz, "Globalization and American Power," *National Interest* (Spring 2000): 46–56.

22.   See Snyder, *Negotiating on the Edge*, 6. It should be noted that Pyongyang did not abide by the terms of the agreement. The North Korean regime seems either to have calculated that the inducement was not adequate to the scale of the concession it was expected to make, or to have sought to pocket the inducement while covertly continuing its nuclear program through other means.

23.   Miroslav Nincic, *Renegade Regimes: Confronting Deviant Behavior in World Politics* (New York: Columbia University Press, 2006), 328.

"Qian wanted a presidential visit in return for support of the resolution; Baker promised only a visit by the undersecretary of state to prepare for a visit by him [Baker] the next year. The Chinese ultimately abstained, permitting passage of the resolution"—apparently, the Chinese calibrated the level of their support for the resolution to the rank of the visiting American![24]

Just the sense of personal prestige afforded by a brief, personal conversation with a high-ranking U.S. official can sometimes erode the intransigence of a foreign negotiator. During the Dayton negotiations, for instance, Kresimir Zubak, president of the Bosnia Federation, felt ignored and refused to attend a signing ceremony—until Warren Christopher chatted with him. "Flattered by the personal attention of the Secretary of State, who met with him for fifteen minutes," recalls Richard Holbrooke, "Zubak said he would attend the signing."[25] Lower down the ladder of officialdom, prestige-enhancing actions by the United States can be equally effective; even the seating arrangement at dinners for the two negotiating teams can be a subtle bargaining chip, with those members of the foreign team who seem more likely to accept American demands being seated next to high-ranking U.S. officials. During negotiations in the 1980s involving dozens of delegations to the Conference on Security and Co-operation in Europe, remembers Ruth Whiteside, Max Kampelman ensured that one or another member of the American delegation "spent some time" with "the bit players" in the talks. "His whole approach to this was you never know when we'll need the Maltese on some very technical point or something like that. And a big part of the idea [of spending time with the bit players] was to find a couple of little things that they wanted, which were mostly inconsequential to us."[26]

While the breadth of U.S. resources allows U.S. negotiators to offer an equally broad array of inducements, the depth of U.S. pockets is probably the single-most effective incentive. Other countries, of course, deploy financial incentives as well. The European Union, for instance, has developed a reputation for wielding not a big stick but a big wallet.[27] Its aid to Palestine alone in 2007 exceeded 550 million euros.[28] But the United States is still the world's most wealthy country, and its negotiators are far from averse to deploying dollars in pursuit of national interests. One of the best-known—and most expensive—examples of economic inducements is the package of grants and military aid that President Jimmy Carter used

---

24. Ross, *Statecraft*, 88.

25. Holbrooke, *To End a War*, 263.

26. Whiteside, interview, 38.

27. See, for example, Parag Khanna, "Waving Goodbye to Hegemony," *New York Times*, January 27, 2008: "Robert Kagan famously said that America hails from Mars and Europe from Venus, but in reality, Europe is more like Mercury—carrying a big wallet."

28. Figure from the European Commission Technical Assistance Office, http://www.delwbg.ec.europa.eu/en/cooperatio_development/aid2007.htm.

to encourage Israeli prime minister Menachem Begin and Egyptian president Anwar Sadat to sign a peace treaty in 1979. As a reward for signing, Israel received $3 billion and Egypt about $1.8 billion annually until the mid-1990s; since then, the figures have declined somewhat but remain substantial. As William B. Quandt has observed, "Both [Israel and Egypt] hoped that the United States would advocate their views in their adversary's capital and would be generous in rewarding any of their concessions made in the course of negotiations."[29] In the case of Egypt, as Robert Satloff and Patrick Clawson explain,

> this aid was essential in countering the inter-Arab isolation and the beleaguered popular mood it suffered for Anwar Sadat's strategic decision for peace. Economically, the assistance . . . was badly needed: Egypt's balance of payments was hemorrhaging. . . . The magnitude of the aid was itself quite large, equal to 10 percent of gross national product . . . paid on an annual basis. In retrospect, the aid was an excellent example of an effective use of foreign assistance, cementing Egypt's new strategic relationship with the United States, providing an important incentive to keeping the peace treaty alive during moments of stress (e.g., the 1982 Lebanon War), and eventually moving Egypt along the path of vital economic reform.[30]

Financial incentives have been no less effective in negotiations with the world's poorer countries. During his self-described "odyssey" in 1990 to rally international support for military action against Iraq, Baker met with the Ivory Coast's foreign minister, Simeon Ake:

> He got right to the point [recalls Baker]. "The major concern in our country right now is really not the Gulf," he said. "It is development. We are having a financial crisis. The G-7 has looked at debt forgiveness. Forgiveness would be extremely helpful."
> As it turned out, Ivory Coast had not been included in a G-7 debt-forgiveness plan agreed to at the Toronto Summit in 1986. "Let me see what if anything can be done," I said. "I will look into what might be done, without promising anything, or tying it to other subjects we have been discussing today—and I know you are not suggesting such." We both knew better, of course.[31]

A day later, Baker met with the Romanian foreign minister to seek his support. "I encountered no resistance from him," comments Baker, "perhaps because the preceding December I had visited Bucharest and delivered $80 million in humanitarian assistance to the new government."[32]

To give another example, when the Soviet Union dissolved in the early 1990s, Washington was alarmed at the prospect of the newly independent Republic of

---

29.   William B. Quandt, "Camp David and Peacemaking in the Middle East," *Political Science Quarterly*, 101, no. 3 (1986): 360.

30.   Robert Satloff and Patrick Clawson, *U.S. Economic Aid to Egypt: Designing a New, Pro-Growth Package*, PolicyWatch no. 324 (Washington, D.C.: Washington Institute for Near East Policy, July 7, 1998), http://www.washingtoninstitute.org/templateC05.php?CID=1202.

31.   Baker, *The Politics of Diplomacy*, 315–316.

32.   Ibid., 316.

Ukraine assuming control of eighteen hundred Soviet nuclear warheads. In July 1993, the Clinton administration

> offered the fledgling nation a substantial economic aid package in return for Kiev's agreement to dismantle some of the former Soviet nuclear missiles and ship the warheads to Russia. When members of the Ukrainian Rada began to argue later that year for retaining the weapons, the United States joined with Russia to negotiate a comprehensive agreement providing economic assistance and security assurances to Ukraine in exchange for a complete removal of all remaining nuclear weapons.[33]

U.S. offers of side payments are not always welcome, however. According to Stapleton Roy, who served as ambassador to China, Singapore, and Indonesia, businesslike American negotiators are inclined to think that their counterparts share their readiness to consider side payments and to regard a negotiation as akin to a business transaction.[34] But if a principle dear to the heart of the other side is at stake, or is believed to be at stake, the negotiator from the other country may refuse to make a deal. The sensitivity of other governments to the appearance of being bought off should not be discounted. In such cases, side payments might still be effective, but they must be presented in such a way that the trade-off between principle and financial reward is hazy or entirely obscured.

Putting the Pressure On

Just as American inducements come in many forms, from the distinctly modest to the almost irresistibly lavish, so do pressure tactics employed by U.S. negotiators. They range from a gentle nudge to implicit or even explicit threats to outright coercion. In many—perhaps most—situations, U.S. officials do not bring out their big guns immediately when faced with a negotiating partner reluctant to accept American arguments, terms, or deadlines. They may prefer at the outset to leave implicit the prospect of heightened pressures. When legalistic or political arguments do not carry the day, they may begin to marshal America's multifarious resources, creating linkages to overwhelm their negotiating partner or rallying international support to emphasize the other side's isolation.

If the other side continues to resist, U.S. negotiators may emphasize the costs of failing to reach an agreement and threaten to walk away from the negotiations or to escalate their demands. If agreement is still elusive, they may explicitly threaten some form of punishment or sanctions; and if all else fails, they may carry through on such threats. At various points in this diplomatic turning of the screw, the United States will impose deadlines and issue ultimatums issued to ratchet up the pressure. Whether or not the other side agrees to make concessions, the

---

33. David Cortright and George A. Lopez, "Bombs, Carrots, and Sticks: The Use of Incentives and Sanctions," *Arms Control Today* (March 2005), http://www.armscontrol.org/act/2005_03/Cortright.

34. Roy, interview.

U.S. side may abruptly raise its demands, "moving the goalposts" in response to domestic political pressure from Congress, parts of the Washington bureaucracy, or special interests in the private sector.

But while American negotiators typically have various forms of leverage available to them, the U.S. side is far from omnipotent. The very entry of the United States into a negotiating process usually indicates that Washington recognizes that negotiation is, if not the only way, then the most cost-effective or politically acceptable approach to achieving its aims. The negotiating counterpart will recognize this and will seek to maximize the concessions or minimize the costs of accommodation. In some cases, domestic political pressures on the counterpart may dictate resistance to any pressure that the United States might bring to bear. In other cases, the counterpart may, like a judo expert, use America's strength against itself; for instance, when a U.S. negotiator applies pressure to secure agreement by a particular deadline, the counterpart may ratchet up its own demands and refuse to sign before the deadline unless those demands are met.

Linkages

Well aware that "every international negotiation is part of a much broader network of negotiations and, explicitly or implicitly, interacts with the network of which it is a part,"[35] American negotiators frequently seek to make this interrelatedness explicit. They do so by creating "linkage" between issues, making progress on one matter contingent on progress on another. Their opportunities for doing so are numerous because the United States has both a broader range of international interests than most other nations and a greater ability to defend and pursue those interests.

The use of linkage has not always been popular with American diplomats. In the late 1960s, when President Richard Nixon sought to link different facets of the Soviet-American relationship—such as arms control, Middle East stability, and the war in Vietnam—his approach "became wildly controversial."[36] As Nixon's national security adviser, Henry Kissinger recalls, "the concept of linkage encountered stormy weather in the foreign policy community," which was accustomed to segmenting foreign policy "into a series of individual, and at times isolated, initiatives geared to highly specific problems." Thanks not least to the leverage created by "achieving a dramatic opening to China," Nixon and Kissinger were able to persuade the Soviets to accept linkage and—perhaps a harder task—persuade Washington to do so as well.[37] Indeed, though linkage often discomfited adherents of the moralistic mind-set, it became the centerpiece of several major negotiations

35.   Victor Kremenyuk, ed., *International Negotiation: Analysis, Approaches, Issues*, 2nd ed. (San Francisco: Jossey-Bass, 2002), 32.

36.   Kissinger, *Diplomacy*, 717.

37.   Ibid., 717–718, 719.

not only in the 1970s but also in the 1980s. For instance, progress on human rights issues in negotiations with the Soviet Union came to be tied to progress on a variety of other U.S.-Soviet fronts; similarly, the policy of "constructive engagement" developed by President Reagan's assistant secretary of state for African affairs, Chester A. Crocker, linked support for Namibian independence to the withdrawal of Cuban forces from Angola.

Since the end of the Cold War elevated the United States to a position of unrivaled power, opportunities to employ linkage and the potency of the tactic have increased. Furthermore, the widespread concern among America's negotiating partners of being overwhelmed by the United States has been accentuated by an erosion of the distinction between "high" politics (e.g., security issues) and "low" politics (e.g., environmental, trade, and social issues). In the post–Cold War world, the boundaries between high and low politics have blurred and linkages have grown legion. This blurring feeds the perception that the United States, with its numerous interests in so many parts of the world, is involved in everything. (And that perception may well be accurate, for when the United States develops an interest in an issue, that issue automatically becomes internationalized.)

The United States is often insensitive to or unconcerned by the relative difference in importance of a given issue: what may occupy a lowly place on the U.S. agenda can be a major national or regional concern to U.S. partners on the other side of the table. Through inattention or indifference, the U.S. side tends to ignore the ripples it can cause by pursuing issues with significant repercussions for its partners.

Gilles Andreani advises foreign negotiators that linkage is best left to Americans: "The tactic known as *junktim*, which consists of linking issues unrelated in substance to gain leverage on a partner, is ill-advised and should be avoided. It is sure to backfire with the Americans, who can usually come up with a number of issues more important to you than to them, which they can then hold hostage to the negotiation at hand."[38]

But linkage can backfire as well in the hands of Americans. During negotiations with China over renewal of its most favored nation (MFN) trading status in mid-1993, President Clinton decided to set additional human rights conditions for the Chinese to meet before MFN status would be granted. Some members of Congress supported this conditionality, but the Chinese were adamant that the trade issue be separated from the United States' human rights concerns. And with the Commerce, Defense, and State Departments keen to settle the issue quickly, and with American corporate interests favoring renewal of MFN status, other members of Congress ultimately sided with the Chinese position in support of U.S. business interests. The issues were delinked in 1994.[39]

---

38. Andreani, "Negotiating with Savoir Faire," 282.

39. Vladimir N. Pregelj, *Most-Favored-Nation Status of the People's Republic of China*, Congressional Research Service (CRS) Issue Brief no. 92094 (Washington, D.C.: CRS, December 6, 1996), http://www.fas.org/man/crs/92-094.htm.

Marshaling international support

The United States has been able to pressure its negotiating counterparts by marshaling international support behind a U.S. position, thereby confronting the other side with the prospect of its isolation and relative weakness. The sheer scale of U.S. political power and its diplomatic machinery makes the coordination of its diplomatic assets especially common and effective. The global network of U.S. diplomatic posts gives the United States the opportunity to advocate its positions in coordinated fashion in capitals throughout the world. The resident U.S. ambassador or *chargé* is able, thanks to recognition of the United States' dominant position, to gain access to the highest officials in a country, and can use that access to press the U.S. case in ongoing negotiations conducted far away. An increase in the overall numbers of U.S. diplomatic posts since the 1990s has expanded the ability of the United States to exert this on-the-spot pressure; the United States continues to have a more extensive network of foreign offices than any other state.[40]

Meanwhile, in Washington various levers of U.S. power can be pulled to indirectly influence ongoing negotiations elsewhere in the world. For instance, the resident foreign ambassador might be invited to the State Department to discuss issues related to the negotiations, or that ambassador might be shown certain material by U.S. intelligence agencies.

Although marshaling international support has not always brought immediate results, it has helped to push a recalcitrant nation toward the negotiating table or a reluctant negotiator toward an agreement. In the mid-1990s, for instance, the Clinton administration sought to orchestrate international pressure on Serbia in a systematic fashion by forming the Contact Group, which was intended to coordinate the diplomacy of the group's members (the United States, France, Germany, Britain, and Russia) toward Serbia and thereby undercut the Milosevic government's efforts to play one major power off against another. The Bosnian peace effort also saw the United States bring international pressure to bear on a single individual—such as the time when the American team at Dayton persuaded British prime minister John Major and French president Jacques Chirac to telephone Bosnian president Alija Izetbegovic to urge him to accept the deal on the table.[41] One of the most notable American efforts to marshal international support in recent decades was the formation in 1990 of a coalition of thirty-four countries (including six Arab states) prepared to commit troops to eject Iraqi forces from Kuwait. Yet, despite such an impressive diplomatic accomplishment, the effort failed insofar as the negotiations to persuade Saddam Hussein to withdraw his troops failed—requiring military action to attain the desired outcome.

---

40.   As noted in chapter 2, as of 2008 the United States maintained 268 embassies, consulates, and missions abroad.

41.   See Holbrooke, *To End a War*, 294.

As in the case of linkage, the tactic of orchestrating international support can backfire if not carefully calibrated to each situation. In 1998, for instance, President Clinton enlisted President Jiang Zemin of China in "lambasting India and Pakistan for [their recent nuclear] tests and suggesting that the United States and China were looking for an additional way of applying the screws to both countries." Strobe Talbott, then deputy secretary of state, recalled:

> Within hours, I received a blistering email from a close [Indian] friend. . . . He thought Washington's attempt to play the China card against India was bad poker and bone-headed diplomacy. . . . He was right. . . . The incident was a classic example of what can happen when the U.S. government pursues, as it does every day, multiple and often conflicting objectives with rival, if not hostile, countries. . . . Our goal with the Indians was to change their policies and attitudes, not to insult, embarrass, or frighten them, and the effect was sure to be a hardening of their position in the dialogue we had just begun.[42]

In recent years, the United States' ability to marshal international support has declined (as discussed in the section "Negotiating Multilaterally" later in this chapter). However, while other nations may be less willing than before to rally to the side of the United States, Washington still retains a greater ability than any other government to enlist the support of the international community.

Sanctions

Sanctions, another U.S. tactic to ratchet up the pressure on other countries, rarely backfire, but they often misfire and usually take considerable time to induce the desired effect. They have long been a favorite tool of U.S. governments, with Washington imposing them on various targets fifty-four times between World War I and 1992. During the 1990s, the White House resorted ever more frequently to sanctions, imposing sixty-one new programs between 1993 and 1999. As of September 2008, the U.S. Treasury's Department of Foreign Assets Control was operating eighteen sanctions programs.[43] From 2001 to 2008, at the United States' urging or with its support, the UN Security Council imposed sanctions (including economic sanctions, arms embargoes, and travel bans) under Chapter VII of the UN Charter on countries including the Democratic Republic of the Congo, Ivory Coast, Sudan, Iran, and North Korea, as well as on terrorist organizations and states and nonstate actors that assist terrorists, and on senior members of Saddam Hussein's regime.[44]

Sanctions, however, fail to achieve their goals more often than not; if they work at all, they usually take a long time to do so; they are very difficult to calibrate and target accurately; they can impose heavy burdens on American corporations that

---

42. Strobe Talbott, *Engaging India: Diplomacy, Democracy, and the Bomb*, rev. ed. (Washington, D.C.; Brookings Institution, 2004), 91.

43. http://www.ustreas.gov/offices/enforcement/ofac/programs.

44. See http://www.un.org/sc/committees.

trade with targeted countries; and their imposition often signals or provokes an end or suspension of any ongoing negotiations with those countries.[45] For all these reasons, businesslike negotiators tend to steer clear of sanctions unless and until all other forms of pressure (short of the use of military force) have failed to sway a negotiating counterpart. Their chief appeal to businesslike negotiators is as a cheap way (for the U.S. government) of being seen to do something on an issue of concern to certain domestic constituencies. For the more moralistic among American officials, however, sanctions can be a way of signaling official displeasure with a behavior or action taken by a foreign state. As Richard Haass has observed, sanctions "satisfy a domestic political need to do something and reinforce a commitment to a norm, such as respect for human rights or opposition to weapons proliferation."[46] And as George Lopez, a leading scholar of sanctions, has remarked, "Sanctions have become a very quick way for people to say to their constituents, 'By God, we did something.'"[47]

Moving the goalposts

American officials are often accused of changing their goals in the middle of a negotiation or after agreement has been reached at the negotiating table, asking their counterpart either to go beyond the concessions they have already made or to make concessions on topics not previously part of the negotiating agenda. In 1992, for instance, North Korea "repeatedly complained . . . that the United States was 'moving the goalposts' by adding democracy, human rights, and missile sales to its original demands for upgrading the dialogue with North Korea."[48] Two years later, *Time* magazine reported that even Saddam Hussein's widely reviled regime was attracting a measure of sympathy "among some foreign diplomats, who agreed with Iraqi U.N. Ambassador Nizar Hamdoon's assertion that the U.S. keeps 'moving the goalposts'" by adding new conditions that Iraq had to meet if sanctions were to be lifted.[49]

Other examples, past and present, abound. In February 2006, for example, "Anil Kakodkar, chairman of India's Atomic Energy Commission and secretary of its

---

45.   A study published in 2008 by the Peterson Institute for International Economics concluded that sanctions were at least partially successful 34 percent of the time. Gary Clyde Hufbauer, Jeffrey Jay Schott, Kimberly Ann Elliott, and Barbara Oegg, *Economic Sanctions Reconsidered*, 3rd ed. (Washington, D.C.: Peterson Institute for International Economics, 2008), 158. That success rate is at least rising. The 1997 edition of the same work found that unilateral U.S. sanctions had worked only 13 percent of the time since 1970. The study also found that sanctions cost the United States (in terms of potential exports) between $15 billion and $19 billion annually.

46.   Richard N. Haass, "Sanctions Madness," *Foreign Affairs* (November–December 1997).

47.   Quoted in Michael Paulson, "US: History of Sanctions Shows Most Haven't Worked," *Seattle Post-Intelligencer*, May 11, 1999, http://www.corpwatch.org/article.php?id=14581.

48.   Leon Sigal, *Disarming Strangers: Nuclear Diplomacy with North Korea* (Princeton, N.J.: Princeton University Press, 1998), 140.

49.   Nancy Gibbs, "A Show of Strength," *Time*, October 24, 1994, http://www.time.com/time/magazine/article/0,9171,981645-1,00.html.

Department of Atomic Energy, accused the US of 'moving the goalposts' in the negotiations on the nuclear accord."[50] Negotiations over another country's nuclear ambitions prompted a similar observation, with U.S. behavior toward Iran's nuclear program being criticized as "essentially a repeat of a previously-established pattern where Iran makes concessions and shows flexibility, only to be met with increased demands."[51]

Not all such complaints are merited, of course. And the United States is not the only country to indulge in this practice.[52] But clearly, raising demands is closer to a regular practice among Americans than an isolated phenomenon. The most common explanation for moving the goalposts focuses on the changing constellation of political and bureaucratic forces within Washington. American negotiating strategies are usually forged through a process of tough interagency bargaining, and if the consensus within the executive branch breaks down because of a change of personnel or of opinion within one or more agencies, then the negotiating strategy may be reformulated in a way that raises the U.S. bottom line.

Shifts in congressional support for a negotiating tack can also lead to an escalation of U.S. demands. As discussed in chapter 5, members of Congress—perhaps under pressure from lobbying groups or constituents—will sometimes urge U.S. negotiators to seek greater and greater concessions during a negotiation. And once a negotiation has been—ostensibly—concluded and an agreement signed, Congress will sometimes press for the agreement to be renegotiated. For instance, President Carter's administration found itself pushed by Congress to renegotiate the Taiwan Relations Act in 1979. The act established quasi-diplomatic relations with Taiwan and was negotiated in the wake of the establishment of full diplomatic relations with the People's Republic of China. When it was presented with the first version, Congress "did not think it was strong enough," recalls Stapleton Roy, and the administration had to strengthen it, even though doing so prompted loud complaints from an already displeased PRC.[53]

On occasion, U.S. officials have decided to up the negotiating ante because of an imprecise but real sense of dissatisfaction with the specific negotiation or the wider

50.   Kakodkar's comments were reported in the *Indian Express*. Cited at http://www.wsws.org/articles/2006/feb2006/bush-f28.shtml.

51.   Cyrus Safdari, "Iran Nuclear Goalposts Moving Again; Another "Paris Agreement" Fiasco? *Iran Affairs* [a blog], http://www.iranaffairs.com/iran_affairs/2007/09/moving-nuclear-.html.

52.   In the cases of Iranian negotiators, for instance, one veteran American negotiator has observed that "the Persians are incredible at moving the goalposts. It is a science in negotiations with Iranians. . . . I used to watch them with foreign companies, and they would get to the point where they thought the deal was made, pop the champagne cork, and then, aaahh, Deputy Minister Ali would call and say, "You know, so-and-so has a problem." And the Iranians would run the companies through this psychological process to the point where the companies would lose all sense of what they had originally said was their bottom line, what they wouldn't do. And in the end, they would be signing deals that they would have sworn a month earlier would not be." Comment made during a meeting about enhancing American negotiating capacities, United States Institute of Peace, April 17, 2009, Washington, D.C.

53.   Roy, interview, 25.

relationship with the negotiating counterpart. Max Kampelman was the lead U.S. negotiator for the three-year negotiating process that culminated in the signing of the multifaceted Helsinki Final Act, which addressed issues ranging from the definition of borders in Europe to human rights matters such as freedom of emigration and reunification of families divided by international borders. When the negotiating parties finally seemed ready to sign the treaty, Kampelman was happy insofar as he had won some hard battles over the language defining human rights in what would be a very influential statement of internationally accepted principles, but he could not help but feel that the United States had not got enough out of the negotiation. He discussed the endgame with Secretary of State Shultz and President Reagan:

> And I remember Shultz saying, "Was all this time worth it for just words?" Reagan thinks about it and then he says something that neither Shultz or I knew. He says, "You know, when I became president . . . I asked Al [Haig] to bring in the Russian ambassador to see me. I said to the ambassador that if his government wanted to have better relationships with me, and I'm a new president now, then I want a signal that they want to turn pages and begin working closely with us. Now let me give you the signal. The Pentecostals..."

Kampelman proceeded to contact the Soviets about "getting people out" of the Soviet Union, including seven Pentecostalists who had taken refuge in the American embassy in Moscow for more than twelve months. Kampelman decided to talk plainly:

> [I] didn't hold anything back. [I told my Soviet contact, Sergei Medvedev] how the three of us [Reagan, Shultz, and Kampelman] met. And I said, "We will not agree to an end to this meeting until we get people out." . . . He exploded, as I knew he would explode. "You can't do that. This is not the way the world works."

In the context of the president's statement, and with the United States applying pressure from other quarters as well, the Pentecostalists were allowed to leave the Soviet Union a few months later.[54]

Another recent president who moved, or tried to move, the goalposts was Bill Clinton. As noted earlier in this chapter, he sought—unsuccessfully—to delay approval of China's MFN status until China agreed to additional human rights conditions. Clinton was more successful in altering the scope of the North American Free Trade Agreement (NAFTA), which had been signed by President George H. W. Bush just before Clinton won the presidential election. Clinton did not insist on renegotiating NAFTA when he entered the White House, but he bolstered the agreement with two complementary agreements on environmental and labor cooperation among Mexico, Canada, and the United States.

Threats

Almost every U.S. action at the bargaining table carries with it an implied threat. America's negotiating partners can hardly forget that the government represented

---

54. Max Kampelman, interview, Washington, D.C., August 6, 2008, 78, 84.

on the other side of the bargaining table possesses the resources—military, economic, political, and diplomatic—to influence, if not to harm, their national interests. They are conscious, too, that America is proud of its standing in the world
and of its conviction that its history and values justify its extensive influence. That
said, the weakest players on the international scene (for instance, failed states such
as Somalia and quasi-states such as the Palestinian Authority) may have so little to
lose that they are almost immune to U.S. pressure, while the pack mentality evident
within some international organizations can embolden small and midsize states to
challenge the United States from a safe distance. But most negotiating partners
are understandably cautious in challenging Washington—thwarting its goals or
offending its pride—especially in bilateral encounters. John Wood, for instance, felt
an unsettling sense of apprehension in dealing with U.S. officials on a fundamental security issue—nuclear weapons policy. His American counterparts left him in
little doubt that Washington was ready to make an example of New Zealand for
its refusal to back down on its policy of denying nuclear-powered vessels access to
its territorial waters. "That apprehension of the preparedness of at least some in
the United States to hang our country out to dry as an example to others," Wood
recalls, "gave rise to more sleepless nights than any other single aspect of these
negotiations."[55]

Yet despite this inherent sense of implied threat, American negotiators tend not
to use *direct* threats—not, that is, unless vital interests are perceived to be at stake
or until other tactics in the U.S. repertoire of pressures have been tried. Part of
the reason for this self-restraint is self-confidence: an expectation that the United
States—stronger than its counterparts in so many ways—will get what it wants
from a negotiation. (Paradoxically, perhaps, weaker countries are often more inclined than stronger ones to use threats. North Korea, for instance, usually seeing
itself as the vulnerable party in a negotiation, employs threats almost reflexively.)[56]
Another explanation is that the U.S. side recognizes that implied or indirect threats
can be more effective than the direct variety. Part of the reason, too, is that the legal
profession from which so many U.S. negotiators spring generally frowns on overt
threats and employs them only sparingly. Career American diplomats are also part
of the international diplomatic fraternity, whose centuries-old norms and informal
sanctions discourage its members from treating one another disrespectfully.

However, when U.S. officials feel obliged to overcome such professional restraint, they prove themselves adept at using a wide variety of direct threats. A
very incomplete list of examples of such threats employed by American negotiators
includes the following:

---

55.   John Wood, "Negotiating within Washington: Thrown in at the Deep End," 224.

56.   Snyder argues that Kim Il Sung's "guerrilla instincts" have bequeathed a "'guerrilla' negotiating style" to
North Korea, a readiness to mask or to compensate for its own weakness with threats; see *Negotiating on the Edge*,
24, 85–86.

- *Threats to disengage from negotiations and leave the parties to their fates.* On the thirteenth day of the Dayton negotiations, Richard Holbrooke warned the Bosnian delegation "that Christopher would consider closing down the talks if we could not make progress" and wrote to Christopher himself, who was about to take a short trip to Japan, that the Americans must convey "the clear message that when you return we must have either closure or closedown."[57]
- *Threats to lay the blame for failure of negotiations on the other side.* During negotiations in 1974 for the disengagement of Israeli and Syrian forces, "Kissinger threatened to blame Israel for any breakdown in negotiations, and threatened as well to withdraw completely from the negotiation process."[58]
- *Threats to penalize or punish.* In its long-running trade negotiations with Taiwan, the United States threatened in the early 1990s to impose trade sanctions against Taiwan under Section 301 of the Trade Act unless Taiwan moved to stop Taiwanese companies pirating U.S. intellectual property such as computer programs and music CDs.[59]
- *Threats to treat the other side as an adversary.* As President George W. Bush said in November 2001, in a joint press conference with French president Jacques Chirac: "Over time it's going to be important for nations to know they will be held accountable for inactivity. . . . You're either with us or against us in the fight against terror."[60]
- *Threats to employ military force.* When fundamental U.S. national security concerns come into play, threats can rise to the level of use of force—from President Dwight Eisenhower's threat of nuclear war against China in 1955 and 1958 if it continued to attack Taiwan[61] to President George W. Bush's threat in 2002 to impose "the severest consequences" on Saddam Hussein unless he admitted possessing weapons of mass destruction.[62]

---

57.   Holbrooke, *To End a War*, 271, 273.

58.   Brian Mandell, "The Limits of Mediation, Lessons from the Syrian-Israeli Experience, 1974–1994," in *Resolving International Conflicts*, ed. Jacob Bercovitch (Boulder, Colo.: Lynne Reinner, 1995), 134. Holbrooke offers another example: Bosnian foreign minister Mohamed Sacirbey claimed that his side needed to renegotiate a deal on which the imminent Geneva discussions depended. "In no uncertain terms," writes Holbrooke, "I told Sacirbey that if he precipitated a failure in Geneva, the United States would hold him responsible and only the Serbs would benefit. It was a harsh conversation . . . and it was overheard by several other people." Holbrooke, *To End a War*, 139.

59.   See Mark Harris, "Taiwan Acts to Stop Fake Chip Makers," *Electronic Times*, April 27, 1998; Chien-pin Li, "Trade Negotiation between the United States and Taiwan," *Asian Survey* 34, no. 8 (August 1994): 692–705.

60.   See "Bush Says It's Time for Action, *CNN.com*, November 6, 2001, http://archives.cnn.com/2001/S/11/06/ret.bush.coalition/index.html.

61.   See Arthur M. Schlesinger, Jr., *The Cycles of American History* (New York: Houghton Mifflin, 1999), 400.

62.   Speaking on the eve of a NATO summit in November 2002, President Bush declared: "Should he again deny that this arsenal exists, he will have entered his final stage with a lie, and deception this time will not be tolerated. Delay and defiance will invite the severest consequences." As reported in "Bush Threatens Attack over Iraqi 'Lies,'" *Guardian*, November 21, 2002.

Security issues are not the only subjects to elicit threats. Insofar as a higher political profile raises the stakes in a negotiation, congressional interest is likely to encourage the use of threats by U.S. officials involved. This helps explain, for instance, the threatening tenor of U.S. trade negotiators in the late 1980s and early 1990s, a period of intense congressional concern over America's trade imbalances with several other countries. In Charles Freeman's memorable—if less than literal—phrase, the nature of those trade negotiations was "comply or die."[63]

Threats alone, however, often fail to generate the desired response. As Robert Art notes in a study of the United States' use of coercive diplomacy, "punishment and denial strategies are difficult to execute" because "the target, especially a highly motivated one, can . . . see threats and limited use [of military force] as signaling weak resolve. After all, if the coercer cares that much about its objective, why pull its punches in the first place?"[64] Positive inducements, Art argues, are probably more effective—and he cites their use by the United States in Laos in 1961, Cuba in 1962, Somalia in 1992, Haiti in 1994, and Bosnia in 1995.[65]

American negotiators have often (but not always) shown themselves well aware that threats are usually most effective when combined with inducements. This recognition is hardly unique to U.S. officials, but it has a more practical expression in the case of American negotiators because the United States has a more varied and potent inventory of incentives and threats than most other players on the international scene. Moreover, given that preponderant powers such as the United States have few qualms about issuing threats, while businesslike U.S. negotiators are generally happier proffering incentives, U.S. diplomacy is well served by the multifaceted nature of the American approach to negotiating.[66]

Even pugnacious negotiators faced with recalcitrant counterparts recognize the value of combining "carrots and sticks" (incentives and pressures). For instance, Undersecretary of State Nicholas Burns, in a speech in April 2007, had the following to say about the Bush administration's strategy for persuading Iran to abandon its nuclear weapons program:

> In looking at how we might deal with the government of Iran, President Bush has said many times, "All options are on the table"—military, economic, and political. In that part of the world, in this type of crisis, you do not want to de-link the threat of force and diplomacy.

---

63.   Freeman, interview, 5.

64.   Robert J. Art, "Coercive Diplomacy: What Do We Know?" in *The United States and Coercive Diplomacy*, ed. Robert J. Art and Patrick M. Cronin (Washington, D.C.: United States Institute of Peace Press, 2003), 364.

65.   Ibid., 396.

66.   Of course, experts can disagree on the proper mix: when former Secretary of State James Baker denounced the Clinton administration's Agreed Framework with North Korea as "all carrot and no stick," his successor Warren Christopher responded that the Apache helicopters, Patriot missile batteries, and Bradley Fighting Vehicles that Washington sent to South Korea the previous year "were not armed with carrots." *Washington Post*, January 25, 1995.

Because we have seen time and again, whether in the Balkans, in Rwanda, in Darfur, and certainly in the Middle East, that the threat of force combined with effective diplomacy is absolutely essential. So we keep all options on the table, but we are focused on diplomacy. We are not seeking a conflict with Iran. And we do believe that diplomacy has a good chance of succeeding if we stick with it long enough.[67]

A reluctance to bluff

The American preparedness to threaten the warring parties in the Balkans in the 1990s stands in marked contrast to the behavior of the major Western European powers, which tried to use incentives rather than threats with the Serbs, partly out of a historically conditioned aversion to the use of force within Europe, partly because of the near impossibility of reaching consensus within the European Union on the use of military force in so complex a conflict, and partly because the Europeans lacked the ability or willingness to follow through on threats. By contrast, the Americans came to see force or the threat of force as essential to bringing the Serbs to the negotiating table and to compelling them to abide by their commitments. And American threats possessed the vital ingredient for effectiveness: credibility.

A reputation for *not* bluffing is a prized and valuable possession for any negotiator, no less than for an American. Without it, indeed, U.S. threats would carry much less weight, which would make them less of a deterrent, which in turn would oblige the United States to follow through on threats far more often.

Richard Holbrooke recounts a time when the American delegation at Dayton departed from this tenet. In a "pathetic" theatrical gambit, the delegation packed their bags and left them in the parking lot to be picked up by a truck, supposedly signaling the end of the talks. As Holbrooke notes, "Everybody saw through our bluff; nobody else made the slightest effort to prepare for departure. Early in the evening, we gave up and brought the bags back to our rooms."[68]

More characteristic of American diplomacy generally was the time Holbrooke threatened to terminate discussions with Slobodan Milosevic over a halt to NATO's bombing of Bosnian Serb positions, unless Milosevic's Bosnian Serb colleagues were ready to withdraw their heavy weapons from around Sarajevo. "Milosevic paused for a moment, perhaps to gauge if this was a bluff. . . . [His hesitation] was over in a few minutes. Milosevic came over to us, asked us to rejoin him, and said that the Bosnian Serbs were ready to negotiate on the basis of our draft."[69]

---

67.   R. Nicholas Burns, "Carrots and Sticks" (remarks presented at the John F. Kennedy Presidential Library, April 11, 2007) published in the *Boston Review* (May–June 2007), http://bostonreview.net/BR32.3/burns.php.

68.   Holbrooke, *To End a War*, 293–294.

69.   Ibid., 151.

Watching the Clock

Among the negotiating characteristics for which U.S. officials are best known by their foreign counterparts, a short-term outlook and a consequent sense of urgency rank very high. During the Paris Peace Talks to end American involvement in the Vietnam War, the U.S. team arrived in Paris and made hotel reservations for one week. Their Vietnamese counterparts leased a château for a year. As the negotiations proceeded, the Americans continually renewed their weekly accommodations.[70]

Several factors help explain this pronounced trait. In broad cultural terms, America is both a "young" country, with relatively limited interest in history, and a business-oriented, industrial society accustomed—unlike traditional peasant economies—to ordering life by the clock: valuing time (which is money), respecting deadlines, sticking to schedules, and so forth.[71]

The nature of the American political system also imparts impatience to the country's foreign policy. "The propensity that induces democracies to obey impulse rather than prudence, and to abandon a mature design for the gratification of a momentary passion," was famously observed in America in 1834 by Alexis de Tocqueville, who also critiqued the ability of democracies to conduct effective foreign policy. "A democracy can only with great difficulty regulate the details of an important undertaking, persevere in a fixed design, and work out its execution in spite of serious obstacles," remarked de Tocqueville. "It cannot combine its measures with secrecy or await their consequences with patience."[72] In the past 175 years, the United States has grown more adept at secret diplomacy (see chapter 4's discussion of back channels), but it has also grown more impatient.

More concrete factors impelling the American sense of urgency include the U.S. electoral calendar. As discussed in chapter 5, all American diplomats and policymakers are mindful of election cycles, which tend to dictate short and fixed negotiating timetables. They are also sensitive to media and political pressures to achieve rapid results in negotiations on issues that have a high domestic public or political profile. Another factor that imparts a sense of short-term preoccupation is the absence of any institutionalized mechanism that brings together the executive and

---

70. See Adler, *International Dimensions of Organizational Behavior*, 219.

71. Some scholars divide culturally determined concepts of time into two broad categories: polychronic and monochronic. According to Michelle LeBaron, negotiators from polychronic cultures tend to start and end meetings at flexible times; take breaks when it seems appropriate; are comfortable with a high flow of information; expect to read each others' thoughts and minds; sometimes overlap talk; and view start times as flexible and not take lateness personally. Negotiators from monochronic cultures tend to prefer prompt beginnings and endings; schedule breaks; deal with one agenda item at a time; rely on specific, detailed, and explicit communication; prefer to talk in sequence; and view lateness as devaluing or evidence of lack of respect. Of the two categories, Americans clearly fit more comfortably in the latter category. However, the fit is far from perfect. For instance, Americans do not always "prefer to talk in sequence," and their appetite for linkage means that they are comfortable dealing with more than one issue at a time. Michelle LeBaron, "Culture-Based Negotiation Styles."

72. Alexis De Tocqueville, *Democracy in America* (Garden City, N.Y.: Doubleday, 1969), 228–229.

the legislative branches to engage in coordinated planning.[73] According to Zbigniew Brzezinski, the efforts to locate such planning in the National Security Council "have resulted in long-term interests being subordinated to the short term. The legislative branch focuses almost exclusively on immediate domestic concerns."[74]

Whatever the underlying cause, American negotiators are renowned for trying to achieve short-term results and for focusing on immediate gains rather than for laying the foundations for enduring relationships or for staking out a position that may not yield concrete rewards until many years later.

Urgency and ultimatums: The up side

Urgency and impatience have both advantages and disadvantages for a negotiator. On the positive side, they encourage officials to work very hard to create diplomatic momentum, break stalemates, and resolve intractable issues.

Another advantage of urgency and impatience is that they make officials highly attentive to windows of opportunity. President Clinton's administration had spent its first years in office hoping the Europeans would handle the Bosnian crisis, and even when events had conspired to push Bosnia much higher up the U.S. foreign policy agenda, the administration still refused to grasp the nettle and act decisively. But quite suddenly, in the aftermath of the massacres of the men and boys of Srebrenica and with Croats pushing back Serb forces, Clinton sensed a window of opportunity to promote a settlement of the conflict. After listening to his advisers in a cabinet meeting, the president declared: "I agree with Tony [Lake] and Madeleine [Albright]. . . . We should bust our ass to get a settlement within the next few months. We must commit to a unified Bosnia. And if we can't get that at the bargaining table, we have to help the Bosnians on the battlefield."[75]

American negotiators strive to communicate this sense of ephemeral opportunity to the other side, suffusing the entire negotiation with a sense of urgency. In February 2003, as the Security Council debated whether to approve a seemingly irresistible U.S. drive to win support for military action against Iraq, the American permanent representative to the United Nations, John Negroponte, warned those council members still reluctant to endorse an attack, "The diplomatic window is closing."[76] American negotiators try to condition their counterparts—even representatives from relationship-oriented nations that try to allow time to build

---

73.   Zbigniew Brzezinski, *Second Chance: Three Presidents and the Crisis of American Superpower* (New York: Basic Books, 2007), 195.

74.   Ibid.

75.   Madeleine Albright, *Madam Secretary: A Memoir* (New York: Hyperion, 2003), 241.

76.   Quoted in Serge Schmemann, "The World: All Aboard; America's War Train Is Leaving the Station," *New York Times*, February 2, 2003, http://query.nytimes.com/gst/fullpage.html?res=9B02E4DE1538F931A35751C0 A9659C8B63&sec=&spon=&pagewanted=1.

personal associations before conducting business—to accept the need for haste or to recognize that the time is unusually propitious for fruitful dialogue. In short, American negotiators define a window of opportunity and then seek to push their counterparts through it.

Washington gave an incoming New Zealand prime minister a grace period of just two months in office before pressing him to present a plan for resolving the impasse over U.S. naval vessels' access to New Zealand waters. "These demands for a game plan, a timetable, a roadmap with signposts that could be ticked off and progress duly measured as the two sides went along, were to become an ongoing theme in our discussions with Washington," observes John Wood.[77]

Two months, however, was an eternity compared with the amount of time Holbrooke gave Bosnian president Izetbegovic on one occasion:

> As Izetbegovic argued, Rosemarie handed me a note warning that we had five minutes left to make our "window" for the last flight of the day, after which we would be unable to get out of Sarajevo until the next day. . . .
>
> Still he hesitated. I pushed a pen toward him. . . .
>
> "Here it is, Mr. President," I said. . . . "We must leave immediately. If you don't sign now, the war will continue." I started to rise.
>
> Izetbegovic took the paper. His hands shook as he held it. Finally, slowly and reluctantly, he signed the document. We shook hands and raced for the airport, taking the document with us and leaving Ambassador Menzies to call Washington with the news.

U.S. negotiators are fond of using their own self-defined deadlines as a means of pressuring the other side to reach agreement. Such a sense of haste might be interpreted as panic on the part of a small country, but a powerful country such as the United States is often able to force weaker nations to abide by its own established deadlines—usually driven by the press of other business and an overloaded schedule. Some deadlines have a symbolic quality and are intended to stoke media interest or apply pressure by associating the outcome of a negotiation with the standing of a particular leader or the significance of an event commemorated on the day of the deadline. For instance, the 1998 Northern Ireland peace talks chaired by former U.S. senator George Mitchell had a target date of April 9. Agreement was actually reached the following day, Good Friday, the start of Easter and a highly appropriate occasion to consummate an agreement intended to resurrect intercommunal peace.

Other deadlines are decidedly practical—albeit not from the point of view of the negotiating counterpart but from the perspective of American domestic politics. President Carter convened the Camp David summit just two months before midterm elections, the timing determined at least in part by hopes that success in

---

77.   Wood, "Negotiating within Washington," 224.

the talks would translate into votes.[78] The imminence of presidential elections in 1988 similarly

> put pressure on all the parties to make tangible progress in the Angola/Namibia negotiations. It increased the pressure on the American negotiator, Chester Crocker, because, although Ronald Reagan was retiring, the Republican candidate, Vice-President George Bush, was obviously anxious to highlight as many foreign policy achievements for the administration as possible in his own election campaign. As for Crocker, who had led the negotiations for such a long time, it was also natural that he would want a personal success before probably leaving office himself.[79]

The upcoming elections, Crocker later commented, were a valuable source of leverage, allowing him to "warn the parties that there would be changes in personnel and the continuity in an eight-year process would be lost."[80]

Impatience and deadlines: The down side

While Americans can parlay their sense of urgency into powerful negotiating pressure, that same impatience also presents some disadvantages. A first disadvantage is that weaker nations are sometimes able to turn the tables when American negotiators are eager to reach an agreement for political reasons—because, for instance, the U.S. president wants to demonstrate the success of his foreign policy to audiences both abroad and at home by signing an agreement during a scheduled visit to a particular country. Such situations allow a negotiating counterpart to exploit the American position by refusing to sign unless the United States offers concessions. In October 1975, for instance, the Chinese pressed Kissinger—during a planning visit to Beijing—against his own departure deadline to agree to an unacceptable draft communiqué being prepared for President Ford to sign during a summit visit two months later. (Subsequently, when the political environment within the United States shifted, the dynamic changed against the Chinese and they accommodated to the American position.)[81]

A second disadvantage is related to the first. When one lays down a deadline, three things can happen, and two of them are bad. The only good outcome for the United States is when the other side caves in and signs on American terms. The two bad outcomes are, first (as just described), that the weaker nation demands and wins U.S. concessions, and, second, that the United States refuses to make those concessions, which leaves the American side with two equally unpalatable alterna-

---

78.   See Berridge, *Diplomacy*, 62, quoting William Quandt. Quandt—and Berridge—also point out that Carter was keen to wrap up a peace treaty between Egypt and Israel before a forthcoming Arab League summit might cause Sadat to "lose his nerve."

79.   Berridge, *Diplomacy*, 62.

80.   E-mail from Chester A. Crocker, July 13, 2008 (on file with the authors).

81.   See Solomon, *Chinese Negotiating Behavior*.

tives: terminating the negotiation without achieving U.S. goals; or continuing the negotiation and thus revealing that the missed deadline was just a bluff.

A third disadvantage with American officials' short-term, impatient approach occurs when they are faced—as they usually are—with a negotiating counterpart with a very different attitude toward time. As Faruk Logoglu explains, this mismatch in approaches can cause serious misunderstandings:

> Being punctual, finishing business on time, not wasting time, using time as planned, and displaying impatience toward those who act slowly are all patterns of American cultural behavior. The Turks, on the other hand, are more relaxed about time and exhibit a tendency to procrastinate. This combination proved to be explosive in the first months of 2003 when the United States was making final preparations for the invasion of Iraq.[82]

The United States, without consulting the Turkish government, sent warships full of troops to the Eastern Mediterranean, in expectations that they would be able to disembark at a Turkish port and quickly make their way to northern Iraq. Meanwhile, the Turkish government sought to delay a vote in parliament on whether to permit U.S. troops to enter Iraq via Turkey. When the vote was finally taken, its negative outcome effectively left thousands of U.S. troops stranded off the coast of Turkey and unable to participate in the invasion. As Logoglu observes, "The differences in the timelines and priorities led to the making of dramatic mistakes on both sides."

Impatience can also be counterproductive by forcing the negotiating counterpart to accede to demands that are politically untenable in the counterpart's own political system. Nazarkin, for instance, cites the example of the START-2 talks held shortly after the dissolution of the Soviet Union, during which President Bush, eager to wrap up an agreement before the end of his first—and, as it turned out, only—term in office, telephoned President Boris Yeltsin and pressed him to order the Russian delegation to abandon its resistance to the U.S. proposal. The short-term result was an agreement that favored American interests and established an unusually early deadline for full implementation. In the long term, however, the "one-sided" treaty met with resistance in the Russian Duma, which took seven years to ratify it. In any event, the treaty was never ratified by the U.S. Senate.[83]

Indifference to history

Some societies pay considerable attention, or at least high respect, to the past; Americans focus on the present and the future.[84] This orientation helps explain why American officials are often accused of being ignorant of or insensitive to their

---

82. Logoglu, "Negotiating Security," 218–19.

83. Nazarkin, "Negotiating as a Rival," 249.

84. According to Donal Carbaugh, the United States tends to be oriented to the present and the near future. See Donal Carbaugh, "Some Distinctive Features of U.S. American Conversation," in *The Changing Conversation*

counterparts' history. Sometimes such accusations are justified. In this volume, for instance, Lalit Mansingh argues that the lack of respect shown by many American officials toward their Indian counterparts for decades after Partition had much to do with the fact that "Americans knew little of India as one of the ancient civilizations of the world, nor did they comprehend its complex, multicultural, multireligious, and pluralistic society. The paradoxical images of India as a land of feudal wealth, mysticism, and destitution continued until the 1990s."[85]

Some accusations of American ignorance of history are misplaced. U.S. officials (especially career diplomats as opposed to political appointees) may in fact have done their homework and delved into the history of their negotiating counterparts' country. However, they may give the impression of knowing or caring little for the weight of that history because they see the past as largely irrelevant to the task at hand, unless history itself is the subject of the negotiation.

This downplaying of the significance of history, it should be noted, is not one-sided. Americans do not dwell on their own history either. While history is a source of pride to U.S. officials, they may know less about their own history than do many of their foreign counterparts. This dearth of knowledge and interest may have something to do with the fact that although the United States is older than most other independent sovereign states, Americans' sense of national identity is of more recent vintage than that of many other peoples, who can look back to pre-colonial, medieval, or even ancient antecedents.

A lack of interest in the historical record extends even to the history of negotiations themselves. As discussed in the concluding chapter of this book, State Department practices and procedures do not encourage the meticulous compilation and organized preservation of negotiating records. Individual negotiators may be keenly aware of their country's triumphs and disasters at the bargaining table, but those individuals tend to take their memories—and sometimes even their records—with them when they return to the private sector or otherwise retire from government service.

Talking across the Table

The advantage of English and the problem with interpreters

The status of English as the primary language of international diplomacy (as well as of the global scientific and business communities) is of great benefit to the United States and other English-speaking countries. U.S. representatives can trust in their mastery of their native tongue to convey exactly what they mean to say—and to

in America: Lectures from the Smithsonian, ed. William F. Eadie and Paul E. Nelson (Thousand Oaks, Calif.: Sage, 2002).

85.   Mansingh, "Negotiating Bilaterally," 256.

figure out what others are really saying. Holbrooke recalls studying a "seemingly conciliatory" letter from a Nikola Koljevic, who had the title "Vice President of Republika Srpska," during a pause in NATO's bombing of Bosnian Serb forces. The letter declared that Koljevic was prepared to "accept conditions" previously laid out by NATO:

> The omission of any definite or indefinite article preceding the word "conditions" was, I argued, a dead giveaway. Where was a word like "all" or even "the" preceding the word "conditions"? I pointed out that the author of the letter was a Shakespeare scholar, and knew perfectly well the exact meaning of words in English. We were startled that anyone in the United Nations or Washington was taking this silly letter seriously.[86]

English's standing as the lingua franca of diplomacy may help to explain why Americans often seem only modestly interested in studying or exploiting the nuances of other languages. This reluctance is most pronounced among U.S. negotiators who are not career diplomats and have not been rigorously trained in foreign languages. But even career diplomats who are fluent in another language can be reluctant to use their linguistic skills. This disinclination seems to be based on a professional concern for precision. According to Ambassador Stapleton Roy, even though he was fluent in Russian, he preferred to speak English to his Russian interlocutors to ensure that he was accurately following the instructions he had been given by Washington. "If you negotiate in the other language," Roy remarks, "you may somehow misrepresent your position."[87]

American negotiators who are not fluent in a local language will, of course, use interpreters—and even those negotiators who are fluent will also use the "buffering" support of an interpreter, to buy time for consideration in exchanges and to provide opportunities for adjustment of position (due to "inaccurate interpretation"). Unfortunately, according to Ronald Neumann, "we have far too few interpreters in places like Afghanistan and Iraq," and among those who are available, "very few of them are properly qualified." At the level of secretary of state, interpreters are "extraordinarily competent," but competence diminishes lower down the bureaucratic ladder. Moreover, observes Neumann, many American negotiators, particularly young ones, "are not well trained or taught to deal with interpreters."

> There are some basic things Americans need to know about dealing with interpreters. You have to use short sentences. You shouldn't have interior parentheses elements in the sentence. You should use active verbs rather than jargon. I had an assistant secretary who . . . used a lot of analogies, and analogies don't translate. I brought this up with him sometimes, and finally I started keeping a little list. On one occasion, I said to him, "Do you realize that in this conversation you have used 'I'm back on the reservation' and 'cross the Rubicon.' What do you think the poor interpreter's going to do with 'cross the Rubicon'? Pause in

---

86.   Holbrooke, *To End a War*, 128.

87.   Roy, interview, 33.

the middle and give a lecture on Roman history and Caesar's decision making and the end of the first republic?[88]

There are other costs for U.S. negotiators of not knowing local languages and of not knowing how to use interpreters effectively. On occasion, had a U.S. official been better briefed on the basic character of his counterpart's language, serious miscommunication might have been prevented. For instance, President Nixon, faced with the allusive, elliptical, and ambiguous character of Japanese, famously took (or intentionally took?) the wrong impression from a comment by Japan's prime minister at a time of high tension over the trade imbalance between the two countries:

> As Prime Minister in 1969, Mr. Sato visited Washington to deflect American anger over a flood of textile imports from Japan, a hot trade issue at the time. The Japanese must exercise restraint in exports, President Richard M. Nixon insisted.
> To which Mr. Sato replied as he looked ceilingward, "Zensho shimasu." Literally, the phrase means, "I will do my best," and that's how the interpreter translated it.
> What it really means to most Japanese is, "No way."
> Mr. Nixon thought that he had an agreement, however, and when Japan continued on its merry export way, he reportedly called Mr. Sato a liar.[89]

Of course, the possibility exists that Nixon heard what he wanted to hear, and thus used linguistic fuzziness to his own advantage. There was no advantage to be gleaned (except for provoking good-natured amusement among Poles), however, when the State Department's interpreter mistranslated President Carter's speech to an audience in Poland in December 1977. Carter declared that he "loved the Polish people," but his American interpreter used Polish wording that implied that the American president "lusted after the Polish people."[90] Such problems are hardly a thing of the past. In the spring of 2009, for instance,

> on her first European tour as secretary of state, Clinton told NPR in Brussels that in discussions with the Russians, "we're going to hit the *reset button* and start fresh." She went so far as to present Russia's foreign minister, Sergei Lavrov, with a red desk ornament representing a reset button, and they both merrily pressed it in a photo-op. Her gag gift was labeled in Russian as *peregruzka*, supposedly meaning "reset," but actually meaning "overcharge"—in the sense of "electrical overload," not meaning "gouging the unsuspecting consumer"—but the American mistranslation gave the Russian diplomat a chance for a sly dig.[91]

---

88.   Neumann, interview, 45–47.

89.   Clyde Haberman, "Some Japanese (One) Urge Plain Speaking," *New York Times,* March 27, 1988, http://query.nytimes.com/gst/fullpage.html?res=940DE5DF1331F934A15750C0A96E948260.

90.   See "Transformations: The Spaces between Words," on the University of Arkansas Web site, http://www.uark.edu/~arsc/FRFall05/translation.php; and Seung Hwa Hong, "Ich bin ein dolmetscher (I am an interpreter)," *Seattle Times,* August 14, 2005. The exact nature of this mistranslation is hard to pin down; different reports give different wording.

91.   William Safire, "Reset Button," *New York Times,* April 1, 2009.

An appreciation of ambiguity, but a preference for precision

While linguistic ambiguity in languages such as Japanese can be so slippery as to defeat American efforts to grasp the real meaning of what is being said, Americans themselves are not averse to ambiguity where there is a perceived advantage in using it. The phrase "constructive ambiguity," after all, is sometimes attributed to Henry Kissinger (among many others), who saw the value of employing deliberately ambiguous language to conceal a failure to agree or to allow each side to claim that it had won a concession from the other and thus move on to other, more tractable issues.[92]

Dean Acheson used the term "Humpty Dumpty words" to refer to diplomatic phrases that "could mean whatever one wished them to mean," like the wording of the lend-lease agreement with Great Britain signed in October 1941.[93] Acheson was obviously thinking of the following exchange in Lewis Carroll's *Alice in Wonderland*:

> "When I use a word," Humpty Dumpty said, in a rather scornful tone, "it means just what I choose it to mean, neither more nor less."
> "The question is," said Alice, "whether you *can* make words mean so many different things."
> "The question is," said Humpty Dumpty, "which is to be master—that's all."

Rather than speaking in rhymes and riddles, however, American negotiators generally prefer to make their position unambiguously clear. As one might expect, given the legalistic bent of many U.S. negotiators, they use language like a scalpel, dissecting their counterpart's proposals and laying bare their own. Neumann notes that "we often have lawyers in our delegations," who are helpful in explaining why one or another American law "makes it impossible for you to do what the other side wants."[94] U.S. negotiators craft and insist upon airtight, legalistic language in agreements, thereby hoping to ensure that the other side implements the agreement exactly as envisaged by the U.S. team. As Yuri Nazarkin comments on the basis of his long experience as an arms negotiator, the other side is rarely in any doubt about what the United States is proposing.

> U.S. negotiating language is usually clear and precise. Even though American negotiators widely use terminology from the worlds of sports and business that gives their language a certain "American flavor," they manage to get their point across. U.S. negotiators expect similar precision from their counterparts. If something is not clear, American negotiators do not hesitate to ask as many questions as they feel are necessary to acquire a full

---

92.   G. R. Berridge and Alan James, *A Dictionary of Diplomacy*, 2nd ed. (Basingstoke, UK: Palgrave-Macmillan, 2003).

93.   Dean Acheson, *Present at the Creation: My Years in the State Department* (New York: W. W. Norton, 1969), 31.

94.   Neumann, interview. Neumann cautions, however, that "if you move from [explaining] to lecturing the other side on law," the other side is likely to become quickly irritated, for which reason Neumann instructs, "Keep [the lawyers] bottled up."

understanding of their counterparts` statements. This creates a solid ground for better mutual understanding.[95]

Nazarkin's equanimity in the face of sporting terminology is not universally shared. David Hannay, for one, calls upon U.S. negotiators to

> eschew sporting metaphors, particularly when the sports in question are not generally played elsewhere. Neither the Americans (nor the British for that matter) are immune from this practice. One wonders, for example, how much time was wasted and irritation caused by the need to understand and explain the term "slam dunk."[96]

Such appeals, however, seem likely to fall on deaf ears. Like Americans generally, U.S. negotiators find sporting metaphors irresistible. Phrases such as "a level playing field," "hitting a home run," "being on the one-yard line," "putting the ball in the other guy's court," and—of course—"moving the goalposts" punctuate the presentations and, especially, the conversations of almost all U.S. officials, from the lowliest to the most exalted. To take just a few examples: Secretary of State James Baker advised President George H. W. Bush against U.S. involvement in the Balkans conflict by observing, "We don't have a dog in that fight."[97] The president's son, President George W. Bush, declared of Tony Blair, who had announced his decision to step down as British prime minister, "He's going to sprint to the wire." Bush's secretary of state, Condoleezza Rice, urged patience in reference to talks with North Korea, explaining, "This is still the first quarter. There is still a lot of time to go on the clock." And Rice's negotiator with the North Koreans, Christopher Hill—after cautioning reporters that "those people who are not Americans ... won't understand this metaphor"—described his private discussions with North Korean officials thus: "It's always like 3 yards, 3 yards, 3 yards. And then it's always 4th and 1, and you make a first down and do 3 more yards."[98]

As most semiologists agree, the metaphors that a government or person employs attest to how that government or person understands and organizes the world.[99] The popularity of sporting metaphors among Americans suggests that they see negotiation as a competitive process that produces winners and losers, but not as a war—not as a no-holds-barred fight to the death. In sports, losers live to play another day; moreover, competitors play according to shared rules and most sides esteem values such as fairness, team spirit, and self-discipline.

---

95.   Nazarkin, "Negotiating as a Rival," 239.

96.   Hannay, "Negotiating Multilaterally," 274.

97.   Quoted in George F. Will, "A Dog in That Fight?" *Newsweek*, June 12, 1995, http://www.newsweek.com/id/117559/output/print.

98.   These examples are taken from "Bush Runs White House with Sports Metaphors," Associated Press, July 15, 2007, http://www.msnbc.msn.com/id/19774480.

99.   For a brief discussion of the fundamentally metaphorical nature of our conceptual system and the impact on diplomacy, see Berridge, *Diplomacy*, 64.

Bluntness

Sports—or at least those most popular in the United States—are physically robust affairs that typically involve some trickery but little outright deception; indeed, American sports fans—and negotiators—value hard-hitting directness more than evasive opacity. These qualities are reflected in the blunt, very unambiguous language that American negotiators employ when it seems advisable to impart precision and clarity to an exchange that otherwise might be obscured with customary diplomatic politesse. For instance, James Baker, a professional lawyer and consummate dealmaker, decided to dispense with rounded or oblique diplomatic phrasing when he drafted a declaration for a NATO summit, a declaration intended to show Gorbachev's domestic foes that NATO was intent on adopting a less threatening posture toward the Soviet Union. The French and British governments objected to the declaration's radical statement that nuclear weapons would be "truly weapons of last resort," but Baker told his NATO counterparts, "We do not need to water down this document. It would be a mistake. We have one shot at this. These are different times. This is not business as usual."[100] In another case, Baker upset everyone at a meeting with French officials by telling them that agreement was a lot further away than it seemed.[101]

Sometimes bluntness seems not only advisable but necessary to make sure the other side—especially a side accustomed to dealing in evasive, self-serving, or ambiguous half-truths and distortions—recognizes what is at stake. Holbrooke found it indispensable in tackling the Balkans. On one occasion he told Milosevic that the United States wanted to be sure "that you understand that we will not, and cannot, compromise" on the question of the participation in forthcoming negotiations of men indicted by the International War Crimes Tribunal:

> "But you need Karadzic and Mladic to make peace," he replied.
> "That is your problem. Karadzic and Mladic cannot go to an international conference. They will be arrested if they set foot in any European country. In fact, if they come to the United States, I would gladly meet them at the airport and assist in their arrest. You have shown us a piece of paper giving you the power to negotiate for them. It's your problem."[102]

Bluntness can help a negotiator establish a reputation for honesty that enhances his or her standing with counterparts, who may wince at the negotiator's unvarnished opinions but who appreciate the fact that the negotiator is unlikely to spring any unwelcome surprises on them. Max Kampelman, when head of the American delegation to the Conference on Security and Cooperation in Europe in the early 1980s, made a point upon occasion of being offensively blunt. When a Romanian representative asked Kampelman for a meeting, Kampelman replied, "I do not want

---

100.   Baker, *Politics of Diplomacy*, 258–259.

101.   Ross, *Statecraft*, 212.

102.   Holbrooke, *To End a War*, 140, 107.

to have any meetings while you people are violating the Helsinki Final Act. I was very blunt with him. And he wasn't that unhappy about it, to be perfectly candid with you." A short while later, Kampelman met the Romanian president, Nicolae Ceauşescu. "I was also very open with him. I told him I liked his representative. I also told him we were going to have problems because I was going to attack him. I leveled straight with him." In response, Ceauşescu "opened up," taking him to a large map on the wall, pointing to where Soviet forces were stationed, and asking, "Doesn't anybody in Washington know that I've got 200,000 [Soviet] troops right next to my country." He also arranged for Kampelman to visit the Romanian town, then part of the Soviet Union, where the American's parents had been born. Kampelman took the same candid approach with the Soviets: "I always maintained a good relationship with the Russians. They knew exactly where I stood because I didn't hide a word. I was very blunt, very open, no secrets."[103]

The line between bluntness and rudeness, of course, can be blurry, and what sounds like straight talking to Americans can sound like arrogance, insolence, or abuse to some negotiating counterparts. On more than a few occasions—especially during trade talks involving U.S. officials who were not career diplomats—American negotiators have been perceived to have overstepped the mark in discussions, offending their counterparts in a fashion that made final agreement harder, not easier, to reach. Koji Watanabe complains of "the confrontational and ill-tempered manner in which U.S. negotiators have approached trade negotiations [with Japan]."[104] Written language can be as offensive, and as counterproductive, as the spoken word. Logoglu recounts a letter from President Lyndon Johnson in 1964 "telling the Turkish prime minister that if Turkey invaded Cyprus, NATO allies might not come to its defense if the USSR attacked Turkey. The language of the letter was harsh. The Turks were hurt, never forgot the incident, and concluded that they should take a broader view of their security needs that went beyond the United States and even NATO."[105]

Americans can also offend their interlocutors unintentionally, simply because American conversational norms run counter to those of some other societies, notably those in the Arab world and Asia. "Americans in their informality and frankness can, if they're not careful, appear disrespectful," observes Ronald Neumann.

Our conversational style is very back and forth, cutting across each other. Many foreign cultures don't have that style. Algerians, for instance, tend to speak in paragraphs, if not pages. When you're speaking, they will listen to you very politely. . . . And then when you're done, they will reply and they expect the same courtesy from you. But an American being very American will jump into the middle of their discussions. Saying "Fascinating point, but I had this other perspective" is really going to tick them off. It appears to be rude and

103.   Kampelman, interview, 41, 43, 49.

104.   Watanabe, "Negotiating Trade," 206.

105.   Logoglu, "Negotiating Security," 215.

dismissive and treating them as your subordinate. That's not the way you get to agreement in negotiations.[106]

If U.S. negotiators sometimes fail to curb their conversational enthusiasm, they tend to do a better job of keeping their darker emotions in check. Such self-restraint makes it all the more impressive to their counterparts when they lose their cool. On one occasion, for instance, Warren Christopher, "a famously polite man who almost never raised his voice or showed personal discourtesy of any sort," refused to shake the hand of Mohamed Sacirbey, the Bosnian foreign minister, when he reneged on an agreement. Instead, Christopher demanded "in a voice barely containing his fury," "What the hell is going on here? . . . I made an agreement with your President just two hours ago." Not surprisingly, Sacirbey was "taken aback" and soon indicated that he would abide by the earlier agreement.[107]

Listening to what is said but not to what is not said

U.S. negotiators have a reputation not only for making sure the other side hears what they say but also for listening to what the other side has to say. In this volume, Logoglu, Andreani, and Mansingh each commend American negotiators for being good listeners, with Mansingh describing Strobe Talbott in terms that could apply to many of his professional colleagues: "He was a careful and patient listener, allowing his counterpart to speak extensively."[108]

U.S. officials, given their cultural propensity for straight talk, are much less accomplished, however, at hearing what the other side is *not* saying. They are also apt to miss or misread ambiguous or indirect messages floating hazily across the bargaining table. In communal, relationship-oriented cultures such as China and Japan, communication is allusive rather than direct; the context in which a message is delivered is as important as the content of the message. By contrast, in individualistic cultures—which the United States exemplifies—language is used directly and explicitly, and context is less important to conveying meaning.[109] Members of individualistic cultures are ill prepared to pick up the nonverbal cues that can play such an important role in communication within communal societies. Thus, U.S. negotiators have upon occasion failed to heed the body language of their Chinese and Japanese counterparts and missed quiet but meaningful signals, such as the seating arrangements at ceremonial functions. Kissinger recalls that when China tried to signal a readiness to discuss rapprochement with the United States, "Beijing's diplomacy was so subtle and indirect that it went over our heads." During

---

106.   Neumann, interview, 12–14.
107.   Holbrooke, *To End a War*, 182, 183.
108.   Mansingh, "Negotiating Bilaterally," 265.
109.   See the discussion of this in Cohen, *Negotiating across Cultures*, chapter 3, esp. 31–33.

the Chinese Independence Day parade in October 1970, Edgar Snow, an American journalist thought in Beijing to possess great credibility in Washington, was placed next to Chairman Mao on the Tiananmen reviewing stand. Two months later, Mao gave Snow an interview, during which the Chinese leader invited the American president to visit China. But both gestures, as Kissinger admits, were "lost on us."[110]

In a similar vein, whereas relationship-oriented cultures are able to tolerate silence during diplomatic exchanges—especially if the alternative is to utter outright disagreement, which is seen as impolite or off-putting—Americans, as Stapleton Roy observes,

> are uncomfortable with gaps in conversation. And in a place like China, or in Asia more generally, that is a real detriment because often the other side pauses a longer time than Americans are comfortable with before they make a point. It is just the practice where there are pauses between exchanges. So you make a point—and you have to be comfortable sitting there until the other person responds. If you have somebody with you who interjects . . . then you don't get the feedback from the other side you are looking for.[111]

Unease in the presence of silence creates another problem. As Michael Blaker explains,

> The Japanese cultural disinclination to utter an outright "No" and to smile and nod to indicate understanding, but not necessarily agreement, has often misled Western negotiators. So, too, has the Japanese use of silence. Silence is perfectly acceptable in Japanese social interactions. Indeed, it is expected of senior officials and respected elders. Non-Japanese, however, tend to misinterpret Japanese silence in the face of a counterpart's proposal as connoting agreement or at least acquiescence. As the UN diplomat Akashi Yasushi remarked, Japanese diplomats have "big ears and small mouths."[112]

Ronald Neumann makes a similar observation about representatives from Arab cultures. They "do not like to disagree with you," he explains. "When an American is talking, they will nod. They will occasionally say 'Yes,' which means 'Yes, I understand.' It doesn't mean 'Yes' [I agree]." He further observes:

> They will often start [their response] by saying "I agree, but." Now, when Americans hear "I agree," they will be looking for small adjustments at the margin of the idea [being expressed]. So, when that phrase is used to introduce what may be a position of complete disagreement, sometimes Americans have trouble following the thought or . . . . they get mad about it and think, "You're lying to me."[113]

According to Foreign Service Officer Michael Lekson, Americans seek to counter the risk of not catching the meaning of words or of misinterpreting silence by having several members of their negotiating team in the bargaining room at the

110.   Kissinger, *Diplomacy*, 725–726.

111.   Roy, interview, 66.

112.   Blaker, Giarra, and Vogel, *Case Studies in Japanese Negotiating Behavior*, 10.

113.   Ibid., 13, 44–45.

same time, on the assumption that at least one of them will perceive what is really being said—or what is not being said.[114]

Negotiating Multilaterally

The multilateral magnifying glass

Although much of what has been said in this chapter applies to U.S. behavior in both bilateral and multilateral settings, the latter also differs in some important ways. Most of those differences are matters of degree, with various American traits evident in bilateral encounters being magnified (or diluted) in negotiations involving multiple players. In some cases, this magnification is "real"—in the sense that certain traits or tactics actually feature more prominently in the American negotiating repertoire—whereas in other instances a particular characteristic is merely more conspicuous.

The U.S. emphasis on generating concrete results rather than building relationships certainly stands out in intergovernmental organizations. In such fora, the ability to leverage carefully nurtured professional relationships can be vital to securing the votes or the consensus necessary to achieve specific policy goals. For this reason, many countries devote considerable energy to nurturing long-term relationships, and assign the same diplomats to the same intergovernmental organization for lengthy periods. Indeed, many of these diplomats are permanently stationed within individual organizations and become significantly acculturated to the behavioral codes of those organizations. A Foreign Service officer, by contrast, typically spends just a few years working at an international organization before being moved to another assignment, which significantly limits his or her ability to develop a network of personal and professional contacts. U.S. political appointees, too, come and go frequently. In the thirty years from 1979 to 2009, the United States had no fewer than eighteen different permanent representatives to the United Nations; the comparable figures for the United Kingdom and the Soviet Union/Russia are nine and six, respectively. Given that many multilateral negotiations drag on for years, the short tenure of American diplomats in such positions means that several different U.S. officials may well participate in the same negotiation.

Awareness of this fact can make U.S. negotiators more impatient than usual, especially because decisions in international organizations are typically made on the basis of consensus, which can take a long time to build. Rather than engage in the slow process of developing consensus, U.S. officials are apt to simply assert the American position. Phyllis Oakley has remarked that her multilateral negotiations at the United Nations were not often negotiations at all. Because the United States was the "leading donor, and the heavy hitter . . . we more or less gave them our

---

114.   Lekson, interview.

position. There wasn't that much negotiation with them as you would expect on a bilateral problem."[115]

This disinclination to adjust the opening American position is reinforced by at least two other factors. In the first place—and as discussed at greater length in chapter 5—an American negotiator will be constrained by the need to adhere to the negotiating strategy agreed upon in Washington after an often protracted process of interagency debate. "The room for maneuver is very little," observes Ambassador Chan Heng Chee:

> We realized this is because of the internal interagency negotiations. The United States takes a longer time than its counterparts to come to a position, but once it has adopted a position, there is little room for change. In effect, the consultations with the various other agencies lock U.S. negotiators into a position. That is why American negotiators keep repeating their position in negotiations until the other side accepts it.[116]

In the second place, an American negotiator will be conscious of being watched not just by his or her bureaucratic colleagues but also by Congress, whose members (again, as discussed in chapter 5) are often suspicious of international organizations, seeing their procedures and rules as an attempt to chain or fleece the world's greatest power and richest country.

As a superpower, the United States is more comfortable negotiating in bilateral settings, where it can more easily flex its political, economic, and military muscle, than in multilateral fora, where its relative diplomatic weight is diminished by the collective strength of other member-states—many of whom exhibit greater resistance to U.S. proposals and voice harsher criticism of U.S. positions than they would dare to express in a bilateral encounter with the world's preeminent power. Such vociferous criticism, of course, only accentuates congressional distaste for multilateral organizations.

A unilateralist among multilateralists?

U.S. exceptionalist and unilateral tendencies are particularly conspicuous within multilateral organizations, which by their very nature emphasize mutual and universal commitments.

The most well-known recent instance of the United States acting in defiance of, or at least without the explicit endorsement of, international opinion was, of course, the decision to invade Iraq despite failing to secure a UN Security Council resolution explicitly authorizing the use of force against Saddam Hussein if he did not comply with earlier UN resolutions. The administration of George W. Bush at first sought to work within the UN framework to achieve its objectives in Iraq. Between

---

115. Oakley, interview, 4–5.
116. Chan, "Different Forums, Different Styles," 191.

September and November 2002, Secretary of State Colin Powell campaigned intensively to win the support of Security Council members for a resolution authorizing the use of military force to rid Iraq of its weapons of mass destruction (WMD). Colin Powell made "150 phone calls to his counterparts at the ministerial level in the course of the negotiations over the resolution. President Bush was also involved in phone calls to other chiefs of state and government, but Powell was the lead negotiator on the U.S. side."[117] And on November 8, the Security Council voted unanimously for Resolution 1441, which, though ambiguously worded, was welcomed by U.S. officials for threatening Iraq with "serious consequences as a result of its continued violations of its obligations" to destroy its stocks of WMD and certain kinds of missiles.[118] Jean-David Levitte, the French ambassador to the United States, declared that "the vote was a success for Colin Powell. He was the artisan of this long negotiation."[119] Yet, as Charles Cogan points out in his analysis of Franco-U.S. diplomacy over Iraq, that success had demonstrated an American tendency to preach rather than persuade:

> The long debate over UN Resolution 1441 illustrates, in schematic terms, a contrast between the U.S. emphasis on moral judgments and the French emphasis on logic and rationality. U.S. insistence that "we were not counting votes," which was a "false issue," but rather attempting to persuade other members to come around to its point of view betrays a characteristic self-righteousness that others, particularly Europeans, tend to perceive as sanctimoniousness and/or hypocrisy.[120]

Moreover, the Bush administration appears to have been determined to bring about "regime change" in Baghdad long before Resolution 1441 came into effect. In other words, the United States looked to the United Nations to validate and facilitate its predetermined plans, not to help shape them.[121] When UN weapons inspectors reported that Iraq was not demonstrating genuine cooperation with Resolution 1441, the United States urged that the time had come to use military force. The Bush administration did press for a second resolution explicitly authorizing such action, but it did so reluctantly—chiefly to help British prime minister Tony

---

117.   Cogan, *French Negotiating Behavior*, 201.

118.   The text of Resolution 1441 is online at http://daccessdds.un.org/doc/UNDOC/GEN/N02/682/26/PDF/N0268226.pdf?OpenElement.

119.   Quoted in Cogan, *French Negotiating Behavior*, 204.

120.   Ibid.

121.   Exactly when President Bush decided to embrace a policy of "regime change" in Iraq is still debated. Those who argue that the decision was made well in advance of discussion of Resolution 1441 point to various sources, including a leaked summary of a British cabinet meeting on July 23, 2002. According to the Downing Street memo, a recent visit by Richard Dearlove, the head of the British foreign-intelligence service, to Washington revealed that "military action was now seen as inevitable. Bush wanted to remove Saddam, through military action, justified by the conjunction of terrorism and WMD. But the intelligence and facts were being fixed around the policy. The National Security Council (NSC) had no patience with the UN route, and no enthusiasm for publishing material on the Iraqi regime's record." The leaked memo was published in the *Sunday Times* on May 1, 2005, http://www.timesonline.co.uk/tol/news/uk/article387374.ece.

Blair subdue British domestic opposition to the impending war.[122] Determined on its own course of action, the United States would not accept a proposal floated by the Chilean president for a thirty-day deadline for Iraq to comply with Resolution 1441—a proposal that the French, who strongly opposed action without explicit UN backing, did accept—because U.S. military plans for an invasion dictated that the invasion be launched before the hot weather set in.[123]

This asserted example of U.S. unilateralism is not quite as clear-cut as it might appear. American officials and scholars asserted both before and after the invasion that Resolution 1441 actually contained all the authorization necessary for military action against a noncompliant Iraq—in other words, the United States had *not* acted without UN approval. Even so, the fact remains that the Bush administration sought a Security Council resolution explicitly endorsing an invasion, failed to get it, and then went ahead anyway. In the eyes of many foreign observers, the U.S. action overrode the lack of support of the international community as a whole.[124]

Other recent examples of this perceived tendency to act apart from an international consensus include opposition to the Kyoto Protocol, the International Criminal Court, and the Ottawa Treaty prohibiting the use of landmines—policies in which the United States was in the minority in multilateral fora. U.S. opposition to these agreements may have been rooted in pragmatic considerations—such as a concern to protect American commercial interests, or to ensure that American troops are not the targets of politically motivated prosecutions—but foreign observers see a common thread running through all such cases: a reluctance to subscribe to the sovereignty-limiting aspects of multilateral institutions.[125]

The impact of personalities

Colin Powell's energetic campaign to secure wide support within the Security Council for America's approach to disarming Iraq reflected not only the high stakes on the negotiating table but also Powell's own character. In that respect, the negotiation over Resolution 1441 underscores a point made near the beginning

---

122.   See, for example, Cogan, *French Negotiating Behavior*, 209, citing a UN official and the *Financial Times*.

123.   Cogan, *French Negotiating Behavior*, 211.

124.   In many quarters of the world, there has been widespread agreement with Kofi Annan's judgment that the invasion was "not in conformity with the UN Charter" and thus "illegal." See BBC, "Excerpts: Annan Interview," September 16, 2004, http://news.bbc.co.uk/2/hi/middle_east/3661640.stm.

125.   American officials played significant roles in the origins of some of these international agreements that the United States is now reluctant to embrace. "In 1899 and 1907, American delegations participated in the creation of the Permanent Court of Arbitration and in the elaboration of the Convention for the Peaceful Settlement of International Disputes. At both conferences, Americans urged the necessity of an international judicial tribunal, which at the urging of Elihu Root, eventually became the Permanent Court of International Justice in 1920 and ultimately the International Court of Justice incorporated into the United Nations Charter." James Truslow Adams and R. V. Coleman, ed., *Dictionary of American History*, vol. 4, 2nd ed. revised (New York: Charles Scribner's Sons, 1942), 232.

of this volume, namely, that negotiating behavior in any given specific context is the product of a combination of factors, one of them being the personalities of the negotiators involved, especially the chief negotiator. That personality seems to matter more than usual at the United Nations. Certainly, several recent U.S. permanent representatives to the United Nations have had strong and strongly contrasting personalities that influenced their working relationships in New York. For instance, Jeane Kirkpatrick and John Bolton (who served in 1981–85 and 2005–6, respectively) earned reputations for being combative and outspoken; many foreign observers saw them as embodiments of an American populist distrust of diplomacy and debate.[126] In contrast, foreign diplomats have described Vernon Walters, Thomas Pickering, and Bill Richardson (1985–89, 1989–92, and 1998–99, respectively) as helpful, open-minded, and concerned to build consensus—and therefore more effective in advancing U.S. interests in the United Nations. Chan Heng Chee, for instance, believes that "it matters whether the American representative or negotiator has a rough and tough personality riding roughshod over others, or whether he or she is a nice jovial person. Jeane Kirkpatrick was apparently not popular. She was seen as too tough. Vernon Walters, her successor, was funny, avuncular, nice, and the United Nations loved him. They also loved Tom Pickering, who mobilized the United Nations during the first Gulf War and sustained its support."[127]

One reason why the personality of U.S. representatives seems to be more important—or at least more commented upon—at the United Nations than in bilateral fora may be that many of the leading American players at UN Headquarters have been diplomatic outsiders and high-profile political figures. Most countries send only trained diplomats to negotiate for them in intergovernmental organizations such as the United Nations, but the United States often sends negotiators who are well-known political personalities. Political appointees bring both advantages (they are often very talented and driven to achieve particular outcomes during their brief tenures) and disadvantages (unschooled in the ways of international diplomacy, they may find it hard to navigate through procedures and may inadvertently provoke resentment by failing to follow institutional conventions). According to David Hannay, another drawback of political appointees is their inclination to play to a domestic audience: "lambasting the United Nations in public speeches or statements may play well on Fox News or among conservative think tanks in Washington, but it tends to infuriate and antagonize those other ambassadors with whom the daily business of multilateral diplomacy must be transacted."[128]

Hannay also points out that while the U.S. permanent representative may be a stranger to the UN Headquarters in New York, he or she is also often a cabinet

---

126. An opinion expressed by a European participant at the United States Institute of Peace workshop on American negotiating behavior held at Airlie House, Warrenton, Virginia, July 2007.

127. Chan Heng Chee, "Different Forums, Different Styles," 196–97.

128. Hannay, "Negotiating Multilaterally," 275.

official and must divide his or her time between New York and Washington, with the latter usually claiming precedence given the importance of cultivating relations with the president and a domestic constituency. As a consequence, the permanent representative is typically both overloaded with work and is something of an outsider to the diplomatic establishment—meaning that U.S. attention to, involvement with, and empathy for the United Nations is diminished.

A global purview

If the professional purview of individual U.S. negotiators can be a mixed blessing in multilateral settings, so, too, can the global purview of the country they represent. As the world's "indispensable power," the United States has to take a position on almost every issue addressed within a multilateral organization. On the negative side, this can present Washington with the difficult tasks of balancing competing policies and interests (for instance, what to do when a country that supplies the United States with vital oil supplies abuses the human rights of its citizens?) and satisfying diverse domestic constituencies (such as the energy industry and human rights activists). It can also overstretch U.S. diplomatic capacities, especially because Washington is often reluctant to delegate significant authority to its negotiators at UN Headquarters or at the headquarters of other intergovernmental organizations. On the positive side, it allows the United States to exploit linkages; with U.S. support crucial to progress in so many different areas of an organization's work, the United States can usually elicit reciprocal support from many member-states on an issue of interest to Washington.

The United States can also be particularly effective when it marshals its considerable assets in support of a negotiating position. As discussed earlier in this chapter, the combination of unrivaled networks of professional analysts, intelligence agencies, and diplomatic posts, preeminent military capabilities, and unmatched political and economic power usually gives U.S. negotiators very considerable leverage. For instance, in trying to rally support among UN Security Council members for a resolution authorizing force to oust Iraqi forces from Kuwait, Secretary of State Baker orchestrated a three-level process that involved the U.S. permanent representative to the United Nations lobbying in New York, the State Department in Washington calling in foreign ambassadors for demarches, and U.S. ambassadors abroad promoting the proposed resolution with their host governments.[129]

* * *

In the 1990s, many informed observers, as well as some eminent U.S. negotiators themselves, predicted that the American approach to bilateral and multilateral negotiations would have to change to accommodate the changes being wrought by

---

129.   See Ross, *Statecraft*, 87–88.

globalization and to function effectively in a diplomatic world that had abandoned the confrontational postures of the Cold War era. In 1997, for instance, Deputy Secretary of State Strobe Talbott declared that "global interdependence is affecting the way virtually all governments think about international relations and practice diplomacy. The more engaged in and affected by the process, the more they must change. For the United States, therefore, the imperative for change is especially powerful."[130] Talbott described a variety of changes that the U.S. government was making in response to increasing globalization and interdependence, among them efforts by the State Department "to hire people who already have experience in areas such as international finance, labor, environmental science, and law enforcement"; closer, systematic cooperation between the State Department and other U.S. government departments and agencies, such as the Departments of Commerce, Defense, and Justice; and efforts by "our diplomats abroad . . . to nurture regional and transregional relationships to a greater extent than ever."

Just six years later, however, insofar as U.S. negotiating behavior had altered, it had shifted by accentuating its unilateral instincts rather than multilateral imperatives.[131] With the U.S.-led invasion and occupation of Iraq as their backdrop, many foreign observers pointed to an American retreat from the negotiating table and predicted a future in which U.S. negotiators would either be unemployed or would leave their businesslike briefcases and legalistic portfolios outside the negotiating room and enter brandishing only the cudgels and scourges of the hegemon and moralist.

Another six years on, the predictions seem to be changing once again, with President Obama stressing the need for diplomatic engagement with states such as North Korea and Iran that had been off-limits to the George W. Bush administration. "I do think that it is important for us to be willing to talk to Iran to express very clearly where our differences are," Obama declared in his first White House television interview, with the network Al Arabiya. "And as I said during my inauguration speech, if countries like Iran are willing to unclench their fist, they will find an extended hand from us."[132] In what has been widely seen as another break with the Bush administration's approach, Obama has also emphasized the importance of building greater international support for diplomatic efforts on issues such as climate change and cleaner sources of energy. In his inauguration speech, for instance, he called on the world's rich countries to recognize that they cannot

---

130.   Talbott, "Globalization and Diplomacy," 72.

131.   Logoglu attributes this to a combination of cultural traits and momentous events: "As the stakes become more important, such cultural traits are more likely to come into play. In the post-9/11 setting, national security has become the number one priority for America. This high sensitivity, in turn, has warped American negotiating behavior, making negotiations susceptible to bouts of temper and loss of patience." Logoglu, "Negotiating Security," 214.

132.   "Clinton: Engagement in Iran's Hands," *First Read*, NBC News, January 27, 2009, http://firstread.msnbc.msn.com/archive/2009/01/27/1762566.aspx.

continue "to consume the world's resources without regard to effect. For the world has changed, and we must change with it."[133]

In recognition of such ambitions, the Norwegian Nobel Committee awarded Obama the 2009 Nobel Peace Prize, citing "his extraordinary efforts to strengthen international diplomacy and cooperation between peoples."[134]

The conclusion to be drawn from all this is that administrations respond in certain measure to international imperatives as well as to the personal preferences of the chief executive. Yet negotiating habits rooted in enduring cultural mind-sets that are themselves sustained by enduring institutional factors persist and impart continuity to American negotiating practice over time. In other words, the traits and tactics identified in this chapter are likely to be displayed and employed by U.S. officials in formal negotiations—whether multilateral or bilateral—despite short-term variations induced by politics and personalities.[135] These behavioral patterns, however, are only part of a more extensive picture of American negotiating practice, which consists not just of the formal negotiations but also of exchanges away from the bargaining table and of negotiations among Americans themselves. It is to these two subjects that we now turn.

---

133.   "Transcript: Barack Obama's Inaugural Address, *New York Times,* January 20, 2009.

134.   Nobel Foundation, "The Nobel Peace Prize 2009," http://nobelprize.org/nobel_prizes/peace/laureates/2009.

135.   As of this writing, foreign affairs pundits have commented on the degree to which the Obama administration is reverting to certain policy positions pursued by its predecessor—despite campaign efforts to distance itself from the practices of the Bush administration.

4

Bargaining away from the Table

Ranging over time, negotiations also extend in space—outside the formal negotiating environment, that is, outside the framework of formal discussions involving the designated negotiating teams and other government officials.

Negotiations conducted away from the bargaining table can take many forms, but all, or almost all, involve a pronounced element of *indirectness*.[1] Certainly, the three forms that are the focus of this chapter—back channels, mass media, and hospitality—share that quality.

Back channels—private or secret contacts that take place outside regular diplomatic channels—may be direct insofar as they involve frank discussion of issues at the heart of a negotiation, but they are indirect insofar as they circumvent, often covertly, the explicit negotiating channel.

By contrast, when it comes to using mass media, the official negotiating team is usually directly involved, but its goal is to communicate with its negotiating counterpart indirectly, inspiring stories, briefing journalists, and otherwise shaping or "spinning" media coverage to influence the negotiating agenda or put pressure on the negotiating counterpart.

The third form, hospitality, does not address the issues at stake in a negotiation directly but rather seeks to create an atmosphere (be it one of sophisticated formality or easygoing cordiality) that will establish a more personal relationship in hopes of making the counterpart more receptive to one's arguments or appeals.

Given the portrait painted in the preceding chapters of American negotiators as explicit, precise, and blunt—sometimes to the point of rudeness—indirectness might seem an anomalous element in the makeup of American diplomacy. In fact, U.S. officials as a whole do not embrace all three forms with unalloyed enthusiasm.

---

1. "Indirectness" does not seem a fair description of, say, track-one-and-a-half or track-two encounters. Such initiatives (e.g., informal intermediaries shuttling between the parties to a conflict or workshops promoting dialogue between civil society leaders from warring communities) are usually conducted outside the formal, official negotiating framework, but they are designed to supplement and support the official negotiators, not to sidestep or undermine them.

Back channels seem to provoke little unease (except for concern that their discovery might undermine the front channel, and except in cases where officials in the front channel sense that they are being circumvented by their competitors in one of Washington's interagency feuds). American negotiators also have few qualms about trying to shape media coverage; even so, they rarely conduct orchestrated media campaigns, partly because the independent-minded American media would likely refuse to cooperate and partly because U.S. negotiators expect to carry the day with or without a supportive press.

Hospitality is an area in which, with some notable exceptions, Americans are notoriously deficient. This curious reluctance on the part of an otherwise hospitable nation to influence negotiating counterparts with entertainment and close attention to their personal comfort may stem from cultural tendencies such as a businesslike focus on substance, a preference for informality, and a populist aversion to governmental "extravagance"—an aversion evident in congressional opposition to the use of public money for official entertainment.

While U.S. negotiators do not exploit any of these three forms of indirect negotiation as much as they might, they certainly do not neglect two of them. Indeed, back channels and attempts to use the media are the most common ways in which American officials negotiate away from the bargaining table. We discuss the third form in this chapter for an altogether different reason: because American officials make only limited use of hospitality, whereas several other major powers exploit its potential to the fullest. Assessing exactly how and why Americans employ—or underemploy—each of these three forms tells us much about American negotiating behavior as a whole.

All of these three forms involve "track-one" actors—that is, official representatives of the U.S. government seeking to influence their negotiating counterparts. The chapter concludes, however, with a brief discussion of three other types of negotiating away from the bargaining table that target other actors: public diplomacy, track-one-and-a-half diplomacy, and track-two diplomacy. Public diplomacy, as its name suggests, seeks to influence opinion in the publics of other countries. Track-one-and-a-half and track-two diplomatic initiatives seek to draw on the expertise, ideas, or influence of private individuals or officials participating on an unofficial basis. Each of these forms of bargaining away from the table has played a role in past negotiations involving the U.S. government and will surely continue to do so, although that role has usually been limited.

Back Channels: An American Infatuation?

Back channels have long been a favored recourse of American officials. More than a century ago, Theodore Roosevelt used multiple back channels while he directed (although he never attended) the Portsmouth Peace Conference to bring a negotiated end to the Russo-Japanese War of 1904–05. For his efforts, President Roosevelt was rewarded with the Nobel Peace Prize in 1906.

Since then, the use of back channels has become highly characteristic of U.S. negotiating behavior—a common, albeit not a routine, expedient of officials trying to secure a deal when the formal front channel is of limited effect, obstructive, or nonexistent. Like furtive love affairs, back channels require and inspire various forms of intimacy. Secret rendezvous, candid disclosures, go-betweens, surprising revelations, bold declarations: such trappings of these diplomatic trysts can help to nurture a sense of partnership and trust between old friends and odd couples alike. But back channels also pose many of the same risks evident in amorous affairs. If they turn sour, they can leave partners with a sense of betrayal and an appetite for recrimination and revenge. And if they are exposed, they can tar participants with a reputation for promiscuity and untrustworthiness.

The White House and National Security Council tend to like back channels because they permit direct contact with their opposite numbers and offer the promise of a frank exploration of issues that might take a long time to navigate through the diplomatic bureaucracy. Back channels are also valued because various negotiating uncertainties can be partly resolved by using the supportive atmosphere of secrecy: uncertainty about any preconditions that will be demanded of the American side before the other side will agree to sit down at the open negotiation table; uncertainty about opposition that exists or will be mobilized (i.e., spoilers) within the ranks of the negotiating counterpart once talks are made known; uncertainty about the true interests and priorities of other parties who cannot or will not reveal or explore them in open channels; and uncertainty about the outcome of negotiations and fear that failure can damage top-level leaders politically.[2]

The State Department looks less favorably on back channels, at least those that entirely circumvent the formal diplomatic process, because they may undermine the authority of the lead negotiator. However, even in Foggy Bottom back channels have their champions. Dennis Ross, a former director of the Policy Planning Staff at the State Department and manager of several negotiations on behalf of secretaries of state, goes so far as to declare that "back channels are an essential part of any negotiation," because they make it possible to explore each side's "mythologies and politically explosive issues . . . in a noncommitting, unquotable, and nonreferral fashion."[3]

Yet back channels are *not* a constant feature of U.S. negotiating behavior—not, anyway, in the sense that the term is used in this book. Ross appears to define back channels very broadly to include any private, off-the-record conversations between high-level players in a negotiation or mediation. But this definition seems too broad to be helpful. For instance, if a private conversation between the publicly

---

2. We are indebted to Anthony Wanis-St. John for this point about uncertainty, a point made in an e-mail to the authors (of April 6, 2009) and in his article "Back-Channel Negotiation: International Bargaining in the Shadows," *Negotiation Journal* 22, no. 2 (April 2006): 125–129.

3. Ross, *Statecraft*, 232.

designated mediator in a peace process and the prime minister of one of the parties to the conflict qualifies as a back channel, of what then does the *front* channel consist? Here, "back channel" is used to mean secret or private contacts between U.S. officials and foreign governments or nonstate actors that are conducted *outside of the formal, overt diplomatic machinery*. One scholar, Anthony Wanis-St. John, characterizes them as "the black markets of negotiation."[4]

This narrower definition still leaves considerable room for variety. A typology of the phenomenon could distinguish among

- back channels in situations in which there is no front channel versus back channels in situations where there *is* a front channel;
- back channels that require complete secrecy to function effectively and others that can tolerate some public exposure;
- back channels intended to assist the work of the official negotiators and those designed to undercut that work;
- back channels that are confined to a particular phase of the negotiating process (such as prenegotiations) and back channels that run throughout all or most phases of the negotiating process;[5]
- back channels designed to help the negotiating counterpart build support for an agreement and those that seek to create or exploit division within the other side; and
- back channels that enhance the status of the other side's lead negotiator and those that are essentially shopping trips in search of alternative interlocutors.

A well-traveled Cold War road

Back-channel communications were particularly in use during the Cold War, for several reasons. First, the tense, distrustful, and conspiratorial nature of the superpower standoff encouraged U.S. policymakers to embrace deniable, covert, and indirect forms of diplomacy. Second, the Byzantine opacity of many communist governments left Americans either unsure of just whom they should be talking to on the other side or eager to exploit potential divisions within the ranks of their opponents. And third, the intelligence agencies, whose modus operandi instinctively favors secrecy, enjoyed considerable influence and were sometimes preferred over the explicit diplomatic actors by U.S. policymakers when handling highly sensitive negotiations. In the 1960s, for instance,

> the CIA chief in Paris, Al Ulmer, was used to convey a warning to de Gaulle about the existence of unnamed Soviet spies at high levels in the French government and in de Gaulle's

---

4. Wanis-St. John, "Back-Channel Negotiation," 120.

5. This particular distinction was suggested to the authors in an e-mail by Wanis-St. John. He also noted that front and back channels are sometimes also used intermittently and sequentially.

own entourage. Such was the suspicion in Washington of Soviet penetrations in France that the United States took the unorthodox action of going directly to de Gaulle on the basis of unproven assertions by a Russian defector.[6]

In another example, in 1973 Henry Kissinger sent the deputy director of the CIA, Vernon Walters, to meet with Palestine Liberation Organization (PLO) representatives at a time when there were no formal relations between the United States and the PLO. The PLO had "killed two U.S. diplomats in Sudan, [and] General Walters was ordered to make it clear to the PLO that the United States would not stand for such behavior. A meeting with PLO representatives was arranged at the palace of King Hassan of Morocco. Walters had known the king since World War II, when he gave him a ride in a U.S. tank."[7] (Walters went on to become U.S. ambassador to the United Nations, an ambassador-at-large, and ambassador to Germany, evidencing the sometimes very close relationship between the diplomatic and intelligence communities, and the fact that intelligence officials are often not mere message carriers but negotiators in their own right.)

Back channels ran between Washington and the capitals not only of allies—including difficult allies, such as the French—but also of rivals. In the 1950s, for instance, the Soviet intelligence organizations, the KGB and the GRU, competed "to develop their own direct lines of contact to the White House, which became known to Americans as 'the back channel' and to Russians as 'the confidential channel.'" At one point in 1960, this channel ran between the head of the Soviet TASS news agency in Washington, who reported directly to Moscow through the Soviet military attaché, and U.S. attorney general Robert Kennedy, the president's brother. President John F. Kennedy valued the information he received from Soviet premier Nikita Khrushchev—at least until Khrushchev used the channel to try to deceive the president about the presence of nuclear missiles in Cuba. Even so, Kennedy still did not close down the channel, which was instead rerouted through the Soviet ambassador to Washington.[8]

While back channels were thus hardly rare at the start of the 1960s, they became almost commonplace by the end of that decade, thanks to President Nixon and Henry Kissinger, who saw them not only as an opportunity for candid discussions with foreign leaders but also as a way of sidestepping individuals and agencies within the U.S. government that disagreed with Nixon's policies or that moved too slowly to keep up with their quick-stepping diplomacy.[9] When Kissinger was

---

6. Cogan, *French Negotiating Behavior*, 143.

7. "Vernon Walters, 85; Ambassador to U.N., CIA Official," *Los Angeles Times*, February 15, 2002.

8. Schecter, *Russian Negotiating Behavior*, 99. See also, Smyser, *Kennedy and the Berlin Wall*.

9. Kissinger set up a complex back channel with West Germany's foreign policy maestro Egon Bahr in the early 1970s, during the Quadripartite talks on the future of Berlin. As Richard Smyser notes, Kissinger wanted to bypass the State Department because he "believed that the State Department professionals would not move quickly enough to get an agreement." Smyser, *How Germans Negotiate*, 110.

Nixon's national security adviser, the National Security Council, which he headed, asked for intelligence and analysis from numerous agencies and departments, all for use in the conduct of the secret negotiations he wanted to undertake in parallel with the official, State Department–run negotiations.[10]

Kissinger developed secret contacts with a variety of countries, most notably China and the Soviet Union. As Soviet ambassador to Washington Anatoly Dobrynin comments in his memoirs:

> This mode of communication continued for many years while I served as ambassador [1962–86], continuing with varying intensity, although it was more restricted during the Reagan era when all contacts went through the Secretary of State.... It provided the freedom of personal chemistry which is an essential of diplomacy, and made it possible to explore unchartered diplomatic territory, which was often what was needed to break the stalemates that characterized the Cold War.[11]

Whereas Kissinger's back channels, in circumventing the State Department, often undercut the authority of the formal channels,[12] other U.S. officials have used back channels in harmony with the work of the State Department, circumventing not U.S. agencies but sluggish or obstructionist actors on the counterpart's side. In negotiating for the withdrawal of Cuban forces from Angola in the late 1980s, for instance, Assistant Secretary of State for African Affairs Chester A. Crocker discovered that the Angolan foreign minister was reluctant to talk to him unless Crocker declared that the U.S. government officially recognized the Popular Movement for the Liberation of Angola (MPLA) government as the government of Angola, which Washington did not. Crocker and his colleagues thus used a variety of intermediaries, including Nigerian businessmen and Mozambican government officials, to reach the Angolan president and engage in what proved to be fruitful negotiations.[13]

Other examples demonstrate that back channels can work well when they run in parallel with, not in opposition to, other U.S. diplomatic efforts. In the negotiations over German unification, observes Dennis Ross, relationships nurtured by U.S. officials from the State Department and the National Security Council with the right-hand men to Russia's and Germany's foreign ministers enabled the Americans "to prevent misunderstandings, to manage them when they occurred, and to condition attitudes of decision makers in private. Without the back channels, the trust that was required to manage the process would have been far more difficult to

10.   Kissinger, *White House Years*, 238–239.

11.   Anatoly Dobrynin, *In Confidence: Moscow's Ambassador to America's Six Cold War Presidents* (New York: Times Books, 1995), 100.

12.   See, for example, Gerard Smith, *Doubletalk: The Story of the First Strategic Arms Limitation Talks* (New York: Doubleday, 1980).

13.   Chester A. Crocker, speaking at the cross-cultural negotiation workshop held at Airlie House, Warrenton, Virginia, in July 2007.

achieve."[14] By confirming and underlining the U.S. position in this way, back channels can help to build mutual confidence.

Sometimes, a back channel can present itself with little warning. In July 1987, for instance, Crocker and his colleagues working to get Cuban forces out of Angola

> received an unofficial go-between bearing a message from [Fidel] Castro to the top level of the administration. The message distilled hours of conversation with the Cuban leader. Castro had chosen his emissary carefully, and he knew precisely which senior administration officials would receive his message. He proposed that Cuba should join the U.S.-MPLA talks.

Somewhat taken off guard by the proposal, Crocker nonetheless managed to use it to American advantage, by sending a "diplomatically correct" reply not only to Havana but also to the MPLA government in Luanda, which knew nothing of Castro's feeler, "stating that it was up to the MPLA to decide how it wished to proceed on the matter of having Cubans at their side in the negotiations." The Americans were able to stoke some dissension between Havana and Luanda, while also bringing the Cubans to the negotiating table. The latter effect had not been the Americans' intention, but it served their interests well.[15]

Back channels may have declined in number since the end of the Cold War, but they have certainly not gone out of fashion. In Franco-American relations, for instance, they have been employed during discussions over a French return to NATO in the mid-1990s and during the crisis over the war in Iraq in 2003. The "blue line"—a direct electronic connection between the Élysée and the White House—is credited with helping to promote good working relations between the two countries' presidents and, below them, the U.S. national security adviser and his or her French counterpart.[16]

A risky route

While the virtues of back channels are many and varied—from strengthening personal ties, to providing an opportunity to float ideas without running the risk of public embarrassment if those ideas are rejected, to enabling communications to be opened with governments with which the United States has no formal relations—they also have several shortcomings. One is the difficulty of maintaining secrecy in an age of intrusive media and "leaky" administrations. When a back channel is exposed, the front channel is usually undermined and discredited—or at the very least embarrassed. "One American diplomat," notes Richard Smyser in his study of German negotiating behavior, "found himself profoundly embarrassed when Kissinger instructed him [during the Quadripartite talks in the early 1970s] to

---

14. Ross, *Statecraft*, 45.

15. Chester A. Crocker, *High Noon in Southern Africa: Making Peace in a Rough Neighborhood* (New York: W. W. Norton, 1992), 355, 357, 358.

16. See Cogan, *French Negotiating Behavior*, 145.

accept a Soviet position that Kissinger had worked out with Bahr and Gromyko [in a back channel] and that the American had rejected only a few days earlier when Moscow had proposed it."[17] Embarrassment was inflicted not just on an individual but on the administration as a whole in December 1989, when the White House revealed that National Security Adviser Brent Scowcroft had made a secret trip to China in July of that year, just a few weeks after the bloody repression of dissent in Tiananmen Square. Scowcroft was sent covertly by President George H. W. Bush to try to limit the damage to bilateral relations and to press for the release of jailed dissidents. Scowcroft later recalled:

> But I went over there—this was a secret trip—I went over there and he [Deng Xiaoping] said, "I'm meeting you as a courtesy because you're an old friend, not because—I'm not the decision-maker now," which, of course, wasn't true. But he said, "I welcome you as an old friend, but I want you to know, this is none of your business. This is an internal affair of the Chinese people, and you're interfering."
>
> And so I said, "You're right. It's an internal affair of the Chinese people. But its ramifications around the world are an issue of great importance to the United States, and that's why I'm here." And then we had a very amicable discussion.[18]

Amicable it may have been, but the conversation was not very productive. "After the Chinese released only a handful of dissidents . . . ," Scowcroft and Bush later wrote, "it became apparent that the entire, slow process [of dissident release] was grinding to a halt—and we had no significant steps to point to in order to justify any normalization of our strained relations."[19] Moreover, the Bush administration was widely criticized for its apparent hypocrisy in condemning the Chinese leadership for the Tiananmen massacre while also seeking to maintain good relations with Beijing.

Another problem of back channels is that they hold the risk of policymakers hearing what they want to hear, rather than acknowledging and accepting the reality of the counterparts' formal position. The problem with such an approach, of course, is that any deal that disregards political reality is likely to fall apart. Logoglu's discussion of the U.S.-Turkish back channel in the prelude to the Iraq War is illustrative:

> The cost of using back channels was high. In a mutually reinforcing process, the American side was hearing only what it wanted to hear and the Turkish side was promising mostly undeliverable results regarding Turkish support on Iraq. The Pentagon planned to send troops overland from Turkey into Iraq. This required authorization from the Turkish Parliament. I kept reminding my interlocutors that the Turkish Parliament was a democratically elected body and that no one could make promises about how it would vote on such a contentious issue that affected Turkey's national security. Yet based on what they were hearing through

---

17.   Smyser, *How Germans Negotiate*, 110.

18.   From the transcript of an interview conducted on October 3, 2007, as part of HBO's *History Makers* series and available on the Council of Foreign Relations Web site, http://www.cfr.org/publication/14397/hbo_history_makers_series.html.

19.   George Bush and Brent Scowcroft, *A World Transformed* (New York: Alfred A. Knopf, 1998), 178–179.

back channels, Pentagon officials were sticking to the assumption that the Turkish case was a done deal. The assumption proved to be wrong.[20]

Back channels also encourage a related American weakness, namely, the tendency to "shop around" for collaborative partners in the counterpart government, for officials who will make a deal on U.S. terms whether or not they actually have the power to deliver on their commitments. In the words of Gilles Andreani, "When meeting resistance from foreign negotiators, the United States may test their credit at home, seek to circumvent them, or have them disavowed by higher authorities. . . . As a rule, Americans will poke around in your home system to find the point of least resistance."[21] Some Middle East diplomats describe veritable shopping sprees by American negotiators, who have established three or four back channels within the main channel within a single week.[22]

Shopping for collaborative partners poses a number of dangers, most of them related to the fact that such explorations are more likely to be mounted when dealing with governments whose internal discipline is weak and lines of authority unclear. One danger is that those interlocutors who are most ready to agree to American terms are probably least likely to be able to deliver an agreement on those terms, either because they lack adequate authority among their constituencies or because the authority that they do possess will erode if they are seen as acceding to American demands. Another danger is widening cracks in the internal unity of the other side until that side splinters into competing factions, none able to reach, much less to implement, an effective agreement. Yet a third risk is that of alienating the original—and probably the most powerful—interlocutor, who understandably will resent being "betrayed" or compromised in this fashion and may well either harden his or her stance or call off negotiations entirely. Finally, there is some risk of imperiling the United States' overall reputation as a trustworthy, reliable negotiating partner. This last risk applies, indeed, to the use of all back channels.

In America's defense, it should be pointed out that when it comes to back channels, it takes two to tango. The number, variety, and longevity of back channels with the Soviet Union, for instance, says as much about Moscow's internal feuding and cynicism toward traditional forms of diplomacy as it does about Washington's own interagency battles and readiness to compromise process for results. To take a more recent example: as Logoglu admits, while the Bush administration preferred to use back channels, "particularly in the early stages of the contacts with the new Turkish government at the end of 2002, . . . the Turkish side was partly responsible for

20. Logoglu, "Negotiating Security," 217–18.

21. Andreani, "Negotiating with Savoir Faire," 283.

22. Comments made by a participant at the cross-cultural negotiation workshop held at Airlie House, Warrenton, Virginia, in July 2007.

encouraging the Americans in this regard, as Erdogan and his party did not trust the bureaucracy and relied at least initially on their handpicked advisers."[23]

The Media: A Changing Balance of Power?

Just as Henry Kissinger gained a reputation as a maestro of the back channel, so in the 1970s he was widely considered to be a master manipulator of the media, brilliantly shaping coverage of foreign policy issues through his ability to regulate and selectively apportion the supply of newsworthy information and through his cultivation of relationships with prominent journalists and editors. For instance, Bernard Kalb and Marvin Kalb, brothers and highly respected journalists, were invited to travel extensively with Kissinger on his diplomatic peregrinations. They produced a sympathetic portrait—a book titled *Kissinger*—of the peripatetic secretary of state, even though Marvin Kalb was included by President Nixon's aides on the president's "enemies list" of political opponents.

Today, however, the media are far more difficult to marshal. Thanks to the communications revolution, which has transformed not only the technology used to gather and disseminate news but also patterns of media ownership and distribution, governments have considerably less control over the supply and distribution of news. Media outlets are far more numerous and varied than before, have a much greater geographical reach, and operate in real time, with "news updates" 24/7—every hour, every day of the week. The Internet has also reshaped the global communications landscape. All kinds of organizations—from al Qaeda to Amnesty International—can reach a global audience swiftly and directly without having to persuade the gatekeepers of public access (media editors and, in many countries, governments) to air their agendas, concerns, and opinions.[24] Once in the public domain, new ideas, information, and misinformation become fodder for an army of "bloggers," who can reshape the perceptions of their readers as well as influence coverage by the traditional media. The concept of "civic journalism," which posits that citizens and communities should be active participants in, rather than merely spectators of, media coverage and democratic processes, has begun to be translated into practice in the Internet age.

When a single individual with a camcorder, access to the Internet, and the luck to stumble on a newsworthy event can influence opinion about that event throughout the world within a matter of minutes, government censors, spokespersons, and spin doctors—not to mention diplomats—are going to have an uphill struggle to shape public perceptions. Nicholas Burns, when he was spokesman for the State

---

23. Logoglu, "Negotiating Security," 217.

24. For a detailed examination of the use made by terrorist organizations of the Internet, see Gabriel Weimann, *Terror on the Internet: The New Arena, the New Challenges* (Washington, D.C.: United States Institute of Peace Press, 2006).

Department during the Clinton administration, observed that "instantaneous reporting of events often demands instant analysis by governments. . . . In our day, as events unfold half a world away, it is not unusual for CNN State Department correspondent Steve Hurst to ask me for a reaction before we've had a chance to receive a more detailed report from our embassy and consider carefully our options."[25]

Compared with the time when Kissinger was in office, the balance of power between the media and policymakers can even seem to have been reversed. Since the protests in Tiananmen Square in 1989 and the famine in Somalia in 1992, the so-called CNN effect has enhanced the power of the media to build public political pressure on a U.S. administration to respond to a foreign crisis or disaster by broadcasting graphic images of the human suffering associated with the crisis.[26] Those images in turn generate demands from the public for government action to alleviate the suffering directly, by providing relief, or indirectly, by negotiating with the governments or parties involved.

The CNN effect can be powerful, but its impact on any given event tends to be short-lived and its power to influence governmental decision making seems to have been exaggerated.[27] The politicization of a foreign policy issue—often through the efforts of special interest groups, such as the representatives of ethnic diasporas or economic interests—can produce a more profound effect, as the American media shapes the parameters of public debate through editorial decisions on what to cover, how often to cover it, and whose opinions to solicit. Even when the American media help set the agenda in this fashion, however, they rarely have a direct impact on negotiations themselves.

Furthermore, although the communications revolution may have significantly changed the relationship between the U.S. government and the public, it has not transformed that relationship beyond recognition. Foreign policy players, including not only the White House and State Department but also individual negotiators, still cultivate media contacts, deliberately leak information, and provide not-for-attribution interviews in an attempt to shape coverage of the issues that concern them.

---

25.   Burns, writing in 1996, quoted in Steven Livingston, *Clarifying the CNN Effect: An Examination of Media Effects According to Type of Military Intervention* (John F. Kennedy School of Government's Joan Shorenstein Center on the Press, Politics and Public Policy at Harvard University, 1997), 2.

26.   See Warren P. Strobel, *Late-Breaking Foreign Policy: The News Media's Influence on Peace Operations* (Washington, D.C.: United States Institute of Peace Press, 1997).

27.   One study of the CNN effect points out that "media coverage of humanitarian crises . . . is typically triggered by official actions and associated with the presence of U.S. troops"—that is, the media have an effect only in situations in which the U.S. government is already active; Livingston, *Clarifying the CNN Effect*, 9. Another study is even more skeptical: "This book shows that the CNN effect implied by Kennan [i.e., that the news media's influence has usurped the traditional function of government policymakers] does not exist. It disappears under the examination . . . of numerous incidents in which the media supposedly played a major role"; Strobel, *Late-Breaking Foreign Policy*, 5.

Of course, the results of such efforts are by no means always predictable, especially when American officials are trying to feed an independent media, whether in the United States or elsewhere. In the mid-1990s, for example, U.S. ambassador to Canada James Blanchard, a former governor of Michigan, was trying to seal a sensitive renegotiation of the aviation relationship between the United States and Canada, referred to at the time as the "open skies agreement." Just as President Clinton was scheduled to sign the agreement in a public ceremony in Ottawa, the imposition of a new tax on U.S. magazines—the beginning of what came to be known as the "culture war" between the two countries—threatened to blow the open skies agreement off the front pages.[28] Blanchard took it upon himself to contact journalists at the five key Canadian media outlets and gave them a "confidential exclusive" on the forthcoming aviation agreement. The media outlets were supposed to embargo the story until a day later, but instead they published it immediately and referred to Blanchard by name or to "a senior U.S. government official." The unauthorized leak to the media

> caused a furious Canadian side to threaten to cancel the deal, but a counterthreat by the American side to make the agreed-upon announcement unilaterally turned back the tide. The last-minute attempt by the Canadian bureaucrats to stall the announcement in the hope of killing the deal was thus thwarted, and the leak actually helped by bringing it all into the open.[29]

American media advantages

Compared with officials from other countries, U.S. policymakers and negotiators have several advantages when it comes to using the media. In the first place, despite the globalized nature of media markets, all of the world's major news channels and newspapers are represented (usually by some of their most accomplished journalists) in Washington, giving U.S. officials unprecedented access to global audiences. Before, during, and after negotiations involving almost any part of the world (the exceptions include that handful of tightly controlled, cloistered states such as North Korea and Myanmar-Burma), American officials can be confident that their views will be reported—albeit not always accurately—in their counterpart's country and region.

Such coverage is usually but not necessarily an advantage for the promotion of U.S. policy. Insofar as American negotiators are seen as implementing a policy that is resented by or otherwise unpopular with the public or government of a negotiating counterpart, their appearance in the media may only stoke local hostility and inspire the counterpart government to adopt an uncompromising stance in the

---

28.   James Blanchard, *Behind the Embassy Door: Canada, Clinton, and Quebec* (Toronto: McClelland and Stewart, 1998).

29.   Robert V. Keeley, ed., *First Line of Defense: Ambassadors, Embassies, and American Interests Abroad* (Washington, D.C.: American Academy of Diplomacy, 2000), 57.

negotiations. In addition, any attempt by the U.S. government to shape media coverage in a foreign country runs the risk of being seen as interference in that country's domestic affairs, which will inflame public opinion and likely make the other side less tractable. Paradoxically, U.S. interests may be well served by low levels of literacy and spotty access to television and radio in some developing countries: media access favors the elites, who may be more receptive to U.S. arguments, and not the masses, who can be fiercely hostile to U.S. influence.

Even so, on balance the ability of U.S. negotiators to get their point of view into the newspapers and onto the airwaves of other countries is an asset. It is an asset that Dennis Ross, for one, wishes he had exploited more fully:

> Looking back at the Middle East peace process during the Clinton years, I believe I was far too cautious in using the media to set a tone and convey messages to all sides and their publics. There were times when clear signs of losing patience would have created a very useful pressure on both sides. . . . I could have employed messages or signals through the media much more than I did.[30]

Secretary of State James Baker drew on America's considerable resources—in this case, its logistical capabilities—to send an unambiguous and positive message about U.S. intentions to the peoples of the suddenly independent states that emerged out of the Soviet Union's collapse in December 1991. In the run-up to the Coordinating Conference scheduled for late January 1992 and intended to marshal international assistance to the states of the former Soviet Union, recalls Baker,

> I wanted to send a very clear signal of support to the Russians, Ukrainians, and others that the entire free world wanted their experiments with democracy, free markets, and independence to succeed. That goal would be partially fulfilled by the makeup of the conference itself. . . . But I wanted to add a touch of drama that would break through the typical media coverage of such an event. I wanted to create a story that might be transmitted by CNN and other international media to help instill hopes in those in the former Soviet Union, while also galvanizing a public consensus (and private efforts) in the United States. Margaret Tutweiler came up with the perfect vehicle: an airlift of medicines and food to every one of the new emerging democracies.

U.S. Air Force planes delivered 38 million pounds of assistance, another manifestation symbol of the sea change in U.S. relations with the former Soviet Union and its former provinces.[31]

Foreign negotiators are usually denied the opportunity to bring comparable pressure to bear on their American interlocutors, not just because they lack the resources to stage a major airlift of humanitarian supplies, but also because the American public evinces only sporadic and very selective interest in foreign affairs. Coverage of international affairs in most of America's national media—beyond the "prestige papers"—is modest, and in local newspapers and television channels it can be downright scanty. In negotiations on subjects at the forefront of

---

30.   Ross, *Statecraft*, 185.

31.   Baker, *The Politics of Diplomacy*, 618.

international news, representatives of other nations and of international organizations sometimes do garner significant coverage. In the case of U.S. negotiators, however, that level of coverage is far more common because of the world media's intense focus on Washington, which in turn reflects America's global influence.

Those traits of U.S. negotiators described in earlier chapters—for instance, self-confidence, professionalism, careful preparation, and active language faculty in English—can serve them well in dealing with the press. Some U.S. negotiators are widely recognized as masters of the craft. Assistant Secretary of State Christopher Hill, for instance, won the following accolade from John Wood for his performance as head of the U.S. delegation to the Six-Party Talks on North Korea's nuclear status:

> Hill's skills in public advocacy through the news media strongly supplemented the direct negotiating contribution he made. . . . Hill was available before and after each negotiating session, calm, measured, firm in setting out the U.S. negotiating line, fair in characterizing the state of the talks, and the positions of the other parties. It seemed to me to have been a very American performance, and one which none of the other negotiators had the confidence or the authority to seek to emulate.[32]

Most American diplomats, however, are a good deal less gifted in this capacity than Hill. In the past, Foreign Service officers were expected to bring with them to their profession a talent for speaking to the press, or else to develop that skill on the job. Such development, however, has always been hindered by the tendency of the State Department and the White House to keep junior and mid-ranking diplomats on a tight leash and to deny them opportunities to hone their skills through opportunities to speak with the media, especially the American media. Overseas, the paucity of Foreign Service officers fluent in non-European languages—such as Arabic, Farsi, Urdu, Hindu, and Pashto—has made it difficult to reach out to mass publics through the vernacular press (as opposed to the elite press). In recent years, however, the State Department has sought to rectify these shortcomings by making "a more intense effort to increase the media savvy of [American] diplomats." As Ruth Whiteside, director of the Foreign Service Institute, explains, "we offer a tremendous amount of media training," ranging from "a lot of on-camera practices and simulations," to courses in managing press offices, to instruction in honing foreign-language skills so that diplomats can answer "hard, rapid-fire questions" during television and radio interviews.[33]

High-ranking career diplomats and political appointees usually are much more comfortable than lower-level Foreign Service officers in front of a camera or a microphone. Such self-confidence and fluency are valuable resources for a negotiator, who may be obliged to speak before congressional hearings and expected to

---

32.   John Wood, "Use of the News Media" (paper presented at a workshop on American negotiating behavior, Airlie House, Warrenton, Virginia, July 27, 2007).

33.   Whiteside, interview.

participate in conferences and workshops organized by the dozens of nongovernmental organizations and think tanks that focus on foreign affairs and call Washington home. They may also be called upon to give interviews to foreign and domestic media and to provide "background briefings" (nonattributable interviews) to journalists. Inevitably, they often develop close contacts with journalists, which can serve them well during negotiations.[34]

Feeding the media

Media attention can be welcome, but the media are always hungry, and the negotiator who neglects to feed them may soon discover that their attention turns elsewhere or their mood turns sour. Fortunately for U.S. officials, there are numerous excellent reasons for offering journalists a healthy diet.

In terms of trying to influence public attitudes, media coverage can help at all stages of a negotiation. Before a negotiation begins, U.S. officials can frame the issues at stake; as it progresses, they can interpret the unfolding course of discussions, responding quickly to counterinterpretations and unexpected developments; and as it concludes, they can characterize the outcome of talks and apportion blame and credit. The very act of speaking to the media—at least if performed in an ostensibly straightforward and open fashion—can help a U.S. negotiator demonstrate his or her "transparency" with the public.

Most of these media-delivered messages are appropriate not only for foreign public opinion, but also for all of the audiences that U.S. negotiators might wish to reach. In most negotiations, there are at least six different audiences that an American negotiator wants to reach through the media: the negotiating team on the other side of the bargaining table; the other side's key decision makers, who are not likely to attend the talks in person; the other side's public; third-party governments and publics, and international opinion makers, such as nongovernmental organizations; the American public; and other players within the U.S. government and bureaucracy. The relative importance of these audiences varies over time and from negotiation to negotiation. One might perhaps expect the first and second of the six groups to be the most important in most cases, but interestingly the fifth and sixth groups—domestic audiences—probably claim that distinction. Whether to advance their department's interests in an interagency dispute (a topic explored in the next chapter), to promote their professional reputations or agendas, or to find out what the U.S. public thinks of a particular policy (in a media-driven society, foreign policy and domestic policy often overlap), American negotiators spend a lot of time talking to other Americans through the media.

---

34.   Richard Holbrooke, for instance, was able to send "a useful signal" to Bosnian Serb leader Radovan Karadzic through CBS's *60 Minutes*' presenter Mike Wallace, an old friend of Holbrooke's. Holbrooke, *To End a War*, 98–99.

Furthermore, this communication is by no means one-way. What the public hears from a negotiator may shape what the public thinks about a particular negotiation and its associated issues, but how the public responds to what the negotiator tells the press will filter back—through the media, Congress, and other avenues—to the negotiator and may shape his or her approach. Similarly, there is an important public "feedback loop" among a negotiator and the secretary of state and the president. The latter two will want to know if the negotiator is doing what he or she has been instructed to do; if not, the negotiator will be asked to correct course or may even be replaced.

On occasion, American officials will seek to tailor a message to a specific group. This is a difficult and risky undertaking, however. Yuri Nazarkin recalls that an article appeared in the *Washington Post* in April 1990 reviewing the state of the START negotiations and containing information that could have come only from someone involved in the confidential talks. Moreover, the article portrayed the negotiations as heavily favoring the American side. Whatever the intended impact of the article in Washington, in Moscow it gave ammunition to conservatives who were seeking not only to stop the negotiations but also to undermine Gorbachev and the entire process of rapprochement with the West. Ultimately, Gorbachev overruled his opponents and the negotiations continued, but the episode, remarks Nazarkin, demonstrates a typical trait of American negotiating behavior: to give absolute priority to domestic requirements and to discount the problems of the negotiating partners.[35]

American negotiators work hard to craft factually accurate but linguistically nuanced messages intended to have the desired impact on one audience without offending another. They also practice the art of shaping the attitude of one audience so as to influence another. For instance, in late 1977 the Carter administration mounted a media campaign aimed at American and Israeli public opinion to bring pressure to bear on the government of Israeli prime minister Menachem Begin to conclude a peace agreement with Egypt.[36]

The media can be a useful tool with which to build momentum. In the negotiations over Angola and Namibia in the late 1980s, Assistant Secretary of State Crocker's media tactic

> was to sound optimistic at press briefings once it was clear that there was a genuine chance of a breakthrough. Any party that then deserted the talks or behaved in an obstructive manner would be the target of attack from the many influential quarters . . . that favoured a settlement. . . . "Once a little momentum was achieved, Mr. Crocker would drive the talks trains faster and faster, briefing journalists on how well negotiations were going and how close to an agreement they were. If the participants tried to stop the train or get off, they would be portrayed as wreckers."[37]

35. Nazarkin, "Negotiating as a Rival," 244.

36. See Berridge (citing Quandt), *Diplomacy*, 68.

37. Ibid.

According to Charles Freeman, Christopher Hill "used press attention [in the Six-Party Talks] to create a sense of movement which may or may not have been accurate but which enabled him to continue a dialogue that otherwise the neoconservatives and others in Washington would have insisted be cut off."[38]

Crocker and Hill could not have employed this tactic so successfully had they not been intimately involved with management of the negotiation. This need for firsthand, on-the-spot knowledge of the nuances and dynamics of ongoing discussions explains why major U.S. negotiating teams dispatched abroad almost always include a press officer.

Media salvos, not blitzes

Careful handling of the media in the run-up to the U.S. invasion of Iraq in 2003 and the tight discipline exercised by the Pentagon on media contacts during the Iraq War shows that it is still possible to corral the media in exceptional circumstances. In this case, the media were almost entirely dependent on U.S. intelligence reports for information on Iraqi weapons of mass destruction before the war, and during the hot war and most intense periods of the insurgency, the environment was extremely dangerous for any journalists not "embedded" with American military units. However, as demonstrated by media coverage of the photographs of the torture and humiliation of Iraqi prisoners by U.S. soldiers at Abu Ghraib, while the media can sometimes be corralled, they cannot be contained for long—especially in the era of 24/7 coverage, real-time reportage, innumerable media outlets, and citizen-journalists, who can now drive the news agenda for mainstream outlets by releasing information from unexpected quarters.

Recognition of this inconvenient fact of diplomatic life is part of the reason why U.S. negotiators seldom seek to orchestrate media campaigns. As just discussed, they certainly do try to pressure their negotiating counterparts via the media in a variety of ways, but the kind of full-scale campaign conducted in 2003 to shape domestic and international coverage of the dangers posed by Iraqi weapons of mass destruction is rarely witnessed, being reserved for issues seen by Washington as vital to U.S. national interests.

John Wood recalls how, in the second half of the 1980s, U.S. officials helped to fire a salvo of negative stories about New Zealand but did not launch a sustained media blitz:

> The U.S. administration tended to use the media reactively, to respond to events, news reports, and government statements from the New Zealand end, and in particular, usually neuralgically, to put the record straight from its perspective at any perceived mischaracterization of U.S. views from New Zealand sources. This frequent bouncing back and forth of claim and counterclaim between the two sides, by proxy as it were through the media, could be

---

38. Freeman, interview, 73–74.

very time-consuming for both sets of officials in Washington to manage, and at times quite disruptive of the negotiating process.

This disinclination to mount media campaigns also derives from a belief that such efforts are largely unnecessary, because the United States has sufficient power to gain its negotiating objectives via governmental procedures, without the influence of public pressures generated by mass media. A similar self-confidence may help to explain the curious reluctance to use hospitality as a component of negotiation management.

Hospitality: An Inelegant Sufficiency

"French negotiators," a senior U.S. diplomat has remarked, "are in the business of winning hearts and minds with a good meal and a good wine. Call it *traiteur* [caterer] diplomacy. . . . using all the finery of French culture and cuisine to wow you."[39]

The Chinese are expert in "the purposeful orchestrations of receptions, sightseeing, cuisine, and music to dazzle . . . guests from afar. . . . Kissinger found himself negotiating the Shanghai Communiqué late at night after a banquet of Peking duck and powerful *mao tai* liquor. As he concluded, 'nothing was accidental and yet everything appeared spontaneous.'"[40] He also quipped to his Chinese hosts, "after a meal of Peking duck I'll agree to anything."

"For Russian negotiators," writes Jerrold Schecter, "well-lubricated lunches, cocktail hours, and dinners provide an opportunity for personality assessment, position probing, and resolution of deadlocks."[41]

But when it comes to American hospitality, as one longtime ambassador to Washington ruefully remarked, "It can be hard to get a coffee."

Few foreign diplomats testify to being impressed, beguiled, or otherwise intoxicated by the measure of hospitality that American officials normally provide

---

39.   Quoted in Cogan, *French Negotiating Behavior*, 148.

40.   Solomon, *Chinese Negotiating Behavior*, 62–63. Kissinger's negotiating counterpart, Zhou Enlai, had instructed one of Beijing's finest restaurants, Quanjude, to provide a twelve-course meal of Peking duck for the secret meeting. "On the first morning of negotiations, when the discussion had reached a stalemate by noon, Zhou, at one point, suggested that before continuing, 'We'd better eat first, or the roast duck will get cold.' . . . . Zhou introduced Kissinger to Quanjude roast duck, showing him the finer points on how to eat it, and after the meal was over led a few toasts with China's best maotai liquor. That afternoon Kissinger began by saying that the US couldn't abandon its 'friend' [Taiwan], and Zhou responded with, 'May I ask, what kind of friend are you afraid of losing . . .?' The discussions proceeded with various points determined, and the rest, as they say, is history." "Zhou zongli de kaoya waijiao" [Premier Zhou's roast duck diplomacy], on the Web site China Quanjude, http://www.quanjude.com.cn/historystory_info.php?auto_id=139.

41.   Schecter, *Russian Negotiating Behavior*, 94. North Korean officials seem to share their Russian counterparts' affection for alcohol. Madeleine Albright recounts a dinner in Washington, D.C., hosted by a North Korean emissary. The dinner "was quite relaxed, perhaps overly so. I spent much of the evening trying to fend off the North Korean delegation's aggressive style of drinking, which appeared to require the constant refilling of glasses and near-continuous toasts." Albright, *Madame Secretary*, 584.

to their negotiating counterparts. To the contrary, many decry the treatment they receive as significantly inferior to that which is customarily offered by numerous other countries, many much poorer and all of them less powerful than the United States. Hospitality—a broad term encompassing the reception, accommodation, and entertainment extended to visiting officials on both informal and formal occasions—is deliberately used by many states as part of the negotiating process.

Why should America downplay the role of hospitality? Some attribute this parsimony to the country's puritan past and populist instincts, the former frowning on luxury of all kinds, the latter critical of any form of governmental extravagance. Ambassador Ronald Neumann says that American hospitality "look[s] kind of cheap" in part

> because we don't have the funds, but also because we don't have the same habit [of wining and dining foreign guests]. . . . Arabs, Iranians, and Afghans, if their means allow, are going to have a table groaning with food, only a small portion of which can possibly be consumed by the simple gathering. . . . In some cases there is monstrous waste. . . .
>
> We grew up in an environment in which we were expected to clear your plate. "The starving children in China"—that kind of morality. . . .
>
> [Ours is] a very different tradition. So, in that sense, yes, we're going to look a little cheap to them. They're going to look a little profligate to us.[42]

The businesslike mind-set may also play a role, insofar as it leads Americans to regard negotiation not as a process of building and nurturing relationships but as a matter of getting deals done by "selling the steak, not the sizzle." Focused on substance, they pay scant attention to opportunities to impress their visitors with prandial pomp and pageantry, to manipulate them with carefully choreographed schedules of meetings and meticulously managed protocol.

Some foreign officials sense an apparent indifference to hospitality among their American counterparts. According to this view, Americans are eminently capable of being solicitous hosts and have no deep-seated objections to being so, but they simply do not see it as an essential element to be orchestrated in the negotiating process. As Neumann says, "I don't think that stuff matters a whole lot to the final result, although relations are important." By no means all U.S. diplomats share this opinion, however. Ambassador Thomas Pickering, for instance, remarks that ambassadors "are expected to do a large amount of entertaining," which "is an enormously effective way of building relationships, getting to know people, establishing new contacts."[43] But the weight of evidence suggests that Neumann's view is the more widely held.

Patrick Kennedy, undersecretary of state for management, describes the State Department's hospitality as "decent": "It's enough; not frugal, not lavish."[44] This

---

42.   Neumann, interview, 59–61.

43.   Pickering, interview, 55.

44.   Patrick Kennedy, interview, Washington, D.C., July 16, 2008, 2.

attitude is reinforced by the stringent rules and fiscal limits of the State Department's hospitality account—itself a reflection of congressional opposition to "extravagant" spending on entertainment. Remarkably enough, the bills for hospitality provided by a U.S. mission abroad are paid directly by the U.S. ambassador who heads that mission. He or she then seeks reimbursement from the State Department, which carefully vets receipts. If, when an ambassador submits a receipt, the yearly budget for "foreign missions and non-executive branch qualified purchases" is already exhausted, the receipt is stamped "Would be paid, except for the absence of funds." The receipt is then only of use to the ambassador as a tax deduction! The State Department, notes Kennedy, "doesn't really have a venue for hospitality—just the eighth floor [of the State Department's headquarters], Jackson Place, Blair House—nothing like the Colbert in Paris."[45] Such penuriousness is compensated for, in many instances, by the appointment of well-heeled political ambassadors to high-profile posts such as Paris and London, where private resources can make up for limited State Department hospitality funds.

Protocol, too, is not an activity to which Americans devote considerable, or at least consistent, attention. Especially for officials from countries that prize formality and etiquette, the absence of a formal greeting for their ambassadors and foreign ministers when they arrive on American soil can be galling. That sentiment can explode into anger and fuel resentment when foreign representatives, especially those off the State Department's radar except when actually engaged in conversations with State Department officials, are subjected to indignities at the hands of U.S. government security procedures. In one case, the defense minister of an Asian country who had just concluded constructive talks with high-ranking officials in Washington was searched and detained at an airport in New York before being allowed to board his flight home. "There, in the presence of the security team that had guarded him throughout [the negotiations], he was strip-searched, he was detained for a good half an hour, and was searched again and again. All the goodwill that had been built up through the successful talks evaporated because of this episode."[46] In another instance, a senior Chinese diplomat being courted in the early days of the normalization effort was outraged when confronted at a domestic airport with the need to go through a magnetometer screening. A confrontation was avoided only when a call to State Department senior officials excused him of the requirement to be screened.

---

45.   Ibid. The Salle Colbert, part of the National Assembly building across the Seine from the Place de la Concorde, is an ornately decorated room capable of holding three hundred people. The French also entertain diplomats and visiting politicians "in the splendor of buildings such as the Quai d'Orsay, the Élysée Palace, and Matignon, [where] the atmosphere is institutional and formal: one observes a strict dress code and does not deal in first names." Cogan, *French Negotiating Behavior*, 147. The Kleber Conference Center, near the Arc de Triomphe, is another impressive venue for international conferences.

46.   As recounted to the authors by a former Indian ambassador to the United States.

In another case, the level of indignity suffered was lower—American military guards ordered the senior French representative to the Dayton negotiations to get out of his car and then searched him using a dog trained to sniff out explosives. The fact that it was inflicted on a senior foreign representative to the Dayton talks not only during those talks but at the site of those talks is telling in that the incident occurred during the American hosts' "most ambitious effort" to provide an opportunity "to break down the barriers of hatred and disgust."[47]

Down-home hospitality

American downplaying of diplomatic hospitality seems to reflect the nature of American culture. That is not to say that Americans are culturally inhospitable—millions of foreign tourists each year would surely disagree—but rather that American hospitality has traditionally leaned toward a simple, informal, and unpretentious style and away from complexity and formality. Coming from a country that prizes informality over pageantry, most American negotiators tend to be more comfortable building relationships with their counterparts in relaxed and informal settings rather than amid the elaborate trappings of regal power or bourgeois refinement. In 1993, the U.S. team negotiating with North Korea in Geneva decided that the best way to get to know their counterparts was to throw a pizza party for the delegation from Pyongyang.[48] In Madrid in 1980, during negotiations on the Conference on Security and Cooperation in Europe, the American delegation "spent a lot of time on hospitality" but "had very little money," remembers Ruth Whiteside. The delegation's head, Max Kampelman, instituted "movie nights," consisting of old cowboy movies and Mexican food. "It was one of the few things the entire Russian delegation would be allowed to come to," Whiteside recalls. "And they absolutely loved it."[49]

Given the right interlocutors, informality can shade into a "freewheeling approach" to negotiations, as John Wood notes of his mid-level exchanges with American officials: "Often one-on-one or in a very small group, usually out of the

---

47.   Holbrooke, *To End a War*, 244. Holbrooke retells the tale with some levity, noting that the Frenchman refused to be mollified by Holbrooke's apologies. "The insult was not simply to him, but 'to all of France.' He would not leave the compound for our dinner—but he would make a formal protest to Washington and consider returning to Paris. 'I will not,' he said, 'be sniffed.' He pronounced it 'sneefed.'" (On two or three occasions in *To End a War*, Holbrooke pokes fun at foreign officials' poor pronunciation of English, a surprising jibe from a professional diplomat and one that lends weight to complaints heard among some of America's negotiating partners about American cultural insensitivity.)

48.   Snyder, *Negotiating on the Edge*, 57. Whether such a modest affair actually impressed the North Koreans is not clear. The North Koreans themselves, when they had hosted their first U.S.-DPRK meetings in Geneva, had provided "elaborate coffee-break settings." Snyder, however, contends that the pizza party "facilitated the negotiating process through the normalization of informal contacts and the development of relationships between officials on the two sides." Ibid.

49.   Whiteside, interview, 39.

office, frequently over coffee, a lunch, or a drink (invariably, with one notable exception, at the New Zealand Embassy expense)."[50]

High-profile exceptions

Informality and thriftiness may be the rule, but there are notable exceptions. Meetings between the American president and other heads of state or government are typically august affairs, organized in European-style protocol and formality—at least until the cameras stop rolling.[51] White House receptions for foreign dignitaries are lavish and ornate, if not always as highbrow as some of those dignitaries might prefer.[52]

Away from the capital—in the rural tranquility of the presidential retreat at Camp David in Maryland, for instance—meetings may be less formal, but they can still feature generous hospitality if one or both of two related conditions are present: the issue under discussion is at or near the top of Washington's foreign policy agenda, and the president or another very high-ranking American official is participating. The former may explain why negotiators from the Middle East tend to have a much higher opinion of the quality of American hospitality than do diplomats from many other countries.[53]

Invitations to the presidential retreat at Camp David are highly prized and can be an effective way of signaling the depth of U.S. support for the invitee and the level of U.S. commitment to reaching an agreement on the issue at hand. The venue, a mountainside pressure cooker, almost certainly helped President Carter secure agreement from President Sadat and Prime Minister Begin in 1978 for an Israeli-Egyptian peace settlement. It did not work as well for President Clinton in 2000, although he sought "to summon the positive mood of the 1978 Camp David summit" with some careful stage setting:

> Barak was assigned to Dogwood, the lodge used by Egyptian President Anwar Sadat, while Arafat was given Birch—slightly closer to Clinton's [cabin], Aspen, the most spacious of the three], a subtle goodwill sign designed to ease Arafat's fear of entrapment—which had been used by Israeli Prime Minister Menachem Begin.[54]

---

50.   Wood, "Negotiating in Washington," 229.

51.   It should be noted that hospitality in Washington is funded by a separate account than the one that covers hospitality provided by the State Department's overseas missions.

52.   In October 1949, on his first trip to the United States, Indian prime minister Nehru "was appalled to observe Americans flaunting their wealth in social conversations. He found the conversation at Truman's White House banquet far from stimulating, the principal topic being the merits of Kentucky Bourbon!" See Mansingh, "Negotiating Bilaterally," 256.

53.   These differing assessments were described at the CCN workshop held at Airlie House Warrenton, Virginia, in July 2007.

54.   Clayton E. Swisher, *The Truth about Camp David: The Untold Story about the Collapse of the Middle East Peace Process* (New York: Nation Books, 2004), 252.

According to Dennis Ross, "inviting [Helmut] Kohl to Camp David in February 1990—the first time a German chancellor had ever been a guest there—was critical for solidifying the Two Plus Four negotiating process . . . and for gaining an unmistakable commitment from the chancellor that unification must take place with the new Germany as a full member of NATO."[55]

Camp David was considered but rejected as the venue for what became the Dayton talks because, as Richard Holbrooke relates, it was considered to be "too close to Washington, too small, too 'presidential,' and too closely identified with the 1978 negotiations between Egypt and Israel." The site ultimately chosen was a good deal less charming than the president's forested retreat, but the care with which it was selected reveals a concern with stagecraft that one might not expect from officials of a nation widely adjudged to be indifferent to diplomatic hospitality, if not theatricality. The Wright Patterson Air Base provided "a physical symbol of American power," but it also provided "five visiting officers' quarters grouped around a central parking lot, only a few feet apart." These "nondescript" buildings "were adequate, but hardly elegant." They were perfect, however, for "true 'proximity' talks; we could walk from President to President in about a minute."[56]

> At the time, it did not sound like an impressive place for an international conference. As Dobbs wrote in *The Washington Post*, "Camp David it isn't." When we told Milosevic the news on October 17, he protested, half-jokingly, that he did not want "to be locked up like a priest.". . . The Europeans, used to negotiations in more opulent settings, literally had no idea where Dayton was, and expressed open unhappiness with a site "somewhere in the middle of America." Carl Bildt worried about the hawkish imagery of a military base. But I thought the reminders of American airpower would not hurt.[57]

Holbrooke's reasoning suggests that, as with the case of down-home hospitality, American negotiators are not as indifferent to making an impression on their counterparts as is widely believed. But the impression they wish to create is not that of an opulent and highly refined diplomatic partner but rather that of a purposeful, businesslike nation, a nation conscious of its power, determined to secure concrete results, and with little interest in protocol flattery or prandial excess designed to awe their interlocutors. American negotiating behavior away from the bargaining table is not very different from its practice within the formal negotiating environment.

Other Forms of Bargaining away from the Table

Three other forms of bargaining away from the table that involve groups or individuals outside of government—public diplomacy, track-two diplomacy, and

---

55.   Ross, *Statecraft*, 40.

56.   Holbrooke, *To End a War*, 204, 233.

57.   Ibid., 204.

track-one-and-a-half diplomacy—have implications for the work of track-one officials. But each also tends to be seen as of limited value to the formal negotiating process. In the case of public diplomacy, its influence on negotiations is so indirect as to be almost impossible to assess. Track-one-and-a-half and track-two efforts are weakly wired into the official negotiating process, and indeed are often viewed with some suspicion by officials determined to ensure that negotiations remain under their control.

Public diplomacy

The United States Advisory Commission on Public Diplomacy defines public diplomacy as "the attempt to understand, inform and influence foreign publics in support of [U.S.] foreign policy objectives."[58] This attempt has been made on behalf of the United States since the days when Benjamin Franklin sought to appeal directly to the British and French publics by laying out the American case for independence in articles published under his own name and various aliases.[59] American public diplomacy was given institutional form in World War II and the Cold War with the establishment of organizations such as the Voice of America (VOA, founded in 1942) and the United States Information Agency (USIA, founded in 1953 and dismantled in 1999, when it was integrated into the State Department and most of its operations placed under the under secretary for public diplomacy and public affairs). The term "public diplomacy" came into popular usage in the mid-1960s and referred to a combination of propaganda and public relations programming designed to "tell America's story to the world"—to promote a favorable impression of the United States, and especially of U.S. culture and values, in foreign societies.

Public diplomacy can take many forms, including efforts to foster bilateral cultural, academic, and civil society ties through exchanges, student scholarships, and exhibitions; through a variety of cultural programs, most of them run or funded by the Department of State (and formerly USIA); and through official efforts to influence public opinion abroad via mass media, such as the radio and television programming produced by the VOA. This latter form is related to the use of the media as discussed earlier in this chapter, but it differs in several respects, all of which limit its usefulness to negotiators. First, public diplomacy typically has broader, more diffuse, and longer-term aims than shaping the outcome of a particular negotiation. Second, it often takes a long time (longer than the course of many negotiations) to have any discernible impact. Third, public diplomacy campaigns are rarely

58.   United States Advisory Commission on Public Diplomacy, *Getting the People Part Right: A Report on the Human Resources Dimension of U.S. Public Diplomacy* (Washington, D.C.: United States Advisory Commission on Public Diplomacy, 2008), 2.

59.   See Injy Galal, "The History and Future of U.S. Public Diplomacy," *Global Media Journal* 4, no. 7 (Fall 2005), http://ics.leeds.ac.uk/papers/vp01.cfm?outfit=pmt&folder=7&paper=2837.

shaped by or coordinated with the efforts of U.S. negotiating teams. Indeed, VOA programming is insulated by the VOA's charter from an administration's editorial control, and VOA broadcasts sometimes contradict government policy on a particular subject, generating confusing signals about U.S. intentions in the minds of negotiating counterparts and their governments.

Public diplomacy can certainly assist American negotiators in a very general way, by helping over the long term to persuade foreign publics to regard an American official's arguments as credible and to assume that his or her intentions are consistent with local interests. It has had an influence on some relatively protracted and high-profile negotiations, such as the U.S. efforts to win international support for its approach toward the reunification of Germany and for the first Gulf War, but that impact is very difficult to measure. Furthermore, insofar as one can estimate its effectiveness, public diplomacy seems to work best in a climate indifferent to or already sympathetic to the United States. Writing of the mid-1960s, one scholar has argued that "public diplomacy could not function in a hostile political climate, in which the deeds and values of the United States were rampantly unpopular."[60] And commenting on the mid-2000s, the same writer asserts, "Neither public diplomacy nor any other facet of soft power can overcome the fallout from the present-day use of hard power," especially when today's global media can quickly spotlight apparent contradictions between U.S. actions and American values as projected by public diplomacy.[61]

This contention is strongly supported by polling data—data that also point to the very fickle nature of international public opinion. The Pew Global Attitudes Project polled twenty-four countries in 2007 and found that in only ten of them did a majority of the public have a favorable attitude of the United States, while fourteen were unfavorably disposed. Just two years later, however, majorities in no fewer than sixteen countries thought favorably of the United States, while the number with unfavorable majorities had fallen almost by half, to eight. According to a report issued by the Pew Global Attitudes Project in July 2009, the marked improvement in "the image of the United States . . . in most parts of the world, reflect[s] global confidence in Barack Obama. In many countries opinions of the United States are now about as positive as they were at the beginning of the decade before George W. Bush took office."[62]

Such sudden and substantial shifts in opinion—driven, apparently, by changes in Washington's declared agenda and public perceptions of senior leaders—underscore the nature of the challenge facing exponents of public diplomacy.

---

60. Ron Robin, "Requiem for Public Diplomacy?" *American Quarterly* 57, no. 2 (2005): 346.

61. Ibid., 351.

62. Pew Global Attitudes Project, *Confidence in Obama Lifts U.S. Image around the World: Most Muslim Publics Not So Easily Moved* (report released July 23, 2009), http://pewglobal.org/reports/display.php?ReportID=264.

Track-two diplomacy

Whereas public diplomacy typically targets large audiences, including entire populations, track-two and track-one-and-a-half diplomacy target small sections of elite opinion. Both of these tracks have come into vogue relatively recently, reflecting the growing complexity of issues that animate contemporary conflicts and the increasing variety of actors involved in them. Their popularity also reflects an increasing belief—among nongovernmental entities, chiefly—of the need to "fill the gaps of high-level, official third-party conflict resolution efforts."[63]

"Track-two" diplomacy is a term coined by Joseph Montville, who defined it as "unofficial, informal interaction between members of adversarial groups or nations with the goals of developing strategies, influencing public opinions and organizing human and material resources in ways that might help resolve the conflict."[64] This interaction is usually facilitated by "unofficial intermediaries [who] work with nonofficial yet influential people from the conflicting sides," people such as parliamentarians, academics, retired diplomats, NGO leaders, journalists, and political activists.[65]

From the perspective of U.S. officials, these endeavors can be especially helpful in brainstorming new approaches to apparently intractable issues and mobilizing support from influential elites for negotiating objectives. New ideas can be fed directly or indirectly into the official negotiating process. From time to time, the State Department encourages the creation of initiatives that bring together individuals of stature who have great expertise in the subject at hand (expertise that U.S. officials may not possess) or who are not themselves government officials but who have close contacts with high-ranking officials.

One of the best-known and longest-lived track-two efforts was the Dartmouth Conference, launched at Dartmouth College in 1960 in an attempt to build some degree of understanding between influential American and Soviet citizens. Over the following four decades, the participants—all of whom had close contacts with policymakers in their respective countries and some of whom who went on to become policymakers themselves—developed a lively and broad-ranging dialogue that had helped the American and Soviet governments avoid misunderstandings, overcome disagreements, and forge new forms of cooperation. Dartmouth's direct influence can be seen in "the achievement of a partial nuclear test ban treaty in 1963, the Soviet reappraisal of the American position on intermediate-range

63.   Diana Chigas, "Negotiating Intractable Conflicts: The Contributions of Unofficial Intermediaries," in *Grasping the Nettle: Analyzing Cases of Intractable Conflict*, ed. Chester A. Crocker, Fen Osler Hampson, and Pamela Aall (Washington, D.C.: United States Institute of Peace Press, 2005), 126.

64.   Joseph Montville, "Transnationalism and the Role of Track-Two Diplomacy," in *Approaches to Peace: An Intellectual Map*, ed. W. Scott Thompson and Kenneth M. Jensen, with Richard N. Smith and Kimber M. Schraub (Washington, D.C.: United States Institute of Peace Press, 1991), 262.

65.   Chigas, "Negotiating Intractable Conflicts," 133.

nuclear weapons in 1981, the reopening of U.S.-Soviet talks in 1983, and changes in the Soviet position on conflicts in the Middle East."[66] Its indirect impact was multifaceted, encouraging participants, policymaking circles, and wider publics to develop a common vocabulary and entertain new ideas and new forms of coopera-tion. Dartmouth also inspired other, similar track-two initiatives, such as the Inter-Tajik Dialogue and the U.S.-China Dialogue.[67]

The willingness of some U.S. officials to consider incorporating the results of track-two diplomacy into official negotiations is interesting from a cross-cultural perspective, indicating perhaps a legalistic respect for expertise and a business-like openness to new ideas. However, many other American officials are far from eager to embrace track-two efforts, which lie outside their control and which can complicate the official negotiating process. For instance, a track-two effort that offers a venue for parties excluded from the official process also presents them with an opportunity to rally opposition to the terms of any deal agreed to between the official negotiators. Furthermore, track-two diplomacy implies some degree of government endorsement of the third party's activities (whether to deliver a message to a foreign government, solicit information from a party to a conflict, or to explore common problems), which presents the U.S. government with the risk that the third party will embarrass Washington by overstepping its authority. It also presents a problem insofar as Washington has to decide which among the numerous individuals and organizations vying to play a track-two role to endorse or encourage—a politically sensitive decision that Washington would often prefer not to have to make. Asked whether track-two discussions are useful to U.S. ne-gotiators, Phyllis Oakley responded, "Well, it depends upon the circumstance. . . . I don't think there is an immediate payoff. It really is [a process of] building for the future."[68]

Track-one-and-a-half diplomacy

Definitions of track-one-and-a-half diplomacy vary, but all distinguish it from track-two diplomacy insofar as it may involve government officials. Roger Fisher has referred to "alternative" negotiations that occur in informal, working sessions, usually with governmental and nongovernmental experts or standing committees participating.[69] These sessions generate or test ideas (they "float trial balloons") or build political support for the objective of a given negotiation. Most definitions

---

66.   James Voorhees, *Dialogue Sustained: The Multilevel Peace Process and the Dartmouth Conference* (Washington, D.C.: United States Institute of Peace Press, 2002), 345.

67.   See ibid., 351–355.

68.   Oakley, interview, 53.

69.   Roger Fisher, "The Structure of Negotiation: An Alternative Model," *Negotiation Journal* (July 1986): 233–235.

envision a role for unofficial parties, be they nongovernmental organizations or individuals, acting either as impartial facilitators or as mediators. Diana Chigas, for instance, offers the following definition:

> In track-one-and-a-half diplomacy unofficial actors (former government officials and religious or social organizations such as the Catholic Church or the Quakers) intervene with official government representatives to promote a peaceful resolution of conflict. Track-one-and-a-half diplomacy typically takes one of two forms: direct mediation and conciliation, in which the unofficial intermediary tries to mediate a settlement to the conflict or specific issues in dispute, or consultation, in which the unofficial third party acts as an impartial facilitator of informal problem-solving dialogue among decision makers or negotiators.[70]

Among the best-known examples of this type of diplomacy is the successful effort by the Rome-based Catholic lay organization, the Community of Sant'Egidio, to facilitate discussions between the warring sides in the Mozambique conflict in the early 1990s. Another example comes from the work of the United States Institute of Peace, which was asked by the U.S. Department of State to facilitate peace negotiations between the Philippine government and the Moro Islamic Liberation Front (MILF). "The State Department felt that the Institute's status as a quasi-governmental, 'track-one-and-a-half' player would allow it to engage the parties more broadly than an official government entity could."[71] The Institute of Peace thus organized the Philippine Facilitation Project (PFP), which ran from 2003 to 2007 and helped the parties come up with creative solutions to difficult problems, such as the definition of "ancestral domain," launched dialogues to promote interfaith cooperation, and conducted training programs for local history teachers and civil society leaders.[72] Given the U.S. government's pursuit of counterterrorism objectives in the region, the State Department would have always found it difficult to win the cooperation of the Muslim community in Mindanao. The PFP initiative was initially regarded with suspicion by the insurgent groups, but gradually was able to build a productive dialogue with both the MILF and the government of the Philippines.[73]

Americans have played leading roles in several other track-one-and-a-half initiatives, but almost invariably in the unofficial capacity of facilitators or mediators—former president Jimmy Carter and the Carter Center at Emory University

---

70.   Chigas, "Negotiating Intractable Conflicts," 130. Other definitions—and other discussions of the pros and cons—of track-one-and-a-half diplomacy can be found in Jeffrey Mapendere, "Track-One-and-a-Half Diplomacy and the Complementarity of Tracks," *Culture of Peace Online Journal* 2, no. 1: 69–74, http://www.copoj.ca/pdfs/Jeffrey.pdf; and Susan Allen Nan, "Track One-and-a-Half Diplomacy: Contributions to Georgian-South Ossetian Peacemaking," in *Paving the Way,* ed. R. J. Fisher (Lanham, Md.: Lexington Books, 2005), 161–173.

71.   G. Eugene Martin and Astrid S. Tuminez, *Toward Peace in the Southern Philippines,* Special Report no. 202 (Washington, D.C.: United States Institute of Peace Press, February 2008), 1, http://www.usip.org/pubs/special reports/sr202.pdf.

72.   Ibid., 2.

73.   Ultimately, the project was (prematurely) terminated when the U.S. embassy in Manila withdrew its support for this track-one-and-a-half effort and official Philippine resistance to an agreement with the MILF compromised the negotiation.

being particularly prominent actors in the track-one-and-a-half mode. The American government has rarely been a party to a negotiation that featured track-one-and-a-half diplomacy. When it has participated, it has usually done so either very briefly—as in the case of the bipartisan team of former U.S. officials dispatched to Haiti just ahead of a U.S. invasion force to persuade the Haitian junta to relinquish power peacefully,[74] or ambivalently, as in the case of Jimmy Carter's visit to Pyongyang in 1994 to meet with North Korean leader Kim Il Sung with the objective of de-escalating tensions between the U.S. and North Korean governments.

Like track-two initiatives, track-one-and-a-half efforts are, potentially, quite valuable from an official U.S. perspective when communications between the United States and another government have been broken for an extended period and relations are hostile. Even in such circumstances, however, U.S. officials are still wary of ceding control over negotiations to others, even (or perhaps especially!) to former American presidents. The Clinton administration gave its support to Carter's visit to Pyongyang but came to feel that the former president had overstepped his authority while there. "As the chilly reception given to Jimmy Carter on his return to Washington from Pyongyang demonstrates, unofficial intermediaries can be seen as interfering with the policies of interested governmental parties or mediators."[75]

* * *

If President Carter's trip to North Korea exemplified why American negotiators rarely and reluctantly use track-one-and-a-half efforts, the same episode also illustrates a far more common phenomenon in American negotiating behavior: Americans vying with one another to determine and implement a negotiating strategy. Almost all countries witness some degree of internal debate over such issues, but the scale and intensity of that debate in Washington puts the United States in a league of its own. As the following chapter reveals, whether engaged in rivalries between different agencies, struggles between the legislature and the executive, feuds between cabinet members, or divisions within delegations, Americans negotiate with no one as passionately and relentlessly as they negotiate with themselves.

---

74. Whether the Haitian episode qualifies as track-one-and-a-half diplomacy is debatable. Jeffrey Mapendere characterized it thus in an article written while he was assistant director of the Conflict Resolution Program at the Carter Center (see Mapendere, "Track-One-and-a-Half Diplomacy," 72), noting that Jimmy Carter, one of the three-man team, was invited to go to Port-au-Prince by Haitian leader Raoul Cédras. However, other accounts note that the team was dispatched by President Clinton—and thus was closer to a track-one venture than a track-one-and-a-half effort (see, for example Robert J. Art and Patrick M. Cronin, "Coercive Diplomacy," in *Leashing the Dogs of War: Conflict Management in a Divided World*, ed. Chester A. Crocker, Fen Osler Hampson, and Pamela Aall [Washington, D.C.: United States Institute of Peace Press, 2007], 304–305).

75. Diana Chigas, "Capacities and Limits of NGOs as Conflict Managers," in *Leashing the Dogs of War*, ed. Crocker, Hampson, and Aall, 557.

5

Americans Negotiating with Americans

mericans who come to [foreign] negotiations cold are quickly aware of the
fact that their most difficult negotiations may be with Washington,"[1] observes Thomas Pickering, one of the most experienced American ambassadors. Veteran Singaporean diplomat Chan Heng Chee puts it even more bluntly:
"If I had to give a ratio, I would say that 20 percent of America's negotiations are
with the foreign party and 80 percent take place at home."[2] Even for seasoned diplomats, negotiating with various agencies within the executive branch and dealing
with Congress are always challenges. As Ambassador Raymond Seitz has noted,

> [T]he American government is very fragmented. We have a peculiar way of governing our-
> selves that puzzles foreigners a great deal. We like our system because it's very democratic,
> but it's often inefficient and confusing, with many competing executive departments and
> agencies, a White House managing the politics, the lack of a cabinet structure for decision
> making, and all the congressional interests. This is not something that is ever going to be
> corrected, and perhaps it shouldn't be, but it makes understanding the nature of our own
> government a fundamental requirement for an ambassador to be effective in the field.[3]

In recognition of this fact, the Foreign Service Institute offers training in the process of "interagency coordination that occurs before a formal negotiation" and in
congressional relations. As Ruth Whiteside points out, American diplomats must
keep "an eye on the Congress," because "at the end of the day you will have a lot
of interested congressional people who know you're negotiating and are constantly
telling you what you can and can't do."[4] Foreign officials, too, must understand the
domestic system that an American official must navigate before and during a negotiation if they are not to be confused and frustrated by the behavior of that official
at the negotiating table.

---

1. Pickering, interview, 10.

2. Chan Heng Chee, "Different Forums, Different Styles," 190.

3. Raymond Seitz, *First Line of Defense: Ambassadors, Embassies, and American Interests Abroad* (Washington,
D.C.: American Academy of Diplomacy, 2000), 51.

4. Whiteside, interview, 25.

This internal aspect of diplomatic negotiation is not unique to the United States. Even within autocratic governments, factions or individuals compete behind the scenes to set their country's negotiating agendas and strategies, if not to directly control the performance of the formal negotiation. In democracies, the competition tends to be more open and to involve many more participants, though exactly how open and how many depends on each country's system and traditions of governance. For example, in Japan, a highly pluralistic society, public policy decisions are reached in "an intensely combative, heavily bureaucratic, consensus-driven process" conducted among a relatively weak executive, extremely powerful government bureaucracies, interest groups, and "tribes" of issue-specific Diet members.[5] The practical consequences for Japanese negotiators bear a striking resemblance to those experienced by American officials:

> The need to reach [an internal policy] consensus means that Japan is slow to reach a negotiating position and is severely constrained from departing from it during negotiations. It enters negotiations with very little room for maneuver, which largely rules out the use of trade-offs, bluffs, and Machiavellian tactics. Anticipatory concessions have already been made at home, in the process of reaching a consensus on an initial negotiating position. When confronted with demands for concessions at negotiations, the Japanese may say in effect, "We already did that!"[6]

Yet, for all the similarities shared by democratic states, the differences between the American domestic system and other systems are pronounced. Americans negotiate among themselves in a way that reflects their country's unique constellation of domestic forces, cultural patterns, and institutions. In the United States, the separation of powers among the branches of government drives the necessity for internal negotiations beyond the degree required in other countries. "Foreigners," observes Phyllis Oakley, "are often amazed at the multiplicity of power centers in the U.S. government."[7] And reflecting both institutional and cultural factors, internal negotiations within the Washington bureaucracies aim not to reach consensus like the Japanese political culture, but to win the support of the relevant stakeholders—especially the president. Furthermore, the game of policy formulation is played to the ticking of an electoral clock, which is recalibrated after congressional elections and completely reset every time a new chief executive moves into the White House.

The executive, conscious of the need to balance competing international and domestic policy objectives, seeks to preserve the maximum negotiating flexibility. Congress, whose members do not share the president's national standing and who are usually more attentive to the concerns of their own constituents and of special interest groups, often seeks to limit the executive's flexibility. According to Dean

---

5. Blaker, Giarra, and Vogel, *Japanese Negotiating Behavior*, 10–11.

6. Ibid., 11.

7. Oakley, interview, 7.

Acheson, who headed the first bureau to deal systematically with Congress on matters of foreign policy:

> What the executive brings is initiative, proposal for action; what the legislature brings is criticism, limitation, modification, or veto. . . . Once it was thought that Congress would press forward with popular initiatives and the President could hold back with more conservative caution. . . . However, today both the complexity and urgency of matters calling for action and the difference in the nature of the constituencies have made the President the active and innovative initiator and the legislators the more conservative restrainers.[8]

While the authority to commence or end negotiations with foreign states lies with the president, the Congress and various executive branch agencies frequently determine the "bottom line"[9] for a particular negotiation, often by working together.

This chapter explores how the structure and internal dynamics of the U.S. governmental system help determine negotiating goals, timetables, and tactics. It begins by examining the influential role played by Congress, a role prescribed in the Constitution, colored by the American public's insularity, and resented by more than a few U.S. presidents—but not without benefits for American negotiators. The chapter then assesses the impact of U.S. elections on the conduct of negotiations with foreign governments, and, in particular, the impact of the electoral calendar and the effects of changeovers in administrations on negotiations, the continuity of negotiating positions, and institutional memory. Moving from the neoclassical splendor of Capitol Hill and the White House to the utilitarian corridors and offices in Foggy Bottom, the Pentagon, and other bureaucratic strongholds in Washington, the chapter explores the intense interagency rivalries for the ear of the president and control of the negotiator's brief. The challenges for a negotiator seeking a particular outcome lie in determining which among all the possible stakeholders are most relevant, and in ensuring that the president has the appropriate level of engagement for the issues at play.

U.S. negotiators are usually constrained, not liberated, by what goes on in Washington both before and during a negotiation. But they cannot escape being blamed for what this internal negotiation produces in the way of negotiating guidance, goals, and outcomes. To the contrary, as the final section of the chapter explains, U.S. diplomats are politically vulnerable to a degree witnessed in few other democracies—a vulnerability that speaks, at least in part, to the fundamental American ambivalence about the entire enterprise of negotiating with foreigners.

A Trammel and a Spur: The Influence of Congress

The U.S. Congress influences the conduct of an administration's negotiations in a variety of ways. Before World War II, the State Department would rarely consult

---

8. Acheson, *Present at the Creation*, 99.

9. Neumann, interview, 12, 15–16, 51; Pickering, interview, 69–71.

with Congress on matters of foreign policy unless—as mandated by the Constitution—the policy dealt with treaty negotiations. Since 1943, however, when it became clear that the cost of the programs planned for postwar European recovery would require hefty congressional appropriations, Congress has acquired a much greater say in foreign affairs. Today, through the annual budgetary appropriations process and oversight responsibilities, Congress can exercise a powerful influence over the goals and implementation of a specific negotiation.

From a negotiator's perspective, Congress often seems intent only on making the diplomat's life harder: rejecting carefully crafted treaties, limiting diplomatic freedom of maneuver, and frowning on pragmatic compromises with foreign powers. Yet Congress can also give a negotiator considerable leverage and a strong incentive to use it when the issues in a foreign negotiation pique the interest of specific members or their constituents.

A powerful constitutional role

From the president down to the most junior diplomat, U.S. negotiators must abide by certain provisions of the U.S. Constitution relevant to the conduct of foreign policy. They receive additional guidance from past practices of U.S. negotiations and decisions of the Supreme Court, which help shape the authorities and scope of responsibility of each branch of government. Although the president is constitutionally empowered to initiate and conduct negotiations with foreign governments, any treaty must be approved by at least two-thirds of the Senate. For non-self-executing treaties, Congress often has to pass implementing legislation to any treaty signed by the president. Hence the president and his administration must keep a watchful eye for possible congressional opposition to U.S. negotiating positions, lest the terms of the treaty be changed in the process of Senate ratification. If the treaty terms change, the executive branch is required to renegotiate the agreement—in effect, moving the goalposts of a settlement.

The Senate—reflecting in many instances an abiding wariness among the American public about making agreements with foreign powers—has made ample use of its constitutional role with respect to treaties, trammeling the executive's room for maneuver on the international stage. The Senate's own Web site notes that in its first two hundred years, the Senate *failed* to approve approximately 10 percent of the fifteen hundred treaties submitted to it. Twenty-one of these were rejected because they failed to receive the required two-thirds majority in a Senate vote. "Most often, the Senate has simply not voted on treaties that its leadership deemed not to have sufficient support within the Senate for approval, and in general these treaties have eventually been withdrawn."[10] In the case of other treaties, the Senate

---

10. http://www.senate.gov/artandhistory/history/common/briefing/Treaties.htm.

has added reservations, understandings, and declarations, collectively referred to as "RUDs." Forty-three treaties have never entered into force because the reservations or amendments were not acceptable either to the president or to the other country or countries party to the treaty. Another eighty-five treaties submitted to the Senate were later withdrawn because no action was taken. The committee process within the Senate means that treaty language submitted by the executive might never make it to the floor for a vote. There have been instances in which treaties have lain dormant within the Senate Foreign Relations Committee for years, even decades, without action being taken.[11] If the president does not resubmit a treaty rejected by one Congress to the next Congress, the treaty is considered to have been withdrawn.

Presidents have sought to escape Senate restraints in various ways. For instance, especially since the end of World War II, they have increasingly resorted to making "executive agreements," which theoretically do not require formal approval by the Senate, although there is heated debate over what subjects can be appropriately negotiated as executive agreements. Today, the United States is a party to more than five thousand executive agreements but only nine hundred treaties.

The negotiations to establish the United Nations Relief and Rehabilitation Administration (UNRRA) during World War II highlight why it may be wise to consult with the Senate early in the negotiating process. When the Truman administration's committee designing the United Nations declaration submitted its ideas to Congress in 1943, Dean Acheson, then assistant secretary of state, anticipated very little interest. After all, the president had briefed select members of Congress without much response. Acheson recalls that he had expected "about as much comment as a Red Cross drive evokes, and [I] could not have been more wrong." Senator Arthur Vandenberg, for instance, was livid at the lack of wider consultation, and his anger blossomed when he was told that the draft agreement would not be submitted to Congress for approval. Reflecting on this political storm, Acheson noted that the administration's mistake, which it never repeated, was to have "failed to bring the Congress into participation in the great endeavor."[12]

Congress's involvement in foreign affairs is not limited to deciding whether or not to approve foreign treaties. The "power of the purse" has long been the primary lever with which Congress—the only body constitutionally authorized to impose taxes and regulate foreign trade—seeks to restrain executive power in both domestic and foreign affairs. When international issues pertain to trade or budgetary matters, Congress has been especially ready to assert its authority. The Senate Foreign Relations Committee and the House Foreign Affairs Committee—and their numerous subcommittees—do not, however, confine themselves to budgetary issues.

---

11. Ibid.

12. Acheson, *Present at the Creation*, 70–71.

They have come to exercise a wide range of functions related to foreign affairs, from expressing their confirmation power over the president's ambassadorial nominees to overseeing foreign aid programs to reviewing peacekeeping mandates. Congress as a whole has legislated a role for itself in a variety of other foreign policymaking areas. For example, the 1973 War Powers Resolution was intended to increase the influence of Congress in decisions about whether or not to go to war.[13]

Congressional interests are understandably most pronounced when American negotiators are pledging not only material but also human resources. "The Hill can never be taken for granted," observes former ambassador to the United Nations Richard Holbrooke. "Without its support, it is virtually impossible to construct and carry out a policy on a controversial issue—and nothing is more controversial than placing American troops in harm's way." Holbrooke and his colleagues relearned this lesson during the run-up to the Dayton peace talks, when Congress ratcheted up its criticism of the Clinton administration's policy, culminating in the House of Representatives, on October 30, 1995, delivering "a serious public blow to the Administration" by "voting three to one for a nonbinding resolution that the Administration not deploy troops in Bosnia without prior congressional approval."[14]

Confronted by such opposition, the Clinton administration tried to reframe the issues in such a way that members of Congress and the American public as a whole would be persuaded of the wisdom of the administration's course. The administration of George H. W. Bush was obliged to do much the same in the buildup to the first Gulf War. Faced with what then-Secretary of State James Baker later described as "the administration's collective inability to articulate a single coherent, consistent rationale for the president's policy" to evict Iraqi forces from Kuwait by force, the U.S. public was by no means convinced of the need to deploy American troops.[15] The Bush administration thus sought to persuade Congress that it had done all it could do short of war to oust the Iraqis, so as to secure a congressional resolution supporting the use of American forces, a resolution that would ease public doubts over the policy. One of the main reasons that Bush and Baker offered Saddam Hussein a last chance to discuss a peaceful settlement to the crisis was to demonstrate to domestic critics that they had, as President Bush repeatedly said, "gone the extra mile for peace." As Baker recalled, "only by offering these meetings

---

13.   In practice, some observers contend, the resolution does not so much limit presidential power as invite presidents to wage whatever military campaign they want to wage for up to ninety days. See Miller Center of Public Affairs, *National War Powers Commission Report* (Charlottesville, Va.: Miller Center of Public Affairs, University of Virginia, July 2008), 21. In 2008, a commission chaired by Warren Christopher and James Baker called for repealing the old statute in favor of a new war powers resolution to clarify the consultation requirements and powers of each branch. See Karen DeYoung, "Ex-Secretaries Suggest New War Powers Policy," *Washington Post*, July 9, 2008.

14.   Holbrooke, *To End a War*, 173, 225.

15.   Baker, *Politics of Diplomacy*, 336.

could we hope to obtain the domestic consensus necessary to wage war."[16] But the initiative had unwelcome effects on the administration's negotiations with foreign powers.

> The overture contributed to speculation among many of our European and Arab allies that we really didn't want to use force and were desperately looking for an escape route. The need for secrecy created an aura of confusion it took us a few days to dispel. In retrospect, it's probably true that Saddam mistook our initiative as a sign of weakness. . . .
>   Among our coalition allies, the Saudis and Kuwaitis in particular were very concerned, fearful that talks might lead to the nightmare scenario of Saddam leaving Kuwait with his full military intact. They were also unhappy about being caught unawares.[17]

Baker had to reassure coalition members that he expected the talks to fail. And when his "meeting in Geneva [with Iraq's deputy prime minister Tariq Aziz] on January 9 failed to produce a breakthrough, opposition on Capitol Hill began to crumble."[18] Five years later, the Clinton administration was faced with similar congressional opposition to the deployment of American troops (this time, to Bosnia), and like Bush and Baker, Clinton and his secretary of state, Warren Christopher, had to spend several months persuading Congress to support sending GIs overseas and into harm's way.

Congress exerts its influence not only directly but also indirectly. For instance, as Koji Watanabe observes, increased politicization of an issue can significantly affect the tenor of negotiations:

> Because the genesis of a trade negotiation is more often than not to be found in Congress, trade negotiations invariably become politicized, making it difficult to achieve businesslike solutions. . . . More often than not [during highly politicized trade negotiations with Japan in the 1980s], U.S. negotiators were high-handed and aggressive, making one demand after another and forcing Japan to reluctantly agree to a series of concessions, some of which had adverse and enduring effects on Japan's economy.[19]

Congress also exerts its influence not only collectively but individually as well. The celebrated example of Representative Charlie Wilson's involvement in covert operations in Afghanistan during the Afghan-Soviet war is an exceptional case of what one member of Congress can achieve,[20] but numerous other senators and representatives make their presence felt in one way or another. Individual representatives and senators comment publicly and lobby privately on international issues of interest to themselves and their constituents. They can quickly turn a local or even a national searchlight on a country or an issue that had previously flown below the media's and public's radar. In January 2007, for instance, Tom Lantos, chairman of the House

---

16. Ibid., 350.

17. Ibid., 351–352.

18. Ibid., 344.

19. Watanabe, "Negotiating Trade," 205.

20. See George Crile, *Charlie Wilson's War: The Extraordinary Story of the Largest Covert Operation in History* (New York: Atlantic Monthly Press, 2003).

of Representatives Foreign Affairs Committee, demanded in a congressional hearing that the Bush administration cut off ongoing negotiations with Malaysia over a free trade agreement (FTA) unless Malaysia's SKS Group terminated a $16 billion deal with the state-owned National Iranian Oil Company to develop oil fields in the south of Iran.[21] The SKS-Iranian deal went ahead, but Lantos's intervention complicated the FTA negotiations.

All in all, the American Congress probably has greater influence on foreign policy than any other legislature in the world. Whether this is an advantage or a disadvantage for the United States, however, is a matter of debate, and depends in no small measure on whether one works on Capitol Hill or in Foggy Bottom. The veteran diplomat Charles Freeman certainly has a negative view of Congress's role. "Foreign policy is inherently an act of discretion," asserts Freeman. "It involves intricate judgments about what is possible and what is not possible and when it is possible and when it is not possible." Only the executive branch can make such judgments, avers Freeman, because Congress "is inherently fickle, it does not have a common view or a single view. . . . It is not well informed about the other side. It is, I would argue, incapable of empathy because foreigners don't vote." Congress also lacks the ability to display discretion because legislation can prohibit or authorize but cannot implement or execute. "The nature of legislation is to establish rigid parameters. Very often in the real world those parameters turn out to be counterproductive." Freeman concludes that "the separation of powers . . . is an impediment to our effective conduct of foreign policy that hasn't mattered very much during the period when we could call the shots, but which will matter more and more as we are relatively less able to call the shots."[22]

To be sure, it can be hard to execute a muscular yet nimble foreign policy while Congress is second-guessing, publicly critiquing, or otherwise involving itself in administration efforts. Henry Kissinger—not a man to welcome interference in his work—certainly did not appreciate what he described as the "finely honed manipulative skills" of Senator Henry Jackson, who used "his masterly grasp of how to manipulate the various branches of government" to effectively tie the hands of successive administrations in their policy toward and negotiations with the Soviet Union.[23] The Jackson-Vanik amendment to the Trade Act of 1974 made the extension of most favored nation trade status to the Soviet Union contingent upon the Soviets allowing all Jews who wished to emigrate from the Soviet Union to do so.

Supporters of the Jackson-Vanik amendment promoted it as the "right" thing to do, as a move to defend the rights of the individual against oppressive states. In most cases, indeed, congressional activism in the realm of foreign affairs is inspired

---

21.   See "U.S. Threats to Halt FTA Negotiations," *Malaysian*, February 2, 2007, http://the-malaysian.blogspot. com/2007/02/us-threats-to-halt-fta-negotiations.html.

22.   Freeman, 61–63.

23.   Kissinger, *Diplomacy*, 747.

more by politics and morality than practicality. At the risk of oversimplification, Congress—within the context of negotiations among Americans—can be seen as representing the moralistic facet of the American approach to negotiation, while the White House and, even more so, the State Department evince the businesslike and hegemonic mindsets. A former ambassador, Monteagle Stearns, argues that "moral judgments on the conduct, whether internal or external, of foreign states come easily to members of Congress and carry few political liabilities at home." He illustrates his contention by noting that "when Congress in 1976 charged the State Department with the responsibility for preparing annual reports evaluating the human rights record of each country receiving U.S. military or economic assistance, the Carter administration welcomed the move," because it squared with its own emphasis on respect for human rights, and it was left to the diplomats to point out "that the administration would have difficulty coming up with an accurate yardstick and applying it with consistent objectivity."[24] Stearns also observes that "even Henry Kissinger, the superrealist, when seeking confirmation as secretary of state before the Senate Foreign Relations Committee in 1973 . . . felt obliged to pay lip service" to a highly moralistic interpretation of American foreign policy, solemnly declaring that "throughout our history we have thought of what we did as growing out of deeper moral values. America was not true to itself unless it had a meaning beyond itself. In this spiritual sense, America was never isolationist."[25]

An insular instinct

As Kissinger well knew, spirituality aside, in many other respects the United States has been an exemplar of isolationism, eschewing "entangling alliances" with Europe up until World War I and then swiftly returning to its isolationist stance almost as soon as that war had ended. Congress traditionally championed the isolationist cause, and Congress's most famous intervention to derail the efforts of U.S. negotiators came when it twice refused to ratify the Treaty of Versailles and declined to join the League of Nations, thus crushing President Woodrow Wilson's dream of making the United States the bulwark of a new, Kantian international system of collective security—and, it may be noted, ensuring that American diplomats had little opportunity to engage in multilateral diplomacy between the wars.

Isolationism thereafter has enjoyed fluctuating fortunes. It was thrown overboard in the wake of Pearl Harbor and sank beneath the waves during the Cold War, but it began to resurface in the early 1990s, only then to disappear again after 9/11. Throughout this period, Congress has continued to display an insular instinct that influences the work of U.S. negotiators.

---

24. Monteagle Stearns, *Talking to Strangers: Improving American Diplomacy at Home and Abroad* (Princeton, N.J.: Princeton University Press, 1994), 9–10.

25. Ibid., 47.

Congress often takes particular interest in—or particular exception to—the work of the United Nations. Foreign ambassadors have sometimes sought to reach out to Congress and reassure its members that decisions taken by the United Nations and by other multilateral bodies will not injure U.S. interests. However, such is Congress's suspicion of the United Nations that negotiations at the UN level have to be handled with great sensitivity. Foreign representatives note that after attempting to negotiate with an American at the United Nations, they are left feeling as though they have been hauled before a congressional hearing.[26]

Congressional skepticism about the value of the United Nations, given Congress's relatively large financial investment in the institution, significantly influences the work of U.S. diplomats in New York. American officials, acutely aware that Congress is watching over their shoulders, are often reluctant to trade concessions with their UN colleagues, to make sacrifices for the sake of building long-term goodwill, and to settle for less-than-perfect agreements. By the same token, however, Congress's interest in what happens at UN headquarters can give American negotiators considerable leverage there. U.S. permanent representative John Bolton, during the George W. Bush administration, was able to push harder for major managerial reforms of the UN system thanks to legislation introduced in both the House and the Senate. The United Nations Reform Act of 2005, authored by Representative Henry Hyde, chairman of the House Foreign Relations Committee, threatened to cut U.S. funding of the United Nations—which accounts for more than 20 percent of the organization's yearly budget—by half unless significant changes were made in the way it is managed. While the bill passed the House, it stalled in the Senate and never became law. Even so, this legislative backdrop allowed Bolton to exert greater influence during his push for reform of the United Nations in 2005.

Bolton's threats also had credibility thanks to previous initiatives by Congress to trim or condition U.S. support for the world body. In 1986, for instance, the Kassebaum-Solomon amendment to the Foreign Relations Authorization Act for FY1986 and FY1987 effectively withheld 20 percent of the U.S. assessed contributions.[27] In 1994, the Clinton administration attempted to reach a "grand bargain" with congressional leaders by seeking to negotiate a package of reforms at the United Nations in return for the legislators' consent to pay off all or most of the U.S. arrears.[28] The deal was finally struck in 1999, and America paid up in 2001, once its conditions had been satisfied.

The extent to which Congress's insular instincts can influence American foreign policy, however, should not be overstated. Faced with a president determined to

---

26. These views were voiced by a number of former officials of foreign countries at the cross-cultural negotiation workshop held at Airlie House, Warrenton, Virginia, in July 2007.

27. Edward C. Luck, "Reforming the United Nations: Lessons from a History in Progress," *International Relations Studies and the United Nations*, Occasional Papers no. 1 (2003): 34.

28. Ibid., 44.

intervene on the international stage, Congress can only do—or want to do—so much. Congress itself is receptive to presidential calls for global engagement when American interests are seen to be at stake. Such unlikely political bedfellows as Franklin D. Roosevelt and George W. Bush have both asserted that America's domestic freedom and security depend on the United States guarding freedom and security abroad. "The present great struggle," said President Roosevelt in a "fireside chat" on February 23, 1942, "has taught us increasingly that freedom of person and security of property anywhere in the world depend upon the security of the rights and obligations of liberty and justice everywhere in the world."[29] Sixty-six years later, Bush declared in his second State of the Union address that "building a prosperous future for our citizens . . . depends on confronting enemies abroad and advancing liberty in troubled regions of the world."[30]

Such assertions resonate, of course, with the moralistic impulse prevalent within American society, but they can equally be seen as pragmatic arguments for intervention overseas—or, to some foreign audiences, as cynical justifications for displays of superpower might. Whatever the driving force behind arguments for engagement, they have often won the day. President Washington may have warned against "foreign entanglements," but "the United States is now a party to so many thousands of international obligations that it takes 510 pages of tiny type to list them all in the 2007 edition of Treaties in Force."[31] Despite the deep veins of isolationist sentiment that have run through both the Democratic Party and the Republican Party, presidents have led the United States into conflicts abroad more than a hundred times in the past century.[32]

The indirect influence of interest groups

Congress's ability to influence negotiations means that those who are in a position to influence Congress—lobbyists, special interest groups, diasporas, and immigrant communities—also have their influence on negotiations, albeit indirectly.[33] Ethnic lobbies in the United States are not only numerous but also, in many cases, sufficiently well organized to be able to deliver electoral support—in terms of votes and campaign funds—to politicians who support their brethren overseas. Sometimes, presidents themselves heed the influence of such lobbies. For instance, according

29.   The full text of this radio address can be found at http://en.wikisource.org/wiki/Roosevelt's_Fireside_Chat,_23_February_1942.

30.   The text of the address can be found at http://www.whitehouse.gov/news/releases/2008/01/20080128-13.html.

31.   Ted Widmer, *The Ark of the Liberties* (New York: Hill and Wang, 2008), xviii.

32.   See ibid.

33.   The influence of ethnic lobbies on U.S. foreign policy is by no means a recent phenomenon, according to a volume of essays on the subject that begins with a chapter on the Spanish-American war: Thomas Ambrosio, ed., *Ethnic Identity Groups and U.S. Foreign Policy* (Westport, Conn.: Praeger, 2002).

to one scholar, Irish Americans played a significant role in encouraging President Clinton to involve himself in the Northern Ireland dispute.[34] (Presidents have also been known, however, to exaggerate to their negotiating counterparts the influence of ethnic lobbies.)[35]

Senators and congressmen sometimes take up an ethnic lobby's cause, which in practice often means introducing legislation or other measures that limit the executive branch's policy choices on subjects of interest to that lobby. Examples of lobbyists successfully influencing negotiations include the 1974 embargo against Turkey, which was supported by the Greek lobby, and the Jackson-Vanik amendment, which was strongly supported by the American Jewish community—and which many U.S. officials of that period, among them Stapleton Roy, consider one of the clearest-cut examples of congressional limitation of diplomatic freedom of maneuver.[36] Phyllis Oakley recalls that when she was negotiating over the issue of Vietnamese refugees in camps in Hong Kong, she felt "constantly" politically vulnerable from pressure exerted by the Vietnamese diaspora, who "had a lot of voting power in California," and who "had built up such political power in the United States" through refugee support groups, veterans' associations, and other NGOs.[37] More recent instances range from the Syria Accountability Act (2003) to the Taiwan Security Enhancement Act (2000) and Section 907 of the Freedom Support Act (1992), which was directed largely at Azerbaijan and which reflected the influence of the Armenian community in the United States.[38]

In some instances, pressure can be brought to bear on an administration *not* to negotiate with a particular country. Congress has been the source of especially

---

34. Joseph O'Grady, "An Irish Policy Born in the U.S.A.: Clinton's Break with the Past," *Foreign Affairs* 75, no. 3 (1996): 2–8. Another study notes efforts by Irish Americans—especially after the Irish potato famine of 1845–47—"to involve Washington in conflict with London, hoping thereby to secure Ireland's independence": Tony Smith, *Foreign Attachments: The Power of Ethnic Groups in the Making of American Foreign Policy* (Cambridge, Mass.: Harvard University Press, 2000), 48.

35. See, for instance, a discussion of President Franklin D. Roosevelt's reasons for telling Stalin in 1943 that he was not interested in losing the votes of some six to seven million Americans of Polish extraction by accepting Soviet dominion over Poland—even though that is more or less what Roosevelt acceded to at the Yalta Conference. Warren F. Kimball, "Principles and Compromises: Churchill, Roosevelt and Eastern Europe (paper presented at the Annual Churchill Conference, Boston, October 28, 1995), http://www.winstonchurchill.org/learn/biography/the-war-leader/yalta-1945, 164. "In fact," writes Kimball,

> Roosevelt grossly exaggerated "the Polish vote" in his statements to Stalin. The claim of six to seven million Polish-Americans—"a genial Rooseveltian exaggeration evidently plucked from the air" in Arthur Schlesinger's phrase—actually translated into less than half that number, many of whom were not voters.
> That hyperbole was, perhaps, a bit more calculated and less genial than it appeared, for it allowed FDR to escape public responsibility for the political fact that he, Churchill, and Stalin's Red Army, together ensured that, in the short run, Poland's independence would depend on Moscow's self-restraint, not Anglo-American guarantees.

36. "The most obvious case [of congressional pressure] would be the Jackson-Vanik Amendment act where Congress essentially imposed on us the provision on Jewish immigration." Roy, interview, 26.

37. Oakley, interview, 18.

38. Brzezinski, *Second Chance*, 198.

fierce and vocal criticism of any rapprochement with Cuba under Fidel Castro, though its actions have not been merely censorious. In the 1990s, two pieces of legislation known collectively as "the Helms Burton legislation" sought to tighten sanctions on Cuba. In the 2000s, however, as Fidel Castro, in declining health, gradually relinquished power, a raft of other legislation has sought to encourage democracy in that country and to support the Cuban people in various ways.[39]

Such a sophisticated interest group influence on foreign affairs is relatively uncommon, however—and reflects, in the case of Cuba, the diversity of opinion among Cuban groups in the United States that has emerged over a period of almost sixty years. More commonly, interest groups seek to work through Congress to influence U.S. negotiating agendas so as to obtain more straightforward and more tangible benefits. Even so, such benefits are often hidden—at least by the negotiators themselves—within the Trojan horse of principle. Koji Watanabe recounts the case of the Strategic Impediments Initiative (SII) negotiations between Japan and the United States in the late 1980s and early 1990s. SII was supposed to root out structural impediments to the benefit of both countries' economies. American negotiators—under pressure from Congress—pushed hard for a change in a Japanese law that restricted the establishment of large department stores, supermarkets, and other stores. "American pressure," notes Watanabe, "helped Japan's Ministry of Economy and Trade decide to opt for revision [of the law]. However, it subsequently emerged that U.S.-based Toys "R" Us had directly asked the USTR and Congress to help it open shops in Japan. Today, Japan has no fewer than twenty-five Toys "R" Us stores."[40]

A two-sided relationship

Foreign diplomats—and many American officials, too—tend to portray the relationship between Congress, on the one hand, and the White House, the State Department, and other parts of the U.S. negotiating apparatus, on the other hand, as fundamentally adversarial, with Congress frustrating, opposing, or undermining the work of U.S. negotiators. In many instances, however, the relationship is complementary and mutually supportive.

In the first place, Congress is a keystone in the constitutional system of checks and balances. And as Chan Heng Chee notes, "the separation of powers provides the opportunity to reexamine policy" and to avoid "hasty and reckless decisions." The fact that American negotiators must "have an eye on how the agreements they work out will play in Washington, especially treaties and agreements that need congressional approval," leads them to "test the market." "Getting a sense of

---

39.   See Mark P. Sullivan, *Cuba: Issues for the 109th Congress*, CRC Report for Congress (Congressional Research Service, December 19, 2006), 13–14, http://www.au.af.mil/au/awc/awcgate/crs/rl32730.pdf.

40.   Watanabe, "Negotiating Trade," 206.

what the market can bear is an important part of the process of negotiation for the American side and frankly for the other side as well, especially in bilateral free trade agreements."[41]

In the second place, as the case of John Bolton's determined pursuit of UN reforms demonstrates, while Congress can impede a U.S. negotiator's flexibility, it can also give a negotiator valuable leverage. American negotiators often use what Phyllis Oakley calls "the shadow of congressional interest over our shoulders as a way of influencing the behavior" of negotiating counterparts.[42] Ambassador Charles Freeman goes so far as to say that

> the most distinctive element of American negotiating style as I observed it and practiced it myself is the tendency to extend American politics abroad by invoking congressional threats. That is, [the negotiator tells his counterpart] "there's this group of mad people who are up on Capitol Hill, and they're utterly irrational, erratic, and unpredictable, and if you don't appease them somehow, the nice guys like me are going to get shoved out of the way, and you are going to confront [unpleasant] consequences."
>
> It's carried to the extent of being almost self-parodying. Jim Baker, for example, never once in my experience employed a different technique of negotiation internationally—except for one other variant: "Your friend, the president, will be embarrassed by the Congress if you don't do this." So it's a very coercive approach, not persuasive at all, but which softens the threat of coercion by attributing it to somebody else.[43]

Threats of this kind are frequently quite real. Stapleton Roy, for example, recalls negotiating a consular treaty with China and being able to defeat a Chinese demand (for a lengthy notification period) simply by pointing out "the fact that the objective circumstance meant that Congress" would not accept such a provision.[44] On occasion, however, such claims are tinged with disingenuousness insofar as the negotiator—or at least the negotiator's superiors—can exert some influence, directly or otherwise, on what the Hill will accept. Congress is very far from being a presidential pushover, but it is also not deaf to appeals and arguments from the president and his lieutenants regarding foreign policy issues. Congressional receptivity to such arguments depends on various factors, including the issue at stake and the level of political understanding or sympathy between the administration and the legislature. But given the right conditions, a president can encourage Capitol Hill to adopt a particular stance on a given issue and then send an envoy to press a foreign government to accept a U.S. proposal carefully designed to match that stance.

Another way in which the administration can use Congress as a source of leverage with a foreign government is to ask congressional leaders to show more or

---

41. Chan Heng Chee, "Different Forums, Different Styles," 190.

42. Oakley, interview, 31.

43. Freeman, interview, 7–8.

44. Roy, interview, 22.

less sympathy toward that government's interest. New Zealand ambassador John Wood recalls that no one in his country "fully appreciated how frequently and effectively administrations of the day had put in a quiet word on our behalf with the congressional leadership, urging them to avoid damaging the interests of such a good friend and ally"—no one, that is, until the administration, annoyed at New Zealand's continuing refusal to rescind its prohibition on nuclear-powered American vessels in its waters, "was no longer prepared to intervene in this way."[45]

A Ticking Clock: The Impact of Election Cycles

Another component of the U.S. political system that both constrains and empowers U.S. negotiators is elections, and more particularly the impact of the electoral calendar and of changeovers in administrations that elections bring. American negotiators, as historian Robert Schulzinger has observed, "operate within earshot of a clock ticking down a president's term."

The electoral calendar

Americans' sense of urgency, their businesslike drive to propose, craft, and wrap up an agreement in the shortest time possible, is driven by the two-, four-, and six-year cycles for elections to the House of Representatives, the White House, and the Senate and by the two-term limit on the presidency. The rationale for this system is, as William Quandt notes, "almost entirely domestic" (keeping representatives in touch with the shifting mood of their constituents) and does little to encourage sound foreign policy.

> In practice, [the electoral cycle] often means that presidents have little time during their incumbency when they have both the experience and the power needed for sensible and effective conduct of foreign policy. The price we pay is a foreign policy excessively geared to short-term calculations, in which narrow domestic political considerations often outweigh sound strategic thinking, and where turnover in high positions is so frequent that consistency and coherence are lost.[46]

Acutely conscious that they have only four, or at most eight, years in which to make their mark on the international scene, and that the outcome of congressional elections can swiftly undermine political support for an administration's foreign policies, presidents have incentives to move swiftly. Each president comes to office with the hope, or a plan, to reshape the realities of the international environment, but by the second year of the term, a more tactically focused agenda typically prevails.

---

45. Wood, "Negotiating within Washington," 227.

46. William B. Quandt, "The Electoral Cycle and the Conduct of Foreign Policy," *Political Science Quarterly* 101, no. 5 (1986): 826.

As presidents near the term's end, they are well aware of the domestic political implications of their foreign policy successes and failures.[47] By the end of their second term (if they attain one), a president's concern to leave an enduring legacy in foreign policy can inspire last-minute efforts to bring negotiations to a successful close, especially negotiations in which they have invested significant political and personal capital or which involve issues that are politically contentious at home. This sense of urgency extends, as Phyllis Oakley has noted, to political appointees in the State Department, who are keenly aware that, "three or four years at most . . . that's what you get."[48] Career officials operate under the time constraints of their three-year rotational cycles. Thus, they cannot escape the pervasive sense that the hourglass of opportunity is forever emptying, that American diplomacy operates under a signboard bearing the motto *Tempus Fugit*.

Few administrations in recent decades have been immune from a feverish desire to mark their passing with a notable triumph or two on the international stage. For example, Madeleine Albright traveled to Pyongyang in October 2000—making her the first U.S. secretary of state to visit North Korea—to test the waters for a presidential visit before Bill Clinton left the White House less than three months later, in January 2001. Clinton almost did go—to sign a joint statement that would commit North Korea to getting rid of its missiles that could reach Japan and beyond—and only opted not to because of the competing demands of "a crash effort to reach closure with the Israelis and Palestinians" before he left office.[49] In July of that same year, Clinton had convened a meeting between the Palestinian and Israelis leaders at Camp David in a bold but ultimately unsuccessful effort to achieve agreement on the "final status" issues that continued to bedevil the peace process. Similarly, President George W. Bush, who for seven years had largely avoided investing diplomatic energy in the Israeli-Palestinian conflict, staged a major—but also unfruitful—Middle East peace conference just before the start of his final year in office.

This sense of time ticking quickly away is a double-edged sword. It cuts to America's advantage insofar as U.S. diplomats can apply great pressure to the other side by arguing—with a good deal of truth—that unless an agreement is reached relatively quickly, it may never be reached at all. As discussed in chapter 3, when the Namibia-Angola negotiations ran into a set of final hurdles in December 1988, the lead American negotiator, Assistant Secretary of State Chester A. Crocker,

---

47.   Quandt ably delineates the foreign policy characteristics of each of a president's four (or eight) years in office. See ibid., 830–835.

48.   Oakley, interview, 54.

49.   Albright, *Madame Secretary*, 597. Albright's account of her visit to Pyongyang and the discussions over Clinton's possible visit to North Korea occupies chapter 27 of her autobiography.

"openly advertis[ed] the fact that a new administration would likely mean a change of personnel and a basic policy review," and "U.S. mediators pressed the Angolans, Cubans, and South Africans not to waste years of effort."[50] The agreements were signed less than two weeks later. Furthermore, from the point of view of a sub-cabinet-level U.S. negotiator who has been laboring in the shadows to advance a neglected negotiation, close presidential involvement can give a stalled negotiation a much-needed authoritative push into the political limelight and propel it towards a successful outcome.

But the pressure of time cuts the other way, as well. In the first place, presidential urgency to secure a legacy can deny U.S. negotiators the luxury of time with which to outlast or wear down their counterparts. Second, it exacerbates the American tendency to opt for short-term fixes over long-term solutions. Third, it gives negotiating counterparts leverage that they are not shy to exploit.

A fourth problem is that it encourages counterproductive haste. Clinton's attempt to force through a final status deal on the Israeli-Palestinian conflict, for instance, has been criticized on the grounds that it was launched too late in his administration to be successful, and that its failure left not only the Israelis and Palestinians but also the next U.S. administration gun-shy of further negotiations. "Clinton," write Daniel Kurtzer and Scott Lasensky, "laid out his boldest ideas for the Israeli-Palestinian peace—the so-called Clinton parameters—much too late, in his final days in office, and in a manner that all but invited the next administration to back away from peacemaking."[51] That next administration, in its turn, also waited too long: "The Bush 43 administration's initiative in 2007 to organize a major international meeting and support renewed Israeli-Palestinian talks also came very late, after some parties had already resigned themselves to wait for the next U.S. administration."[52]

As William Quandt observes, "election years rarely witness great success in foreign policy. Carter struggled in frustration with the Iranian hostage crisis. Reagan withdrew ignominiously from Lebanon after more than 250 Marines had died." Nixon was "the great exception to this pattern," but Quandt attributes his success in no small part to the fact that Nixon had served as vice president for eight years "and thus came to the Oval Office with much more knowledge of world affairs than other presidents."[53]

---

50. Chester A. Crocker, "Peacemaking in Southern Africa: The Namibia-Angola Settlement of 1988, in *Herding Cats: Multiparty Mediation in a Complex World*, ed. Chester A. Crocker, Fen Osler Hampson, and Pamela Aall (Washington, D.C.: United States Institute of Peace Press, 1999), 229.

51. Kurtzer and Lasensky, *Negotiating Arab-Israeli Peace*, 35.

52. Ibid., 50–51.

53. Quandt, "The Electoral Cycle and the Conduct of Foreign Policy," 835.

Changeovers in administrations

Once an election has occurred, the realities of foreign conflicts and their problems for negotiators do not disappear. Instead, if the White House has a new resident (especially one who lacks substantial experience in foreign affairs), negotiators face at least three new difficulties—as well as fresh opportunities.

One is that it often takes several months before a new administration is up and running. In the interim, negotiations may stall or flounder because of inattention, indecision, lack of policy guidance, or procrastination in Washington. Richard Schifter—like his Soviet negotiating counterpart Anatoly Adamishin—contends that a vital year to advance U.S.-Soviet relations was lost in the transition from the Reagan to the Bush administrations, a year in which a new group of foreign policy advisers and officials reassessed U.S. policy toward the Soviet Union in general and toward Mikhail Gorbachev and his policy of perestroika in particular. Eventually, the new secretary of state, James Baker, and the new president decided to sustain their predecessors' policy of supporting Gorbachev, but by the time they came to that conclusion, the Soviet premier's domestic standing had spiraled downward while the Americans offered neither support nor advice:

> Secretary Shultz, as he left office, had been concerned about the outlook of the new administration, in which "realists," such as Brent Scowcroft, the new National Security Advisor, would play a significant role. While President Bush and Secretary Baker did not belong to the "realist" camp, they had sufficient doubts about the Reagan-Shultz policies to allow for a pause in the development of U.S.-Soviet relations that would permit conducting a "top-to-bottom policy review." In the meantime, as he came to note, President Gorbachev felt like the bride left at the altar.[54]

A second difficulty is that the progress already made in ongoing negotiations is likely to be reassessed, if not repudiated, by the incoming administration, which may well decide to pursue a significantly different policy. Indeed, the chief determinant of a new president's policy often seems to be "anything but [the previous president's policy]." For instance, according to an article in the *New York Times* in April 2007,

> Once upon a time, the Bush administration was a strict adherent of what some privately called the ABC—Anything But Clinton—approach. . . . Bush administration officials came to power in 2001 taking pains to distinguish themselves from their immediate predecessors. One of the first things President Bush did was to get rid of the State Department's special Middle East envoys. . . . A few days later, [White House spokesman] Mr. Fleischer went even further to drive a stake into the heart of the Clinton approach, [blaming it for creating] "unmet expectations in the region . . . that resulted in violence."[55]

---

54.   Adamishin and Schifter, *Human Rights, Perestroika, and the End of the Cold War*, 251.

55.   Helene Cooper, "Look Who's Reboarding That Clintonian Shuttle," *New York Times*, April 1, 2007, http://www.nytimes.com/2007/04/01/weekinreview/01cooper.html?_r=2&oref=slogin&oref=slogin.

In the case of very protracted negotiations, U.S. policy can shift not just once but several times. Schulzinger cites the decades-long negotiations over the Law of the Sea Treaty as an example of "how shifting domestic political dynamics can affect the outcome of a specific negotiation." The Senate declined to ratify the treaty during Carter's presidency; Reagan withdrew it; Clinton renegotiated its terms but the Senate still declined to ratify it; and it remained unratified throughout George W. Bush's eight years in office.[56]

Even as policy shifts from administration to administration, so does the manner in which it is implemented. The moralistic but increasingly beleaguered tone of the Carter administration in its final year gave way to the combative tenor of the early Reagan administration, just as the Clinton administration's multilateralist rhetoric gave way to the unilateralist assertions of the Bush administration. American diplomats engaged in ongoing negotiations may have to display considerable dexterity to accommodate themselves to such changes in tone and style without endangering their credibility as reliable, consistent negotiating counterparts.

A third problem is the loss of institutional memory as one set of political appointees exits the scene, permanently erasing many of their computer files and taking with them—usually to presidential libraries—many if not most of the records relevant to particular negotiations. Those documents are then scattered among numerous archives, making it difficult if not impossible for negotiators to retrieve and reassemble the record to determine the precise history of a protracted negotiation. In the colorful phrase of Ambassador Freeman, the nature of the U.S. political system "essentially gives the government a frontal lobotomy every four or eight years, [leaving us] blissfully unaware of our transgressions against our word."[57] In May 1967, for example, as Egyptian-Israeli tensions mounted in the run-up to the Six Day War, Israel reminded U.S. officials of commitments made to Israel by the Eisenhower administration ten years earlier, when Israel had withdrawn from the Sinai. The State Depart ment, however, literally had no record of those guarantees, and a researcher had to be dispatched to the Eisenhower Presidential Library in Abilene, Kansas, to unearth the relevant documents. Retrieving the files took three or four days.[58] As Samuel Lewis, the former U.S. ambassador to Israel and head of policy planning in the State Department, put it, "One of the hardest things to do is to walk into a foreign ministry, talk to somebody, and realize they've been working on [an issue] for 40 years, and they have every file. You've been working on it for one year, and you have no files, nor does the State Department."[59]

---

56.   Schulzinger, "American Presidents and Their Negotiators," 178.

57.   Freeman, interview, 23.

58.   This incident was mentioned by Itamar Rabinovich at the United States Institute of Peace workshop on American negotiating behavior held at Airlie House, Warrenton, Virginia, in July 2007.

59.   Comment made during a meeting about enhancing American negotiating capacities, United States Institute of Peace, April 17, 2009, Washington, D.C.

Such archival disorder hardly seems to square with a legalistic mindset—not, that is, until one recognizes that history effectively begins anew for each administration, which enters office disinclined to preserve the achievements—and the records—of its predecessor. The contrast with, say, the Chinese system of record keeping is marked. When Henry Kissinger was negotiating with Deng Xiaoping in 1975, for example, Kissinger repeated something Mao Zedong had said to him in an earlier conversation. Kissinger, however, somewhat misquoted Mao—an error that was brought to Deng's immediate attention by a Chinese official seated behind him who held a small notebook in which Mao's exact words from that conversation had been faithfully recorded.[60]

Interagency rivalries can also undermine good record-keeping practices. "Competition behind the scenes within the administration [of George W. Bush] was so intense that there were even breakdowns in the normal record-keeping process," observes one study of U.S. diplomacy in the Middle East. "The study group was repeatedly told that careful records were not always maintained and shared in the Clinton and Bush 43 administrations. . . . Meticulous record keeping is particularly vital in the Arab-Israeli conflict because the parties themselves—especially Israel—do so zealously."[61]

The Impact of Interagency Rivalries

A U.S. negotiating team's room for maneuver, already limited by the need for congressional approval and by the electoral timetable, is further restricted by the labyrinthine and competitive nature of Washington's foreign policy agencies. The State Department, the Defense Department, the Treasury, the Justice Department, the U.S. Agency for International Development, the National Security Council, the Central Intelligence Agency, and the Office of the United States Trade Representative—and their relevant subordinate offices—all have a stake in international negotiations. The size of that stake varies according to the subject of a given negotiation and the identity of the negotiating counterpart, but the agency with the largest stake will not necessarily have the largest say in setting and implementing the negotiating strategy.

Instead, when the prospect of an international negotiation appears on Washington's radar screen, some or all of the foreign affairs agencies are mobilized and engage in often intense and protracted negotiations with one another to set the goals and strategy of the international process. The winner is the agency that persuades the president—or, if the president is not engaged, his most senior lieutenant—that its approach will yield the greatest diplomatic or political benefits.

---

60. Author's personal recollection.
61. Kurtzer and Lasensky, *Negotiating Arab-Israeli Peace*, 54.

The interagency struggle rarely ends with the president's decision, however. Once a negotiating strategy is decided, a team made up of representatives of the competing agencies will be entrusted with implementing it, and those representatives will "watchdog" each other to make sure that the lead negotiator sticks to the course already plotted in Washington. They will usually present a united front at the bargaining table, but their allegiance to their individual agencies is greater than to the negotiating team, and team members will send frequent reports to their respective agencies that provide ammunition for their bosses to continue the struggle for supremacy back in Washington.

A disputatious system

America's foreign policy bureaucracy, in its modern form, took shape during the presidency of Franklin D. Roosevelt, when numerous agencies and thousands of experts employed by the government came to be involved in the making of foreign policy. "Roosevelt," comments Robert Schulzinger, "presided over this sprawling bureaucracy . . . with charm and guile. He relished and encouraged competition among government agencies. Only he had complete information and a clear idea of the ultimate goals of his diplomacy. He delayed decisions until the last minute."[62]

Almost seventy years later, many features of this system are still evident, some even in exaggerated form. To be sure, differences—both temporary and permanent—can be discerned. Some presidents have evinced much less interest in foreign policy, or in its details, than did Roosevelt, and have allowed some of their lieutenants to exercise greater decision-making power. The bureaucratic context has become more complex and less flexible. The number of players involved in foreign policy disputes has increased, with agencies such as the Office of the United States Trade Representative coming to play important roles in negotiations on subjects within their purview. And the National Security Council, established by President Harry S. Truman in 1947, has provided a forum for discussing foreign policy matters and for coordinating policies among agencies. In many important respects, however, the system remains the same: presidents still exercise decisive power and agencies still compete intensively to convince the president that their proposed strategy is the most beneficial or most expedient course of action.

In many cases, as both American and foreign observers recognize, the most difficult negotiations for the United States are the interagency discussions that take place before the U.S. negotiating team ever leaves Washington. The degree of difficulty is compounded by the ferocity and longevity of personal and institutional rivalries between some of the players. In the first years of the twenty-first century, the most intense—or certainly the most visible—interagency rivalry was between

---

62.   Schulzinger, "American Presidents and Their Negotiators," 170.

the Department of Defense (and the vice president's office) and the State Department. Faruk Logoglu describes a "deep divide and disconnect between the State and Defense Departments in the months leading to the invasion of Iraq." Instead of dealing chiefly with State Department personnel, as Logoglu, like other foreign ambassadors, was accustomed to doing, he had most of his conversations with the administration from early 2002 until early 2003 through the Pentagon. "The State Department was largely out of the picture. It was as if Foggy Bottom had disowned the Iraq issue and was resigned to the Pentagon running the show. . . . The curious interdepartmental disconnect meant that the administration was handling the issue at reduced capacity, without the full benefit of the knowledge and experience of the State Department."[63]

The State-Defense rivalry is hardly recent. In the Reagan administration, Secretary of Defense Caspar Weinberger and Secretary of State George Shultz engaged in a bitter feud, with the tension between them described by Jeane Kirkpatrick, the U.S. ambassador to the United Nations, as "palpable." "For months," reported *Time* magazine in December 1984, "Shultz and Weinberger have been giving Reagan conflicting advice on some of the gravest issues of U.S. policy. Lately they have been carrying on what amounts to a public debate. . . . In part, the dispute is institutional: the State Department's diplomats and the Pentagon's brass often view the world from different vantage points. The Pentagon's insistence on a voice in foreign affairs also is a perennial sore point."[64] But personal animosities added fuel to the fire, as did sharp policy differences. For instance, Weinberger's determination not to use force unless stringent conditions were met infuriated Shultz, who remarked in his memoirs, "to Weinberger, as I heard him, our forces were to be constantly built up but never used"; the Weinberger doctrine was a "counsel of inaction bordering on paralysis."[65] The feud spilled over into several ongoing negotiations, including arms control talks with the Soviet Union. (This clash was echoed to some degree during the Balkans conflict in the 1990s. In his memoir *My American Journey,* Colin Powell recounts a discussion he had when he was chairman of the Joint Chiefs of Staff with Secretary of State Madeleine Albright. "What's the point of having this superb military that you're always talking about if we can't use it?" she asked. "I thought I would have an aneurysm," Powell writes. "American G.I.'s were not toy soldiers to be moved around on some sort of global game board.")[66]

Arms control was the venue for another outbreak of State-Defense rivalry six years later. Yuri Nazarkin recounts a story from 1990 in which, from a Soviet perspective, Secretary of Defense Cheney, as "part of the broader game against the

---

63. Logoglu, "Negotiating Security," 216.

64. See George Church, Bruce van Voorst, and Johanna McGeary, "Force and Personality," *Time*, December 24, 1984, http://www.time.com/time/magazine/article/0,9171,951381-2,00.html.

65. George P. Shultz, *Turmoil and Triumph: My Years as Secretary of State* (New York: Scribner's, 1993).

66. Colin Powell, *My American Journey: An Autobiography* (New York: Random House, 2005), 609.

START Treaty being played in Washington," spread an allegation that Secretary of State Baker had been manipulated by the Soviets.[67] Cheney may have done no such thing, but it is reflective of the U.S. bureaucracy's reputation for feuding that Nazarkin and his colleagues were convinced that a simple misunderstanding was being exploited by Cheney as part of a political struggle within Washington.

While interagency rivalries are sometimes waged in public, more typically they are conducted behind closed doors, and an image of a unified American negotiating team is projected to the negotiating counterpart. Moreover, while differences of opinion among agencies are inevitable, sometimes those differences are minor, and the image of a united front is an accurate reflection of a solid consensus of opinion. John Wood, for instance, anticipated that "once the administration had pushed the national security button, New Zealand representatives could expect to encounter a united policy front among the key U.S. agencies concerned." His expectation was correct. Throughout the negotiations on New Zealand's exclusion from its waters of U.S. nuclear-powered or -armed vessels, there was "no discernible evidence . . . of those differing agency views that sometimes offer the foreign negotiator greater scope for inducing a more nuanced and muted outcome from the U.S. system."[68] As noted in chapter 1, one characteristic of American culture is that once the quarterback or the coach has called the play, the team—despite its internal rivalries—goes into action in a coordinated fashion.

Wood's experience, however, is not one that foreign diplomats often encounter or one that many American insiders would recognize as typical. More characteristic is the following description—based on documents held at the Reagan Library and the Margaret Thatcher Foundation—of the climate within the U.S. foreign policy decision-making system in July 1981, just seven months into President Reagan's first term and thus, one might have expected, still something of a honeymoon period for the administration's key players:

> Inter-agency rivalry, as well as the President's narrow escape from assassination in April, had bitten deeply into the first year. When the NSC met to take the first steps [on the issue of a Siberian gas pipeline being built by the Soviet Union to supply Western Europe] on 6 July 1981 decisions still seemed a long way off, if not altogether out of reach: Al Haig's State Department and Caspar Weinberger's Pentagon were so bitterly at odds that they couldn't even agree on paperwork describing the key issues, while the options on the table were susceptible to 180 permutations, with ten interested agencies holding distinct opinions on every one. And time was pressing, because the outlines of a policy needed to be in place for the President to put before the allies at the Ottawa G7, 19–21 July.[69]

In this case, as in most cases, each agency's goal was to see its preferred policy win the day, which meant trying to persuade the president to adopt that policy.

---

67. Nazarkin, "Negotiating as a Rival," 248.

68. Wood, "Negotiating within Washington," 225.

69. Margaret Thatcher Foundation, "The Polish Crisis of 1981–82," http://www.margaretthatcher.org/archive/us-reagan%20(Poland).asp.

The president, however, is by no means always above the fray himself. Sometimes, indeed, he may be the target of an agency's campaign—not to persuade him to adopt a new policy, but to discredit a policy he already favors. Kissinger recounts how "Kremlinologists" and "arms controllers" in the foreign policy bureaucracy, passionately opposed to President Nixon's plan to link arms negotiations and political issues, "chipped away at the [president's] policy . . . in leaks to the press. Though not 'authorized,' these leaks were never disavowed. . . . These cumulative pressures . . . were never posed as a head-on challenge; instead, a series of tactical, day-to-day comments were used to edge matters toward the position preferred by the bureaucracy."[70]

While presidents are not always immune from bureaucratic struggles, it *is* in the president's power to influence the extent of those struggles. Indeed, the single-most important factor determining the intensity of interagency strife during a given administration is the president's decision about how to "play" the system and whether he encourages or discourages competition among cabinet-level officials. Like Franklin D. Roosevelt with his cunning mastery of cabinet politics, some presidents actively promote competition. Announcing his selections for the top foreign policy positions in his administration, then President-elect Barack Obama was asked "how he would avoid having a 'clash of rivals' rather than the smoothly functioning team he portrayed." Obama responded by saying that "he expected 'vigorous debate' and described himself as 'a strong believer in strong personalities and strong opinions. . . . There are going to be differences in tactics and different assessments and judgments made. That's what I expect; that's what I welcome. That's why I asked them to join the team.'"[71]

Other presidents favor one particular agency and may even delegate considerable authority to it. Especially during his first term, President George W. Bush gave the Office of the Vice President and the Department of Defense a considerable degree of influence over the foreign policymaking process.[72] Still other presidents adopt a hands-off approach. President Reagan, for instance, did not encourage but toler-

---

70. Kissinger, *Diplomacy*, 718.

71. Karen De Young and Michael D. Shear, "Obama Names National Security Team," *Washington Post*, December 2, 2008. Obama's rival for president, Senator John McCain, expressed similar sentiments during the presidential campaign, saying he welcomed "competing opinions" and "a certain amount of tension" within a decision-making apparatus, because it made sure that a candidate, or a president, reached "fully informed decisions." Adam Nagourney and Jim Rutenberg, "Embracing a Free-Form Style, McCain Leads a Camp Divided," *New York Times*, August 10, 2008.

72. "Cheney and Secretary of Defense Donald Rumsfeld have managed to keep a heavy 'thumb on the scales' of high-level deliberations, particularly on critical issues such as Iraq." I. M. Destler, reviewing Donald Rothkopf's book *Running the World* on the workings of the National Security Council; "The Power Brokers," *Foreign Affairs* (September–October 2005), http://www.foreignaffairs.org/20050901fareviewessay84513/i-m-destler/the-power-brokers.html.

ated the intense rivalry between Secretary of State Shultz and Secretary of Defense Weinberger.[73]

A variety of initiatives have been launched over the course of many decades to reduce the level of dissension within Washington's foreign policy apparatus and to foster a more unified and coordinated approach. The establishment of the National Security Council (NSC) in 1947 has been the most ambitious and arguably the most successful step in this direction, but to some extent the NSC has only provided another stage on which agencies are able to play out their policy feuds.[74] In an attempt to bolster its effectiveness, in 1989 the NSC established the Principals' Committee (which, unlike the NSC, meets without the president and the vice president but does include their chiefs of staff) as the "senior interagency forum for consideration of policy issues affecting national security."[75] (At the same time, the Deputies' Committee and eight policy coordinating committees were also formed.) The small size of the committee has streamlined the decision-making process in many instances, but it has by no means put an end to interagency rivalries. Bob Woodward's book *Plan of Attack*, which offers a behind-the-scenes account of the run-up to the war on Iraq launched in 2003, reveals that at several meetings of the Principals' Committee, Secretary of State Colin Powell expressed concern about inadequate planning for postwar management of Iraq and "all kinds of unanticipated and unintended consequences" of an invasion, but failed to stimulate a discussion of the subject. At one meeting, Vice President Cheney brushed aside Powell's question by simply saying, "Not the issue."[76] The Principals' Committee may have been a valve that allowed the leading players to air their views, but by all reports it did not function in that way. The real business of deciding policy went on in one-on-one meetings with the president.

The makeup of negotiating teams

Personal and professional frictions have always shaped the conduct of American negotiating teams, as Schulzinger reminds us with his story of the five-member delegation sent to Ghent in 1814 by President Madison to negotiate with the British.

> John Quincy Adams was irritated that his fellow commissioners enjoyed a good time. He grumbled that "they sit after dinner and drink bad wine and smoke cigars." Clay told him not to be a prig and that part of a diplomat's job was to provide and enjoy hospitality. Adams

---

73. See, for instance, Strobe Talbott, "America Abroad," *Time*, August 28, 1989, http://www.time.com/time/magazine/article/0,9171,958426,00.html.

74. An excellent insider's history of the NSC is Donald Rothkopf, *Running the World: The Inside Story of the National Security Council and the Architects of American Power* (New York: Public Affairs, 2005).

75. National Security Presidential Directive no. 1, "Organization of the National Security Council System," February 13, 2001, http://www.fas.org/irp/offdocs/nspd/nspd-1.htm.

76. Bob Woodward, *Plan of Attack* (New York: Simon and Schuster, 2004).

then joined the rest in attending the plays, receptions, dinners, and card parties the residents of Ghent provided for the Americans.[77]

Such endemic clashes of personalities can be compounded by conflicting bureaucratic loyalties in the case of negotiating teams made up of officials from two or more agencies. Indeed, interagency teams often reflect and perpetuate the rivalries of the agencies—and their heads—from which the team members are drawn.

Such internal dissension is by no means inevitable, however. The level of dissension that accompanies interagency wrangling over negotiating goals and strategies does *not* necessarily carry over into relationships within the negotiating teams that Washington dispatches to implement those strategies. Carl Bildt, the European Union's special envoy to the former Yugoslavia, has remarked that "the U.S.—when it sorts out its own mess in Washington—has the capacity to act. . . . Europeans are good at coordinating with each other, while the U.S. is not, but our internal coordination takes up all our time, and you are more decisive when you get your act together."[78]

Crocker contends that interagency teams can be very effective, as they were in the Bosnian peace process in the 1990s and in the initiative he led in the 1980s to negotiate peace in Angola and Namibian independence. He notes, too, that the administration of George W. Bush "used a similar approach to end Libya's pursuit of weapons of mass destruction (with the help of the British) in late 2003 and to negotiate the 2005 north-south agreement in Sudan. This model also facilitated the partially successful six-party talks with North Korea." Interagency teams, explains Crocker,

> save top government officials from being overwhelmed by the daily (if not hourly) demands of statecraft for months on end. This model, however, can only succeed when the executive branch is relatively united, the lead envoy is given real responsibility, and the effort is spearheaded by a person of relentless perseverance who can operate in choppy political, congressional, interagency, and diplomatic waters. Its success depends on a clarity of purpose, a commitment to the principle of delegation, and backing from the top.[79]

In most cases, American teams project a united front, especially when their leaders go to pains to instill a sense of discipline and common purpose. Holbrooke's Bosnia team was tightly knit and highly disciplined:

> Complete trust and openness among all seven of us were essential if we were to avoid energy-consuming factional intrigues and back channels to Washington. This presented difficulties for representatives of those agencies—the NSC, the JCS, the Office of the Secretary of Defense—that often distrusted or competed with one another and whose representatives normally send private reports back to their home offices each day. . . . We succeeded in avoid-

---

77.   Schulzinger, "American Presidents and Their Negotiators," 162.

78.   Quoted in Holbrooke, *To End a War*, 242.

79.   Crocker, "The Art of Peace: Bringing Diplomacy Back to Washington," *Foreign Affairs* (July–August 2007), http://www.foreignaffairs.org/20070701fareviewessay86414/chester-a-crocker/the-art-of-peace-bringing-diplomacy-back-to-washington.html.

ing this problem, in part because our team was so small, and in part because we shared all our information internally and developed close, even intense personal relationships.[80]

Another relatively streamlined team was the one Dennis Ross assembled to negotiate peace between the Arabs and Israelis, and which met daily (when not on the road) "to plan what we were doing and to make sure that nothing was going on in the administration that might be inconsistent with what our diplomacy required."[81] The team, however, was widely judged to be "too insular and largely cut off from traditional State Department and interagency support structures," according to an assessment of U.S. diplomatic management of the Middle East peace process. Furthermore, the team "had superior expertise regarding Israel, but far less expertise and experience in dealing with the Arabs." As a consequence, it was seen by the Arabs as biased toward Israel and suffered from inadequate cross-cultural expertise:

> The lack of cross-cultural negotiating skills was so acute toward the end of the Clinton period that the State Department's top Arabic translator, a talented and well-connected individual, was drafted into sensitive diplomatic dealings with senior Arabs. The decision seemed based on expediency and a sudden awareness that the absence of Arab expertise was handicapping U.S. diplomacy.[82]

Ross's and especially Holbrooke's teams were unusually small given the sensitivity of the process they were trying to manage and the importance the administration attached to the conflicts they were trying to end. Less sensitive negotiations, however, are usually staffed by large teams drawn from various bureaucratic quarters. Reflecting legalistic and businesslike respect for thorough preparation, professional acumen, and the power of facts and figures, teams are staffed not only with seasoned diplomats but also lawyers and technical experts in the subjects to be discussed. Just as President Wilson took a staff of hundreds with him to Paris to negotiate the Treaty of Versailles, eighty years later President Clinton "assembled experts from the Office of the Trade Representative and the State, Commerce, and Treasury Departments to join in the drafting of the charter of the 180-nation World Trade Organization, ratified in 1999."[83]

The impetus for multidisciplinary teams is not merely cultural, just as the rationale for multiagency teams is not purely political. As Strobe Talbott noted while he was deputy secretary of state, "the multitude, magnitude, and complexity of transitional issues" demands that the State Department "rethink the way we recruit and train" people so as to broaden the professional backgrounds and skill sets of American diplomats. "Globalization," Talbott added, "has also increased the need for other departments and agencies of the U.S. government to play an active role in pursuit of American interests abroad—and for the State Department to

---

80. Holbrooke, *To End a War*, 111.
81. Ross, *Statecraft*, 139.
82. Kurtzer and Lasensky, *Negotiating Arab-Israeli Peace*, 52–53.
83. Schulzinger, "American Presidents and Negotiators," 181.

cooperate more systematically with them. This cooperation has been particularly close on matters of economics, defense, and law enforcement."[84]

Even in multiagency teams, one agency usually plays a leading role. In such cases, the style of the U.S. negotiating effort will likely mirror the internal culture of the lead agency as well as the personality of the lead negotiator. For instance, the Office of the United States Trade Representative has a reputation for conducting trade negotiations in a combative, confrontational, and abrasive fashion. "USTR negotiators," observes Koji Watanabe, "are closely watched by Congress, which makes them more aggressive toward their counterparts, more dismissive of Japan's concerns, and less inclined to compromise. The State Department and the Treasury are generally more moderate in their approach, more prepared to focus on the larger bilateral relationship, and less willing to endanger that relationship by pushing hard on a single issue."[85]

A short, tight leash

In the eighteenth and nineteenth centuries, U.S. officials often enjoyed considerable freedom of action and authority when negotiating agreements with foreign officials on behalf of their government, especially if they were distant from the United States and thus effectively out of operational contact with Washington. As communications have improved, diplomatic autonomy has dwindled, and today the kind of latitude allowed Commodore Matthew Perry in the 1850s in his negotiations with Japan is rare indeed.[86]

Proximity to Washington, however, significantly limits a negotiator's flexibility. "It often seemed to me that the simple fact of being in the same time zone as their own capital was a handicap for the U.S. negotiators," comments David Hannay, reflecting on his experiences as British permanent representative to the United Nations and on the "cumbersomeness and slowness" of American diplomacy in New York. Whereas the British Foreign Office allowed its UN mission significant flexibility in deciding how best to pursue a specific policy goal, U.S. negotiators at the United Nations in New York "often receive instructions slowly and late and in the form of fully worked-out texts formulated in Washington that take more account of reconciling interdepartmental tensions there than of accommodating the views of others who are being asked to sign up to a particular policy."[87]

---

84.   Talbott, "Globalization and Diplomacy," 75.

85.   Watanabe, "Negotiating Trade," 206.

86.   See Schulzinger, "American Presidents and Their Negotiators," 164–165.

87.   Hannay, "Negotiating Multilaterally," 275.

Even negotiators in distant time zones, however, find that Washington usually keeps them on a short, tight leash. Very few negotiators enjoy the kind of latitude allowed Max Kampelman when he was entrusted by Presidents Carter and Reagan to negotiate the Helsinki Final Act in the early 1980s. Kampelman "never asked for permission" from Washington before taking a tactical step. "I assumed," says Kampelman, "that the United States knew what I was doing and liked what I was doing."[88] Far more typical was the experience of Richard Burt, the chief U.S. negotiator in Geneva in the early 1980s during negotiations for the Strategic Arms Reduction Treaty. Burt "would send suggestions to the administration on how to resolve the sticking points. He would reach tentative deals with his Soviet counterpart, Yuri Nazarkin, only to have them slapped down by Washington, often on personal instructions by [National Security Adviser Brent] Scowcroft."[89]

This lack of room for maneuver does not, of course, go unnoticed by foreign negotiators on the other side of the bargaining table. Indeed, it forms one of the most common refrains in their assessments of American negotiating behavior. And, as the following observation from Gilles Andreani illustrates, foreign officials customarily attribute this rigidity to Washington's decision-making process. "Late demands are unwelcome" to any country's negotiators, notes Andreani, but "they tend particularly to irk the Americans, whose decision-making process is slow and cumbersome, and whose ability to take into consideration the viewpoint of other countries is limited. They dislike surprises, especially if their consequence should be to reopen decisions painfully arrived at in Washington."[90] Andreani also notes that those U.S. officials "most opposed to your viewpoint in the first place can use the irritation provoked by your late demands to unwind the previously agreed U.S. position, and engineer something worse for you"—as happened to France when it was trying to get a European, rather than an American, appointed as the head of NATO's southern command.[91]

---

88.   Kampelman, interview. Another example is Holbrooke, who, as he recognized himself, was given by Secretary of State Christopher an unusually high degree of authority and responsibility during the Bosnia negotiations. Holbrooke, *To End a War*, 115, 239.

89.   Nazarkin, "Negotiating as a Rival," 246–247, quoting Michael R. Beschloss and Strobe Talbott, *At the Highest Levels: The Inside Stories of the End of the Cold War* (Boston and London: Little, Brown, 1993), 373.

90.   Andreani, Negotiating with Savior Faire," 282. John Wood makes a similar point. According to Wood, "There is a strong tendency for American officials to show up at the negotiating table with an opening position close to or even at their bottom line, with the explanation implicit or explicit: 'This is the best we can get for you from our system, and you'd better believe it.'" Wood, "Negotiating within Washington," 225–226.

91.   The case of the Franco-American dispute over NATO's southern command is discussed in detail in Charles Cogan, *French Negotiating Behavior*, 163–186.

A Convenient Target: The Political Vulnerability of American Negotiators

A caste of cowboys and scapegoats

> The elephant may be big, but it has feelings. The first feelings you must take care of are those of the U.S. negotiators themselves. They have often spent credit at home expressing your concerns, as they ask for some leeway in their negotiating position to accommodate them. What they come back with may be insufficient, and at times minuscule to the point of looking offensive. But sometimes, blood has been spilled in Washington to get there. Therefore, you should first recognize the efforts of your counterpart, who may have paid a price for the concessions, before dismissing them as insufficient.[92]

Andreani's advice to foreign negotiators draws attention to the fact that while American negotiators can seem impregnable to their counterparts' arguments and indifferent to their pleas, U.S. officials are far from invulnerable to criticism from their fellow Americans.

This vulnerability in itself is hardly remarkable; accusations of professional incompetence are routinely lobbed in all sorts of fields of endeavor. In the case of American negotiators, however, the critical arrows fired at them are often barbed with accusations, not of professional shortcomings, but of indiscipline, insubordination, and even disloyalty—of political or even cultural misdeeds. Of course, political appointees—selected on the basis of their political allegiances—are natural targets for political criticism. But why should career diplomats attract such brickbats?

One reason is institutional in nature, and stems from the structural tension created between diplomats and politicians with the establishment of a professional foreign service in the 1920s. Since then, diplomats have been something of a class apart, a separate caste with its own professional code and with concerns not necessarily shared on Capitol Hill or in the White House. Indeed, as discussed earlier in this chapter, the interests of the politicals and the professionals can often conflict: while Congress or the president looks for unambiguous assertions of American interests, professional diplomats look for the negotiating leeway needed to attain practical agreements—which usually entail compromises. In such a situation, the political community not surprisingly sometimes sees the diplomatic community as an obstacle to the attainment of political goals—and is not shy about voicing that opinion.

A second explanation for the criticisms leveled at career officials is that they are an easy target. Diplomats don't have a domestic constituency able to protect them from accusations that, for example, they have been too soft on one or another foreign negotiating counterpart. Even the State Department, on occasion, gives its diplomats only weak political support.

---

92.   Andreani, "Negotiating with Savoir Faire," 286.

A third explanation has to do with the fundamental American ambivalence toward negotiation and the keen sense of American exceptionalism discussed in chapter 2. Negotiation itself is seen as un-American insofar as it involves compromise rather than resolute adherence to principle. And diplomacy is seen as even worse, for it may involve a suspect bartering of American values and interests for foreign benefits of dubious worth. From the perspective of either values or interests, individual diplomats, whatever their personal rectitude, are vulnerable to censure simply because they are the agents of these un-American trade-offs between principle and pragmatism.

Monteagle Stearns notes an interesting tendency for presidents and secretaries of state to deflect such attacks by wrapping themselves in the imagery of the pioneering American West.

> By temperament and tradition, we are less likely to regard diplomacy as the achievement of national objectives by means short of the use of force than as compromising objectives that the use of force would more reliably achieve. In the circumstances, it is not surprising that presidents and secretaries of state so often resort to images of the western frontier when they discuss American foreign policy. Dean Rusk said of the Cuban missile crisis, "we were eyeball to eyeball and the other guy blinked"; in an interview with an Italian journalist Henry Kissinger compared himself to the "lone cowboy"; spokesmen for the Nixon administration described its withdrawal strategy from Vietnam as "backing out of the barroom shooting." The language in each case is intended to suggest uncompromising diplomacy and the ability to go it alone.[93]

Back in the days of the Western frontier, however, diplomats—even ones who behaved like "lone cowboys"—did not escape criticism. Schulzinger cites the example of Nicholas Trist, dispatched by President James K. Polk in 1845 to negotiate an end to the U.S. war with Mexico. When the political climate in Washington shifted, Trist was recalled. "Trist, however, ignored the recall" and concluded a peace treaty with Mexico. The treaty "split the Democratic Party—to which both Polk and Trist belonged. Polk's presidency ended in disarray, and Trist returned home to financial ruin and political oblivion."[94]

Stearns draws a comparison between Europe, where foreign policy failures are laid at the feet of the governments who devised the original plans, and the United States, where "American career officials are sometimes held more accountable by the legislature (and the courts) for failed policies or policies of dubious legality than are the political officials who authored them." In the American system, claims Stearns, the temptation exists "to shift the blame for bad policy decisions to career officials, as the Bush [41] administration tried to do when its courtship of Saddam Hussein exploded in the Gulf war."[95] April Glaspie, U.S. ambassador to Iraq in 1989, has been seen by some as a scapegoat for the Bush administration's failure to

---

93. Stearns, *Talking to Strangers*, 5–6.

94. Schulzinger, "American Presidents and Negotiators," 163.

95. Stearns, *Talking to Strangers*, 43.

anticipate that Saddam Hussein would invade Kuwait. Glaspie met with Saddam just before his forces, then massed in the south of Iraq, moved into Kuwait. She told him that the United States did not take a stand on Arab-Arab conflicts, and added that Iraq's dispute with Kuwait should be settled by peaceful means. In an interview in March 2008 with a Lebanese newspaper, *Dar al Hayat*, Glaspie said she harbored no resentment at being accused of having given Saddam a green light to invade: "It is over. Nobody wants to take the blame. I am quite happy to take the blame. Perhaps I was not able to make Saddam Hussein believe that we would do what we said we would do, but in all honesty, I don't think anybody in the world could have persuaded him."[96]

In the same administration, Ambassador Winston Lord was accused by National Security Adviser Brent Scowcroft of mishandling the president's visit to China in February 1989, during which a leading Chinese dissident, human rights activist Fang Li Zhi, was invited to the president's farewell dinner but in the event was barred from attending by the Chinese police. The incident severely embarrassed the president, who had campaigned—in part—on his ability to manage the relationship with China. Lord resented being scapegoated for the contretemps. He claimed that the invitation to the Chinese dissident had been approved by the White House and senior State Department officials, and he was reported to have sent a highly secret letter to Scowcroft protesting as much.[97]

Parochialists, traitors, and perverts

One accusation that has long been leveled at negotiators is that of "parochialism," or "localitis." Perhaps the first American diplomat to attract such charges was Benjamin Franklin, whose sympathy toward his French hosts prompted one contemporary fellow American diplomat, Ralph Izzard, to declare that "the political salvation of America depends upon recalling Dr. Franklin."[98]

Two hundred years later, as Stearns observes, charges of localitis are "still leveled at American diplomats who are deemed more familiar than they should be with a particular foreign culture."[99] Sometimes, the charges come from abroad. For instance, a candidate for political office in Brazil diagnosed "an acute case of what diplomats call 'localitis'" in the behavior of U.S. ambassador Donna Hrinak in 2003, who publicly applauded the global antiwar movement and went along with the suggestion of the Brazilian government to meet with Iraq's ambassador in

---

96. As reported in Glenn Kessler, "Ex-Envoy Details Hussein Meeting," *Washington Post*, April 3, 2008.

97. See James Mann, *About Face: A History of America's Curious Relationship with China, from Nixon to Clinton* (New York: Alfred A. Knopf, 1999), 180–183.

98. Stearns, *Talking to Strangers*, 26.

99. Ibid.

Brasília, "just weeks before U.S. Secretary of State Colin Powell requested that all countries expel Saddam Hussein's diplomats."[100]

Often the accusations come from much closer to home—from fellow American officials. During the crisis in East Pakistan in 1971, for instance, Kissinger felt that the U.S. ambassador to India, Frank Keating, was a victim of localitis and failed to see through New Delhi's insincerity about reaching peace with Pakistan.[101] According to Charles Freeman, localitis is still alive and well, albeit in a more sophisticated form, with the Foreign Service containing

> subcultures which correspond to the foreign cultures on which they're focused. Chinese specialists tend to be optimistic and strategic in their thinking. Russian specialists tend to be pessimistic, despairing, and very hard-edged. Japanese specialists tend to be subtle and soft and nonconfrontational. . . . Experience in negotiation with a particular other culture . . . [results in negotiators becoming] acculturated to the other side and taking on the cultural characteristics of those with whom they're interacting.[102]

Accusations of localitis can have little or no impact on a negotiator's performance—to the contrary, they may enhance his or her standing and effectiveness with representatives of the country whose interests the negotiator is said to favor. Sometimes, however, such charges, even if entirely unfounded, can undercut a negotiator's credibility with other interlocutors and with the negotiator's own colleagues and superiors, and prompt a reassignment. Even so, they are less damaging, personally and professionally, than accusations of political disloyalty, which at best can leave a negotiator distracted, isolated, and fearful of doing anything that might be seen as confirming the charge and at worst can abruptly terminate a career.

The political vulnerability of U.S. negotiators was never greater than during the years when Senator Joseph McCarthy pursued his search of communists within the executive branch. Diplomats were ideal targets for McCarthy's witch hunt for several reasons, all of them connected to the nature of their profession: they had extensive foreign contacts and had often spent years living abroad; they had access to the highest levels of America's political system but were not quite part of that system; and they conducted negotiations, which necessarily involved offering concessions or at least trying to understand the point of view of the other side.

One group was attacked with particular vehemence: the "China Hands," a dozen or so leading China scholars and diplomats who were accused of having "lost China" to the Communists in 1949 by denigrating the Nationalist government of Chiang Kai-shek. Spurred on by Chiang's American supporters, McCarthy and his allies began in 1950 to attack the State Department's Far Eastern Division, which

---

100.   Gerald Brant, "How Brazil's Lula Is Fooling the World," *Brazzil*, May 2003, http://www.brazzil.com/p130may03.htm.

101.   According to Anthony Quainton, a former U.S. ambassador who served in India and Pakistan. See Khalid Hasan, "General Yahya Agreed to Withdraw Forces," *Daily Times*, July 3, 2005.

102.   Freeman, interview, 87–88.

he claimed was composed of "individuals who are loyal to the ideals and designs of Communism rather than those of the free, God-fearing half of the world." At one point, McCarthy claimed he had a list of more than two hundred names of people who were shaping American foreign policy even though they were "known to the secretary of state as being members of the Communist Party."[103] Over the course of four years of congressional hearings, the China Hands were accused of sabotaging American efforts to prevent the collapse of the Nationalist government and of trying to infiltrate communist agents into the U.S. intelligence services so as to subvert America. Despite the absence of any evidence of "crimes" greater than that of arguing that the Chinese Communists were not simply Soviet stooges and were likely to defeat the Nationalist government in an impending civil war, many of the China Hands were dismissed from the State Department, most notably John Service. The 1950s also witnessed a purge of one thousand State Department officials suspected of being homosexual.[104]

The patriotic paranoia and social hysteria that colored the 1950s have since subsided, and professional diplomats have rarely had to defend themselves from the kinds of accusations of political disloyalty wielded by Senators Joseph McCarthy and Kenneth Wherry. Political attacks on diplomats, however, have continued in one form or another, with negotiators being subject to a range of criticisms from a variety of political corners. In February 2007, for instance, John Bolton, a political appointee in several administrations, publicly lambasted Christopher Hill, the lead U.S. negotiator in talks with North Korea on its nuclear program, for making "a very bad deal" with the North Koreans. Despite the fact that Hill's negotiating brief had been approved by the president and the secretary of state, Bolton directed his fire at the career diplomat:

> I'm just going to say I hope the president is not yet fully briefed. He has a few hours to consider this. It really—it sends exactly the wrong signal to would-be proliferators around the world, if you hold out long enough and wear down the State Department negotiators, eventually you get rewarded, in this case with massive shipments of heavy fuel oil for doing only partially what needs to be done to complete dismantling of their nuclear program.[105]

---

103.   E. J. Kahn, *The China Hands: America's Foreign Service Officers and What Befell Them* (New York: Viking, 1975).

104.   This purge is described in David K. Johnson, *The Lavender Scare: The Cold War Persecution of Gays and Lesbians in the Federal Government* (Chicago: University of Chicago Press, 2004).

105.   From an interview with Wolf Blitzer on CNN, aired February 12, 2007, transcribed at http://sweetness-light.com/archive/john-bolton-blasts-north-korean-nuclear-weapons-deal.

Part III

Historical Perspective

6

American Presidents and Their Negotiators, 1776–2009

Robert D. Schulzinger

O ver the course of more than two centuries, American presidents and their principal advisers have tried, with varying degrees of success, to manage foreign policy in an increasingly challenging international environment and with the support of an ever more complex bureaucratic system. In the eighteenth and nineteenth centuries, when communications between Washington and U.S. negotiators abroad were difficult and slow, American diplomats had wide personal latitude to conduct negotiations. With the communications revolution of the twentieth century and the rise of the United States to global power status, however, presidents became more deeply involved in directing the performance of their envoys. In certain circumstances—usually in crisis situations—presidents have conducted negotiations themselves. Presidents also play a major role in setting the broad outlines of foreign policy and in structuring the bureaucratic context within which policy is formulated and implemented.

During any given period, the extent of presidential involvement in international negotiations has, of course, varied widely and been influenced by the president's personality, his foreign policy experience, his management style, and—not least— his view of the role of the United States in world affairs. Customarily, presidents have concentrated on the issues of "high policy," primarily matters of national security, war and peace, and major economic issues. Matters of "low policy," tactical issues concerning trade and commerce, migration, science, technology, and the environment, among many other subjects, have usually been the domain of subcabinet officials. Indeed, most U.S. negotiations are conducted by officials who have no direct relationship with the president.

The relationship—direct or indirect—between presidents and their negotiators has been significantly shaped by three factors:

- *The confidence that presidents have had in their envoys.* When presidents have trusted U.S. negotiators and considered them close personal advisers, the diplomats have often had the authority to reach agreements. Alternatively, presidents sometimes have grown estranged from, lost confidence in, or outright despised their own envoys. In such cases the diplomats have come home disgraced or been left to twist in prevailing political winds.
- *The confidence that the public has had in a president's foreign policy.* When a president's foreign policy goals or methods have been popular, U.S. negotiators have generally had the political support needed to reach successful agreements. When the public has turned against a president's foreign policies, however, negotiations have often been thwarted and agreements blocked.
- *The ability of negotiators to influence their superiors in Washington or the public.* Occasionally, American envoys have succeeded by mobilizing public opinion in favor of their negotiating positions, using allies in Congress and the press to build support for their positions.

Presidents and their negotiators operate in a political environment whose moods and tempo can significantly influence the content and pace of foreign policy initiatives. The importance of international issues in U.S. politics fluctuates; and when the public has been seized with a foreign affairs issue, the room for maneuver of a president and his senior advisers may be severely limited. Presidential election cycles and the alternations of political parties have also driven policy initiatives— either by spurring a president to attain results before his term ends or the complexion of Congress changes, or by inspiring an administration to distance itself from the policies of its predecessor.

The interaction between the domestic political scene and the prevailing geopolitical landscape has also shaped the foreign policies and negotiating approaches of U.S. presidents. Americans have embraced conciliatory negotiating styles when the president and the public have felt relatively secure and believed they could influence the realities of world politics. The American negotiating style has been more bluntly demanding during times when the United States has felt threatened in its security or by major economic trends. Periods in which the United States has clearly been the dominant world power have also witnessed efforts to spread American ideals—often characterized as "freedom," "democracy," and "the promotion of human rights." In such circumstances, American foreign policy has tried to transform the realities of life abroad, with U.S. officials pressuring foreign governments to follow American leadership.

Despite the myriad shifting forces that have shaped U.S. negotiating behavior over time—from changes in communications technology and the rise and fall of ideologies, to recalibrations of the military balance of power and the development of a professional foreign service—one constant has been the paramount role of the president. As chief executive, he (and, in due course, she) sets forth not just his administration's strategic objectives but also, of critical importance, the character of the bureaucratic process—the interagency context—within which policy is formulated and implemented. Some presidents have encouraged rivalry, or "creative tension," among their senior advisers—only to find in many cases that bureaucratic rivalries have produced destructive policy feuding. Others have distanced themselves from such rivalry, often with equally negative effects. Still others have dominated the foreign policy process, imposing bureaucratic discipline or managing foreign policy formulation and implementation out of the White House.

It is to such variations in presidential foreign affairs leadership that this chapter now turns.

The Era of Personal Diplomacy, 1776–1898

From the founding of the Republic until the end of the nineteenth century, presidential involvement in negotiations was relatively weak. Diplomacy was conducted primarily by nonprofessional diplomats who often had wide negotiating latitude. Many of these people were highly skilled and quick to learn the nuances of other cultures and styles. Many had close relations with presidents or other high-ranking officials back in the United States; some did not. At times these nonprofessional diplomats promoted distinct political agendas. The United States often employed negotiating teams from competing government departments who were at odds with one another.

The pattern of Americans negotiating with themselves before they negotiated with their foreign counterparts was set during the Revolutionary War, before there was a president or a United States of America. The American diplomats in Paris in the 1770s and 1780s, set a precedent of accomplished envoys bickering among themselves. Benjamin Franklin was the most prominent of the American representatives. He charmed the French with his combination of scientific accomplishment, philosophical range, practicality, homespun wisdom, and, above all, a fresh republican style. His face appeared on medallions popular throughout France. One praised his scientific and political genius: *"Eriuit Coelum Fulum Septrumque Tyrannis"* ("He snatched the lightning from heaven and the scepter from tyrants.")[1]

Franklin's celebrity in France and his strongly pro-French sentiments went down badly with his American colleagues. John Adams, an accomplished lawyer

---

1. H. W. Brands, *The First American: The Life and Times of Benjamin Franklin* (New York: Doubleday, 2000), 551.

and prominent revolutionary pamphleteer, lacked Franklin's cheeriness; meanwhile, Adams's awkwardness bothered Franklin. Adams objected to Franklin's life "of continual dissipation." He could not stand the fact that "on Dr. F. the eyes of all Europe are fixed, as the most important character in American affairs in Europe. ... neither L. [Arthur Lee, another commissioner] nor myself are looked on with much consequence."[2] For his part, Lee thought Franklin was too close to the French. Indeed, he was, at least at the beginning of the war, when the success of the American cause depended on successfully negotiating a military alliance and a commercial treaty. But as the fortunes of the Americans improved on the battlefield, due in part to French aid, Franklin charmed the British peace negotiators, too. The Treaty of Paris of 1783 was a personal triumph for Franklin. His success in no small measure resulted from his personal connections to French and British officials as well as the high regard in which he was held by the Congress in Philadelphia.

Personal frictions among American negotiators or between diplomats and presidents also shaped the conduct of peace negotiations in the first half of the nineteenth century. President James Madison sent a five-member delegation to Ghent in 1814 to negotiate with the British. He selected men from different regions and political parties, and of different backgrounds. Rep. Henry Clay of Kentucky was one of the original war hawks who had urged the conflict. John Quincy Adams, a brilliant man, was the son of John Adams who had been at Paris with Franklin and a former ambassador to Russia. Jonathan Russell was the ambassador to Sweden. Albert Gallatin was a Swiss-born financier and a former secretary of the U.S. Treasury. James Ashton Bayard was a Delaware senator. John Quincy Adams was irritated that his fellow commissioners enjoyed a good time. He grumbled that "they sit after dinner and drink bad wine and smoke cigars."[3] Clay told him not to be a prig and that part of a diplomat's job was to provide and enjoy hospitality. Adams then joined the rest in attending the plays, receptions, dinner, and card parties the residents of Ghent provided for the Americans. The American delegation had a significant advantage over the British. The Americans, three thousand miles from the capital in Washington, had full power to work out a treaty, while the British had to refer all issues home to London. (Indeed, the U.S. negotiating team decided on its own to ignore several of the demands set forth in their original instructions.) After several months of back-and-forth exchanges, the two sides agreed on a peace treaty reestablishing conditions to those that existed before the war.[4]

A different pattern emerged during the U.S. war on Mexico from 1846 to 1848. In this conflict the single American negotiator—Nicholas Trist—had explicit

---

2. Ibid., 549.

3. Samuel Flagg Bemis, *John Quincy Adams and the Foundations of American Foreign Policy* (New York: Knopf, 1949), 191.

4. Bradford Perkins, *The Creation of a Republican Empire, 1776–1865*, vol. 1 of *The Cambridge History of American Foreign Relations*, ed. Warren Cohen (New York: Cambridge University Press, 1993), 143.

instructions that he followed, but his commitment to his original mission eventually landed him in trouble with President James K. Polk, whose appetite for Mexican land grew as the war went on. The president lost confidence in his envoy and recalled him; yet the diplomat simply ignored his order to return home and negotiated a treaty without authority from his government.

Trist was an experienced diplomat with political connections. Married to Thomas Jefferson's granddaughter, he had served eight years as consul in Havana and spoke Spanish. He had also previously served as chief aide to President Andrew Jackson and, in 1845, as the chief clerk in the State Department. In the midst of the war in 1847, Polk sent Trist with the army to Mexico to negotiate a peace settlement that would include the cession of Texas and the purchase of California. Polk selected Trist for his impeccable Democratic Party credentials. The president believed he would foil efforts by General Winfield Scott, an ardent Whig and a likely presidential contender in 1848, to take credit for success in the war. At first, Trist the Democrat did clash with Scott, but as the war wore on the diplomat and the general formed a partnership. Their collaboration enraged Polk, who came to want more Mexican territory than he had originally instructed Trist to attempt to buy. Like many Americans of his day, Trist expressed racist contempt for dark-skinned Mexicans, whom he labeled a "degenerate race." Still, he came to believe that either a long occupation or total annexation of Mexico (as expansionists advocated) would invite international condemnation and end "the Jeffersonian vision" of a peaceful republic.[5]

Trist got along with the Mexican president, Manuel de la Peña y Peña. Peña had been appointed president by the Mexican Congress after Mexico suffered defeats on the battlefield, had served previously in that office, and now was willing to sell off part of his country. He found Trist to be courteous and appreciated his ability to speak Spanish. Trist's apparent success in ending the war further irritated Polk. He wrote that Trist had "managed the negotiation very bunglingly and with no ability."[6]

On Polk's orders, Secretary of State James Buchanan recalled Trist to Washington. Trist, however, ignored the recall and concluded a peace treaty with Mexico more or less along the lines of Polk's original instructions. The Treaty of Guadalupe Hidalgo was popular in the United States, but it split the Democratic Party—to which both Polk and Trist belonged. Polk's presidency ended in disarray, and Trist returned home to financial ruin and political oblivion. His negotiation had succeeded, yet he felt like a failure. Trist's story is unusual, for rarely have U.S. negotiators who have been disavowed by their superiors achieved their diplomatic goals.

---

5. Wallace Ohrt, *Defiant Peacemaker: Nicholas Trist in the Mexican War* (College Station, Tex.: Texas A&M Press, 1997), 136.

6. Ibid.

His distance from Washington during the war and the changing conditions on the battlefield enabled him to take matters into his own hands.

Even greater distance and weak communications between Washington and other countries enabled other mid-nineteenth century U.S. diplomats to negotiate with little supervision from the capital. When the United States expanded its reach to East Asia in the 1840s and 1850s, the U.S. envoys Caleb Cushing and Matthew Perry exercised substantial independence in dealing with Chinese and Japanese officials. Cushing came to China in the wake of Britain's Opium War, telling a Boston audience that his mission was "in behalf of civilization, and that, if possible, the doors of three hundred millions of Asiatic laborers might be opened to America."[7] In the Treaty of Wanxhia, one of the notorious unequal treaties, he obtained through negotiation the same privileges of extraterritoriality that the British had gained by force.

Perry's mission to Japan originated in the American acquisition of ports on Mexico's Pacific coast in the aftermath of the war with Mexico. Secretary of the Treasury Robert Walker noted in 1848 that "by our recent acquisitions in the Pacific, Asia has suddenly become our neighbor, with a placid intervening ocean inviting our steamships upon a track of a commerce greater than that of all of Europe combined."[8] Secretary of State Daniel Webster, a prominent leader of the Whig Party, hoped that the explosive rivalry between slave states and free states might be dampened by expanding overseas trade. Webster sent Perry to the Japanese emperor bearing a letter from President Millard Fillmore. In it, Fillmore sought to impress upon the Japanese the power of the American military and modern technology. He pointed out that "our steamers can now reach the shores of your happy land in less than twenty days." The United States wanted some of Japan's "abundance of coal," which "our steamships, in going from California to China, must use." Fillmore asked that "our people be permitted to trade with your people, but we shall not authorize them to break any laws of your Empire."[9] Perry sought out the advice of some of the few writers on Japan before he departed. Webster gave him "full discretionary powers," which meant that he could threaten the Japanese with force to obtain a commercial treaty.[10]

Perry thus came to Japan in 1853 with threats as well as gifts. Upon his arrival, he demanded that Fillmore's letter be delivered to the emperor, and promptly went on to China, telling the Japanese he would return with more ships ready for battle if Japan did not agree to a treaty. He returned with a bigger fleet in 1854, seeking to intimidate the Japanese with both the threat of force and American technology—in

---

7. John M. Belohovak, *Broken Glass: Caleb Cushing and the Shattering of the Union* (Kent, Ohio: Kent State University Press, 2005), 155.

8. Quoted in Walter LaFeber, *The Clash: A History of U.S.-Japan Relations* (New York: Norton, 1997), 11.

9. Quoted in ibid., 12.

10. Ibid.

the form of a telegraph machine and a miniature steam train. The Japanese reluctantly agreed to a treaty, opening two ports to American ships and accepting the presence of a U.S. consul in Japan.

Negotiating as a Great Power, 1898–1932

Issues other than foreign affairs consumed most of the attention and energy of presidents from the Civil War to the 1890s. But by the turn of the nineteenth century to the twentieth, U.S. industrial power had enhanced the American presence on the global stage. U.S. presidents became more deeply engaged in foreign affairs and the public more interested in the conduct of U.S. foreign relations and diplomacy. The United States competed with the other European and Asian great powers for overseas empire, territory, and influence.

Ironically, the man who presided over America's transition to global power had himself never been abroad. But as a former congressman and governor of Ohio—a growing industrial powerhouse—President William McKinley took a keen interest in international affairs, especially issues of trade and economics. In fact, during his first administration, U.S. exports to the world almost doubled, from $833 million in 1896 to $1.488 billion in 1901.[11] McKinley's role in the conduct of the Spanish-American War marked several noteworthy transitions in presidential diplomacy: first, before, during, and after the conflict, he had to contend with a new and powerful form of public pressure whipped up by metropolitan newspaper chains, which were growing politically influential; second, during the war, he was able (and willing) to exert hands-on control over both American foreign policy and military strategy through a special "war room" equipped with telephone and telegraph connections; and third, he took a personal role in the negotiations ending the war because he recognized that his secretary of state, William Day, an old friend from Ohio, knew little of the world. Although McKinley relied on the U.S. ambassador to Great Britain, John Hay, to explain the U.S. position to British, French, and Spanish officials in Paris, McKinley believed that the peace treaty would set the parameters of an expansive American geopolitical role. He conducted the negotiations himself in Washington.

McKinley's successor, Theodore Roosevelt, started from the premise that the United States was a great power, the equal of the Europeans. He asserted American interests in many regions of the world. He also greatly enlarged the practice of projecting U.S. power and ideas into disputes in which the United States was not directly involved. In the century after Roosevelt's presidency, many successive presidents followed Roosevelt's practice of helping other nations resolve disputes that threatened to make the world unstable or unsafe for American interests.

---

11.   Kevin Philips, *William McKinley* (New York: Times Books, 2003), 87.

Roosevelt mediated a war and a dispute that could lead to war among the other great powers, organizing a peace conference in the summer of 1905 to resolve the Russo-Japanese War. The conference met in the comfortable seaport of Portsmouth, New Hampshire, rather than sweltering Washington. Roosevelt did not go to Portsmouth personally, but he met several times with the Japanese and Russian ambassadors at his summer home on Long Island. He sympathized with Japan and brokered a settlement validating their military successes. The next year Roosevelt played a major role at the Algeciras conference, resolving a dispute between France and Germany over Morocco. Roosevelt relied on Henry White, the U.S. ambassador to Italy, whose previous service in a variety of countries made him the closest thing the United States had in the early twentieth century to a professional diplomat, to present the U.S. point of view at the conference. In Washington, the president used his personal friendship with German ambassador Baron Speck Von Sternberg (he affectionately called him "Specky") to achieve an agreement.[12]

The administration of Woodrow Wilson marked the first full-blown marriage of America's growing power and presence abroad with exceptionalist ideals. Wilson proclaimed that his administration's "new diplomacy" would be based on democratic principles, expand American ideas of individual liberty, and be open and transparent. It would, at least in principle, forgo the use of material force against smaller powers, promote the peaceful arbitration of disputes, and encourage economic interdependence. A former university president and charismatic orator, Wilson combined high-mindedness with high passion. He had mixed relations with U.S. ambassadors abroad and secretaries of state, often used personal representatives, and involved academic experts in planning, but most of all he personally conducted negotiations.

Wilson intervened militarily in the Mexican revolution after the United States failed in several heavy-handed efforts to determine Mexico's president. In the process, Wilson recalled ambassador Henry Lane and sent a personal friend, John Lind, the former governor of Minnesota, and William Bayard Hale, a journalist for the *New York Times*, to monitor developments in Mexico. At one point President Wilson sought to warn the European powers against supporting one faction in the growing Mexican civil war, but Secretary of State William Jennings Bryan declined to send the telegram of instructions to his ambassadors. Bryan feared direct European intervention. Thwarted by his own Secretary of State, Wilson outlined his Mexico policy in a widely circulated speech in which he promised that Mexico would soon be free of "foreign interests," a thinly veiled reference to British banks and petroleum companies.

---

12.   Howard K. Beale, *Theodore Roosevelt and the Rise of America to World Power* (Baltimore: Johns Hopkins University Press, 1956), 384.

Wilson's deepest involvement in negotiations came during World War I. He articulated U.S. positions on the causes of the current war and international conflict in general, arguing that secret diplomacy and competing alliances were largely to blame. When the United States declared war on Germany, Wilson insisted that his country fight as an Associated rather than an Allied Power, because he wanted to position the United States on high moral ground and thus allow him to promote disinterested postwar plans to reorder global affairs. His calls for a radical reformation of world politics made him extremely popular around the world, at least temporarily. But his ambitious plans also set him apart from more traditional diplomats at home and abroad, and growing skepticism in Congress about the practicality of his vision ultimately doomed his strategy.

Wilson led the U.S. delegation to the Paris Peace Conference in 1919. A staff of hundreds accompanied him, including dozens of academic experts on geography, economics, politics, and world affairs organized into a quasi-governmental body known as The Inquiry that was supposed to give professional, nonpartisan advice on shaping negotiation. Unfortunately, Wilson included no prominent Republican political leader in his delegation, which limited domestic bipartisan support for his peacemaking efforts.

Wilson appealed directly to the European public to force their leaders to endorse his vision of a reformed world order. An American living in Paris said the "enthusiasm and affection" of the crowds was "the most remarkable demonstration . . . on the part of Parisians that I ever heard of." The reaction of French leaders, however, was mixed. The foreign minister said, "We are so thankful that you have come over to give us the right kind of peace." But Premier Georges Clemenceau told Wilson, "we too came into the world with the noble instincts and the lofty aspirations which you express so eloquently. We have become what we are because we have been shaped by the rough hand of the world in which we have to live and we have survived only because we are a very tough bunch."[13]

As the peace conference went on, Wilson personally conducted negotiations with the heads of government of Great Britain, France, and Italy. He compromised on many of the key items of his liberal and generous peace plan in order to gain the assent of the European leaders to his proposal for a League of Nations that would replace the old pattern of rival military alliances with a system of collective security. Wilson relied less and less on the other official U.S. delegates, including his confidant Colonel House. The Inquiry produced thousands of pages of plans for borders, political institutions, reparations, and the structure of the new international organization, the League of Nations. Yet few of their proposals made their way into the final peace treaty—to the great frustration of The Inquiry staff.

---

13.   Margaret Macmillan, *Paris, 1919: Six Months That Changed the World* (New York: Random House, 2001), 16.

Many on the staffs of the American and British delegations who had been in-spired by Wilson's reformist vision turned harshly against him for the political compromises he made in efforts to win support for the League of Nations. They complained that he tried to do it all alone and had been bested in negotiations by European leaders who did not share his commitment to international reform. John Maynard Keynes, a sharp-minded and sharp-tongued young member of Britain's Treasury delegation, also castigated Wilson for being outsmarted by his counter-parts: "The president's slowness amongst the Europeans was noteworthy." Keynes wrote later, "there can scarcely have been a statesman of the first rank more incom-petent than the president in the agilities of the conference chamber."[14]

The Treaty of Versailles that Wilson crafted was never ratified by the U.S. Sen-ate. It failed because some of Wilson's ardent supporters were disillusioned with the retreats he made at Paris from his idealistic agenda. In addition, the Republi-can Party, which had regained control of Congress in 1918, was lukewarm at best to Wilson's liberal internationalism and did not wish to hand him or his party a victory before the 1920 election. The U.S. public initially responded well to Wil-son's speeches in the summer of 1919 in which he pleaded for ratification. Failure to ratify would, he said, "break the heart of the world."[15] Yet after he suffered a stroke, his ability to shape public or congressional opinion diminished. The verdict of the election of 1920, which Wilson hoped would be a solemn referendum on the League of Nations and the Treaty of Versailles, was that the United States need not embark on an ambitious program of serving as the arbiter of international affairs.

Unhappiness among foreign affairs experts with Wilson's solo-presidential ne-gotiations provided momentum to the movement to establish a professional for-eign service for the United States. Since the beginning of the twentieth century, advocates of U.S. power, reformers of international law, and promoters of a general international organization had argued that the United States needed a permanent corps of diplomats. Reformers noted that European states staffed their embas-sies with career diplomats knowledgeable in the languages and cultures of their host countries and experienced in the practice of diplomacy. The United States, on the other hand, selected most of its overseas representatives from among a presi-dent's friends and political supporters. Fewer than one hundred men (there were no women among them) made their careers as professional diplomats or consuls. In 1924 the Rogers Act established the Foreign Service of the United States, consist-ing of diplomatic and consular branches. From then on, U.S. missions abroad were staffed increasingly with professionals.

Career Foreign Service officers brought many skills to their diplomatic assign-ments. They were educated in international affairs and eager to learn the culture,

---

14.   John Maynard Keynes, *The Economic Consequences of the Peace* (New York: Harcourt, Brace and Howe, 1920), 43.

15.   John Milton Cooper, *Breaking the Heart of the World: Woodrow Wilson and the Fight for the League of Nations* (New York: Cambridge University Press, 2001), 433.

languages, politics, economics, and societies of other peoples. Yet, the profession-alization of the foreign service also created some structural tension between career diplomats and the domestic political process. Presidents, their White House advisers, members of Congress, and prominent writers in the press often expressed disdain for Foreign Service officers. At times of high domestic tension over foreign affairs, critics of the Foreign Service sometimes accused its members of being disloyal and advocates of policies adverse to American interests.

The Republican presidents of the 1920s engaged less in high-level diplomacy, relying more on experts in different fields. The first two, Warren Harding and Calvin Coolidge, were men of limited vision and little international experience who largely left foreign affairs to their secretaries of state. Herbert Hoover was both talented and well traveled. But the Great Depression overwhelmed his presidency, leaving little room for international affairs.

Both Harding and Coolidge enlisted special envoys from the world of business to help them avert a potentially dangerous confrontation with Mexico over the right of U.S. firms to drill for oil on Mexican land. In 1923 Harding appointed Thomas Lamont, a partner of J. P. Morgan, as special envoy to restore diplomatic relations broken since the U.S. military intervention of 1917. In 1927, Coolidge resisted advice from U.S. oil executives to threaten Mexico with the possibility of armed intervention to restore their drilling rights. He chose conciliation instead, selecting an old college friend, Dwight Morrow, as his ambassador to Mexico in 1927 to work out a deal that would avoid a confrontation between U.S. bankers and oil companies and the Mexican government. The appointment of Morrow—like Lamont a partner at J. P. Morgan (which had helped to finance much of Mexico's external debt)—initially raised some eyebrows because of the inherent conflict of interests. (*Time* magazine reported that a waggish Senator George Higgins Moses of New Hampshire called Morrow's posting "a capital appointment.")[16] But Morrow, a seasoned troubleshooter, soon won over his critics in the United States and Mexico, negotiating a deal that recognized the ownership rights of oil and mineral properties Americans had obtained before the adoption of the nationalist Mexican constitution of 1917.[17] Morrow used a banker's toolkit of negotiating techniques—personal connections, recognition of his counterparts' national sensitivities, and a desire to reach an agreement with economic benefits. His deal was not permanent, however, lasting only until 1938, when a more nationalist Mexican government banned foreigners from owning or leasing Mexican oil properties. Still, by pursuing modest aims Morrow averted a crisis in U.S.-Mexican relations in a way that brought economic benefits to each side.

---

16. "The Cabinet: Morrow and Tomorrow," *Time*, October 3, 1927.

17. Claude M. Fuess, *Calvin Coolidge: The Man from Vermont* (Boston: Little Brown, 1940), 408–414.

The Growth of a Modern Foreign Affairs Bureaucracy, 1933–45

The shape of the modern U.S. government's foreign affairs system took form during the administration of President Franklin D. Roosevelt. The foundations were laid during the New Deal and the structure emerged fully during World War II. Roosevelt was personally and deeply involved in creating foreign policy, determining military strategy, and negotiating with allied leaders. The amount of attention he devoted to issues was limited only by the number of hours in a day. He paid most attention to high policy concerns. Numerous agencies had a role in creating U.S. foreign policy. The War, State, and Treasury Departments; the Office of Strategic Services (OSS, established in 1941—the predecessor of the Central Intelligence Agency); and the White House all sent officials abroad. During the war, the Treasury and War Departments and the OSS presented competing plans for the future occupation of Germany. The State and War Departments had conflicting visions of the future of Japan. State and Treasury had differences, later resolved, over a new international economic and monetary order. The War Department, the State Department, and the White House differed over the future of Southeast Asia. The State Department and the White House had subtle differences over the shape of the United Nations, the successor to the League of Nations. Thousands of experts—diplomats; military officers; professors of international affairs, history, geography, and economics; scientists; journalists; religious leaders; and business executives—participated in developing the proposals. Most worked for the government. The war also stimulated the growth of nongovernmental organizations interested in foreign affairs. The New York–based Council on Foreign Relations, which had its origins in The Inquiry of the 1919 Paris Peace Conference, provided hundreds of studies to the State and War Departments on the nature of the postwar world.

Roosevelt presided over this sprawling bureaucracy and bustle of nongovernmental activity with charm and guile. He relished and encouraged competition among government agencies. Only he had complete information and a clear idea of the ultimate goals of his diplomacy. He delayed decisions until the last minute to maintain initiative and control. When Keynes came to Washington to negotiate Lend Lease aid in the summer of 1941, he was struck by the interagency competition and control exercised by the president. Keynes reported that "in a negotiation lasting weeks, the situation is entirely fluid up to the last minute. . . . I liken [the Americans] to bees who for weeks will fly around in all directions. . . . and at last, perhaps because the queen in the White Hive has emitted some faint, indistinguishable odor, suddenly swarm to a single spot, in a compact, impenetrable bunch."[18]

---

18.   Quoted in Christopher Thorne, *Allies of a Kind: The United States, Britain, and the War against Japan, 1941–1945* (New York: Oxford University Press, 1978), 115.

The process was disorderly, but it produced numerous results that shaped the post–World War II world. U.S. negotiators were most successful in large multilateral meetings where they came with the largest staffs, equipped with the most extensive briefing books, and provided the most material and military incentives to their partners. The United Nations, the international organization created at the Dumbarton Oaks and San Francisco Conferences (1944 and 1945), was intended to be the center point of the postwar security system. The International Monetary Fund and the International Bank for Reconstruction and Development (World Bank), created at the Bretton Woods Conference (1944), became primary instruments for engaging the economic order. The way in which the United States, Britain, and France managed the postwar occupation of Germany was largely decided in the 1944–45 meetings of the European Advisory Commission. American negotiators succeeded at these meetings through the weight of their numbers, the detail of their proposals, and their ability to set agendas and make the conferees work from their drafts.

Roosevelt employed a variety of negotiators from within and outside the government. He was not close to either of his two secretaries of state, Cordell Hull (1933–44) or Edward Stettinius (1944–45). His impression of many members of the newly created Foreign Service was that they were insular and lacking in vision. Consequently, he sent trusted personal advisers on sensitive diplomatic missions. Harry Hopkins negotiated with the British and the Soviet Union during World War II. The U.S. ambassador to Moscow, Averell Harriman, a successful business executive and banker, formed a personal relationship with Soviet leader Josef Stalin, which facilitated communication with the difficult ally on matters of wartime policy.

Roosevelt knew international matters, had traveled widely, and had supreme confidence in his own skills as a negotiator. He favored Wilsonian goals, but believed that Wilson had failed as a diplomat. Wilson, in Roosevelt's view, had been too aloof from his counterparts. Roosevelt excelled at personal diplomacy at the summit level. He thrived on meeting government leaders at home or in exotic settings. He loved banter and jokes. He and Winston Churchill formed a close friendship from their first summit in the Atlantic in August 1941 through several White House visits and wartime summits, to the final meeting of the Big Three at Yalta in February 1945. After their first face-to-face encounter, Churchill reported to the cabinet, "I have established warm and deep personal relations with our great friend."[19]

Roosevelt's most complicated relationship was with Stalin. The president sometimes teased Churchill in front of the Soviet leader to indicate that the United

---

19.   Quoted in Warren Kimball, *Forged in War: Roosevelt, Churchill, and the Second World War* (Chicago: Ivan Dee, 1997), 98.

States did not share the British leader's long-standing animosity to Communism and the Soviet Union. Churchill, sensitive to Britain's declining international position, found the needling humiliating. Roosevelt regularly—if disingenuously—told the press of his disagreements with his friend Churchill and how he and Stalin saw eye-to-eye. He told reporters aboard the USS *Quincy* en route back from Yalta how he had raised the possibility of international trusteeship for French Indochina after the war: "Stalin liked the idea," he said. "China liked the idea. The British don't like it. It might bust up their empire." (Although Indochina was French, Churchill feared that the decolonization of one European empire would set a precedent for the end of Great Britain's own empire in Asia.)

Secretary of War Henry Stimson did not like the idea of international trusteeships for French Indochina either, because he wanted French and British military cooperation to stabilize post–World War II Southeast Asia. The plan never saw fruition because Roosevelt died before he fully articulated and reached agreement with the other major wartime leaders on his vision. He expected differences to arise between the coalition partners in the postwar world, but he believed his personal rapport with Churchill and Stalin and the great resources the United States could deploy would keep the alliance together.

Negotiating during a Time of Containment and Consensus, 1945–68

Roosevelt's successor, President Harry Truman, had neither FDR's personal relationships with other world leaders nor his skill in mastering the burgeoning U.S. government bureaucracy. Truman relied far more on his subordinates than did Roosevelt. The views of George F. Kennan, a professional Foreign Service officer and one of a small group of Soviet experts, helped fashion the policy of "containing" an expansionist Soviet Union. Truman often seemed in awe of his second secretary of state, George C. Marshall, who served in 1947–49. He relied heavily on the advice of Secretary of State Dean Acheson, who dominated the conduct of foreign affairs in Truman's full term (1949–53). (Acheson, meanwhile, wrote in his memoirs with tender exasperation about Truman's occasional gaffes—including the time that the president initially went along with British prime minister Clement Atlee's suggestion that neither the United States nor the United Kingdom use nuclear weapons without first consulting the other. As Acheson put it in discussing his dislike of summits, "When a chief of state or head of government makes a fumble, the goal line is open behind him.")[20] During Truman's administration, hopes faded for postwar harmony among the wartime victors as the world entered a transition to the Cold War confrontation between the United States and the So-

---

20. Dean Acheson, *Present at the Creation: My Years at the State Department* (New York: Norton, 1969), 480, 484.

viet Union. Truman and Stalin met once, at Potsdam in July 1945. The two leaders seemed to get along well personally (Truman thought Stalin was highly intelligent, well read, well prepared, and funny), but deep policy divisions opened over reparations for war damages and the future of Germany.

Truman, like Acheson, disliked Roosevelt's informal and personal handling of foreign affairs. They were not alone. Several expert commissions advocated reforms to reduce the confusion, mixed signals, and multiple lines of authority favored by FDR. Congress responded with legislation to enhance the position of career diplomats and define more clearly the lines of authority in foreign affairs. The Foreign Service Act of 1946 promised career diplomats greater opportunity to rise to the rank of ambassador. The National Security Act of 1947 was a sweeping reorganization of foreign affairs agencies designed to diminish interagency rivalry and provide the president with an orderly process to receive advice on international affairs. It organizationally separated the Air Force from the Army and put each branch of the armed forces (the Army, Air Force, Navy, and the Marine Corps) under the auspices of a civilian secretary in a newly created Department of Defense. It established a Central Intelligence Agency as successor to the wartime Office of Strategic Services to collect and analyze information and conduct clandestine operations abroad. It set up a National Security Council headquartered in the White House to coordinate all agencies involved in foreign affairs.

In the first presidential administration of wartime military leader Dwight Eisenhower, U.S. officials saw little prospect of resolving the Cold War and continued to use international forums to try to outmaneuver the Soviet Union in the court of public opinion. Eisenhower devoted his final years in office to seeking détente with Soviet leader Nikita Khrushchev, but the efforts failed in the face of deep distrust and animosity. A summit conference scheduled for May 1960 in Paris broke up before it began when Khrushchev publicly denounced the United States for sending manned reconnaissance flights through Soviet air space.

The growing volume of diplomatic activity during the Cold War created difficulties for U.S. government officials in keeping track of conversations, agreements, or promises made to other governments. Many understandings were not codified as treaties requiring Senate ratification or even executive agreements binding the administration that made them. The problem was especially acute when an administration from one party was replaced by one from the other: records of official conversations often were taken out of Washington with the departing president to be relocated in a presidential library. For example, in 1957, in the wake of Israel's successful attack on Egyptian forces in the Sinai Peninsula in 1956, the United States insisted that Israel withdraw from the captured territory. Secretary of State John Foster Dulles assured Israeli foreign minister Golda Meir that the United States would keep open the Strait of Tiran to provide access to Israel's southern port of Eilat. In May 1967 a crisis erupted between Egypt and Israel when

Egyptian president Gamal Abdel Nasser closed the strait to ships bound for Eilat. Israel's foreign minister Abba Eban reminded Secretary of State Dean Rusk of Secretary Dulles's guarantee of access to Eilat. The State Department searched its archives but could not find a record of the commitment. The assurance was eventually found in the Eisenhower Presidential Library in Abilene, Kansas.

Similarly, when Eisenhower met Khrushchev at Camp David in September 1959, the Soviet Communist Party chairman said that he was committed to signing a peace treaty that would recognize the German Democratic Republic's control over access to West Berlin. When President John F. Kennedy subsequently met with Khrushchev in Vienna in May 1961, Kennedy was shocked by what he thought was Khrushchev's belligerent demand to resolve the issue of access to West Berlin with a formal treaty. Kennedy was unaware of what the Soviet leader had told his predecessor, and the White House could not find any record of Khrushchev's statement to Eisenhower.

During some of the periods of highest tension of the Cold War, the United States used confidential channels and special envoys to draw back from the brink of war. During the Cuban Missile Crisis of October 1962, President Kennedy and his brother Attorney General Robert F. Kennedy used multiple irregular relationships to communicate with the Soviet leadership. Apart from Robert Kennedy's "off-line" meetings with Soviet ambassador Anatoly Dobrynin, the White House also employed ABC news reporter John Scali to transmit to Soviet intelligence agents the most sensitive messages on American proposals to end the crisis. Unlike Eisenhower, Kennedy also relied more on his staff and less on formal meetings of his cabinet, and was reluctant to delegate power outside the Oval Office and a small circle of trusted aides. Kennedy was particularly scathing about the State Department, telling journalist Hugh Sidey in 1961 that the department "is a bowl of jelly. It's got all those people over there who are constantly smiling. I think we need to smile less and be tougher."[21] Kennedy often relied on trusted senior advisers such as Averell Harriman. He deployed Harriman to Moscow in July 1963 to negotiate a Limited Nuclear Test Ban Treaty. In 1968 Harriman also served as President Lyndon B. Johnson's lead negotiator with North Vietnam in an effort to end the war in Vietnam.

From an Era of Negotiations to the End of the Cold War, 1968–89

The Vietnam War overwhelmed President Johnson. The bipartisan consensus over the need to contain the Soviet Union and its allies that had guided U.S. foreign

---

21.   Arthur Schlesinger, Jr., *A Thousand Days: John F. Kennedy in the White House* (Boston: Houghton Mifflin, 1965), 406.

policy since the Truman administration eroded in the divisions over the drain-ing conflict in Southeast Asia. Richard M. Nixon won the presidential election of 1968 with appeals to voters frustrated by the stalemate in Vietnam. During the campaign he claimed to have a secret plan to end the war, and in his inaugural address he asserted that "after a period of confrontation, we are entering an era of negotiation."[22] Nixon was suspicious of the political affiliations of the federal bureaucracy in general and the State Department in particular. He and Henry Kissinger, his national security adviser, centralized control over the conduct of for-eign affairs in the White House.

Détente with the Soviet Union was at the center of Nixon's strategy for an era of negotiations, and in a maneuver designed to pressure the Soviet leadership with a major shift in the global balance of power, he secretly initiated a diplo-matic approach to the Chinese communist leadership in parallel with heightened communications with the Soviets. Kissinger opened perhaps the most celebrated confidential or back channel of the entire Cold War era with Soviet ambassador Dobrynin. The two men met regularly in the evenings at the Soviet embassy. They addressed each other as "Henry" and "Anatoly" and spoke for hours over glasses of vodka. Kissinger made it clear that important matters went through him and not the secretary of state, William Rogers, or the professional negotiators in the State Department. Arms control was a central element in the new relationship, and Kissinger asserted to the Soviet envoy that he and the president, not the official U.S. delegation to arms control talks, made the important decisions. Dobrynin re-ported to the Kremlin that Kissinger requested that he instruct Vladimir Semenov, the leader of the Soviet arms control team negotiating with Gerard Smith, the head of the Arms Control and Disarmament Agency, "not to talk to Smith about all of these discussions through our confidential channel. [Smith] doesn't know anything about this" channel, Kissinger said.[23]

Nixon then energized the Soviet negotiations by secretly dispatching Kissinger to Beijing in mid-July 1971 for talks on normalizing Sino-American relations. Kissinger and Chinese foreign minister Zhou Enlai found common cause in countering Soviet "hegemony" and in conducting diplomacy outside the bounds of their respective foreign affairs bureaucracies. Kissinger called Zhou one of the most impressive officials he had ever met. At his first secret meeting with Zhou, Kissinger said that Nixon had asked that his initial mission be kept secret "so we can meet unencumbered by bureaucracy, free of the past, and with the greatest

---

22.   Richard M. Nixon, "Inaugural Address," January 20, 1969, available online at John T. Woolley and Gerhard Peters, *The American Presidency Project* (Santa Barbara, Calif.: University of California [hosted], Gerhard Peters [database]), http://www.presidency.ucsb.edu/ws/?pid=29644.

23.   Henry Kissinger and Anatoly Dobrynin, memorandum of conversation, March 12, 1971 (USSR version), in *Soviet American Relations: The Détente Years, 1969–1972* (Washington, D.C.: Government Printing Office, 2007), 307.

possible latitude."[24] They agreed that Nixon would visit China in February 1972. The Soviet leadership, shocked by revelation of the U.S.-China opening, soon agreed to a Nixon-Brezhnev summit in Moscow in May 1972.

Despite the months of intensive preparations that preceded the Moscow summit, the meetings had a rushed and improvised quality. Nixon wanted it that way. He told Kissinger not to complete work on several of the agreements to be signed at the summit in order to heighten the drama back home. As a result Nixon and Kissinger and their Soviet counterparts at the summit worked long into the night. They excluded Secretary of State Rogers from the conversations (as they had done when Nixon visited China in February). Nixon and Brezhnev signed several agreements and a treaty at the Moscow summit limiting the deployment of antiballistic missiles.

Cementing new relationships with China and the Soviet Union were just two of several high-profile diplomatic episodes in Nixon's era of negotiations. From 1969 to 1976, Kissinger was the nation's premier negotiator. He conducted talks with adversaries and friends through a variety of front and back channels. In addition to détente with the Soviet Union and the dramatic opening to China, Kissinger negotiated an ultimately failed peace agreement with North Vietnam and commenced a peace process between Israel and two of its Arab neighbors, Egypt and Syria. This whirlwind of high-profile activity gained Kissinger a domestic and international celebrity that no previous U.S. official, with the possible exception of Benjamin Franklin, had enjoyed.

Kissinger's status as a diplomatic miracle worker faded in the twilight of the Nixon administration. Détente was widely popular at home in the summer of 1972, but Nixon's and Kissinger's secrecy and tight control eroded the initial enthusiasm for their foreign policies. Domestic political opposition to détente mounted in 1973 and 1974 in the face of deep distrust of the Soviet Union and its military buildup. Some opponents criticized Nixon and Kissinger for ignoring Moscow's abuse of it citizens' human rights. Senator Henry M. Jackson took up the issue of Soviet emigration restrictions. In 1974 Congress passed the Jackson-Vanik amendment to the Trade Expansion Act, which barred the extension of most favored nation trade status to the Soviet Union unless it permitted the free emigration of Jews and other religious minorities. Kissinger told prominent journalists that Senator Jackson, the amendment's principal sponsor, was cynically manipulating the fortunes of Soviet Jews for his own personal political gain. Once Congress began debating Jackson-Vanik, Kissinger pointed out—and the press, generally supportive of détente, reported—that the number of Jews permitted to emigrate dropped from 50,000 per year to under 20,000. In Nixon's final summit

---

24.   Zhou Enlai, Henry Kissinger, et al., memorandum of conversation, July 9, 1971, in *Foreign Relations of the United States, 1969–1976*, vol. 17, *China 1969–1972* (Washington, D.C.: Government Printing Office, 2006), 361.

with Brezhnev in June 1974, both Kissinger and Nixon explained to Soviet leaders that the Jackson-Vanik amendment was a petty domestic political matter that they would not let stand in the way of improved relations between the United States and the Soviet Union.

This prediction that domestic American criticism of the Soviets' violations of their citizens' human rights would fade proved to be inaccurate. Opposition to détente increased during the administration of Gerald R. Ford. In the summer of 1975 Senator Jackson was joined in his opposition to détente by former California governor Ronald Reagan, who was preparing to challenge Ford for the Republican presidential nomination. Jackson, Reagan, and numerous conservative columnists criticized Ford for declining to receive Soviet dissident writer Aleksandr Solzhenitsyn at the White House. They lambasted Ford for going to Helsinki to sign the Final Act of the Conference on Security and Cooperation in Europe. Meanwhile, human rights groups such as Amnesty International and the forerunner of Human Rights Watch were beginning to attract more attention to the cause of human rights worldwide, generating heightened public pressure and creating a foundation for greater foreign policy activism by nongovernmental organizations.

After Kissinger left office, political controversy intensified in the United States over the aims and methods of U.S. foreign policy. No one in subsequent administrations held diplomatic center stage the way Kissinger had. Succeeding administrations sometimes continued negotiations begun by their predecessors, but at other times they suspended work or abandoned earlier agreements in hopes of obtaining results more in line with their domestic political positions. As the presidency changed hands between the Republican and Democratic parties, officials from other nations sometimes were unsure whether what they considered to be commitments made by one administration would be sustained by the next.

When Jimmy Carter campaigned for the presidency in 1976, he decried Nixon's and Kissinger's penchant for secrecy, centralization of foreign policy, and negotiations run out of the White House and their indifference to human rights abuses in other countries. As president, he supported Soviet-American détente that would reduce the dangers of nuclear war and, at the same time, embed the Soviet Union in a universal system of human rights. Soviet leaders were puzzled by Carter, because he seemed at once more conciliatory and yet more belligerent than his predecessors. The Soviets suspected that Carter was not serious about arms control. Three years passed before the United States and the Soviet Union agreed on a SALT II treaty, which was similar to the deal that Kissinger had worked out in 1976. Carter and Brezhnev held their only summit in May 1979. By that time Carter was politically fading and Brezhnev was ailing. Secretary of State Cyrus Vance told the president not to expect much give and take with the Soviet leader. "Actual negotiations on central issues" were unlikely, Vance said, because Brezhnev "is old, human, and emotional."[25] Although Carter and Brezhnev signed a SALT II treaty, Carter's political position at home was so weak that he never submitted the treaty to the Senate for ratification.

At the same time, Carter enjoyed a number of diplomatic successes by building on negotiations begun in previous administrations. He employed a special negotiator, business executive Sol Linowitz, to complete work on two treaties returning the Panama Canal to Panama. He pressed forward with negotiations on a Law of the Sea Treaty begun during the Nixon administration. He selected Elliot Richardson, a veteran of numerous high-level positions in the Nixon administration, as the chief U.S. delegate to the Law of the Sea negotiations. Representatives from the Environmental Protection Agency and the Departments of State, Defense, Treasury, Commerce, and Justice negotiated among themselves, businesses, and representatives of dozens of nongovernmental organizations to produce a compromise among security, commercial, mining, and environmental interests—reflecting the growing complexity of international issues.

The subsequent decades-long saga of the Law of the Sea Treaty demonstrates, as well, how shifting domestic political dynamics can affect the outcome of a specific negotiation. As the negotiations proceeded, domestic political opinion turned against the treaty. Some critics charged that it limited the business prospects of private U.S. firms. The Senate declined to ratify the treaty in 1979; and Carter's successor, Ronald Reagan, withdrew it from consideration on the grounds that it deprived private American firms of the right to profit from mining the deep seabed. Eleven years later, at the beginning of the Clinton administration, the United States returned to multinational negotiations over the Law of the Sea. The Navy urged ratification of the treaty to protect the rights of passage of U.S. warships. Clinton submitted the treaty for ratification in October 1994, a few weeks before the congressional election in which the Republican Party captured both houses of Congress. The new Republican majority in the Senate declined to ratify the treaty; it remained unratified in 2009.

Carter's most impressive achievement in personal diplomacy occurred when he mediated between Israel and Egypt in an effort to normalize their relationship. Convening a twelve-day summit at Camp David between Israeli prime minister Menachem Begin and Egyptian president Anwar Sadat in September 1978, Carter displayed personal sympathy for each side and developed a friendship with Sadat. He knew the minutiae of the dispute. He offered aid in the billions to both sides to conclude a formal agreement. He subsequently traveled to the Israeli and Egyptian capitals to make sure the Camp David framework was formalized in a peace treaty.

---

25.   Quoted in Melvyn P. Leffler, *For the Soul of Mankind: The United States, the Soviet Union, and the Cold War* (New York: Hill and Wang, 2007), 315.

Carter's personal involvement in Middle East peacemaking became a model of presidential diplomacy for many, but not all, of his successors.

After Ronald Reagan defeated Carter for the presidency in 1980, Carter seemed unlikely to be the model for anything. In his first term, Reagan turned away from détente with the Soviet Union, casting doubt on the value of arms control agreements, and he heightened tensions with Moscow by characterizing the Soviet Union as an "evil empire." Yet he sharply reversed course after Mikhail Gorbachev became general secretary of the Soviet Communist Party in 1985. The regular summit meetings between U.S. presidents and Soviet leaders that had characterized the Nixon and Ford administrations resumed. Reagan met Gorbachev five times in four years, including in Washington in December 1987 to sign a treaty removing all intermediate nuclear forces from Europe. Reagan called the agreement "a landmark in postwar history." Gorbachev described it as a way for the two powers to "build a bridge to the future." Addressing Gorbachev, Reagan spoke both of the ideological divide between the two superpowers and his desire for cooperation: "Between us, there has . . . been a profound competition of political and economic philosophy, making us protagonists in a drama with the greatest importance for the future of all mankind." But now, like Nixon before him, Reagan said it was time "to move from confrontation to cooperation . . . . We can coexist as do two wrestlers in a ring if necessary, but we would much prefer to coexist as partners and as friends."[26] Friends they became. When the two leaders met in Moscow in June 1988 and in New York in December, they called each other "Ron" and "Mikhail."

The Reagan administration made an equally surprising shift in policy when it changed from opposing international agreements to protect the environment to take the lead in negotiating the Montreal Protocol on Substances That Deplete the Ozone Layer in 1987. The chief American negotiator was Richard Benedick, a professional Foreign Service officer who immersed himself in the science of the dangers to the earth's climate posed by chlorofluorocarbons (CFCs). He assembled a team of officials from the State Department and the Environmental Protection Agency and scientists "drawn out of their laboratories and into the negotiating process." He recalled that they "had to assume an unaccustomed and occasionally shared responsibility for the policy implication of their findings."[27]

Benedick reported regularly to the White House Domestic Policy Council to maintain support from the president. Nonetheless, at one point he had to face down an attempt by Secretary of the Interior Donald Hodel, waged in the White House and in the press, to unseat him as lead negotiator. But this effort at an antiregulatory putsch failed, with President Reagan signing off on a decision memo that transmitted his approval of the U.S. negotiating position in an "Eyes Only"

---

26. Quoted in ibid., 401.

27. Richard Elliot Benedick, *Ozone Diplomacy: New Directions in Safeguarding the Planet*, enlarged edition (Cambridge: Harvard University Press, 1998), 5.

cable to Benedick (who later wondered if there was any connection between Reagan's decision and his operation months earlier to have some skin cancer removed from his face).[28]

The U.S. negotiators worked with the United Nations Environmental Program (UNEP) to raise public awareness of the dangers of CFCs. The State Department kept more than sixty U.S. embassies around the world briefed on the state of the treaty negotiations and instructed them to use the local press to raise awareness of the problem of ozone depletion. The negotiators produced a flexible and dynamic treaty that responded to changing environmental conditions. When the treaty was signed, Mostafa Tolpa of the UNEP predicted that its mechanisms for adjusting to changing environmental conditions "will—very likely—become the blueprint for the institutional apparatus designed to control greenhouse gases and adaptation to climate change."

The Post–Cold War World

In the 1990s, following the collapse of the Soviet Union, the United States was the world's undisputed superpower. The presidents of the era made personal relations with international leaders a centerpiece of their foreign policies and negotiations, which increasingly involved large multilateral gatherings to address complex economic, scientific, and social issues. Moreover, although the United States was dominant militarily, the end of ideological conflict with the Soviet Union in some ways only amplified the need for Washington to seek international legitimacy for any application of military force. The United States assembled large international coalitions in support of the use of force, in the Gulf War of 1991, the Bosnian War of 1995, and the Kosovo War of 1999. After the victory in February 1991 over Iraq in the Gulf War, President George H. W. Bush put together an international peace conference to settle the wider Middle East conflict. The Middle East peace conference convened in Madrid in October 1991 with representatives from Israel, Egypt, Jordan, Syria, and the Palestine Liberation Organization (PLO) at the same table. It prepared the way for the Oslo Accords between Israel and the PLO signed on the White House lawn on September 13, 1993.

President Clinton also sponsored peace conferences following military engagements. After the Bosnian bombing campaign of 1995, the United States called the leaders of Bosnia and Serbia to a meeting at Wright-Patterson Air Force Base in Dayton, Ohio, to mediate an end to the Bosnian civil war. Choosing an isolated site away from Washington helped the talks succeed in creating an independent Bosnia. As the lead negotiator, Assistant Secretary of State Richard Holbrooke formed

---

28.   Richard Elliot Bendick, "Science, Diplomacy, and the Montreal Protocol," in *The Encyclopedia of the Earth*, http://www.eoearth.org/science,_diplomacy_and_the_Montreal_protocol.

a personal relationship with Slobodan Milosevic, teasing, cajoling, and threatening the Serb leader in a high-pressure effort to conclude a settlement. After six days of bargaining, Holbrooke told Milosevic on November 6, "You may be enjoying Dayton, but we Americans want to go home. We can't stay here beyond November fifteenth." Later, Milosevic balked at a proposal for the contending ethnic groups to share power in the capital, Sarajevo, in a version of what the Americans called the District of Columbia (D.C.) model. The Serbian leader said "these people would kill each other over who would run the day care centers." Fed up with what he considered Milosevic's refusal to bargain, Holbrooke grabbed a draft proposal on the D.C. model from Milosevic's hands, threw it in an ashtray, and told him, "If you don't like this proposal, this is what we'll do with it. But that's the end of it. We'll go back to our original proposal—an undivided Bosnia." Holbrooke said Milosevic laughed at the theater and said he world reconsider.[29] Two weeks later the Americans presided over a ceremony at which the Serbs and Bosnians agreed to share power in Bosnia. Four years later, Holbrooke failed to persuade Milosevic to remove his nation's troops from the province of Kosovo where the ethnic Albanian Kosovars suffered under Serb domination. The United States then organized a six-week-long NATO bombing campaign to force the Serbs out of Kosovo.

Throughout the pre-9/11 post–Cold War period, issues on which the United States negotiated continued to expand beyond traditional security concerns. The number of U.S. negotiators also grew and their expertise became more specialized. Trade and environmental issues gained prominence. In 1992, for example, George H. W. Bush participated, somewhat reluctantly, in a landmark environmental conference convened by the United Nations in Rio de Janeiro that drew more than a hundred world leaders. Bush's administration also negotiated the North American Free Trade Agreement with Canada and Mexico in 1991 and 1992. The Clinton administration pressed Congress to ratify and pass enabling legislation for NAFTA over the objections of a sizeable portion of Democratic Party legislators and Democratic-leaning interest groups. Clinton assembled experts from the Office of the Trade Representative and the State, Commerce, and Treasury Departments to join in the drafting of the charter of the 180-nation World Trade Organization, ratified in 1999.

This practice recalled earlier efforts by Presidents Woodrow Wilson and Franklin D. Roosevelt to negotiate with the support of technical experts, grounded in facts and figures and schooled in the law. During the world wars and again in the 1990s—periods in which the power of the United States was unrivaled—presidents employed specialists to flesh out the details of broad agreements designed to re-order international relations. As had occurred in some earlier eras, Clinton's grand design—to embrace globalization—proved to be unpopular with key elements of

---

29.   Richard Holbrooke, *To End a War* (New York: Random House, 1998), 248, 249.

his own party. The Clinton administration employed dozens of environmental scientists to draft the 1997 multinational Kyoto Protocol on Climate Change. But the political climate in Washington had changed, and a Republican-controlled Congress declined to endorse the agreement.

Clinton invested more personal time and energy in his last year in office in trying to forge a peace between Israel and the Palestine National Authority (PNA) than he did on any other issue, foreign or domestic. He relied on the advice of an eclectic group of Mideast experts. Three, Dennis Ross, Daniel Kurtzer, and Aaron David Miller, had worked on Middle East issues for previous presidents and secretaries of state going back to the 1980s. A fourth, Martin Indyk, had been a scholar and pro-Israel advocate before he joined the staff of the National Security Council. Clinton convened a two-week summit meeting with Israeli prime minister Ehud Barak and PNA president Yasser Arafat at Camp David. Clinton flattered, persuaded, and bargained, but unlike President Carter in 1978, he failed to bring the two leaders to agreement.

After Camp David II broke down in acrimony, Clinton continued his personal involvement in the Mideast peace negotiations until his last days in office. A bloody uprising against the Israeli occupation of the West Bank and Gaza erupted in September 2000. Clinton dispatched Secretary of State Madeleine Albright to the Middle East and Europe to calm the fighting and bring Barak and Arafat back to the negotiating table. In December, Clinton presented an American proposal to bridge the divide separating Barak and Arafat on the thorniest issues: the border between Israel and an independent state of Palestine, the final status of Jerusalem, and the future of Palestinian refugees.

Previous American presidents had avoided setting forth drafts of what a final settlement should look like, but Clinton decided to go for broke with less than a month to go in his term and with the prospect of ending a century-long conflict seemingly within reach. But his personal approach failed. Barak's political support at home was gone, and Arafat lacked backing for an agreement in the complex politics of the Arab world. Clinton was surprised that his personal involvement, his charm, and the personal prestige of the president of the United States were insufficient to bridge the differences between Israel and a nascent state of Palestine.

The terrorist attacks of September 11, 2001, shocked the country—and the administration of George W. Bush—into an assertive mood of self-defense. In the context of initial domestic and international sympathy and support for the United States, President Bush adopted an aggressive response to the unprecedented security threat from extremist elements in the Muslim world. Military action in Afghanistan in 2002 to remove the Taliban regime drew wide support; yet the administration failed to gain explicit United Nations backing for its subsequent removal of the Saddam Hussein regime in Iraq, despite Saddam's repeated rebuffing of UN resolutions calling for him to permit unfettered international inspection of his suspected WMD programs. The United States used international forums to make its case, not to negotiate common positions against Iraq. In February 2003, Secretary of State Colin L. Powell went before the UN Security Council with pictures and intercepted telephone calls which, he assured the world body, proved that Saddam was hiding weapons of mass destruction.

Powell, however, was unable to persuade the United Nations to adopt a resolution explicitly authorizing force. Hans Blix, the United Nations' chief weapons inspector, had himself counseled against such a resolution, since Saddam was allowing UN units some access to sites where banned weapons were suspected. Facing vetoes by France, Russia, and China, the Security Council declined to pass a resolution authorizing the United States to use force against Iraq. French foreign minister Dominique de Villepin addressed the Security Council and warned the United States: "The outbreak of force in this area which is so unstable can only exacerbate the tensions and fractures on which the terrorists feed."[30] The council chamber erupted in cheers and applause at these words, much to the disgust of U.S. ambassador John Negroponte.[31]

In time, the revelation of flawed intelligence over Saddam's presumed nuclear weapons program, the escalating violence and expanding insurgency that followed the quick toppling of the Saddam regime, and skepticism over the forceful effort to promote regime change and democratic governance in a Muslim country eroded public support for America's international standing to unprecedentedly low levels.

The Bush administration, nonetheless, pressed ahead with a global "war on terrorism." With the resources of the world's sole military and economic superpower, and despite the cooperation of a network of more than ninety countries, the administration seemed determined to defend American security on a unilateral basis—and its rhetoric, its policies on detainees and interrogations, and a few spectacular blunders, such as abuse of Iraqis held at Abu Ghraib prison, turned much of world opinion against it.

Bush's first term was characterized by disdain for negotiated approaches to dealing with hostile regimes—the "axis of evil," North Korea, Iran, and Iraq—and rejection of several high-profile international agreements such as the Kyoto Protocol on Climate Change. The president also drew back from formal diplomatic efforts at Middle East peacemaking. He believed that his predecessor, President Clinton, had committed too much prestige and energy into a failed personal effort to broker an Israeli-Palestinian peace agreement.

---

30. Dominique de Villepin, in his address on Iraq before the UN Security Council, March 19, 2003, http://www.un.int/france/documents_anglais/030319_cs_villepin_irak.htm.

31. "Envoys Abandon Scripts on Iraq and Bring Emotion to U.N. Floor," *New York Times*, February 15, 2003.

Yet into his second term, George W. Bush returned to more traditional efforts at diplomatic problem solving. He succeeded in activating a "six-party talks" framework for dealing with North Korea, supported European efforts to engage the Iranian regime in talks on its nuclear program, and deployed Secretary of State Condoleezza Rice to the Middle East in efforts to reactivate an Arab-Israeli peace process. As the last year of his term approached, in November 2007, the president convened representatives of more than forty countries and international organization at Annapolis, Maryland, in an effort to produce a framework agreement for a settlement. These efforts, like those of most prior administrations, failed to achieve their aims, but they did leave the administration's successors a framework for continuing to address these issues.

In the presidential election campaign of 2008, Democratic Party candidate Barack Obama put forward a foreign policy platform designed to draw a contrast with the asserted failings of the outgoing Bush administration. Obama pledged to engage bilaterally adversaries such as North Korea and Iran, and to reenergize U.S. diplomacy. He sought to devise a coordinated international response to the sudden emergence of a global economic crisis, and put special emphasis on nonmilitary issues such as climate change and energy security. In office, he restored to cabinet rank the position of U.S. ambassador to the United Nations, and he appointed a number of politically influential special envoys to concentrate on the Middle East peace process, dealings with Iran, the post-Iraq security challenges emanating from "AfPak" (Afghanistan and Pakistan), genocide in the Darfur region of Sudan, and climate change. Some skeptical observers believed the proliferation of high-profile special representatives diminished the stature of Secretary of State Hillary Clinton. She rebutted the criticism, saying it would be "diplomatic malpractice not to have people of stature and experience handling some of our most difficult problems on a day-to-day basis."[32]

Whether these diplomatic initiatives succeed in resolving highly complex challenges to American security and foreign policy interests will be evident only in time. What can be said as of the writing of this chapter is that in time-honored fashion the transition to a new administration involves initiatives designed to contrast with the perceived failings of its predecessor. As both candidate and president, Obama has stressed the need to return to high-profile diplomacy in seeking results, even at the cost of overriding standing bureaucratic processes. Measured by public opinion polls, the country—and the world—have welcomed these changes. But given the range of complex challenges facing the administration, the test will be what concrete results these initiatives will actually yield.

---

32. Secretary of State Hillary Clinton, interview by David Gregory, *Meet the Press*, NBC, July 26, 2009, http://www.msnbc.msn.com/id/32142102/ns/meet_the_press/page/3/.

Conclusion

From the time of the founding of the Republic to the beginning of the twenty-first century, American presidents and their negotiators have developed their own style of diplomatic interactions with other nations. When one administration gives way to another—especially when there is a change of political parties—there is often a dramatic alteration in foreign policy and diplomatic approach as a new president rejects the presumed failures or foibles of his predecessor. These shifts, however, are often temporary, sometimes have more to do with rhetoric than substance, and always occur alongside a considerable, if overlooked, degree of continuity in negotiating style. Almost all presidents, for instance, are acutely aware of the length of their terms and focus on obtaining results quickly, within the context of electoral cycles. And as presidential popularity fades in the latter months of a term due to domestic problems, foreign policy initiatives are often undertaken to create "legacy" accomplishments.

Over the centuries, the number and complexity of international negotiations involving American interests has expanded enormously. Yet even here there is more consistency than change. In the first century of the Republic, American negotiators explained that their country's democratic political institutions, its expanding economy, new technology, and increasing territory gave significant weight to its positions in diplomatic exchanges. As U.S. power and international involvement grew in the twentieth century, American negotiators were ever more likely to base their positions on the special character of the United States. In the Cold War and post–Cold War eras, they drew strength from American military and economic power, the sturdiness of its political institutions, and the worldwide appeal of its culture. Many times in the late twentieth and early twenty-first century, U.S. negotiators have either explicitly or implicitly stressed the exceptional or even unique characteristics of American politics and society. This presumption of exceptionalism has reinforced American negotiators' propensity to urge or even demand that its negotiating partners adapt the businesslike, results-oriented approach of the U.S. economic system, if not to pressure foreign governments to conform to U.S. standards and U.S.-style democratic political practice.

Another constant is the influence of a political system of divided powers. The president is paramount in matters of foreign policy and national security, but Congress has its say in diplomacy through its powers of investigation, confirmation of ambassadorial appointments, ratification of treaties, and fiscal control. The public also has its say in foreign affairs, especially when economic issues are in play or in matters of war and peace. Public views, amplified and mediated by a critical press, have often set the foreign affairs agenda and modified what presidents and other executive branch officials have sought to obtain in negotiations with other governments.

In the last hundred years the United States has developed an increasingly well-educated corps of officials who negotiate with other powers. These are career civil and military servants from a variety of government agencies. In addition to these professionals, the U.S. government has regularly drawn on the skills and political standing of private individuals brought into the government for limited terms as senior officials. These men and women tend to compete with one another for policy influence and diplomatic involvement. This contest helps to shape the character of the interagency process, and often has meant that more negotiating goes on *inside* the U.S. government among various competing interests and agencies than occurs *between* the United States and its international interlocutors. Complicating the situation further for professional diplomats is the tendency of all presidents to conduct crises or breakthrough negotiations outside established bureaucratic channels and to the exclusion of well-informed junior officials. President Kennedy's handling of the Cuban Missile Crisis and President's Nixon's management of the China opening are more the rule than the exception.

Despite the complex and extensive degree of organization of the U.S. government, American negotiators are highly personal in their conduct. This individualized aspect of negotiating behaviors has been especially important at the level of presidents and their most senior diplomatic advisers. They are politicians in the traditional sense of the word. They like meeting-face-to-face, and they trust their own judgment about whether they can do business with a foreign counterpart. They tend to favor concrete agreements based on practices developed in business and the law. Most of all, they like results, sooner rather than later. American presidents and their negotiators have been, and will continue to be, impatient. Democrat or Republican, realist or exceptionalist, they all operate within earshot of a clock ticking down a president's term.

Part IV

Foreign Perspectives

7

Different Forums, Different Styles

Chan Heng Chee

nyone who has negotiated with the United States knows it comes to the table clearly aware that it is the world's only superpower, a hegemon. The United States understands its power and seeks to wield commensurate influence. These days, it faces a great deal of resistance to its dominance and has to work harder to achieve its negotiating goals. The United States is a country that was founded to allow the expression of freedom and liberty, values it seeks unabashedly to promote. The United States regards these values as "truths" and believes they are wanted and welcomed by everyone. It is unique in that its foreign policy is chiefly about the promotion of values. Americans believe American power should be used to change the world. The war in Iraq has tempered this feeling, but the self-confidence and deeply held belief that American values are superior and worth promoting will return again.

Since the realization of the Manifest Destiny, American power has not been harnessed for the acquisition of new land or the colonization of new territories. And until the twentieth century, it was not overtly harnessed for securing favorable access to international markets. The present order is an outcome of World War II, where American participation turned the tide of defeat and laid the foundations of a Western alliance for the promotion of a liberal, democratic, secular, and free-market system. Indeed, American power today is harnessed principally for the maintenance of a Western-oriented and American-centered international order. These goals were particularly evident in the era of the Cold War, and the drive to maintain them remains the dominant impulse at a time when emerging power centers are challenging American dominance and the established rules of order.

American negotiating style and behavior flow from the reality of its superpower status: the United States is the largest economy in the world, has the most powerful military in the world, and is a fount of technological innovation and creative ideas.

Now let me say something that might shock some readers: Americans don't really negotiate and don't know how to negotiate very well. Americans often present their views at a forum and negotiating table using a very direct approach and expect the other party or parties to accept them or adjust to them. In short, they will try to talk to the other party until it accepts their proposal.

When I ran this thesis by a U.S. State Department official, his response was, "You are right. We don't negotiate. We negotiate with ourselves. The negotiations are all internal—in the interagency process. It is exhausting, so when I come to you to present you with a proposal, often I want to say, 'Hey, this is the best we can get. You'd better believe it.'" Another official, formerly of the Department of Defense, agreed wholeheartedly with this view. If I had to give a ratio, I would say that 20 percent of America's negotiations are with the foreign party and 80 percent take place at home.

America's political structure greatly affects the style and behavior of its negotiators. The U.S. Constitution was not written with the United States as a superpower in mind. It is certainly not conducive to the conduct of foreign policy by a superpower. Some American constitutional scholars of course may argue to the contrary, that the purpose of the system of checks and balances was precisely to impede hasty and reckless decisions and that the separation of powers provides the opportunity to reexamine policy. Indeed, American administrations and their negotiators have an eye on how the agreements they work out will play in Washington, especially treaties and agreements that need congressional approval. For example, as many observers have noted, Assistant Secretary of State Christopher Hill was forced to conduct two negotiations at the same time in the Six-Party Talks over North Korea: one with the other five parties to the talks, and the other with his own administration. Testing the market and getting a sense of what the market can bear is an important part of the process of negotiation for the American side and frankly for the other side as well, especially in bilateral free trade agreements.

American negotiating style and behavior change according to the forums in which U.S. officials are working. Bilateral negotiations are conducted differently than negotiations with regional multilateral negotiations, which in turn are different from negotiations with multilateral institutions such as the United Nations. It also makes a difference whether America is negotiating with a friend or competitor, ally or adversary.

In negotiations with a friend or ally, the United States assumes shared strategic goals and considers the devil to be in the details. Agreements are meant in part to demonstrate the existence of a strong relationship with the negotiating partner, and thus achieving them has political value. For instance, the U.S.-Israel Free Trade Agreement (FTA) and the U.S.-Jordan Free Trade Agreement were seen to be largely political and strategic treaties designed to underscore existing bilateral relationships. When the United States negotiates with Singapore, it understands that both parties share strategic goals. To be sure, Singapore is a country that professes a free-market outlook, similar to the United States.

When negotiating with multilateral bodies, the U.S. approach varies not only relative to bilateral negotiations but also according to the character and stature of the body with which it is dealing. The United States regards the Association of Southeast Asian Nations (ASEAN), for instance, as an important regional grouping worthy of a distinct American approach, particularly if the negotiations are not about a treaty or over a legally binding document. The United Nations is an entirely different multilateral forum, one that features not only allies and friends but also countries whose interests are hostile to the United States. Therefore, U.S. negotiators adopt a separate approach to it.

This chapter discusses these different approaches. The following observations and analyses of these various U.S. negotiating styles are based on my experience as Singapore's permanent representative to the United Nations and Singapore's ambassador to the United States, my involvement in negotiations over both the U.S.–Singapore Free Trade Agreement and Strategic Framework Agreement, and my participation in facilitating Singapore's position on issues related to ASEAN and Asia-Pacific Economic Cooperation (APEC). I have also discussed some of these negotiations with Singapore's negotiating teams to gain further insight.

Bilateral Negotiations: The United States–Singapore Free Trade Agreement

Whether in multilateral or bilateral forums, the U.S. negotiating style is legalistic and totally professional. The U.S. bureaucrat masters his or her brief very well. The room for maneuver is very little. We realized this is because of the internal interagency negotiations. The United States takes a longer time than its counterparts to come to a position, but once it has adopted a position, there is little room for change. In effect, the consultations with the various other agencies lock U.S. negotiators into a position. That is why American negotiators keep repeating their position in negotiations until the other side accepts it. There is no room for ambiguity. The United States seeks clarity. (So does Singapore, though its negotiators are more likely to allow a little room for ambiguity.) Most countries are legalistic when core interests are at issue. The United States is legalistic on every issue that is binding.

These traits were on display during the negotiations for the United States–Singapore FTA, which were launched in 2000 under the Clinton administration and completed in 2003 under the Bush administration. I sat through some intellectual property (IP) negotiations and saw firsthand that the U.S. negotiators were very legalistic and could tolerate no ambiguity in language in the agreement. They wanted everything explicit. Although both the United States and Singapore are countries that understand openness and rule of law and transparency, there is a difference in approach over IP issues between the more economically developed country and the less economically developed country. The leader and innovator, the more-developed country seeks to gain access to markets and to protect its IP rights. The less-developed country seeks to protect local industry and consumers, and is less attuned to the concepts of rights and ownership of intellectual creation. Sudden additional costs to local industry and consumers are involved if new arrangements are introduced. Singapore wanted more room for negotiation over the agreement, arguing it might need time to ramp up to the higher standards. In the end, we found a compromise, but the discussions were tense and Singapore had to make the adjustment. It understood that the IP regime was at the heart of the American interest in the FTA. The United States realized that Singapore understood the requirements of a modern knowledge-based economy and would be the best partner to work out a template with because of mutual interests.

The dispute over chewing gum was well publicized during the FTA negotiations. Although it was not a serious issue for the United States, representing a question of market access, it was a serious issue for Singapore, falling into the realm of what a sovereign country could decide as a social rule. The Singapore government decided to ban the sale of chewing gum in Singapore following the discovery in 1991 that the country's newly introduced Mass Rapid Transit train system had broken down because a passenger had stuck chewing gum over an electronic eye that controlled sliding doors. Because chewing gum has never been an iconic sweet in Singapore as it is in the United States, there was very little public fuss within Singapore over the ban.

In negotiations personality matters, and this was clearly the case in the dispute over chewing gum. I dealt with deputy U.S. trade representative Jon Huntsman, Jr., and U.S. trade representative Robert Zoellick. Both were understanding of Singapore's sensitivities but prodded us along in friendship. In the end we settled on *modest* access, that is, access for sugarless gum for medicinal purposes. Neither side wanted this issue to be the deal breaker for the FTA. The Singapore side yielded a little on an issue that was seen as a social principle, and the United States got half a loaf—acceptance by Singapore of a market-access principle. In other words, the United States compromised, but only because Singapore also compromised and because U.S. negotiators recognized that it would be very hard to get Singapore to remove the ban completely.

What we did not expect was that the deal breaker could have been the issue of capital controls. We encountered a purist free-market approach from the U.S. Treasury Department, which insisted that no form of capital controls be included in the agreement. Since the Asian financial crisis, no government in Asia could afford to forgo the flexibility to deal with an exchange-rate crisis. Singapore wanted some tools in the toolbox allowed under the General Agreement on Trade in Services.

The free flow of capital was a central tenet of the Bush administration, particularly within Treasury. It was not only an ideological issue but also one that engaged U.S. commercial interests. The impasse was resolved when both sides stopped arguing whether capital controls were a legitimate macroeconomic policy and focused on the extent to which Singapore should be subject to claims for damages by affected investors.

On the whole the FTA negotiation experience for Singapore was a good one. Singapore and the United States entered the negotiations as friends and came out of the negotiations as friends. They are alike in that both of their economies are open and both share the same view of the international economic system. They were two friends negotiating a deal based on give and take. And in the case of the IP negotiations, Robert Zoellick did not let the perfect become the enemy of the good.

The Singapore negotiators learned a great deal about the U.S. political process during this exercise. They were impressed by how well business corporations used the system in lobbying for their interests and by how the U.S. administration negotiates for real market interests.

In the case of the negotiations over the FTA, the United States adopted a tough but businesslike approach. It was prepared to be flexible with Singapore if Singapore was also flexible. Both parties leaned forward. The United States saw Singapore as a template for future negotiations. It was tough on IP but did not push fully on chewing gum, because it was not a question of Singapore protecting a market. Both sides compromised on capital controls to avoid the collapse of negotiations.

Regional Forums: Negotiating with ASEAN

The United States has shown much greater patience and accommodation in negotiations with the regional group ASEAN than in the multilateral setting of the United Nations. ASEAN and the United States have had a long history of engagement and have worked together since World War II, including during the United States' military involvement in Southeast Asia in the 1960s and 1970s.

Originally a regional grouping of five noncommunist, free-market countries in Southeast Asia (Indonesia, Malaysia, the Philippines, Singapore, and Thailand), ASEAN was always viewed as a friend of the United States and the Western alliance during the Cold War and has since expanded to include all ten countries of the region. Some ASEAN members, such as Thailand and the Philippines, are American treaty allies, while Singapore is regarded as a close defense partner. Malaysia and Indonesia are moderate Muslim countries whose importance to the United States has been enhanced since 9/11. The addition to ASEAN of Vietnam, a communist country, has been considered a good thing, as the regime has been seen to be taking the road to economic openness and regional integration. Myanmar's entry into ASEAN has proved more controversial for U.S. engagement with the regional organization because of the nature and record of Myanmar's ruling regime.

No American administration has attempted to negotiate an ASEAN-wide agreement or treaty because of the diversity of its members: their political systems and their differing levels of economic development. A U.S.-ASEAN FTA has been talked of, but it remains something to be worked for in the distant future, if at all. In the second term of the George W. Bush administration, an ASEAN-U.S. Enhanced Partnership was negotiated, but this was more a statement of intent than an agreement. No legally binding agreement was possible as the United States would not sign an agreement with ASEAN member Myanmar. Although the Office of the United States Trade Representative (USTR) launched the U.S.-ASEAN Trade and Investment Framework Agreement (TIFA) process in 2005, it is a work in progress with no firm timeline. To avoid difficulties with Congress—including congressional opposition to signing an agreement with Myanmar—the U.S.-ASEAN TIFA was crafted as a memorandum of understanding (MOU) and not as a legally binding document. Even so, USTR came to work on three priority areas with ASEAN: the ASEAN Single Window (ASW), which potentially offered cost savings to ASEAN and U.S. businesses through compatible customs documentation and procedures; pharmaceutical policy harmonization; and sanitary and phytosanitary (SPS) policies to help ASEAN countries gain market access to the United States. Other areas listed for later discussion included best practices on intellectual property rights (IPR), best practices on investment and services liberalization, and a plurilateral agreement on multichip integrated circuits—all measures of strong concern to U.S. business interests.

The USTR was trying to help ASEAN achieve higher transparency and international standards, which in turn would have facilitated the movement of goods and stimulated U.S. businesses to enter ASEAN markets. It would also have spurred foreign direct investment and helped ASEAN exports gain entry into the U.S. market. ASEAN would have become a stronger and better investment and trade area. USTR officials were clear about what they wanted. They visited ASEAN countries many times to sell their point of view. Some countries considered the conditions to not be feasible. Because of the diversity of ASEAN, the regional grouping has not been able to react in a timely fashion to bring this negotiation to fruition. As a work in progress, the trade and investment framework reflects the reality of difficulties in U.S.-ASEAN negotiations.

Similarly, the Plan of Action to Implement the ASEAN-U.S. Enhanced Partnership was developed as a statement of intent rather than as an agreement or treaty. The document consists of an inclusive list of priorities that captures what ASEAN countries want in their cooperation with the United States and vice versa. The focus of cooperation includes political, security, and economic cooperation; health;

scholarships; communications; technology; transportation; energy; and environmental management. It gives priority to areas such as promotion of good governance and combating corruption, IPR protection, and collaboration between small- and medium-size ASEAN enterprises and U.S. companies. ASEAN countries clearly wanted scholarships, assistance in disaster management, and programs to improve their capacity to fight pandemics. Each side found something it wanted of the other. Since this was about assistance and cooperation to enhance development and the obligations were not treaty obligations, there was less need for traditional negotiation. Negotiations were more a question of enumerating the areas both sides wished to work on. Since there are ten member countries in ASEAN, both sides recognized that some areas of cooperation would be harder to implement than others.

These two initiatives were pursued by both sides as a way to underscore U.S. engagement with the region, at a time when China, India, Korea, and Japan were raising their regional diplomatic profiles. The competitiveness and contagious regional context may have facilitated the accommodation of diverse interests. The objectives and the products sought were realistic, because the United States understood what was achievable with ASEAN. U.S. representatives came to the region, listened to concerns, returned to their drafts, and attempted to accommodate diverse interests. As statements of aspirations and intent, the agreements allowed for looser negotiations than would occur over legally binding bilateral free trade agreements or treaties.

The United Nations

The United States probably finds the United Nations the hardest forum within which to negotiate. The countries that comprise the United Nations, especially the smaller countries, see the United States as tough and demanding. I think the United States has to behave so because it has many interests to accommodate at home and because there are many interests opposed to—if not hostile to—the U.S. standing in the world forum. In fact, the United States is frequently and sharply criticized there by member countries who would never dare take such whacks at the United States in a bilateral setting in Washington. Without the benefit of cover that the United Nations provides, they invariably speak in a more measured tone toward the United States in one-on-one forums.

It is at the United Nations that American negotiating behavior is most tested. The United States has a clear set of interests to defend, especially within the Security Council. These interests include issues related to the use of force, peacekeeping, and nuclear proliferation and policies related to Israel, Iran, and Iraq. UN matters also speak to many constituencies—nongovernmental organizations, Congress, media, think tanks, and the administration. As a result, the American negotiator must try to satisfy all these constituencies. This probably explains why the United

States takes documents seriously, demands clarity, and has little tolerance for ambiguity. The documents at the United Nations, especially in the Security Council, are legal documents; there is an obligation to implement them and financial contributions are involved, so great care is taken over every increase and every measure proposed. This care is especially valued by the United States because it is the largest financial contributor to the United Nations, paying 22 percent of the regular budget and much more to the peacekeeping budget. American diplomats at the United Nations have to make sure that they are not caught offside with Congress.

The United States does not put great store by the United Nations. As a superpower, it prefers to work bilaterally, allowing it to exert greater influence than in multilateral settings. Superpowers do not need multilateral institutions as much as small countries do. The careers of U.S. diplomats are made at bilateral postings and by covering bilateral matters, not at multilateral postings. The U.S. weakness in negotiating at the United Nations is seen in its inability to understand groupings, such as the Non-Aligned Movement and the Group of 77 (G-77), and how they operate. I know this because I have spoken to American diplomats. The United States does not know how to lobby. It often lobbies too late; it demarches at too junior a level to be effective in the national capitals; and it even demarches via e-mail! And, when it does lobby hard, it often does so in too visible a manner (e.g., lobbying for Guatemala over Venezuela during the UN Security Council election in 2006) or in a manner (demanding rather than requesting) that puts off the party being lobbied.

Some countries like the American style of negotiation, with U.S. diplomats making clear what their redlines are. Singapore sees the United States' style as upfront and direct, but Singapore is quite upfront and direct itself and knows its own redlines. Other countries are not as open or upfront; their position keeps shifting and the room for maneuver keeps narrowing. I am told that, following the arrival of John Bolton as the U.S. permanent representative to the United Nations in 2005, the room for negotiation with the United States was zero. (Bolton was seen as an ideologue and neoconservative.) During his tenure, what you were presented with in the opening offer *was* the redline. The minimalist position became the maximalist position. I understand that Bolton's successor, Ambassador Zalmay Khalilzad, was quite different. He let the other party feel there was some room to maneuver. I am told he went down well, conveying a sense that he was listening to the concerns of the other side. But in the end, there was often little difference in the substantive positions taken by the two diplomats.

Of course, personalities significantly affect the style and process of the negotiation. It matters whether the American representative or negotiator has a rough and tough personality riding roughshod over others, or whether he or she is a nice jovial person. Jeane Kirkpatrick was apparently not popular. She was seen as too tough. Vernon Walters, her successor, was funny, avuncular, nice, and the United Nations loved him. They also loved Tom Pickering, who mobilized the United Nations during the first Gulf War and sustained its support. Of course, the power of the United States is such that its point of view will usually carry the day at the United Nations—in the end. But it is a question of whether the countries like you and give in to you or whether they go along with you and resent you for it.

In his book *Surrender Is Not an Option*, Ambassador Bolton details how he negotiated at the United Nations,[1] illustrating the points I have been making about negotiating style. Ambassador Bolton arrived at the United Nations on August 1. He was clear he had a mission to fulfill and he immediately set out to negotiate changes to the Outcome Document that was to be presented at the World Summit scheduled for mid-September. This document would outline a new reform vision of the United Nations—from the U.S. perspective, a more efficient, better-managed, and more-prudential United Nations. The United States wanted to replace the existing Human Rights Commission. It was also against funding the Durban II Conference Against Racism out of the UN budget, even though the vast majority of member countries supported the conference.

The United States justified this position by stating that Durban II was anti-Semitic. Ambassador Bolton's demands came about a month before the document was to be finalized after an eight-month process. He presented more than three hundred amendments, all cleared with the interagency process in Washington; and he objected to the length of the document, which was about forty pages. He wanted it reduced to three-to-four pages. Bolton also objected to the process of using a facilitator, that is, a leader appointed to meet with a number of interested countries in informal settings or in a working group to work on sections of the document. This was a fairly well-established UN process to solicit views efficiently and to arrive at the "best approximation of a consensus." Instead, Bolton proposed a direct multilateral negotiation that eliminated the usual leaders, arguing this was a more genuine negotiation, and what he called "garbage language" entrenched in UN documents. The problem was that the language represented careful but imperfect compromises on difficult issues that the 193 members had achieved after a tedious process.

Naturally, coming in at the late hour to reopen discussion of the whole document, Bolton and his approach did not go down well with the rest of the United Nations. In the end the United States insisted on a three-to-four-page document for the heads of state. As the summit date approached and the multilateral negotiations continued, there was no agreement and whole sections had to be left out of the document.

Ambassador Bolton's push for UN budget reform is another illustration of a unilateral approach to negotiation. Amid burgeoning UN expenditures and corruption charges, in particular the oil-for-food scandal, Congress demanded serious

---

1. John R. Bolton, *Surrender Is Not an Option: Defending America at the United Nations and Abroad* (New York: Threshold Editions, 2007).

UN reforms or else the United States would cut back its assessed contributions. Congressman Henry Hyde's bill in 2005 threatened to cut the U.S. contribution by 50 percent if the United Nations did not fulfill thirty-two of thirty-nine conditions the bill had laid down.

Bolton sought to impose management reforms by focusing on the budget review. A budget cap on expenditures was already in place in December 2005, at Bolton's behest, but with the growing eruption of global crises and conflicts and new mandates, the developing countries saw the need to lift the budget cap at the end of June 2006. As decisions are generally made by consensus in the General Assembly's Fifth Committee, U.S. agreement was seen to be essential, especially since the United States is the United Nations' largest contributor. In this instance, the European Union tried to broker a compromise between the United States and G-77, but the United States rejected this. Bolton wanted to cut back the mandates, including "politically sensitive" mandates. In fact, he said that if he could, he would have renegotiated the entire UN program, evaluating each and every one of its activities and mandates. The G-77 wanted to lift the cap on the six-month budget without any conditions. Although the United States could mobilize support from Japan, the second largest contributor, and other JUSKCANZ countries (an acronym for Japan, the United States, Korea, Canada, and New Zealand), the G-77 had the numbers. In the end the United States, supported by the rest of JUSKCANZ and the European Union, voted against the lifting of the budget cap. The G-77, however, with its numerical majority, prevailed in the vote.

Although Ambassador Zalmay Khalilzad was considered to be easier to work with, UN members could not fail to notice that on the issues themselves, the actual negotiating positions did not differ from those under his predecessor. The 2007 62nd UN General Assembly's Fifth Committee adopted the regular budget by a vote of 141–1, which was then followed by a vote of 142–1 at the plenary meeting. The negotiations were tough but performed with a sense of purpose and cooperation. In the end, the United States could not accept the inclusion of funding for Durban II. This was basically a difference between the United States and the G-77. This Fifth Committee vote was significant because it was the first to be taken since 1988 and the second to be taken since the first UN General Assembly in 1946. The budget is usually adopted by consensus. Ambassador Khalilzad later told journalists that the U.S. vote was driven less by budgetary considerations than by concerns that Durban II would be anti-Semitic.

Conclusion

The United States comes to the negotiating table with clear positions and objectives that have been internally settled with different agencies within the administration. It is not inclined to change its positions, because to do so would mean unraveling the internal deal. This gives the impression to its negotiating partners that the United States is inflexible and tough. But, as I have noted, the United States deals differently when it negotiates with an ally versus an adversary, or in a friendly multilateral forum versus a hostile one.

Even when dealing with a friend, U.S. negotiators show flexibility only after stonewalling in the hope of forcing the other side to give in. The United States plays a tough game, but in the end will compromise if the result has strategic advantages, as demonstrated in the conclusion of the United States–Singapore FTA. The Six-Party Talks with North Korea, to take an example not covered in this chapter, showed a much more flexible United States, one willing to compromise to bring about a successful outcome, which the George W. Bush administration greatly desired. Assistant Secretary of State Christopher Hill worked creatively to find compromises that were acceptable and that could be sustained. He also managed to gain the confidence of the North Koreans, the Chinese, the South Koreans, and the White House.

The question Americans need to reflect on is whether the negotiating style with which they have come to be identified can or should be changed, so that they can better achieve their objectives and at the same time win greater influence and strengthen relations with countries globally. I, for one, believe that the American approach can and should change. It is a question of style. After all, personalities matter in diplomacy and negotiations. Where the United States has been successful, it has shown a little less of the unilateralist approach and a little more readiness to engage in multilateral consultations and to compromise.

In his first year in office, President Barack Obama has articulated a new approach and tone for America's engagement with the world. Rejecting unilateralism, he has emphasized the need for dialogue—to talk even with "rogue states," to consult with others, and to work with multilateral forums because, as he told the UN General Assembly in September 2009, "it is my deeply held belief that in the year 2009—more than at any point in human history—the interests of nations and peoples are shared."[2] Under the Obama administration, the United States has reengaged with the United Nations, paid its bills, and joined the Human Rights Council. This is a good start. But only time will tell if this means that America's negotiating style will become more nuanced than before or perhaps change yet more dramatically.

---

2. "Remarks by the President to the United Nations General Assembly," Office of the Press Secretary, White House, September 23, 2009, http://www.whitehouse.gov/the_press_office/Remarks-by-the-President-to-the-United-Nations-General-Assembly.

8

Negotiating Trade: A Bitter Experience for Japanese Negotiators

Koji Watanabe

ike Mansfield, who served as the U.S. ambassador to Japan from 1977 until 1988, would often remark that "the Japanese-American relationship is the most important bilateral relationship in the world, bar none."[1] Many people, especially in Japan, agreed with him. The relationship involved significant economic interdependence and a close security alliance between the world's two largest economies. Japan was the United States' largest trade partner except for Canada, while the United States was Japan's largest trade partner, bar none. Further, the two countries' security relationship constituted an enduring and steadfast linchpin of peace and security in East Asia.

Despite this close security and economic relationship, severe trade friction developed between the two economic giants in the late 1980s and early 1990s. It became so serious that many Americans began to perceive Japan's economic power as "a greater threat to our future than the Soviet Union's military might."[2] The cause of the friction was no mystery: a major trade imbalance between the two countries.

Background to the Trade Dispute

A chronology of Japan-U.S. economic negotiations since 1970 indicates the kinds of subjects that have occupied negotiators over the past four decades (see box). The chronology also reveals the fluctuating intensity of negotiations, which gathered momentum in the 1970s and reached a crescendo in the second half of the 1980s

---

1. Ambassador Mansfield started using this description in the early 1980s. See Mike Mansfield, *My Recollections* (Tokyo: Nihon Keizai Shimbun, 1999), 89.

2. "Rethinking Japan," *BusinessWeek,* August 7, 1989, 51.

Chronology of Japan-U.S. Economic Negotiations, 1970–2007

1970–72   Textiles—export control

1972–74   Steel—voluntary export restraint (VER)

1973–79   General Agreement on Tariffs and Trade (GATT) Tokyo Round

1977   Color televisions—orderly marketing arrangement (VER)

1978   Beef and oranges—agreement to liberalize/expand Japanese imports

1980–99   Telecommunications—Nippon Telegraph and Telephone procurement arrangement

1981–84   Automobiles—VER

1985–86   Electronics, medical equipment, pharmaceuticals, telecommunications, forest products, transport equipment—Market Oriented Sector Selective (MOSS) discussions

1985   Plaza Agreement

1986   Semiconductor agreement

1987–93   Machine tools—VER

1988   Beef and oranges—final agreement, import quotas abolished

1989   Cellular telephones—Cellular Telephone Agreement

1989   Structural Impediments Initiative (SII) begins—wide-ranging discussions on issues such as pricing mechanisms, exclusionary business practices, government regulation, export promotion, saving-investment patterns

1989   Construction market, telecommunications, artificial satellites, supercomputers, wood products—all the subjects of the Office of the United States Trade Representative (USTR) appeals

1990   SII final report

1991   Semiconductors—negotiations for new agreement

1993   Intellectual property rights, government procurement, insurance, flat glass, financial services, automobiles and parts—Miyazawa and Clinton agree to initiate Comprehensive (Framework) Consultation

1996   GATT Uruguay Round concludes; World Trade Organization established

1997   Semiconductors—agreement reached

1998   Enhanced Initiative on Deregulation and Competition Policy starts

2001   Japan-U.S. Economic Partnership for Growth launched

2002–7   Regulatory Reform and Competition Policy Initiative

and the early 1990s. As Japan's proportion of the U.S. trade deficit rose, so did U.S. pressure for trade negotiations.[3] When the American economy began to enter a recession in the early 1980s, that pressure became acute.

In the 1970s, Japan's manufacturing industry became increasingly competitive, and Japanese exports to the U.S. market surged. This prompted mounting pressure from the U.S. Congress for import restrictions on Japanese products. Thus started negotiations on what the American side liked to call "voluntary" restraints on Japanese exports to the United States. Intensive negotiation led to restraints first on textiles and then on steel exports, which were followed by an "orderly marketing arrangement" for the export of color televisions into the U.S. market.

Toward the end of the 1970s, in response to a widening trade imbalance between the two countries, U.S. pressure grew for Japan to negotiate to open its agricultural market and especially to liberalize its markets for beef and oranges. This was a new and shocking development for the Japanese, because Japan was the largest importer of U.S. agricultural products, and the U.S. Department of Agriculture had always supported Japanese interests.

The next subject for negotiation became voluntary restraints on Japanese automobile exports. Negotiations started in 1981 and lasted for four years, during which Japanese car manufacturers had to restrain their exports to the U.S. market, leading eventually to the shifting of a substantial portion of their manufacturing plants to locations within the United States.

After a sharp fall at the outset of the 1980s, Japan's share of the U.S. trade deficit steadily increased throughout the decade, reaching almost 45 percent in 1989, and then, after a modest one-year decline, rocketing up to more than 66 percent in 1991. From the mid-1980s onward, the U.S. attitude toward trade negotiation with Japan became highly politicized, reflecting a deep sense of malaise in the U.S. establishment about the future of the U.S. economy and a U.S. perception that Japan was a major threat to the U.S. economy.

Despite the Plaza Agreement of 1985, which saw the U.S. dollar depreciated substantially in relation to the Japanese yen, the U.S. trade balance did not improve. For the first time in more than seventy years, the United States became a net debtor nation, while Japan became the largest creditor nation. Americans began to denounce the Japanese economic system as a fundamentally closed one and complained that the U.S. system was wide open to foreign imports.

---

3. Japan's share of the U.S. trade deficit grew from 50.4 percent in 1980 to 70.8 percent in 1981, dropped temporarily—to a low of 31.4 percent in 1984—but then rose steadily to 66.4 percent in 1991 and did not fall below 30 percent until 1996. See Department of Commerce, "Japan's Share in the U.S. Trade Deficit," in Ministry of Foreign Affairs, "Japan-U.S. Economic Relationship," http://www.mofa.go.jp/region/n-america/us/economy/relation.pdf.

In 1985, the MOSS (Market Oriented Sector Selective) negotiation began, aimed at liberalizing the Japanese markets for electronics, medical equipment, pharmaceuticals, telecommunications, forest products, and transportation equipment. Semiconductors and cellular telephones were also taken up.

In 1989–90, the Structural Impediment Initiative (SII) started. The SII's underlying assumption was that the trade imbalance reflected structural impediments on *both* sides. The SII thus involved two-way negotiation: the U.S. side raised such issues as Japan's savings-investment pattern, pricing mechanisms, exclusionary business practices, and *keiretsu* (business groupings); and the Japanese side raised topics such as the United States' savings-investment pattern, corporate behavior, export promotion, labor training, and research and development.

In 1993, newly elected U.S. president Bill Clinton agreed with Japanese prime minister Kiichi Miyazawa to establish the Japan–United States Framework for New Economic Partnership, which pledged the two nations to negotiate how to reduce the trade imbalance and promote cooperation in areas such as intellectual property rights, insurance, flat glass, and automobiles and auto parts. The major feature of the agreement was a compromise establishing "objective criteria for policy efforts," a formulation that was adopted after the Japanese rejected an American insistence on obtaining concrete results and introducing numerical targets as managed trade.

As it turned out, however, by the middle of 1990s the intensity of trade negotiations started diminishing, reflecting in large measure structural changes in Japan-U.S. economic relations, with the stagnant Japanese economy ceasing to be perceived as a threat to the rejuvenating U.S. economy.

Lessons Learned from the Trade Negotiations

The experience of trade negotiation with the United States in these years was painful and frustrating and left a bitter aftertaste. It taught Japanese negotiators five lessons about how their American counterparts conduct negotiations.

Lesson 1: Trade negotiations are different—no give and take

American officials employ a distinctly different approach when negotiating over trade and economic issues than when negotiating over security affairs. More often than not, Americans see trade and economic negotiations as a zero-sum game in which one side gains and the other loses, whereas in security affairs, the United States deals with Japan as an ally, as a partner whose interests converge with the Americans. In trade negotiations, Americans extract concessions from the Japanese side by threatening import restrictions and offer no quid pro quo.

Lesson 2: The superpower is self-centered

Even in trade negotiations, the United States exudes a strong sense of pride and power as *the* superpower. Exhibiting high-handedness, self-centeredness, and impatience, American negotiators cite their own domestic constraints while ignoring the domestic difficulties of their negotiating counterparts. U.S. officials often refer repeatedly to congressional pressure for import restrictions or antidumping measures, citing various pieces of new trade legislation. At the same time, Americans seem to be almost indifferent to established multilateral norms such as those embodied in the General Agreement on Tariffs and Trade (GATT), as if unapologetically taking the approach that "we are the only superpower, so we can break the rules if we want to." This unilateralist aspect has markedly diminished since 1995, when the World Trade Organization (WTO) instituted a dispute settlement mechanism.

Lesson 3: Congressional interest makes negotiators more aggressive

Because the genesis of a trade negotiation is more often than not to be found in Congress, trade negotiations invariably become politicized, making it difficult to achieve businesslike solutions. This politicization was most pronounced in the 1980s, when congressional pressure to use Section 301 of the 1974 Trade Act against Japan (which allows the United States to impose sanctions against countries whose practices or policies in some way burden or restrict U.S. commerce) intensified drastically; with the U.S. economy slumping and the trade imbalance with Japan rising, the United States went on the trade offensive. As the chronology shows, the period featured tough Section 301–inspired negotiations over construction markets, telecommunications, artificial satellites, supercomputers, wood products, and so forth. More often than not, U.S. negotiators were high-handed and aggressive, making one demand after another and forcing Japan to reluctantly agree to a series of concessions, some of which had adverse and enduring effects on Japan's economy. For example, faced with the threat posed by Section 301, Japan had to agree to liberalize its commercial artificial satellite market—a move that has impaired the competitiveness of the artificial satellite industry in Japan over the long term.

In the SII in which I was personally involved, Japan resisted congressional efforts to have Japan designated as a Section 301 country, but Japan did agree to discuss structural and systemic issues, such as increasing Japan's level of public investment and encouraging the Japanese public to save less and spend more. SII was an unprecedented exercise in the sense that it was a two-way negotiation and involved, by design, each party meddling in the other party's domestic affairs, with

America condemning Japan's kitchen, so to speak, for being too small and Japan criticizing America's dining room for being too big.

Congress was deeply interested in the progress of SII, not least because major U.S. corporations were interested, and congressional pressure forced U.S. negotiators to make some demands that raised the eyebrows of their Japanese counterparts. For instance, one of the major issues raised by the American side concerned Japanese distribution systems and a Japanese law that restricted the establishment of large-scale stores (department stores, supermarkets, and so forth) so as to protect small- and medium-size shops in Japan. Opinion within Japan was already divided on whether to modify the law, and the American pressure helped Japan's Ministry of Economy and Trade decide to opt for revision. However, it subsequently emerged that U.S.-based Toys "R" Us had directly asked the Office of the United States Trade Representative (USTR) and Congress to help it open shops in Japan. Today, Japan has no fewer than twenty-five Toys "R" Us stores.

Lesson 4: Different agencies negotiate differently

The State Department used to play a leading role in trade negotiations with Japan, but since the 1980s the USTR has played the dominant role. This changing of the guard has had a significant impact on the tenor and content of negotiations because USTR negotiators are not diplomats and are closely watched by Congress, which makes them more aggressive toward their counterparts, more dismissive of Japan's concerns, and less inclined to compromise. The State Department and the Treasury are generally more moderate in their approach, more prepared to focus on the larger bilateral relationship, and less willing to endanger that relationship by pushing hard on a single issue. They are naturally less interested than the USTR in Section 301: indeed, they were helpful in organizing SII so that it functioned independently of Section 301.

Lesson 5: Personalities affect negotiations

Japan-U.S. negotiations on security affairs in the mid-1990s owed a great deal to the insight, tact, and leadership of individuals such as William Perry and Joseph Nye, who made remarkable contributions toward consolidating the Japan-U.S. alliance in the aftermath of the tragic incident of a U.S. serviceman raping a Japanese woman in Okinawa. The cooperative and friendly manner in which security negotiations have generally been conducted stands in marked contrast to the confrontational and ill-tempered manner in which U.S. negotiators have approached trade negotiations. As noted above, U.S. trade negotiators are not diplomats. In the 1990s, most were lawyers, and lawyers are said by training not to have a clear negotiating target; rather, they focus on process and on formulating arguments to support possible outcomes—a trait that in the case of trade negotiations with Japan translated into a tendency to keep moving the target further and further away as the negotiation proceeded.

American negotiators do not have to be charming and courteous to win the appreciation of their Japanese counterparts, but they do have to be clear-sighted and establish a clear conception of the point at which they will be prepared to settle. For example, there was one American trade negotiator who had a reputation as a bully and wore a baseball hat in the negotiating room. Few Japanese liked him—at least not to begin with. However, in the end, he proved to be a very effective negotiator, one who managed to keep the negotiations on a clear course from the early stages onward so as to be prepared to settle the negotiation as soon as the Americans had attained their objectives. I remember that he had a habit of abruptly stopping discussions so that the U.S. side could caucus among themselves before proceeding further, thereby ensuring that he could always represent the consensus of the U.S. negotiating team.

In connection with the personality issue, it is commonly recognized that U.S.-Japan relations have been blessed by the presence of highly respected American ambassadors such as Mike Mansfield, Walter Mondale, Howard Baker, and Tom Foley, all of whom were powerful political figures able to talk directly with the U.S. president or secretary of state by just picking up a phone. In the case of trade negotiations, special mention should be made of Ambassador Mansfield, who worked tirelessly during the late 1970s and most of the 1980s to persuade both Japanese and Americans to settle various trade issues amicably.

A Lesson Learned from Security Negotiations

At the same time that Japanese diplomats were learning these five uncomfortable lessons about U.S. negotiating behavior during trade negotiations, they also were taught a sixth—and equally painful—lesson in a negotiation over security. Specifically, while Americans are almost always direct in stating their interests and demands, they become yet more forthright when budgetary and other financial issues are on the table. Americans are, indeed, remarkably blunt about presenting the bill.

Perhaps the best-known but also most painful example of this trait in relation to Japan occurred during the first Gulf War of 1990–91. When Saddam Hussein invaded Kuwait in 1990, Japan wished to make a material contribution to the U.S.-led coalition forces by providing, as requested by Washington, air and sea transportation, medical teams and facilities, and other assistance. But as it turned out, Japan was not able to deliver its contribution because neither the government nor the public was prepared to participate in such an international military endeavor. As for air and sea transportation, the use of military resources was considered out of the question for constitutional reasons, and a request for civilian air and sea transportation by the government was rejected by firms and labor unions simply because of the lack of precedents and fear of involvement in the war.

I was personally involved in that failed operation, which constituted the most frustrating experience in my foreign service career. Then our frustration was compounded by an abrupt demand from the U.S. Treasury for $9 billion in cash to compensate for Japan's failure to contribute to the Desert Storm operation. Japan agreed to pay and funded that sum by raising taxes. To make matters even worse, when the Kuwaiti government put a one-page advertisement in the *New York Times* thanking all the countries that had helped to liberate the country, Japan's name was conspicuously absent.

That was a real trauma, and it taught us a very bitter lesson about the need to be prepared for a similar situation in the future. When 9/11 occurred and the United States decided to launch a military operation in Afghanistan, Japan immediately decided to send naval vessels to the Indian Ocean to supply fuel and fresh water to U.S. ships and other coalition vessels. Moreover, when the United States decided to invade Iraq in 2003, Japan dispatched its Self-Defense Forces contingents to Iraq for logistic and humanitarian purposes.

The United States' blunt presentation of a huge military-related bill to Japan recently recurred, suggesting a pattern. Japan and the United States agreed to move a substantial portion of Marines from Okinawa to Guam. Out of the blue, Japan was reportedly presented by the United States with a bill for $25 billion to cover the cost of relocating the military base. I have asked my colleagues: "Has there been any other instance in which the cost of removing U.S. bases was paid by another country?" The answer I have received is short and simple: "None." Japan has agreed to pay $6 billion.

Toward a New Era: From Trade Friction to Cooperation

The experience of negotiating over trade during the late 1980s and early 1990s has left an unwelcome memory among Japanese diplomats and bureaucrats. Fortunately, however, the bitterness that stemmed from negotiations on subjects such as the FSX fighter aircraft and semiconductors has since given way to a much more cooperative and harmonious relationship. Four factors explain this change.

First, Japan's share in the U.S. trade deficit has declined and now accounts for little more than 10 percent. As it has declined, China's share has increased, standing at almost 30 percent in 2006. As with Japan in the 1980s and 1990s, the United States has started to raise with China the issue of their trade imbalance.

Second, Japan and the United States are becoming more economically interdependent. Mutual investment has been encouraged, as in the case of the automobile industry. Many firms are also engaging in joint development of new products; for instance, 30 percent of the body (notably the carbon fiber components) of Boeing's new 787 Dreamliner is being produced in Japan.

Third, the dispute settlement mechanism established in 1995 by the WTO has successfully drained the vehemence from most trade disputes. Had the dispute settlement mechanism existed in the 1980s, probably half of the issues related to Section 301 could have been tabled to the GATT, and Japan probably would have won at least half of the cases.

The fourth and probably most important factor is that the Japanese economy is no longer considered a threat. In the 1980s, the U.S. economy was in a slump while the Japanese economy was thriving. To add insult to American injury, Japan sometimes behaved insensitively during those years, as when a Japanese firm purchased Rockefeller Center in New York. That period is over. While Japan experienced stagnation in the 1990s (what is now called the "lost decade" in Japan), the United States managed to transform its economy, centering it on information technology and a very strong competitive service sector.

* * *

Two final points deserve to be noted. First, while U.S. negotiating behavior on trade issues has fairly been criticized for being high-handed and self-centered, that behavioral pattern may have been occasioned by the Japanese way of negotiation and the decision-making process within Japan's bureaucracy. Japanese negotiating teams are composed of members from a variety of different government agencies, and teams operate on the basis of strict consensus. Achieving consensus on a negotiating position is a time-consuming and arduous process. In addition, the Japanese bureaucracy tends to look askance at teams that reach agreement quickly, taking a quick settlement as evidence that Japan's negotiators have not fought hard enough or long enough and have instead accepted a suboptimal agreement. Such a negotiating style may well have provoked impatience and annoyance among Americans, who characteristically prefer to see negotiations progress rapidly.

Second, while Japanese negotiators did not welcome American pressure and impatience, both certainly had the effect of prompting reform and liberalization of the Japanese economy. That positive process would probably have taken longer to occur in the absence of *gaiatsu* (foreign pressure) from the American side. This realization has helped to dispel some of the bitterness created by the painful negotiations in the 1980s and 1990s.

9

Negotiating Security: The Pushy Superpower

Faruk Logoglu

U ntil the attacks of September 11, 2001, the overall objectives of American foreign policy had been to protect and preserve national security by warding off potential threats abroad and to make the world more amenable to American interests. American involvement overseas aimed mostly to help resolve regional conflicts, enhance U.S. economic interests, and promote democracy and human rights. Homeland security was of little concern. Instead, U.S. policymakers focused on disputes in such places as the Middle East, the Caucasus, and the Balkans. Access to secure and inexpensive oil and gas resources was a top priority.

The style of American foreign policy before 9/11 put less emphasis on the use of force and more on diplomacy and multilateral efforts. Euro-Atlantic solidarity was sound and provided a basis for transatlantic cooperation. The Russian Federation was largely hapless; although China and India were visible on the horizon, they were not yet viewed as serious contenders for global influence. In other words, the United States was enjoying its status as an unrivaled superpower, feeling safe at home and exercising leadership around the globe. In the unipolar world, life was good for America.

While generally imperial in essence, American negotiating style in the pre-9/11 period was not necessarily overbearing or pushy. The United States knew it could afford to be generous, flexible, patient, and accommodating. Many of the abrasive features of American behavior did not have to rise to the fore.

This all came to an abrupt and violent end on September 11. That day, America forever lost its insular innocence. Permanently scarred, feeling vulnerable and less safe, America was never again to be the same. National security, which had always been a paramount preoccupation for Americans, mainly because of perceived threats emanating from instability or aggression in other countries, metamorphosed into a domestic question of life or death. The change in perspective reordered the nation's priorities, leading to the establishment of the Department of Homeland Security, a first in the country's history, and the restructuring of the various national intelligence agencies.

In this chapter, drawing on my firsthand experiences with American diplomats and officials, I intend to delineate the American approach to national security in the post-9/11 setting and to highlight how the events of that day affected specific patterns of behavior on the part of American negotiators.

The New World after 9/11

The characteristics generally attributed to American officials and diplomats include impatience, arrogance, attentiveness, insularity, legalism, naïveté, friendliness, flexibility, risk taking, pragmatism, preparedness, and cooperativeness.[1] Over the years, I have found that these various and sometimes conflicting attributes indeed characterized American diplomatic behavior. Americans were generally well prepared for their meetings. They had clear goals and objectives and their "talking points" were concise and targeted. As long as negotiations stayed smooth and remained within the margins of the agreed interagency positions, American officials performed with skill and efficacy. American diplomats are friendly, informal, and straightforward. They are very time conscious, results oriented, and businesslike and pay little attention to extracurricular activities or the cultural traits of their interlocutors. A prime strength of American diplomacy is the use of the English language. The language used is invariably clear, precise, and functional. There is, however, a pronounced legalism about their demeanor, usually accompanied by a marked preference for American notions and concepts of the law.

By all accounts, 9/11 affected deeply the style and orientation of the George W. Bush administration and the American way of handling issues, particularly security questions. National security became the main driver of American diplomacy. President Bush introduced his 2002 National Security Strategy by observing that the United States had entered a new world where "the only path to peace and security" was "the path of action."[2] The 2006 National Security Strategy started with the chilling announcement that "America is at war." The president identified the

---

1. John W. McDonald, "An American View of the U.S. Negotiating Style," *American Diplomacy*, March 2001, http://www.unc.edu/depts/diplomat/archives_roll/2001_03-06/mcdonald_negot/mcdonald_negot.html. For a very concise description of American negotiating behavior, see Nigel Quinney, *U.S. Negotiating Behavior*, Special Report no. 94 (Washington, D.C.: United States Institute of Peace Press, 2000).

2. *The National Security Strategy of the United States of America* (Washington, D.C.: White House, 2002), introduction and p. 31.

protection of the security of the American people as his "most solemn obligation."[3] Today, America is still a nation at war, in Afghanistan and Iraq. Even with the change in administration and the accompanying change of rhetoric, the psychology generated by this backdrop of war doubtlessly continues to affect the American negotiating style in more ways than one.

September 11 reinforced U.S. exceptionalism and relegated the art of statecraft to the backbenches of American diplomacy. The temptation of the United States to use its superpower status and the proclivity of the country to act unilaterally became stronger. The American people felt violated by 9/11 and the Bush administration began to feel that the end justified the means in responding to the challenge of terrorism.

This altered mood became most evident as the Bush administration made up its mind to invade Saddam Hussein's Iraq. In the various phases leading up to the start of the war in Iraq in March 2003, the United States did try to marshal support from its allies in Europe and elsewhere as well as at the United Nations. The effort was probably in earnest because even the neoconservative thinkers who spearheaded the decision to go to war in Iraq recognized the value of garnering international support and legitimacy. American officials tried to persuade their European colleagues, but they got cold shoulders from the two leading continental powers, Germany and France. Washington also engaged in diligent diplomacy at the United Nations to develop a broad coalition against Saddam, but this effort, too, failed to produce the level of support that the United States was seeking. It would not be fair to accuse the Bush administration of planning to go it alone from the outset, or to say that Americans were only playacting with the international community. Had the major European countries been more responsive to Washington's overtures and the UN Security Council been more amenable to swiftly passing the appropriate resolutions, the story of Iraq's occupation might conceivably have been quite different—and for the better.

One lesson to draw from this early U.S.-Europe-UN episode regarding Iraq is that when the United States fails to get what it wants through standard diplomacy, the behavior of American leaders and diplomats tends to become more "Americanized," with cultural characteristics weighing in more heavily. In the eyes of their interlocutors, the "nice guy" begins to turn into an "ugly American." Of course, in all cultures, when things go nicely, better qualities come to the fore. The reverse is also probably true. In the case of American negotiators, the initial degree of cordiality and warmth depends also on how much they covet the desired outcome. This behavior reflects a childlike naïveté on the part of Americans: one behaves in good humor when expectations of the desired outcome are still high, but one becomes

---

3. *The National Security Strategy of the United States of America* (Washington, D.C.: White House, 2006), introduction.

increasingly upset when what one wants seems to be slipping out of reach. As the stakes become more important, such cultural traits are more likely to come into play. In the post-9/11 setting, national security has become the number one priority for America. This heightened sensitivity, in turn, has warped American negotiating behavior, making negotiations susceptible to bouts of temper and loss of patience.

A striking illustration of what happens when things go the right way for American diplomacy was the lightning decision by Turkish president Turgut Ozal to join the war against Saddam in 1991 and to shut down the oil pipeline that ran into Turkey from Iraq. These actions probably preceded any actual demands by the United States and presumably aimed to win a stake for Turkey in the post-Saddam Iraq. Certainly, this gesture endeared the Turkish president to President George H. W. Bush, so much so and so fast that they became and remained close friends until Ozal's passing.

The Turkish Experience

My tour as Turkey's ambassador to Washington started just two weeks after 9/11 and finished at the end of 2005. The period was a particularly challenging one in Turkish-American relations. The U.S. "war on terror" and the issue of Iraq dominated America's agenda. Toward the end of 2001, it was already becoming clear that the United States intended to attack Iraq to remove Saddam Hussein from power. As a U.S. ally, partner, and friend that shared a long land border with Iraq, Turkey was a prospective prime player for any eventual operation against Iraq.

These circumstances set up a period of excruciating negotiations between Turkey and the United States, a process that started slowly at the beginning of 2002, steadily accelerated, and peaked in the first weeks of March 2003. While the weight of technical negotiations was in Ankara, the high-level political encounters were taking place mostly in Washington, allowing me to observe American officials' handling of the Iraq problem, the strengths and weaknesses of their approach, and the impingement of culture upon the whole process.

As a global superpower, the United States sets its interests, priorities, and timelines differently than does a regional player such as Turkey. The difference in scale and perspective may largely explain why the two sides at times find it hard to reach agreement, even when they share similar views. Once the United States determines its policy requirements on a given issue, it pursues those goals relentlessly.

The security relationship between Turkey and the United States dates back to the end of World War II, when the Soviet Union, after refusing to renew the 1923 Friendship Treaty with Turkey, began to make demands regarding Turkey's straits. With the onset of the Cold War, the Americans, given the strategic importance of Turkey and the straits and in line with the containment strategy of the Truman Doctrine, came to support the Turks and made Turkey a beneficiary of the

Marshall Plan. Turkey joined NATO in 1952, in large part as a reward for having sent troops to Korea in the fight against communism. The circumstances of the Cold War helped forge enduring security bonds between the United States and Turkey, with Turkey acting as the crucial eastern outpost of the Atlantic Alliance. The defense/security bond steadily developed into a complex web of relations, with Turkey receiving considerable military assistance from the United States.

However, the relationship was hardly free of troubles and tests. The first test occurred with the Cuban Missile Crisis in 1962, when the United States secretly agreed to withdraw its missiles from Turkey in return for the Soviet withdrawal of its missiles from Cuba. There was no prior consultation with the Turks. Even though the removal of the Jupiter missiles did not endanger Turkey's security, the incident left Turks with a lasting impression that the United States could not be wholly trusted. The second test came in 1964, with President Lyndon Johnson's letter telling the Turkish prime minister that if Turkey invaded Cyprus, NATO allies might not come to its defense if the USSR attacked Turkey. The language of the letter was harsh. The Turks were hurt, never forgot the incident, and concluded that they should take a broader view of their security needs that went beyond the United States and even NATO. The third test was the U.S. arms embargo (1975–78) that followed Turkey's intervention in Cyprus in 1974 to rescue and protect the minority Turkish Cypriots against ethnic cleansing by the majority Greek Cypriots. The Turks learned from the embargo that lobbies (in this case, the Greek lobby, supported by the Armenians) could distort U.S. policy choices. More recent causes of strain arose in the context of the 1990–91 Gulf crisis and before the invasion of Iraq by the United States in 2003. In both cases, Turkey invoked help from NATO against possible retaliatory attacks from Iraq. The NATO response was lukewarm and slow. The Turks put part of the blame on Americans for failing to push European allies harder on the issue.

With its secular democracy, strong army, and Western orientation, Turkey is a vital ally and key partner for the United States in many areas. Today, Turkey and the United States have converging security interests in the Middle East, Iraq, Iran, Afghanistan, the Caucasus, the Balkans, and Central Asia and also in energy matters. However, this backdrop of negative memories—of what the Turks see as instances of American betrayal, lack of resolve, infidelity to solemn commitments, and abandonment—makes the Turkish-American security relationship fragile and sensitive, despite its continuing importance to both sides.

The invasion of Iraq provides a striking example of the rift that can result from the difference in the politics of scale for Turkey and the United States. The Bush administration, once it made up its mind to topple Saddam's regime, began to court Turkey's support. In the initial stages, the American approach was measured and mindful of Turkish views and needs. But as the date—known to the Americans but not to the Turks—of the planned invasion approached, the Americans became increasingly strident. They at first used the elements of soft power to cajole Turkey. Although it is the practice to open the White House only to heads of state or government, President Bush made an exception for Tayyip Erdogan in December 2002, inviting him to the White House even though he was only the chairman of a political party. (Erdogan's party had just won the elections in Turkey, but he was not yet heading the Turkish government—that was to come a few months later.) To keep up White House tradition, however, Bush received Erdogan in the Roosevelt Room, not the Oval Office.

The Distinctive Patterns of American Diplomacy

Several interesting patterns of behavior that emerged during this prewar period are worth noting, because they shed light on the workings of American diplomacy. One was the deep divide and disconnect between the State and Defense Departments in the months leading to the invasion of Iraq. Ordinarily, a foreign ambassador spends most of his or her time at the State Department. But this was not the case for me. From the beginning of 2002 until the first months of 2003, most of the conversations on Iraq between the Turkish embassy and the administration took place at the Pentagon, where I was frequently summoned. The State Department was largely out of the picture. It was as if Foggy Bottom had disowned the Iraq issue and was resigned to the Pentagon running the show. Given the oddness of the situation, I made a point of regularly informing the State Department of our conversations at the Pentagon.

The curious interdepartmental disconnect meant that the administration was handling the issue at reduced capacity, without the full benefit of the knowledge and experience of the State Department. Many of the mistakes made by the United States in Iraq are probably attributable to the fact that the Pentagon was not equipped to run a country in a postinvasion setting. One negative windfall was that during this critical period, there were no high-level American visits to Turkey to solicit its support. The State Department kept out of the fray and Defense Secretary Donald Rumsfeld stayed in Washington. Had Secretary of State Colin Powell, given his stature and the respect he commanded in Turkey, visited Ankara to win over the Turkish leadership, the outcome of the vote in the Turkish Parliament on whether to permit American troops to cross into Iraq from Turkey might have been different.

Another distinctive pattern of behavior was the effort to overwhelm the Turkish side with a staged show of political power and a level of diplomatic representation significantly higher than the accustomed practice. In addition to President Bush's unusual reception of Erdogan at the White House, Undersecretary of the Foreign Ministry Ugur Ziyal met with not only his counterparts in the State and Defense Departments but also with Defense Secretary Rumsfeld and Vice President Dick

Cheney during his visit to Washington in August 2002. Similarly, when I was invited for a meeting with then Deputy National Security Adviser Stephen Hadley, I was surprised to see present in his office all the deputy secretaries of the major departments involved with the issue of Iraq. Most ambassadors in Washington hardly ever get to meet American officials of such rank and certainly never a select group of them in a single meeting. On February 1, 2003, I was invited to the Pentagon for what I thought to be a meeting with Deputy Defense Secretary Paul Wolfowitz, but I found Secretary Rumsfeld himself sitting at the other end of the table from me. The coup de grâce of this effort was dealt on February 14, 2003, when President Bush received at the Oval Office the visiting Turkish minister of foreign affairs and state minister for the economy (Yasar Yakis and Ali Babacan, respectively) and personally engaged in "negotiations" with them. American presidents do not meet with appointed officials unless there is a very special reason for them to do so.

These various demonstrations of high-powered diplomacy pointed to the keen, irrepressible desire of the Bush administration to obtain Turkey's support in connection with the imminent invasion of Iraq. But the net effect of this behavior was probably negative. It led the Turkish side to mistakenly believe that Turkish backing was indispensable for the United States and that the United States would not and could not undertake the proposed military operation against Iraq without Turkey's support. This perception on the part of the Turks accounted for the long delays in the technical-level bilateral negotiations, as the Turkish side tried to get the best possible political, military, and economic/financial terms. The delay itself helped to increase anxiety in Turkey, among the public, in government, and in the parliament, about a new war in Iraq.

In the course of the Turkish-American diplomatic encounters over Iraq, there surfaced a notable defect in the American negotiating profile. This weakness is likely structural and chronically afflicts the American body politic. I refer to the American proclivity to prefer back channels over established lines of communication. Americans are infatuated with, even fascinated by, intelligence. They have less respect for information that comes through formal channels. Particularly in the early stages of the contacts with the new Turkish government at the end of 2002, the administration preferred to work the back channels. The Turkish side was partly responsible for encouraging the Americans in this regard, as Erdogan and his party did not trust the bureaucracy and relied at least initially on their handpicked advisers.

The cost of using back channels was high. In a mutually reinforcing process, the American side was hearing only what it wanted to hear, and the Turkish side was promising mostly undeliverable results regarding Turkish support on Iraq. The Pentagon planned to send troops overland from Turkey into Iraq. This required authorization from the Turkish Parliament. I kept reminding my interlocutors that the Turkish Parliament was a democratically elected body and that no one could make promises about how it would vote on such a contentious issue that affected Turkey's national security. Yet based on what they were hearing through back channels, Pentagon officials were sticking to the assumption that the Turkish case was a done deal. The assumption proved to be wrong: on March 1, 2003, the Turkish Grand National Assembly did not give its approval to the government's request to permit U.S. troops into Turkey. As a result, Turkish-American relations suffered a serious setback from which they have yet to recover.

The preference for back channels is something that partially reflects another trait in American negotiating behavior—unilateralism. There is an innate cultural tendency to believe that the American way of doing things is the right and best way and that a "go-for-it" attitude is a sufficient condition to achieve one's goals. This is a healthy social attribute that probably helps account for the greatness of American society. When it comes to matters of foreign policy, however, this tendency usually means that Americans are not paying enough attention to what their interlocutors are saying. It also means a trigger-happy readiness to use sanctions, including military force, to obtain the results they want. In the context of Turkish-American encounters on Iraq, the United States frequently pushed for early acceptance of American expectations and requests regardless of the reservations of the Turkish side. The United States was not necessarily arrogant or unpleasant, but it was always clear that in the velvet glove, there was an iron fist.

Naturally there were also some other cultural factors at play. One was the non-historical mindset that pervaded the American approach to the complex Iraqi issue. America is a young nation that evolved into a superpower in a relatively short span of time. It is only natural that Americans do not always have a sense of history, given what they learn in schools, the content of their media, and their cultural emphasis on the present and the future. Nevertheless, this lack of appreciation for the historical dimension of foreign policy issues can be a serious handicap for American policymakers and negotiators. In the course of our long conversations, the American side mostly ignored Turkish warnings about mishandling Iraqi realities. Early on, the Turkish side emphasized how important it was not to disenfranchise the Sunnis, not to portray them as hostile, and not to call the areas where they lived the "Bermuda Triangle." The United States did not heed this advice because it saw the Shias and Kurds as America's natural allies and the Sunnis as Saddam's supporters. This simplistic diagnosis did not serve U.S. interests in Iraq well and led to many costly mistakes. Had the Bush administration sought a more constructive relationship with the Iraqi Sunnis from the beginning, the course of events in Iraq might well have been different.

The differing perception of time was yet another factor that affected the progress of Turkish-American negotiations. America is a time-conscious society, putting much value on the clock. Being punctual, finishing business on schedule, not wasting time, using time as planned, and displaying impatience toward those who act slowly are all patterns of American cultural behavior. The Turks, on the other hand, are more relaxed about time and exhibit a tendency to procrastinate. This combination proved to be explosive in the first months of 2003 when the United States was making final preparations for the invasion of Iraq. The Bush administration was pressing the Turks for a "yes" or "no" while the Turkish government was trying to delay its response for as long as possible. The fact that the Turkish leadership had other priorities in mind did not help. The question of Cyprus and the accession negotiations with the European Union had greater urgency, as did an ongoing economic recovery program. The Iraq issue was comparatively low on Turkish leaders' lists, especially since Turkish public opinion was heavily set against a new armed conflict in neighboring Iraq. After all, Turks were still feeling the devastating effects of the economic losses from the previous Gulf War.

The differences in timelines and priorities led to the making of dramatic mistakes on both sides. In the weeks preceding the March 1 vote in the Turkish Parliament, the United States sent warships loaded with troops to the Eastern Mediterranean for eventual disembarkation at the Turkish port of Iskenderun on the premise that they would make their way to northern Iraq. The United States chose to do this without consulting the Turkish side. The Americans were impatient and wanted to push Turkey into an early decision. Already on September 18, 2002, Deputy Defense Secretary Wolfowitz was telling the visiting Turkish foreign minister that the United States wanted a Turkish decision on the "northern option" (American troops entering into Northern Iraq from Turkey) within a "matter of weeks." Turkey, on the other hand, agreed to what was called "site preparations" by the United States at various seaports and airports as a prelude to facilitate the movement of American troops through Turkey into Iraq. This was actually another step by Turkey to gain more time and defer the final decision in the parliament. The Americans, with some justification, thought that the site-preparations agreement meant Turkey's consent and that cooperation on Iraq was on track. In retrospect, I understand that the process of improvement of these facilities should have begun only if the Turkish government felt that the American request for troop deployments in Turkey would be allowed.

However, the "no" vote of the Turkish Parliament changed the entire atmosphere overnight. One lasting effect of this episode was that the American officers and troops on the naval ships that kept waiting for Turkey's decision subsequently blamed Turkey for their idling in the Eastern Mediterranean. In live call-in programs on American national TV channels, some of these troops would ask me why Turkey had "betrayed" the United States, its ally and friend. One of these officers, probably acting out of revenge, was responsible for the infamous and most unfortunate incident that occurred in Suleymaniye, Iraq, on July 4, 2003, when American forces "detained" Turkish officers and soldiers, placing sacks over their heads. To the Turks, the incident showed how abrasive the Americans could be. The incident also highlighted the deep importance Turks attach to their soldiers' honor.

One other point to note is the American tendency to apply American terms and metaphors to the behavior of others. This kind of "Americanization" is generally irritating to the other side and occasionally leads to misunderstandings of American motives. For example, at the Oval Office meeting with the two Turkish ministers on February 14, 2003, President Bush used the American colloquial expression "horse trading" to describe the hard bargain that his visitors were driving over the financial terms of Turkish cooperation. It was a well-meaning effort at levity on the part of the president, but it unleashed a lot of negative imagery in the Turkish media. Numerous cartoons in the American media also depicted the Turks as "selling" their cooperation for money, hurting Turkish sensibilities and perhaps unfavorably affecting the votes of some members of the Turkish Parliament.

The very pushy linkage by Washington of any American financial aid and compensation to Turkey with Ankara's "full cooperation"—that is, total acquiescence by Turkey to American demands on Iraq—was also unhelpful. This pressure not only reduced Turkey's range of choices regarding its level of cooperation but also led to the request of unreasonable financial amounts by the Turkish side in return for cooperation (the highest U.S. offer was $25 billion; the highest pronounced by Turkey was more than $90 billion).

Conclusion

This episode in Turkish-American relations, which got its start after 9/11 and whose repercussions continue today, is full of lessons about what to avoid when discussing matters of war and peace. Topping the list is the need to be aware of the history of a given issue. Being patient, working with reliable lines of communication, avoiding back channels, and controlling unilateral tendencies in order to be aware of the needs and concerns of the other side are also important. Further, paying particular attention to differences in priorities and timelines is critical to obtaining a desired and balanced outcome from any negotiations.

Although 9/11 has accentuated certain long-standing and rather negative American cultural traits in the context of American negotiating behavior, given the singular importance of the presidency in the American system and his or her powerful influence as a trendsetter, the advent of a new presidency could rehabilitate the strengths and merits of American diplomacy. Indeed, America is likely to fare much better with a president who, while aware of the power and greatness of America, acts not with the intemperance and impatience of a crusader, but with a sense of measure, prudence, and humility.

10

Negotiating within Washington: Thrown in at the Deep End— A New Zealand Diplomat Looks Back

John Wood

E ach country's relationship with the United States of America is *sui generis*, something to be managed in its own terms. But in that task, vital to all countries because of America's unique superpower status and global predominance politically, culturally, economically, and militarily, it would seem only wise to draw on the experience of others. It is, after all, reasonable to suppose that common threads of behavior and approach, both determined and institutionalized by America's unique history, culture, and legal and political environment, will be discernible as we examine how the United States negotiates, formally and informally, within its own system and with the outside world. Such observations should provide valuable lessons for each country's attempts to optimize its bilateral relationship with the United States. In the complex and fiercely competitive world of Washington, diplomatic representatives, especially from smaller states such as New Zealand, need all the help they can get.

Reviewing as dispassionately as possible the New Zealand experience of dealing with the United States over the course of my own negotiating career, I had no difficulty in tracing the main outlines of a distinctive American approach to negotiating internationally, and in empathizing with the accounts of others seeking to come to grips with the U.S. system. On the other hand, going back closely over the New Zealand track record revealed differences in both the nature of the bilateral relationship with, and the negotiating style of, the United States compared with the more common norms of experience. An explanation of those anomalies might in itself be instructive, but it might also suggest that, in their interaction, NZ-U.S. relations have proved sometimes an exception to the general rule.

The Nuclear Divide

I cut my teeth negotiating in the American system from 1984 to 1987 as the senior career Foreign Service officer and, for a short but critical time, chargé d'affaires at the New Zealand embassy in Washington's Observatory Circle. The first years in particular of this period were a tumultuous and even traumatic time for New Zealand's relations with the United States. Reverberations from it continue until this day.

At issue was the declared nuclear policy of the government in New Zealand, newly elected in July 1984, which the Reagan administration held to be inimical to America's national security interests. U.S. opposition to New Zealand's antinuclear stance centered on two contentions: a unilateral determination by Washington that in banning access to its ports of nuclear weapons and by nuclear-propelled vessels, New Zealand was placing itself in breach of its obligations to the United States under ANZUS, the trilateral security treaty between Australia, New Zealand, and the United States; and that through the policy itself and the way it was proposed to be administered, New Zealand, notwithstanding its status as U.S. ally, was mounting a direct and unacceptable challenge to America's global policy of neither confirming nor denying (NCND) any aspect of the deployment of nuclear weapons.[1]

Both sides quickly realized that these developing policy differences set them on a collision course. Nearly two years of intensive negotiation followed, much of it conducted behind the scenes on a daily basis on the ground in Washington between middle-ranking American and New Zealand officials, punctuated by higher-level encounters from time to time in the two capitals or more usually elsewhere, on the margins of international meetings.

The Search for Accommodation

In the initial phases these encounters were exploratory, with each side testing out the other side's positions and the firmness with which they were held. It seems very clear to me now that more alarm bells were jangling at this early point than either side recognized. Fundamental differences in negotiating approach, derived ultimately from the very different democratic systems institutionalized in each country, quickly came to the fore. It seemed perfectly reasonable to the U.S. side, for example, to invite the New Zealand prime minister to campaign to change or overturn a major policy position on which his government had just been elected, and for appointed American officials to deliver to him rather stern homilies about the responsibility of political leaders to shape popular opinion, not follow it. From

---

1. This chapter is not intended to discuss in all their complexity the issues under negotiation between the two countries at this time or give a blow-by-blow account of the negotiations themselves. For both of those the reader is referred to Malcolm Templeton's masterly account in *Standing Upright Here: New Zealand in the Nuclear Age, 1945–1990* (Wellington: Victoria University Press, 2006).

the reverse perspective, qualified indications of political intention all too often and too easily acquired the status of commitments entered into by the New Zealand side as far as the United States was concerned. Dashed expectations would produce, at a minimum, disappointment on the U.S. part and resentment from New Zealand at any implication of bad faith.

The focus soon shifted to examining, in seemingly endless permutation, the area of overlap between the two sets of policy concerns in order to recommend a mutually acceptable way forward, one that would allow each side to maintain with public credibility the integrity of its policy position, while providing for a return to "normality" in security cooperation and thus averting a breakdown in this area of the relationship.

The stakes were high, and the tensions palpable. I believe that New Zealand is still the only country formerly in full-fledged alliance with the United States no longer to have that status—to have had its membership in the club of America's allies neither withdrawn nor canceled, but suspended. But as young professionals at the New Zealand embassy, my colleagues and I found it was a heady time too: there we were at the center of a developing crisis, acting under direct personal instructions of the prime minister to try to achieve an accommodation with the United States, but with no precedents to guide us and therefore with more than the usual discretion to bring to the day-to-day exchanges.

Superpower Sensitivities

The first realization I gained from early discussions with counterparts in the State Department, the National Security Council, and the Department of Defense was just how seriously the United States regarded these emerging policy differences, and how difficult, perhaps even impossible, it would be to negotiate a resolution of them other than on American terms. The judgment had already been made by the United States that the issues raised went to the heart of America's national security policy, and by implication for the U.S. officials involved, were not therefore open for negotiation in any conventional sense of the term. The risk as seen by the United States was erosion of the key security principle, NCND.

Nor did New Zealand's traditional preferred status in Washington as a close ally seem to cut us much if any negotiating slack when the issues at stake were considered to have implications for global alliance management and U.S. conduct of the Cold War. To the contrary, the point was made that America's allies should expect to be held to a higher standard of understanding and cooperation than other countries when it came to countering the threat of communism and supporting nuclear deterrence.

This U.S. attitude was usually conveyed more in sorrow than anger: a refrain in our exchanges was that if the issues involved had concerned only New Zealand

and the United States, then such was the nature of the bilateral relationship that doubtless an accommodation could be reached. The risk was, however, that the New Zealand antinuclear "disease" would spread to other allies (such as Japan), a risk unacceptable to the United States and one that it felt compelled to head off at the pass.

The second reality that became quickly evident in the American negotiating approach was that this clash of nuclear policies and interpretation of alliance responsibilities had created a situation that the United States was not prepared to see drift along unresolved. What a subsequent secretary of state, Warren Christopher, delicately used to refer to more than a decade later as the "unfinished business" in the bilateral relationship had, after limited time for assessment and reflection by the New Zealand government, to be addressed and concluded. That grace period turned out to be not very long at all: within two months of his assuming office, our prime minister was being urged by the secretary of state to disclose his intentions and plan for resolving the impasse.

These demands for a game plan, a timetable, a road map with signposts that could be ticked off and progress duly measured as the two sides went along, were to become an ongoing theme in our discussions with Washington. They seemed to me characteristically American and have been commented on as such by other U.S. negotiating partners. I now realize however that they also reflected the faltering trust between the two leaderships.

One has to assume that, in applying consistent pressure on the New Zealand authorities to reach a settlement, U.S. officials were calculating that an outcome more or less on U.S. terms was both achievable and likely. Sometimes to us on the ground it seemed otherwise: no doubt a positive result to the negotiations was the preferred U.S. outcome, but I gained the distinct impression from some interlocutors that rather than compromise a fundamental American security principle, or allow New Zealand in U.S. eyes to become an alliance free rider, it might be better to make an example of our country *pour encourager les autres*. That apprehension of the preparedness of at least some in the United States to hang our country out to dry as an example to others gave rise to more sleepless nights than any other single aspect of these negotiations.

It may well have been a related desire to demonstrate to other countries that the United States was moving to solve the New Zealand case and on track to securing a return to "normal" in the bilateral security relationship, and that the U.S. would come up from time to time with a "sort of, deadline" for progress. In my experience, most set deadlines are artificial ones, and these were no exception.

An impatience to tidy up business and force issues to a conclusion even at the risk of a suboptimal outcome has on occasion seemed to me not just an understandable response to the multitude of issues and demands pressing on a great power, but almost an instinctive reaction on the part of U.S. negotiators. It is easy to see why some foreign observers have regarded this negotiating trait as characteristic of the American way of business and perhaps life.

A House Undivided

Once the administration had pushed the national security button, New Zealand representatives could expect to encounter a united policy front among the key U.S. agencies concerned. This indeed proved to be the case throughout, with no discernible evidence, at least in a collective negotiating context, of those differing agency views that sometimes offer the foreign negotiator greater scope for inducing a more nuanced and muted outcome from the U.S. system.

The State Department, led in New Zealand's case by the Bureau of East Asian and Pacific Affairs, and our principal interlocutor, could be expected to place greater weight than other agencies on relationship considerations, and the National Security Council, and to an extent those with responsibility for international security affairs in the Defense Department, tended to take the more strategic view. But in general there were no divisions, and indeed at critical moments in the U.S. interagency process, the views of those who felt most affected by the issues and therefore most strongly about them, such as the Joint Chiefs of Staff and the U.S. Navy, to my observation tended to prevail and become administration policy. This process was impossible for a foreign representative directly to affect, and even indirect attempts to influence the interagency debate—which of course we felt compelled to make—could be fraught.

I should add that, in the New Zealand experience and rather contrary to other accounts I have seen of the U.S. bureaucratic system at work, this firm and united policy stance on the part of the principal agencies was backed up throughout by extremely efficient staff work and coordination. Very rarely for New Zealand had we been caught up in discussions that were regarded by the United States as significant for its own national security. The number of key senior U.S. officials involved at any point was in fact quite few. I never made representations to them or took New Zealand visitors to see them without finding them both fully informed in advance of the content of our discussions with their colleagues, and singing very much from the same song sheet.

Negotiating with Oneself

On issues requiring engagement with other countries or international organizations and involving U.S. vital interests, it has often been observed that the U.S. system spends at least as much time negotiating with itself as it does with the other party. There is a strong tendency for American officials to show up at the negotiating table with an opening position close to or even at their bottom line, with the explanation implicit or explicit: "This is the best we can get for you from our system, and you'd better believe it."

During a protracted negotiation, such as I am describing, one is always very conscious of this parallel negotiation process going on. The proceedings can be tightly held and take on quite extraordinary dimensions. Only long after the event, for example, did our embassy become aware even of the existence of a U.S. National Security Council directive of October 1985, signed off by the president, which took important decisions about the future of the relationship with New Zealand that to an extent still apply. It was longer still before the text became public—located by an American academic in the U.S. National Archives, as it happens. The contents were never made formally available to the New Zealand authorities (the U.S. administration may well have considered that the gist had been conveyed to them orally often enough).

The significance of this interagency dimension underlines the desirability if not necessity for the countries and causes under debate to have a powerful champion or champions within the U.S. system itself. Our own lack of a champion within the interagency process remained an issue as late as my final term as ambassador in Washington from 2002 to 2006, as we sought to become a bilateral free-trading partner of the United States, a role for which we were and are eminently qualified.

In the negotiations on nuclear issues, the U.S. side was led by assistant secretaries of state and defense who were both thoroughly professional and, in my judgment, sympathetic. By that I mean, while of course tough advocates of the administration position, they were also concerned to give the New Zealand side a full and fair hearing, were prepared to extend to us the benefit of the doubt when that seemed deserved, and, I was told, argued in favor of continuing to negotiate when others around and more particularly above them were no longer inclined to persevere.

I am convinced we never had the sort of champion referred to above within the interagency process who at a critical point in the deliberations would have been prepared to argue forcefully that there was an absolute and enduring value to the United States from the New Zealanders—that their contribution and the relationship with them was such that the negotiations simply should not be allowed to fail. We are all aware of countries that routinely benefit from that role being played on their behalf from within the U.S. system—a role that can provide a safety net in troubled times or, more creatively, a springboard for relationship initiatives.

Dealing with Congress

An important part of the responsibilities of the New Zealand embassy staff in Washington, as negotiations with the administration proceeded, was to (1) keep the relevant committees and subcommittees of the U.S. Congress directly and accurately informed of the New Zealand government's policies and our conviction that, notwithstanding our antinuclear stance, we were fulfilling our responsibilities as a U.S. ally and (2) request patience, understanding, and the benefit of any doubt as we sought to negotiate a mutually satisfactory resolution to the issues with the U.S. government. We pulled in extra resources to help with these tasks.

Despite the considerable degree of general goodwill toward New Zealand that has been built up on the Hill over the decades, in a number of respects, some of it unexpected, we found the Congress increasingly tough-going as the negotiations wore on. The administration understandably was keeping Congress fully briefed from its perspective on the dispute with New Zealand. There has always been an inclination on the part of U.S. elected representatives to defer to government leadership on matters of foreign policy, and this tendency was only reinforced when, as in this instance, the national security dimension was added.

Some within the Congress who had other axes to grind with New Zealand, especially in terms of market access, sought to take advantage of our difficulties on the security front and introduce unhelpful legislation. This had always happened at the best of times, but I do not think anyone in New Zealand fully appreciated how frequently and effectively administrations of the day had put in a quiet word on our behalf with the congressional leadership, urging them to avoid damaging the interests of such a good friend and ally. In current circumstances and until our differences were resolved, the U.S. government was no longer prepared to intervene in this way. It was incumbent rather on ourselves to scent the dangers and mount our own defenses against them. For the first time, we walked the corridors of Congress on our own.

An unexpected complication would arise on occasion from well-intentioned attempts by members of Congress to intervene in the NZ-U.S. relationship and the ongoing negotiations. This typically took the form of engaging directly in the public debate on the issues in New Zealand, usually provoking an adverse reaction, or in anticipating that the negotiations would fail and then seeking prematurely from the point of view of the two governments to define what the basis for a new security relationship might be.

After June 1986 when, following a meeting in Manila with the New Zealand prime minister that effectively brought negotiations to an end, Secretary of State George Shultz announced, "We part as friends, but we part." New Zealand and U.S. officials came, somewhat ironically, to share the same objectives as far as the Congress was concerned. From the beginning, the U.S. administration had made it clear that the dispute with New Zealand was confined to security issues, that other aspects of the relationship including the economic were separate from it, and that even if port access on terms acceptable to the U.S. Navy could not be resolved, trade sanctions were not envisaged.

This stance was a great source of reassurance to the New Zealand authorities throughout and one honored in the aftermath by the United States, but it was strictly in negotiating terms to the American disadvantage. The New Zealand government had inherited an economy on the verge of bankruptcy and had initiated a massive economic reform program. It was rightly apprehensive about any prospect of an increase in international protectionism against the country's exports. In the aftermath of the meeting in Manila, officials from both countries, especially those of goodwill from the United States, worked very hard and successfully to persuade Congress to confine its response to the failed negotiations to the security area and not advance any legislative measures advocating economic retaliation.

The Media

Dealing with the U.S. media throughout this period proved rather problematic for the New Zealand embassy. It had always been difficult if not impossible for a small, distant country in good standing with the United States to attract any media coverage there at all. It was unwelcome, to say the least, to be on the receiving end of a flurry of media references to the emerging dispute, based almost exclusively on official U.S. sources. That said, I did not detect at any time a media campaign programmed in support of the U.S. negotiating position, or any disposition on the part of U.S. officials, to engage in public in Washington in discussion of the issues with New Zealand representatives. Quite to the contrary, when programs such as the *McNeil/Lehrer NewsHour* or Ted Koppel's *Nightline* tried to set up such encounters, U.S. officials would make it clear that if New Zealand were to participate, they would not. They had no wish to create a David Lange versus Goliath scenario from which, in terms of public perception, only New Zealand could benefit.

Rather the U.S. administration tended to use the media reactively, to respond to events, news reports, and government statements from the New Zealand end. It would move, usually neuralgically, to put the record straight from its perspective at any perceived mischaracterization of U.S. views from New Zealand sources. This frequent bouncing back and forth of claim and counterclaim between the two sides, by proxy as it were through the media, could be very time-consuming for both sets of officials in Washington to manage and at times quite disruptive of the negotiating process.

As an embassy, we never succeeded in channeling the enormous amount of American goodwill toward New Zealand and the high regard for our international contribution (as revealed in correspondence at the time and in polling over the years) into consistently helpful media commentary. Any effort to channel that support was somewhat constrained by the New Zealand position that, while our antinuclear policies were reasoned and deeply held and we were prepared to explain and defend them, we were not in the business of international proselytizing and our policies were not designed for export.

Going the Extra Mile

It would be misleading to leave this account without emphasizing again the energy, creativity, and relative open-mindedness that mid-level U.S. officials were prepared to bring to the process of jointly examining formulas to produce programs of action that might have provided a sufficient basis for an outcome under which each country could credibly claim to have adhered to its policy principles and yet avoided an open rupture. This fact may seem somewhat surprising given the well-known U.S. dislike of ambiguity and nuance in language when it comes to negotiated outcomes that it will be required to implement, but it was so.

This informal and freewheeling approach to the lower-level exchanges was also characteristic of their composition and context: often one-on-one or in a very small group, usually out of the office, frequently over coffee, a lunch, or a drink (invariably, with one notable exception, at the New Zealand taxpayers' expense). This process was all very "disownable" in the final analysis as far as principals on both sides were concerned, but it was also capable of producing agreement on a way forward to recommend to them.

Meltdown and After

It may be in retrospect that policy positions were so rigidly held and in such opposition on both sides that creative ambiguity was never going to work, and that no such negotiated outcome was possible. One or two observers afterward claimed that to have been their assessment all along. I recall one National Security Council official reflecting that he had watched the negotiating process "unfold with all the inevitability of a Greek tragedy." All I can say is that the process did not seem like that to those of us most intimately involved. I would go further and claim that the two sets of negotiators were able at least at one critical point to come up with agreed recommendations to their principals that, with the necessary degree of political commitment on both sides, could have led to the outcome we had been instructed to try to find.

As it happened it was at the New Zealand end that the proposed way forward proved too much for the political traffic to bear. The New Zealand cabinet, in the absence of the prime minister, rejected a proposed visit by a U.S. Navy vessel, a proposal that had been developed by officials as both the precursor and an integral part of a negotiated accommodation. As a result, the prospects for success became that much more difficult and distant. After the initial dust had settled, exploration continued, but positions became more rigid on both sides and in fact began to diverge further.

Mutual trust and confidence had become harder to sustain, especially from the American perspective, after a meeting in Wellington between Secretary Shultz and Prime Minister David Lange in July 1984. It seems likely that Shultz and Lange were each listening strongly for what he wanted to hear from the other, and that both left the meeting under a misapprehension.[2] When Lange's subsequent actions did not match Shultz's expectations, the secretary of state came to believe that the prime minister had gone back on his word, a cardinal sin in the eyes of American diplomats who valued straight talking and expected commitments to be honored. With confidence in Lange and patience both worn down, Shultz effectively called the negotiations to a halt at their meeting in Manila.

The Consequences of Failure

The United States took action against New Zealand to sever bilateral military cooperation and severely constrain intelligence cooperation and to unilaterally suspend the United States' obligations to the defense of New Zealand under the ANZUS Treaty. Of these security-related measures, the most damaging was and continues to be the prohibition on training and exercising between our two armed forces, despite their joint deployments in any number of international conflicts over the intervening years. It was confirmed that trade policy issues were to be dealt with in trade policy terms.

However much anticipated these measures had been, they understandably created sourness in the relationship, although more in capitals and among the defense forces than between officials on the ground in Washington who had a mutual interest in stabilizing the situation and limiting any unintended wider damage. At my time of leaving Washington, I described the state of the relationship as one of "uneasy equilibrium."

What our authorities were not told formally, and something which only emerged through attempts to conduct business as usual on trade and agricultural policy, was

---

2. The occasion was Shultz's presence in Wellington for an ANZUS ministerial meeting, which did not however involve the incoming prime minister, whose government had been elected but not yet sworn into office. According to one report, "Mr Lange apparently gave assurances that he wanted to maintain the ANZUS relationship and tried to ease potential diplomatic conflict. He wanted to buy time as his own party was still wrestling with the nuclear ships issue. The Americans thought they had a promise from Mr Lange and later claimed they were betrayed when nuclear-armed and propelled ships were banned." (From an obituary of H. Monroe Brown, U.S. ambassador at the time and a participant at the meeting: Hank Schouten, "Ambassador's Post Was No Sinecure," *Dominion Post*, Wellington, June 22, 2006.)

The actual records of this critical early meeting are patchy, and there are other somewhat differing accounts of what took place. It is clear that Shultz had a stern message to deliver, and that in response Lange may have held out the possibility of change—over time—in aspects of his party's antinuclear policies, most likely that relating to nuclear propulsion. What does seem implausible is that Lange would or could have given any firm undertaking to Shultz to put into reverse a key policy on which he had just been elected.

that henceforth New Zealand—downgraded by the United States from the status of ally, but supposedly retaining that of friend—would be denied access to the administration for its ministers and officials, and its ambassador, above the rank of assistant secretary. One consequence of this was to throw even more weight of responsibility than usual on the embassy to remain engaged with the U.S. system, but at the same time narrowing the scope for it to do so. For the balance of my time in Washington every invitation that came into the embassy was accepted, no matter how tangential the occasion or the organization, in continued efforts to stay in touch with U.S. representatives, to snatch a few words with a cabinet official or even the president on whom we New Zealanders were no longer permitted to call.

It may seem perverse to some to have curtailed in this way dialogue at senior levels, at the very time when there has been a breakdown in a significant area of the relationship, and sure enough the effect was to place things in cold storage for a number of years. It was to be more than a decade before a New Zealand prime minister called on the United States president.

Picking Up the Pieces

Fortunately for me, by the end of 1987 I had moved on to become ambassador to Iran, and I did not experience the full frustration of trying to operate in Washington within these constraints on access and free dealing, unique among U.S. "friends." Indeed, by the time I returned in 1994 as ambassador to the United States in my own right, I was to be the first real beneficiary of the outcome of a unilateral review of the relationship with New Zealand signed off on by President Bill Clinton in March 1993—and at his insistence made a little more forthcoming than officials had first proposed. The principal outcome of this was to restore contact and dialogue between the two countries at all levels and in all areas including military. Within a year of my arrival we had taken advantage of these restored freedoms to rebuild the political relationship with the highly symbolic first prime ministerial Washington visit in eleven years, a process completed with President Clinton's state visit to New Zealand in 1999.

In a number of ways contact and negotiation within Washington from 1994 to 1998 was a very positive experience. The economic relationship had been given a formal structure under a bilateral Trade and Investment Framework Agreement, the negotiation of which I had led as deputy secretary of foreign affairs and trade between Washington assignments. The New Zealand economy was still in the full flood of its reform process, offering great scope for increased involvement by U.S.-based multinational corporations. And in the Washington embassy we worked up the concept for a bilateral free trade agreement with the United States and had this adopted as a priority for the relationship by the New Zealand government. Added to the restoration of the political relationship already described, these economic developments led to a warming of the atmosphere in which to operate and some renewed interest on the U.S. side in dealing constructively with New Zealand.

There was, however, continuing disappointment as well. Despite New Zealand's staunch record of peacekeeping and military deployment in the Middle East and Bosnia, including alongside U.S. forces, the constraints on interaction, particularly joint exercising, remained in place. And overall the "unfinished business" of the continuing standoff over nuclear policy proved time and again to limit the scope of ambition for constructive improvement in relations. The elephant did not forget nor change its national security policies with revolutions in the United States political cycle.

Washington Revisited

Going back for a second and final four-year term as ambassador in Washington from 2002 to 2006, in the immediate aftermath of the terrorist attacks of September 11, 2001, meant a return not only to a negotiating environment of which I had had by then a great deal of experience, but also to familiar faces from the Reagan era and the failed negotiations of the mid-1980s. This was both an advantage in picking up the threads of New Zealand's business in the United States and a disadvantage.

On the positive side I was known by first name, through shared experience by a surprising number of key U.S. officials who now held very senior positions in the first-term administration of President George W. Bush. That was good for access and frankness of dealing. I recall more than one occasion when because of a policy difference or simply an instance of grating tonality, the bilateral situation seemed to call for quick and candid discussion at quite a senior level in Washington. The American interlocutors I best knew from the past were those most likely to make themselves available and to cut directly to the chase.

The background of those previous negotiations also resulted in my own government having sufficient ground for confidence in my U.S. connections to allow me perhaps an unusual degree of freedom in responding from the New Zealand side to the occasional bump in the road. It meant also, however, that those same senior administration officials were intimately familiar with the past twenty-year history of NZ-U.S. relations and continued to feel strongly about the issues. Not only did the elephant not forget, but at critical points it would start to remember.

The Exception or the Rule?

In revisiting this critical chapter in diplomatic relations between New Zealand and the United States, and reliving my own times as negotiator in Washington in the context of a wider examination of American negotiating behavior, inevitable questions arise about how typical or representative of U.S. norms the Kiwi experience really was.

Standing right back and concentrating on the (failed) outcome of the negotiating process, one might conclude very typical indeed: a dispute arose between the United States and a small ally over an issue that Washington had determined to be vital to its national security interests; it entered in a brisk and businesslike way into negotiations designed to reach an accommodation, essentially on U.S. terms, having first obtained interagency agreement on policy and tactics, and the support of other key components of the American system, notably the Congress; the United States kept the pressure on and set its own successive deadlines for settlement; but when a painstakingly crafted outline agreement—which nonetheless Washington probably viewed as lying at the outer edges of its narrowly limited negotiating mandate—failed at the first hurdle in Wellington, the United States lost patience and walked away. The secretary of state put the negotiations to a definitive end. Recrimination and retaliatory measures followed. A hitherto close alliance relationship was unilaterally downgraded in the interests of global relationship management and the effective prosecution of the Cold War.

This sequential account of U.S. negotiating behavior I have given—in a fairly crude outline—would be recognized by many of my foreign colleagues with experience negotiating in Washington as comparable to their own experience and as reflecting traits of the American system and character, as well as of course the size, superpower status, and global responsibilities of the United States.

Still, what has emerged most clearly from the mists of my negotiating memories is a perception of the quite extraordinary lengths the U.S. side went to throughout to keep the negotiations with New Zealand going. When very early on in the piece, for example, I remarked to the senior responsible American official that, given the starkness and force with which he had just reiterated the U.S. position on the policy issue in dispute with New Zealand, it was hard if not impossible for me to see a logical pathway forward to an accommodation. He was quite taken aback and urged both his own and New Zealand officials present to go away and keep trying.

This disposition on the U.S. part to negotiate quietly, behind the scenes, with the New Zealanders rather than simply to maintain a full frontal assault on our position, was sustained, as I have noted, for many months despite all the political vicissitudes and fluctuations in mood. The decision to negotiate in private was responsible, I believe, not just for the cooperative and even creative disposition of those U.S. officials with whom we were in discussion on a daily basis, but also for the uncharacteristically freewheeling approach they were prepared to take toward ideas and suggestions for an accommodation. Middle-ranking State Department officials are not in my experience by nature or training incautious, especially when the issues seem clear-cut from the U.S. perspective and, as in this New Zealand case, they could not have assumed their principals would have approved the lines they were pursuing.

Why was this so? Why, if I am right, did the United States in contrast with its more usual disposition in negotiating with smaller partners, seem prepared to go that extra mile with New Zealand even, as remarked earlier, to the extent of denying to itself from the outset use of the potent tool of linkage?

There will be a number of explanations. The influence of the personalities and the affinities of the respective negotiators, for example, can never be discounted. But the compelling answer is it seems to me a more fundamental one, which rests squarely in the nature of the NZ-U.S. relationship and experiences shared by the two countries in the several decades before the dispute arose in the mid-1980s.

The United States has historically enjoyed intimately close bilateral relations with a number of countries, that with the United Kingdom being characterized as "special." This relationship formed the nucleus at the plurilateral level of the closely knit five-nation grouping that also includes Canada, Australia, and New Zealand (CANZUKUS). This grouping evolved on the basis of shared history, ethnicity, language, culture, and values, and cooperation toward common ends. It seems self-evident that when contentious issues would arise between the United States and any member state of this inner grouping, it would go to extra lengths to try to resolve them.

New Zealand was also, as has been noted, a partner in the trilateral ANZUS treaty, a key part of the formal security infrastructure put in place in the Pacific under the leadership of the United States after WWII. Alliance management, both for its own sake and especially within the Cold War context, would similarly call for special efforts on the U.S. part to ensure that what could almost be perceived as family disputes between members of this alliance grouping were settled in house.

Finally, it is worth recalling that the NZ-U.S. bilateral relationship, as well as the mutual knowledge and understanding and personal relationships between the two countries, had been greatly intensified by shared experiences within the Pacific in the lead-up to the nuclear dispute, including WWII itself, the founding of the United Nations in San Francisco, the Korean War, emergencies in Southeast Asia, and Vietnam. The contribution of New Zealand to these efforts, on occasion disproportionate to its size, was widely known and appreciated in Washington. The president himself would have been aware of it from his California perspective, and his vice president, secretary of state, and secretary of defense all had had direct wartime experience of the Pacific Theater, extending to New Zealand as host of major U.S. forces throughout.

Of course, at the end of the day, special efforts, going the extra mile, and catalytic creativity between officials on both sides were not enough. One could speculate I suppose about the apportionment of responsibility for failure, and more appositely given the subject of this volume, whether it was inherent in the negotiating approaches of either or both of the two protagonists, that resolution of the dispute on mutually acceptable terms proved not possible. A lingering question in my mind, perhaps befitting someone who has spent a career negotiating internationally from positions reflecting the inherently weak hand of a small country, is: Did size in the end make the difference? Would negotiations have been broken off in the way they were if the United States had been dealing not with New Zealand but instead with an Australia or a Canada? Was it inevitable that, in any U.S. calculus about risks to competing alliance relationships, a Japan would inevitably outweigh a New Zealand?

11

Negotiating as a Rival:
A Russian Perspective

Yuri Nazarkin

My diplomatic career was devoted, to a large extent, to negotiations on arms control and nonproliferation. It started in the multilateral sphere (nuclear nonproliferation and chemical and biological weapons) and extended into bilateral talks on a strategic arms reduction treaty (START). Naturally, the main counterpart of the Soviet Union and later the Russian Federation was the United States. I had an opportunity to deal with American negotiators, both bilaterally and multilaterally, through different periods: the confrontation and détentes of the Cold War, Gorbachev's "perestroika," and the first post-Soviet years. After my retirement in 1995, I continued working as a scholar with various think tanks, including the Carnegie Endowment for International Peace's Moscow office. This chapter is based both on my academic observations and on personal recollections of various episodes of negotiations.[1]

In assessing the efficiency of U.S. negotiating behavior, one needs to keep in mind that behind U.S. negotiators lies the political, economic, and military power of the United States. While diplomats of Ruritania or Concordia must rely mainly on their negotiating skill, American diplomats have always had an extra advantage at the negotiating table: the mightiest state in the world behind them. This does not mean that the U.S. government can afford to send bad diplomats to negotiate. American negotiators are adept at using the same methods, tools, and tricks that are in the diplomatic arsenals of all countries. But they can also draw on U.S. power to twist arms. Such behavior was not possible when they negotiated with

---

1. I did not use documents in official state archives. Thus, I cannot claim that every detail is absolutely precise. I have tried, however, to present my stories and judgments as accurately as possible.

the world's other superpower—the Soviet Union. It became possible, however, after the USSR's demise in the early 1990s. Now, as Russia regains its assertiveness, circumstances are changing yet again.

Despite all the ups and downs in the U.S.-Soviet/Russian relationship, the field of nonproliferation has always remained an oasis where both sides, due to common interests, cooperated to keep other countries from acquiring nuclear weapons. Contacts in this field were not interrupted even in the worst periods of Cold War confrontation. In contrast, talks on arms control—that is, on limitations and reductions of existing weapons—depended on the temperature of bilateral relations. U.S. behavior in negotiations during confrontational periods was characterized by political maneuvering and the desire to score political points. The Soviet side behaved in the same fashion. However, in better times—before 1992—the United States did try to reach agreements, and this necessitated compromise.

After the demise of the Soviet Union, when President Boris Yeltsin and his foreign minister Andrey Kozyrev were seeking political support from the United States, they made substantial concessions in negotiations. The United States began to rely more on pressure and arm twisting than on compromise. However, when Yevgeny Primakov replaced Kozyrev in January 1996, he took a more independent stand. Russian-American negotiations on arms control and other security matters became more balanced. During George W. Bush's presidency, a hegemonic approach became the starting point of American diplomacy, and the United States all but stopped participating in arms control negotiations.

Usually, a negotiation involves three levels of negotiators: those who sit at the negotiating table, ministers/heads of agencies, and heads of state. The structure of this chapter roughly parallels this hierarchy, examining in turn the behavior of diplomats, the influence of ministerial interests and interagency rivalries, and the overall strategic direction of negotiations.

The chapter first sketches the general characteristics displayed by American diplomats at the negotiating table: professionalism, straightforwardness, pragmatism, conceptual argumentation, and toughness. I also analyze American negotiators' skill at reaching compromises, which depend upon confidential discussions, as well as their use of leaks, which of course violate confidentiality.

Diplomats do not negotiate in a vacuum: negotiators on both sides are responsive to the interests of various ministries, agencies, and political and industrial groupings. As this chapter discusses, these interests influence negotiating behavior not only directly but also indirectly, because negotiators try to use the internal differences on the other side while taking into account their own internal agendas.

The chapter concludes by examining recent shifts in U.S. negotiating strategy and the prospects for the future.

General Characteristics of American Negotiating Behavior

Having dealt with American negotiators during the Cold War and after, I want to emphasize that their interpersonal behavior remained the same, despite changes in relations between our countries. We professionals treated each other as professionals, not as politicians.

Our American counterparts were very good professionals. In all my negotiating experience, I encountered only one exception, a political appointee who came to international multilateral negotiations from domestic politics. Without his advisers he was completely lost. All the others—from ambassadors to junior diplomats—were competent, well prepared, and highly qualified.

As a rule, ambassadors had broad political vision, at least within the framework of the subject under negotiations, and were quite skillful in defending and explaining the positions of their country as well as in pushing forward their instructions. On support levels, strict specialization existed. If an adviser or an expert of an American delegation was approached on a question that was out of his or her sphere of responsibility, he or she preferred to name the right person to approach rather than to give his or her own judgment. This trait deserves respect and inspires trust. It promotes confidence in the reliability of those opinions that are given.

American negotiating culture has an efficient reporting system from lower to upper levels. Juniors report promptly to their superiors, and their reports help the latter to control them. If you give some information or judgment to junior American diplomats, you can be sure that they will immediately report it to their superiors. Of course, this is mandatory for any national delegation participating in negotiations, but unfortunately not every delegation has an equally effective system.

Another positive trait of American negotiators is their straightforwardness—whether expressing positive or negative views. They always strive to ensure that they are 100 percent understood. This is not typical for diplomats of some other countries, who sometimes prefer to preserve their options by deliberately leaving their statements open to different interpretations.

U.S. negotiating language is usually clear and precise. Even though American negotiators widely use terminology from the worlds of sports and business that gives their language a certain "American flavor," they manage to get their point across. U.S. negotiators expect similar precision from their counterparts. If something is not clear, American negotiators do not hesitate to ask as many questions as they feel are necessary to acquire a full understanding of their counterparts' statements. This creates a solid ground for better mutual understanding.

Another trait of American negotiators that deserves mention is pragmatism. I say this despite the many hours I spent in conceptual debates with my American counterparts, who would defend their positions by insisting on the conceptual logic of the U.S. approach. Conceptualism, however, was used just for practical reasons—to support arguments for the U.S. position—not for the actual business of negotiating compromises and agreements. For instance, in the 1980s Washington proposed the concept of strategic stability to help U.S. negotiators argue against multiple independently targeted reentry vehicles on intercontinental ballistic missiles (MIRVed ICBMs) and defend the development of antiballistic missile (ABM) systems. This concept had a certain logic, but it also had a weak point: during the 1960s, the U.S. side had proposed a different concept to defend the opposite position when Washington stopped the ABM project and launched programs of MIRVed missiles. This made our task of counterargumentation easier; we took the American conceptual arguments of the 1960s and used them against their conceptual arguments of the 1980s. (The Americans defended the reversal of their position on the basis of technological progress, but I strongly suspect that the real reason was the growth of influence of those parts of the U.S. business establishment that were involved in developing ABM components.)

The conceptual rhetoric of U.S. negotiators sometimes came close to sermonizing, particularly at multilateral forums, but their arguments usually remained rooted in logic rather than in ideology. A common American tactic was to present the U.S. position as constructive and flexible and the Soviet or Russian position as just the opposite. Fortunately, the United States used its conceptual argumentation mainly for the record at official meetings for the benefit of domestic audiences. At informal encounters, our American counterparts preferred a pragmatic approach and looked for compromise solutions.

Of course, American negotiators were not free of political posturing. But I cannot say that this trait was unique to them. All negotiators posture. Especially during the Cold War, rhetoric, polemics, and browbeating were the norm at public forums and plenary sessions. Following instructions, I myself made numerous political posturing statements at plenary sessions of the Geneva Conference on Disarmament as well as at plenary meetings of bilateral negotiations.

Did the U.S. side bluff? It was certainly not a usual practice, but sometimes the United States did bluff. Here is an example: During negotiations for the convention banning chemical weapons in the framework of the Conference for Disarmament, many countries, including the United States, long blamed the Soviet side for blocking progress by opposing mandatory on-site inspections. These were, indeed, necessary for effective verification of the Chemical Weapons Convention. In 1987 the Soviet delegation received Moscow's permission to accept mandatory inspections. Everybody was happy, except the U.S. delegation, which was not prepared for this move. It took some time until it received instructions permitting it to include corresponding provisions into the draft convention. As my American counterpart admitted later, after retirement, his delegation had instructions to criticize the Soviet position, but it had no permission to accept mandatory on-site inspections.

I believe this might have been explained by the sensitivity of American private chemical corporations for such inspections.

Were our American counterparts purely businesslike or did they develop personal relationships with us? This depended on the individual. Some were formal; others were inclined to develop close social contacts. Regardless of the level of our personal relationship, all of them were very tough negotiators. They defended their positions with real skill and ingenuity. But when they saw that their proposal had no chance of being accepted by the Soviet side, they were equally skillful in looking for compromise solutions.

Reaching Compromises

When negotiations are at a stalemate, delegations are usually instructed to report to their respective capitals with recommendations on how possible changes in their positions might lead to achieving an agreement. In such instances, they are permitted to reach agreements ad referendum.

This practice was very broadly used in the Soviet-American negotiations on START. A search for such ad referendum agreements usually started with "thinking aloud" during informal encounters such as lunches, meetings over a cup of coffee, Sunday hikes in the countryside around Geneva, and talks after tennis matches.

Because of the very complicated and multifaceted nature of the subjects under negotiation, so-called package deals were a useful gambit. Ambassador Richard Burt, the head of the U.S. delegation, and Ambassador Linton Brooks, his deputy, who later replaced him, were very inventive in using such packages. Since U.S. negotiators often used such package deals, I will explain how they worked in greater detail.

Usually a compromise can be reached when each side concedes halfway toward the other side. However, some issues cannot be settled by halfway compromises and instead require unequal compromises (not 50–50, but, let us say, 80–20 or 30–70), or they call for take-it-or-leave-it approaches. In the START talks, when take-it-or-leave-it issues presented themselves, the sides would sometimes make an "exchange of concerns": one side would agree to drop its unacceptable proposal if the other side would reciprocate by dropping its own unacceptable proposal. In START talks the sides often combined such controversial issues in one package. Such deals usually followed two basic rules: (1) the whole package should be well balanced; (2) both sides should proceed from the assumption that nothing is agreed upon unless everything is agreed upon.

A dozen or more package deals were agreed during the START negotiations, with each package containing between four and ten—or even more—components. These highly technical deals would look something like this: (1) side A drops its proposal X, which is unacceptable to side B; (2) side B drops its proposal Y, which is unacceptable to side A; (3) side A accepts proposal Z of side B; (4) side B accepts proposal W of side A; (5) side A concedes 80 percent and side B concedes 20 percent on issue V; (6) side B concedes 80 percent and side A concedes 20 percent on issue U.

U.S. negotiators' inventiveness and willingness to reach compromises did not mean that they were not tough. Quite to the contrary, U.S. negotiators were quick to pocket the other side's concessions if they were not properly connected with reciprocal concessions from the U.S. side. In one instance, which overshadowed the START-1 negotiations for four years, from 1986 to 1990, the Soviet side felt that the U.S. side had pocketed a Soviet concession (made during the Reykjavik summit between President Ronald Reagan and General Secretary Mikhail Gorbachev) on accounting rules for nuclear warheads that were not long-range air-launched cruise missiles (ALCMs) on heavy bombers, without making good on a reciprocal concession to accept the Soviet definition of long-range ALCMs ("long-range ALCMs should mean an ALCM with a range in excess of 600 km"). This gave the United States a substantial advantage in the number of nuclear warheads. The U.S. side, however, denied that it accepted the Soviet proposal on this definition; eventually, it came around to doing so.

Confidentiality and Leaks

As all negotiators know, premature disclosure of information about ongoing discussions can impede or even undermine the delicate process of reaching a negotiated agreement. However, this does not mean that no information is given to mass media. The problem is how to remain within limits of confidentiality.

When meetings are public, each side tries to score political points by demonstrating its positive, constructive position while emphasizing the negative aspects of the other side's stance. Usually this behavior is counterproductive to reaching agreements. When negotiations are confidential, as the START talks were, each side will sometimes seek to apply pressure on the other side and to gain political points by appealing to the public. This can be done through press conferences, interviews, and publication of articles by "independent" journalists. In the case of such articles, it is difficult to prove that the other side has deliberately leaked information, but I am convinced that even in democratic countries (just as in authoritarian ones), the possibility of unintended leaks is close to zero.

During the Strategic Arms Limitation Talks (SALT), particularly during the SALT-2 talks in 1973–79, the American side quite often appealed to the public either officially or through the media. The Soviet side reciprocated by explaining its own position. And no wonder, that was the Cold War. In the late 1980s, when the Cold War was all but over, American propaganda became more restrained but leaks continued.

Before and after each round, which would normally last two or three months, the heads of both delegations usually arranged press conferences, sometimes joint, sometimes individual, and gave interviews and briefings. My counterparts, Richard Burt and his successor Linton Brooks, were very careful and objective in presenting issues that we faced at the negotiations. I behaved in the same fashion. We had no problems with this kind of dealing with media. However, I recall two cases when American leaks gave us a headache.

In December 1989, when the talks in Geneva were interrupted by the Christmas holidays, I happened to be in Washington. I stayed there one night to talk informally with Richard Burt on the problem of sea-launched cruise missiles (SLCMs), which were a sticking point in our negotiations. The Soviet side regarded these missiles as strategic and insisted on including them in the treaty. The United States disagreed. My task was to probe the possibility of a compromise solution, though I had no formal instructions on this account, except Vice Minister Viktor Karpov's personal advice.

My talk with Burt was conducted in the spirit of "thinking aloud" (i.e., whatever one said did not constitute a commitment). Our discussions led me to believe that although the United States would never agree to include SLCMs in the treaty, it was possible to establish certain limitations outside of its text. Of course, this idea required thorough consideration in Moscow with the General Staff and the navy before it could be tried in practice.

A few days later I read in the *New York Times* an article by arms control reporter Michael Gordon disclosing the contents of my confidential conversation with Burt and concluding that the Soviet side was prepared to meet the U.S. position on SLCMs. This was absolutely inappropriate and violated the understanding of "informal probing."

In Moscow, while Karpov appreciated the results of my probing, our generals and admirals, referring to Gordon's article, condemned me for "violating official instructions" and used this article to block any changes in our position on SLCMs, thereby complicating the preparation of the treaty.[2] The unauthorized disclosure was, in short, completely counterproductive.

When I met Burt in Geneva, he apologized for the article and asserted that he had not leaked the details of our conversation. He was probably being truthful, because such disclosures could only complicate negotiations, which was not in his interest. Of course, I never knew who leaked the information or why someone leaked it. I suspect, however, that the leak was to demonstrate to a domestic audience the persistence and success of American diplomacy.

---

2. The problem of SLCMs was solved much later on the same basis that I discussed with Burt in December 1989.

Another example took place the following year. On April 2, 1990, the *Washington Post* published an article by Jeffrey Smith reviewing the state of the START negotiations. The article was based on information that had not been disclosed before due to the confidential nature of the negotiations. It was evident that the author had been well briefed. Yet while he presented the details correctly, his overall picture was distorted, because the article was silent about compromise and focused on Soviet concessions. It portrayed the treaty under negotiation as of benefit to the United States alone. Even more so than the previous case, this one demonstrates a prominent trait of American negotiating behavior, namely, to give priority to domestic requirements and to ignore the problems of the negotiating partner.

It was a critical period for arms control, because both in Washington and in Moscow the political fight over the START Treaty had reached its peak. I do not know whether the one-sided article helped to strengthen the position of Washington doves. But in Moscow it was used as a pretext to stop the negotiations.

Oleg Baklanov, the Central Committee secretary for defense, who was one of the main political adversaries of Gorbachev,[3] used this article to press his position to the Soviet political leadership about the "treacherous nature" of the START talks. He argued that "even Americans themselves say that the treaty is completely in their interests." His purpose was to block the negotiations and damage Gorbachev's political position. Fortunately Gorbachev managed to overrule Baklanov, and the negotiations continued.

Playing on Our Internal Differences

Perhaps because they were so conscious of their own interagency struggles, U.S. negotiators looked for opportunities to exploit political differences and divisions within the Soviet side. Consider my experience as the leader of the Soviet delegation to the talks on nuclear and outer space armaments. The negotiations consisted of three tracks: intermediate-range nuclear forces (INF), START, and ABM and outer space. After the INF Treaty was concluded in 1987, the last two tracks remained. I took them on when I joined the talks in 1989. The formulation "ABM and outer space" was a compromise between the U.S. insistence on ABM and the Soviet proposal to prohibit the deployment of weapons in outer space. Over the course of the negotiations, the United States was angling to secure advantages for its Strategic Defense Initiative (SDI). On our side, we were trying to keep the ABM Treaty in its original form and to reject its "broad interpretation" without damaging our interest in concluding START. We were also insisting on the demili-

---

3. Later, in August 1991, he joined the putsch against Gorbachev and upon the failure of that adventure was imprisoned.

tarization of outer space, but that was totally unacceptable for the U.S. side, particularly because some ABM components were supposed to be outer space–based.

On the Soviet side, we had three major players in the field of arms control: the Foreign Ministry, the military leadership, and the industries involved in arms production. The last of these included some laboratories and technical centers that maintained the only ABM system around Moscow as permitted by the ABM Treaty. The scientists and engineers who worked there were interested in expanding their activities beyond the strict limitations of the treaty—and the Americans evidently were well aware of their interest.

During the ministerial meeting in Wyoming in September 1989, Secretary of State James Baker invited the Soviet side to send a group of Soviet experts to visit two American laboratories involved in SDI research in Los Alamos and San Juan Capistrano. Evidently, the American side intended to give Soviet ABM lobbyists an argument in favor of ABM research and development and against the ABM Treaty, in hopes of weakening our position on ABM and outer space.

Secretary Baker stressed that the invitation did not imply any reciprocity. This was a clever move, because our defense scientists and engineers were eager to see what their American colleagues were doing, but our rules of secrecy would be an obstacle to inviting Americans to tour our own laboratories. The bait was swallowed, and the group of ten experts headed by myself visited both laboratories.[4]

I think the first part of the American plan was a success: our experts were inspired by U.S. achievements in an area that was very close to their hearts and sought more funds for their own work. However, this did not change the Soviet position at the negotiations. We continued to defend the ABM Treaty in its original form, as it had been concluded in 1972, as well as to insist on the prohibition of the deployment of weapons in outer space.

Influencing Soviet Attitudes

The next case that I am going to present relates to a situation when the United States succeeded in influencing the views of key figures on the Soviet side.

In the 1960s, upon the initiative of Secretary of Defense Robert McNamara, secret discussions about the ABM system took place within the U.S. administration. As Anatoly Dobrynin, the former Soviet ambassador to Washington, recalls, "On January 16, 1964, less than two months after [Lyndon] Johnson had taken office, William Foster, who was McNamara's soul mate and director of the Arms Control

---

4. By the way, the last on the list of visiting experts (in accordance with the hierarchy) was Professor V. A. Tepliakov, who was showered with praise and special treatment at Los Alamos as the discoverer of the principle that was the basis of the project "Beam Experiment Aboard a Rocket" (BEAR), which was a part of SDI. I was impressed with the deep and sincere respect demonstrated by American scientists toward Tepliakov (frankly, I had been unaware of his role in this field).

and Disarmament Agency, had a long conversation with me at lunch. He argued it would be feasible for both nations to renounce building a major ABM system."[5] These confidential contacts were continued for more than three years by both Foster and McNamara. "I sent Moscow numerous reports on the ABM system but received no formal reaction," Dobrynin writes.[6] He testifies further that Brezhnev "pointed out that McNamara made sense when he argued that the ABM system could be overwhelmed by increasing the number of offensive missiles." However, he adds: "In Moscow there was no consensus within the government. Some ministers led by [Prime Minister] Kosygin believed that ABM systems were clearly designed to protect human life, and no negotiations were needed to prove it. How could one refuse to protect people against missiles?"[7]

In July 1967 the Soviet delegation headed by Kosygin came to New York to participate in the UN emergency session on the Middle East. This occasion was used for a meeting between Johnson and Kosygin. Although the official agenda of the summit focused on Vietnam and the Middle East, McNamara decided to take the opportunity to convince Kosygin of the need to ban ABM systems. When he raised this issue, Kosygin's initial reaction was absolutely negative. "Defense is moral, aggression is immoral," he retorted.[8] But the more McNamara spoke, the more seriously and attentively Kosygin listened to him.[9] Of course, he did not give any definite answer, but in Moscow he reported this discussion to the Politburo in a positive way, in contrast to his previous position. Thus a central obstacle to negotiations on an ABM ban was overcome, and in 1972 the ABM Treaty was concluded, to the benefit of both the United States and the USSR, and international security as a whole.

Behind-the-Scenes Internal Differences and Their Impact upon Negotiations

Any delegation participating in negotiations on sensitive matters is influenced by differences within the upper political echelons in its capital. This makes the negotiators more cautious in their behavior. Neither the U.S. delegation nor ours at the START talks was an exception.

"In Geneva," write Michael R. Beschloss and Strobe Talbott, "Richard Burt, the chief U.S. START negotiator, was frustrated. He would send suggestions to

---

5. Anatoly Dobrynin, *In Confidence: Moscow's Ambassador to America's Six Cold War Presidents* (New York: Times Books, 1995), 149.

6. Ibid., 150.

7. Ibid.

8. Ibid., 165.

9. Besides Dobrynin's memoirs, I received valuable information about this event from Victor Sukhodrev, who was interpreting the conversation. Sukhodrev is sure that it was a turning point in Kosygin's position on ABM.

the administration on how to resolve the sticking points. He would reach tentative deals with his Soviet counterpart, Yuri Nazarkin, only to have them slapped down by Washington, often on personal instructions by [National Security Adviser Brent] Scowcroft."[10]

We experienced such complications even on compromises that had been reached at the ministerial level. I refer to heavy missiles. The Soviet Union had 304 SS-18 heavy missiles, and the United States had no heavy missiles. The U.S. side wanted those missiles to be eliminated and banned. The Soviet side insisted that SS-18s be treated on equal footing with other intercontinental ballistic missiles. The solution to this issue was found at the ministerial meeting in October 1990 between Secretary of State Baker and Foreign Minister Eduard Shevardnadze.

The package on heavy missiles included the elimination of 50 percent of heavy missiles, a ban on heavy ICBMs of a new type, and a few other minor restraints on heavy missiles. But our instructions provided for the inclusion in the treaty of a right to deploy additional silo launchers for heavy ICBMs to replace those that have been eliminated.

Burt was reluctant to accept this provision. He blocked the whole package and took time out to consult with his deputy and advisers. After that he said that he was prepared to recommend to his secretary of state acceptance of the whole package on heavies, including the right to replace silos, but he also wanted the Soviet side to explain its motives for keeping this option open. My instructions did not throw any light on this, so I replied that it was indeed possible that we would offer an explanation, but that it would take time to obtain one because we would have to send a cable to Moscow and wait for a reply. I added: "If you wish to finish with heavies today, I can give you my own explanation right now, but informally." He agreed, and I explained that we might need to replace launchers in case of an accident or disaster such as an earthquake or in the event of internal political developments dictating the relocation of silos within the Soviet Union. Minister Shevardnadze was glad that we did not need to send a cable to Moscow. Secretary Baker also looked satisfied with Burt's report to him. They confirmed our package. But unfortunately that was not the end of the story. And its continuation was rather dramatic.

A few days later I met Burt in Geneva; he was extremely gloomy. He told me what happened after the ministerial meeting. The day after the meeting, U.S. defense secretary Richard Cheney had visited Moscow (the visit had been scheduled long before and had nothing to do with the START talks). At the meeting with Defense Minister Dmitri Yazov, Cheney asked him why the Soviet side was going to replace silo launchers of heavy missiles. Yazov replied that it had no such plans.

---

10.   Michael R. Beschloss and Strobe Talbott, *At the Highest Levels: The Inside Stories of the End of the Cold War* (Boston, London: Little, Brown and Company, 1993), 373.

Indeed, at that time there were no such plans, though the General Staff wanted to keep this option open for the future. The agenda of the ministers' meeting did not contain arms control items, and Yazov did not have at hand his arms control experts who could remind him about the agreement on heavy missiles reached in New York two days earlier.

When back in Washington, Cheney spread the allegation that Secretary Baker had been deceived by the Russians. It took time to settle this very unpleasant situation. It was resolved after Yazov and Shevardnadze sent a formal letter to Cheney and Baker, which explained that although at present the Soviet side had no plans to redeploy silo launchers for heavy ICBMs, that possibility could not be ruled out for the future either for technical reasons or "in connection with internal political developments that are taking place in our country."

Why did Cheney play this card? I assume that it was part of the broader game against the START Treaty being played in Washington.

Mistakes in Strategy

As this chapter has shown, I have a high regard for the professionalism of American negotiators and for U.S. negotiating tactics. As for U.S. strategy, however, my evaluation is more critical. The main blemish in U.S. negotiating strategy is that short-term interests usually prevail over long-term ones. This can probably be explained by the fact that American politicians give higher priority to their domestic political interests than to foreign policy considerations. Sometimes, the quick achievement of positive negotiating results that may be advantageous domestically turns out to be counterproductive from the perspective of longer-term security interests. Two examples illustrate this point.

The first concerns U.S. strategy for arms control negotiations between 1985 and 1991. If one accepts the argument that a good negotiating strategy is one that sees negotiations within the context of a general, long-term global strategy, then the United States made a few strategic mistakes in these years. The United States assessed correctly Gorbachev's desire to end the Cold War, helped him accomplish it, and benefited from his readiness to make concessions. However, the United States overdid its pressure on Gorbachev to obtain more concessions, undermining Gorbachev's domestic position, which, I am sure, was not in the U.S. interest. The United States insisted on the inclusion of Soviet SS-23 tactical missiles in the INF Treaty,[11] and it rejected all of Gorbachev's compromise proposals on the utilization of the Krasnoyarsk radar station, which had to be eliminated in accordance with the ABM Treaty.

---

11. The treaty banned missiles with ranges between 500 and 5,500 kilometers. The range of SS-20s was 400 kilometers, but the Americans alleged that their range was 500 kilometers. Gorbachev agreed to include them into the treaty.

The second example concerns the negotiations on the further reduction and limitation of strategic offensive armaments in 1992—the START-2 talks. It took only a few months to negotiate the treaty. The American negotiators had strict instructions to finish the treaty before George H. W. Bush left office. When their Russian counterparts tried to defend their positions, the Americans complained to Washington, and President Bush telephoned President Yeltsin and pressed him to order the Russian delegation to concede to Americans demands. The outcome was a draft treaty that heavily favored the United States. Specifically, the draft provided for complete elimination of heavy ICBMs and the complete prohibition of MIRVed ICBMs, which were the main leg of the Russian strategic triad, while leaving untouched MIRVed sea-launched ballistic missiles (SLBMs), which were the main leg of the U.S. strategic triad. The draft also established a deadline of January 1, 2003, for achieving the aggregate levels of armaments after the reduction provided for by the treaty, instead of the usual practice of setting a deadline a number of years after the treaty's entry into force.

Because of these and other shortcomings, the draft encountered a lot of resistance in the process of ratification in Russia. It took seven years before the Russian Duma would ratify the treaty, and it did so only after the draft was amended and reservations were added. The U.S. Senate did not vote on the amended treaty. Thus, START-2 did not enter into force. In other words, the U.S. negotiators' impatience and desire to gain one-sided advantages through exerting pressure on their Russian counterparts achieved nothing of concrete, practical value.

Looking Ahead

During the administration of George W. Bush, American unilateralism and egocentrism exacerbated the country's difficulties in adopting a long-term perspective and weakened its negotiating skills. If the United States can dictate to its negotiating counterparts, why should it look for compromises?

Although the United States and Russia concluded a treaty on strategic offensive reductions (SORT) in 2002, this agreement did not require any negotiations in the real sense of the word. This document contains only unilateral declarations by President George W. Bush and President Vladimir Putin to reduce their respective operationally deployed strategic offensive warheads. These declarations of intent are not identical, the subject of the treaty is defined very vaguely, there are no implementation procedures, and no verification is provided for. In other words, the "treaty" label is purely symbolic and does not correspond with the contents of the document.

I do not know whether this approach has resulted in U.S. negotiators losing the ability to understand their counterparts' positions and losing interest in finding mutually acceptable win-win solutions. I hope not. Perhaps those talents will once again become important to U.S.-Russian negotiations. Russia seems likely to continue its efforts to establish itself as a country not susceptible to external pressure—to say nothing of external domination. Russian economic growth, the reinforcement of Russian military capabilities, and the rise of Russian nationalism all support this expectation.

President Obama's first steps, particularly the negotiations with Russia on a new treaty to replace the START agreement, inspire hopes that we may enter a new era of productive arms control negotiations. If so, Obama will have to overcome strong opposition from supporters of American unilateralism. Moreover, this new era is likely to be different from the earlier era, although exactly how it will differ is uncertain. Perhaps, the United States will continue to act like a hegemon but will also seek to soften its image by displaying a constructive approach to international cooperation on security issues. This will require U.S. participation in international discussions on security issues in venues such as the Conference on Disarmament. In this case, American diplomats will need to specialize in diplomatic maneuvering—not in reaching agreements on the basis of compromises. Another scenario would see U.S. foreign policy returning to the spirit of balanced negotiation and showing willingness to compromise. If this happens, the professionalism and skills of the negotiators of the 1970s and 1980s will again be in demand.

12

Negotiating Bilaterally: India's Evolving Experience with the United States

Lalit Mansingh

When the United States and India exchanged diplomatic ties in 1941, six years ahead of Indian independence, it was seen as a promising augury for lasting ties between the world's two largest democracies. But events, as they unfolded, belied the high expectations on both sides. Despite their best efforts, Washington and New Delhi failed to achieve a minimal level of understanding that could have led to substantive cooperation on political and economic issues.

At the beginning of the Cold War, India did not count as an important state for the Americans. They saw it as a country mired in poverty and preoccupied with intractable internal problems. India's policy of nonalignment was unacceptable to Washington. The policymakers at the State Department, the Pentagon, and the White House concluded that India was not relevant to U.S. strategic interests. As Steve Cohen put it, "India was an object of American charity, not strategy."[1]

By the end of the Cold War, American strategists began to look at India differently. In 1994, when the United States was the world's unchallenged superpower, Henry Kissinger was contemplating the inevitable decline of American power in the twenty-first century. A new balance of power, he predicted, would require the United States to share its influence with "Europe, China, Japan, Russia and probably India."[2] By the turn of the century, the word "probably" had quietly been dropped. Studies conducted by think tanks such as the Asia Society and the

---

1. Stephen Cohen, *Emerging Power: India* (Washington, D.C.: Brookings Institution, 2001), 4.

2. Henry Kissinger, *Diplomacy* (New York: Simon and Schuster, 1994), 23.

Council on Foreign Relations were urging the United States to pay more attention to India as an emerging power.

The rethink on India eventually reached the policymaking levels in the administration and in the first years of the new century a new, more cooperative and mutually respectful relationship between the United States and India began to take shape.

This chapter traces the evolution of this relationship through six brief case studies. Each explores a significant episode in Indo-U.S. relations between 1962 and 2008 and reveals the impact on bilateral diplomacy of cultural differences, cultural misunderstanding, and—in more recent years—cultural awareness.

The case studies forcefully establish the importance of cross-cultural understanding in resolving disputes and promoting friendly relations. Raymond Cohen and others have rightly questioned the assumption that—in the words of I. William Zartman and Maureen Berman—"there is a single, universal paradigm of negotiation and that cross-national differences are stylish and superficial." The belief in a universal model is an element of what Cohen describes as the "low-context" communicating style of the United States.[3]

Washington's problems with India for those first fifty years arose of out its inability to comprehend that India's cultural and national sensitivities outweighed its desire to conclude favorable "deals" with the United States. As the case study on U.S. food aid to India demonstrates, American leaders were baffled that while Indians were desperately in need of food, they would not explicitly ask for it. And further, when they received food, they appeared reluctant to express their appreciation. "With an acute sense of natural pride," Cohen has commented, "India developed a unique strategy for saving face: it would accept needed assistance, but it would not say please or thank you."[4] This is a telling example of a genuine cultural gap, between Eastern face-saving and Western expectations of good manners.

To many American leaders, India's claims of moral superiority and demands to be treated on equal and equitable terms appeared pompous and overbearing. In 1981, for instance, India vigorously protested the U.S. decision to suspend the supply of nuclear fuel for the Tarapore nuclear plant and insisted on the United States fulfilling its contractual obligations. It was galling for the Americans when India pointed to the hypocrisy of the nuclear powers accepting no limits to their stockpiles of fissile material while objecting to India's nuclear program. India was equally vehement in criticizing the double standards of the nuclear powers when the Nuclear Non-Proliferation Treaty (NPT) was extended indefinitely in 1995. It took American negotiators a long time to appreciate that the frequent Indian recourse to the moral high ground was not a negotiating ploy, but a genuine demand for fair and equitable treatment.

---

3. Raymond Cohen, *Negotiating across Cultures: International Communication in an Interdependent World* (Washington, D.C.: United States Institute of Peace Press, 2004), 20, 36–38.

4. Ibid., 93.

The American approach to negotiations can best be described as "mercantile," a reflection perhaps of the strong entrepreneurial tradition of the United States. As in business negotiations, each case is considered a deal, with an implied bottom-line. As negotiations proceed, concessions are offered, losses are minimized, and a bargain is eventually reached.

Within this overall mercantile approach exist two quite different negotiating styles: coercive and persuasive. The "coercive negotiator" typically expects his counterpart to appreciate and respect the overwhelming strength and power of the United States. He or she is often poorly informed about the history, culture, and national sensitivities of other countries, and neither understands nor cares about cultural nuances. The coercive negotiator's typical normal approach is, "I'll be happy if you agree with me. I'll hammer you if you don't." A major weakness of this approach is that it tends to discount powerful natural sentiments such as ideology, patriotism, historical experience, suspicion, and paranoia—each of which can offset the seemingly obvious benefits of a good deal.

The "persuasive negotiator," by contrast, is typically well informed about the background of the country with which he or she deals. This negotiator is sensitive to the concerns of interlocutors and treats them with equality and respect. The coercive American negotiating style prevailed for much of the first five decades of Indo-U.S. relations; it was only after the end of the Cold War that U.S. diplomacy noticeably shifted to the persuasive style.

"A Half Century of Misunderstandings, Miscues and Mishaps"

The late Senator Daniel P. Moynihan, a former U.S. ambassador to India, aptly summarized the first five decades of Indo-U.S. relations as "a half century of misunderstandings, miscues and mishaps."[5]

Much has been written on the underlying causes of the state of tension between the two countries. The record of official dialogue and negotiations suggests three major contributing factors: ideological differences and conflicting perceptions of national interest; the impact of the key personalities on both sides; and finally, cultural misperceptions that distorted negotiating behavior.

Ideological differences

A major reason for the estrangement between New Delhi and Washington was the fundamental conflict in their world views and consequently a perception of incompatible national interests. With the onset of the Cold War, the United States identified international communism as the principal threat to its national security and to the existence of the free world. It expected India, as a newly independent nation

---

5. Daniel P. Moynihan, quoted in Dennis Kux *Estranged Democracies: India and the United States, 1941–1991*, (New Delhi: Sage Publications, 1993), xviii.

wedded to democratic values, to be its natural ally in the ideological battle against the Soviet bloc.

India, however, differed with the American world view and preferred to remain nonaligned. While the United States, using a network of military alliances, proceeded to throw a cordon sanitaire around the Soviet Union, India led a formidable global opposition against military blocs through the Non-Aligned Movement (NAM), the largest group of sovereign states outside the United Nations.

These ideological differences persisted between Washington and New Delhi throughout the Cold War period. John Foster Dulles declared nonalignment "immoral" and incompatible with friendship with the United States. For India, nonalignment remained an article of faith.

Differences erupted over a succession of major issues: China and its claim to a permanent seat in the United Nations; the Korean War; the Indochina crisis; the Hungarian uprising, the Vietnam War, and the Soviet presence in Afghanistan. Both sides remained adamant and uncompromising in upholding their respective principles.

The influence of key personalities

With the exception of Dwight D. Eisenhower, John F. Kennedy, Jimmy Carter, and Ronald Reagan, American leaders during the Cold War were seen by Indians as indifferent or hostile toward their country. A prominent figure in the gallery of "unfriendly" American leaders was Dulles, the U.S. secretary of state under Eisenhower. Indian accounts portray him as a malevolent, ayatollah-like figure who issued *fatwa*s against nonalignment and who sought to isolate India by inducting Pakistan into U.S. military alliances. "John Foster Dulles," recalled T. N. Kaul, who served in Washington as a junior diplomat in the Harry S. Truman years and went on to become India's ambassador to Washington and then foreign secretary, "was a fanatic, a dogmatic and self-righteous missionary turned politician."[6]

Interestingly, the United States had equally negative perceptions of Indian leaders such as Nehru and Krishna Menon. Arthur Schlesinger, Jr., has commented that "Nehru's talent for international self-righteousness led Kennedy in some moods to view him as almost the John Foster Dulles of neutralism."[7]

Two other American leaders share with Dulles a reputation for bias and hostility toward India: Richard Nixon and Henry Kissinger. It was no secret that Nixon was splenetic with regard to India and loathed Prime Minister Indira Gandhi. Declassified White House documents have revealed conversations between Nixon and Kissinger that contain derogatory and insulting remarks about Mrs. Gandhi.

6. T. N. Kaul, *Reminiscences, Discreet and Indiscreet* (New Delhi: Lancer Publishers, 1982), 155.

7. Arthur Schlesinger, Jr., *A Thousand Days: John F. Kennedy in the White House* (Boston: Houghton Mifflin, 1965), 438.

The antipathy was reciprocated: Kaul, for instance, has scathingly referred to Henry Kissinger's "double dealing, double talk and double think."[8] Not surprisingly, Indo-U.S. relations reached their lowest depth during the Nixon presidency.

Apart from the Nixon years and some other notable exceptions, however, Indian diplomats serving in Washington generally found a friendlier reception at the White House through the national security adviser's office than at the State Department. As recently as the 1990s, professional American diplomats displayed a conspicuous lack of respect toward Indian officials. For example, former foreign secretary J. N. Dixit recounts his interactions with Robin Raphel, who was nominated by President Bill Clinton in 1992 as the assistant secretary of state in a newly created Bureau of South Asian Affairs while she was serving as a counselor in the U.S. embassy in Delhi. While India saw the establishment of the bureau as a signal that the United States was taking it more seriously, Raphel, in her farewell call on the then foreign secretary, surprised him by declaring that "Clinton was not deeply interested in Asia, especially in the sub-continent." She then made the demand that she must meet the Indian prime minister to convey a message from the U.S. president. It is not common practice for heads of government to receive relatively junior diplomats, but because Raphel persisted and refused to meet even the foreign minister, the prime minister's office relented and a meeting was arranged. As for the U.S. president's urgent message, there was not any![9]

On taking up her new post in Washington, Raphel created a greater storm in Indo-U.S. relations. She declared that the Instrument of Accession between the Maharaja of Jammu and Kashmir and the Government of India of October 1947 (on the basis of which the state joined the Indian Union) was not considered politically or legally valid by the United States. This statement and the generally hostile attitude of Raphel toward India cast a pall over Indo-U.S. relations during Bill Clinton's first term.

The impact of cultural differences

A third and major factor that adversely affected Indo-U.S. relations were the cultural differences between the two countries. They had few historical contacts, and their ruling elites derived their impressions and images from secondhand sources, particularly from the British.

Harold Isaacs, a journalist, undertook a comprehensive study at the Massachusetts Institute of Technology on American attitudes toward India and China and published it in 1958 under the title *Scratches on Our Minds*. The average American's idea of India, according to Isaacs, amounted to "maharajas, jewels, wealth,

---

8. T. N. Kaul, *The Kissinger Years: Indo-American Relations* (New Delhi: Arnold-Heinemann, 1980), 58.

9. J. N. Dixit, *My South Block Years: Memoirs of a Foreign Secretary* (New Delhi: UBSPD, 1996), 191–193.

snake-charmers, elephants, tigers, tiger-hunts, cobras, snakes, monkeys." The few American missionaries who worked in India in the early twentieth century were culturally ill-equipped to understand the deep philosophical insights of Hinduism. They saw it as a debased, heathen religion steeped in centuries-old social traditions. Many of Isaac's interviewees associated Indians with blacks and viewed them with racial prejudice.[10]

As a consequence, Americans knew little of India as one of the ancient civilizations of the world, nor did they comprehend its complex, multicultural, multireligious, and pluralistic society. The paradoxical images of India as a land of feudal wealth, mysticism, and destitution continued until the 1990s. U.S. cultural misperceptions of India were not only real; they were also a potent factor for creating misunderstanding. As Robert Goheen, a former U.S. ambassador to India, observed, "There are vast differences in the cultural background of Americans and Indians, which sometimes lead to differing expectations and ways of interpreting experience."[11]

While honest efforts were made to reach out to the other side in the early years, they failed to produce results because the gap was too wide to bridge. The following account of Nehru's efforts to understand America is illustrative.

In October 1949, Nehru, as prime minister of India, went on his first visit to the United States. Intended to be his discovery of America, it ended up as his disappointment with America. Washington found it difficult to understand his "Asian personality" and his complex intellect. Nehru's own reactions reflected his British education and the prejudices of the British elite. He was appalled to observe Americans flaunting their wealth in social conversations. He found the conversation at Truman's White House banquet far from stimulating, the principal topic being the merits of Kentucky bourbon! Nehru "found the United States too cocksure about the rights and wrongs of the Cold War, too insensitive to the aspirations of the colonial peoples and too patronizing in dealing with India."[12] Two subsequent visits by Nehru did not improve on his earlier impressions of the United States.

At other levels, Americans found their Indian interlocutors to be snobbish and condescending. Raymond Cohen cites the testimony of three U.S. diplomats who had served in India. One stated that Indians walk around with a "chip on their shoulder." Another said that New Delhi "looked down on U.S. diplomats with 'Anglophilic snobbery' as a bunch of 'country bumpkins—brash and comic, if well meaning.'" A third diplomat described "a Krishna Menon syndrome compounded of a mixture of arrogance and hypersensitivity," which was found at all levels of

10. Harold Isaacs in M. V. Kamath, *The United States and India, 1776–1996* (New Delhi: Indian Council for Cultural Relations, 1998), 191–192.

11. Quoted in Cohen, *Negotiating across Cultures*, 20.

12. Kux, *Estranged Democracies*, 69.

the Foreign Ministry, "from junior official to minister."[13] Whether accurate or not, this portrayal of Indian officials pointed to a serious communication gap on the diplomatic front.

The Indian perception of American negotiators in the early years was a mirror image of the perceptions described above. American officials were seen as arrogant, self-righteous, condescending, and culturally insensitive.

John Foster Dulles was the original archetype of the Ugly American. Citing Dulles as an example of "cultural ignorance and strategic short-sightedness," Harold Gould describes the following conversation between Dulles and columnist Walter Lippmann at a Washington dinner party in the fifties:

> "Look Walter," Dulles said, "I've got to get some real fighting men into the south of Asia. The only Asians who can really fight are the Pakistanis. That's why we need them in the alliance. We could never get along without the Gurkhas."
>
> "But Foster," Lippmann reminded him, "The Gurkhas aren't Pakistanis, they are Indians."
>
> "Well," responded Dulles, unperturbed by such nit picking, and irritated at the Indians for not joining his alliance, "they may not be Pakistanis, but they're Muslims."
>
> "No, I'm afraid they are not Muslims either, they are Hindus."
>
> "No matter," Dulles replied, and proceeded to lecture Lippmann for half an hour.[14]

* * *

The following four case studies illustrate how cross-cultural and cross-national differences led to serious misunderstandings during the Cold War. All of these cases, it should be noted, had strong political overtones—and political issues seemed particularly susceptible to cultural miscommunication. In the same period, India and the United States signed scores of agreements on subjects such as agriculture and technology transfer after negotiations where cultural misunderstandings were refreshingly absent. When it came to high stakes and high politics, however, negotiations were considerably less businesslike and less successful.

Case study 1
1962: Arm twisting and dithering with arms supplies

In 1962, China invaded the northern borders of India. For India it was an act of betrayal and a national humiliation; for Prime Minister Nehru, a great loss of face. Yet, confronted with this massive threat to India's security, he swallowed his pride and appealed to the United States for assistance. In two separate letters to President Kennedy in November 1962, Nehru requested a dozen squadrons of U.S. fighter aircraft, air defense, and communications equipment to protect Indian cities, and two squadrons of B-47 bombers, flown by U.S. pilots, to strike at Chi-

---

13.   Cohen, *Negotiating across Cultures*, 47.

14.   Harold A. Gould, "U.S.-India Relations: The Early Phase," in *The Hope and the Reality: U.S.-Indian Relations from Roosevelt to Reagan*, ed. Harold A. Gould and Sumit Ganguly (Boulder, Colo.: Westview Press, 1992), 36–37.

nese positions along the border. The U.S. embassy in New Delhi estimated that India urgently required military equipment worth $500 million.

For the United States, the situation was not merely a vindication of its warnings to India about the Communists. It was also an opportunity for a breakthrough in relations. Had the United States responded promptly and assisted India in building up its military strength against China, India very likely would have reviewed its foreign policy and come closer to the United States. That did not happen.

The U.S. did indeed send some military supplies, mostly light arms and communications equipment. They were, however, far short of what India needed to meet the Chinese threat.

Unable to forge a consensus within his administration, Kennedy made a serious blunder in turning to Britain—India's erstwhile colonial master—for advice in assessing India's plea for help.

Washington made a further error of judgment in assuming that a vulnerable India could be pressured into accepting a settlement on Kashmir as a quid pro quo for military assistance.

The U.S. administration continued to dither. In November 1963, a year after the Indian request, the U.S. administration had still not decided on military assistance to India. According to Chester Bowles, the U.S. ambassador in New Delhi, President Kennedy called a meeting on November 26, 1963, to finalize the aid package. The meeting was destined never to take place as Kennedy was assassinated before that. The arms supplies to India did not take place either.

The expectations of a Kashmir settlement were also doomed from the beginning. U.S. officials were naive in believing that a proud and sensitive India would bargain its territory in return for a promise of arms.

The long delay in processing India's request for military assistance convinced India that the United States was not a dependable friend in need.

U.S. ambassador Galbraith had warned President Kennedy in a telegram that if the administration continued to drag its feet, "we will have no progress in Kashmir and no Indians either." That is exactly what happened. As Galbraith commented, "a great opportunity to bring India into a much closer working association with the West" was missed.[15]

Case study 2
1965–66: Bargaining with food

Devastating famines were frequent during British colonial rule. The biggest of them, the great Bengal famine of 1943–44, took a toll of 3.4 million lives. Thus,

---

15. Quoted in Kux, *Estranged Democracies*, 212–213.

dealing with a chronic food shortage was one of the major national challenges faced by a newly independent India in the early fifties.

The United States must be credited for protecting India from famine for two decades after independence. The Green Revolution, launched with American assistance, eventually transformed India into a food-surplus country.

The food grains supplied to India from the United States during this period were worth $4 billion. It would be difficult to cite a better instance of American humanitarian concern and generosity, and equally difficult to find a worse public relations disaster for U.S. foreign policy.

There are two possible reasons why this potential success story turned so horribly sour. First, there was a cultural difference, which created a sense of discomfiture for the Indians at the beginning of the process. The bigger cause, however, was an unfortunate and inappropriate decision taken by President Lyndon Johnson to use food shipments as a coercive lever to change India's agricultural and foreign policies.

The cultural differences emerged in 1949 when Nehru went on his first official visit to Washington. With a request for food assistance clearly on his agenda, he mentioned it only obliquely to President Truman. In the Indian tradition, an explicit request—especially for food—would be equivalent to begging. This was contrary to the newborn nation's pride and self-respect!

Necessity compelled the Indians to overcome this inhibition and send a formal request for food aid. President Truman responded positively, but a fresh misunderstanding arose when American officials floated the idea of bartering strategic material from India in return for wheat. It raised suspicions that Americans were using food to extract concessions from a hapless people. This was sorted out, but then Truman encountered stiff opposition from the U.S. Congress on food aid to India. The delayed American responses stoked Nehru's frustration and suspicions.

The eventual passage of PL-480 (Food for Peace) in Congress made it easier for India to receive uninterrupted food supplies during the Eisenhower and Kennedy administrations. By the time Lyndon Johnson became president, India was receiving close to 5 million tons of food annually from the United States.

But, in June 1965, Johnson ordered a halt to routine food shipments and asked for a "hard new look" at food aid for India. He was not convinced that India was doing enough to boost its domestic food production. He was also unhappy with India's stand on Vietnam.

This was the beginning of Johnson's "short tether" policy, which outraged Indians and mystified senior administration officials in Washington. As Dennis Kux has described, managing food to India became an "intense, obsessive, personal involvement for Johnson. . . . For the next two years Lyndon Johnson, in effect, became the U.S. government's 'desk officer' for PL-480 food aid to India."[16]

---

16.   Kux, *Estranged Democracies*, 243.

In 1965 India suffered its worst drought in a century and in 1966 the monsoons failed again. With famine around the corner, it was a nail-biting period for the Indian leadership. Johnson remained unmoved. Ignoring the pleas of Agriculture Secretary Orville Freeman and Secretary of State Dean Rusk, Johnson continued to impose on India what he himself called a "ship-to-mouth" existence. In December 1966, Prime Minister Indira Gandhi, as sensitive to "begging" as her father, made a desperate telephone call to Johnson to release the shipments of wheat. As recalled by an aide, she exclaimed angrily after the conversation, "I don't want us ever to beg for food again."

The fact that India achieved an agricultural surplus by the early 1970s can hardly be regarded as a vindication of Johnson's "ship-to-mouth" strategy. India viewed this as an attempt to bargain with food destined for its hungry millions and an act of monumental insensitivity. What should have been one of the biggest success stories of U.S. foreign policy sadly turned into a diplomatic calamity.

Case study 3
1971 Bangladesh: Gunboat diplomacy against an emerging nation

Nineteen seventy was a watershed year in the history of Pakistan. In December, Pakistan's military dictator General Yahya Khan conducted the first-ever democratic elections in that country. The National Awami League led by Sheikh Mujibur Rahman secured a majority of the seats in the National Assembly.

The results did not please Yahya Khan because Rahman, a leader from the Bengali speaking province of East Pakistan, was not acceptable to the political elite of Pakistan. After several rounds of desultory negotiations, Yahya arrested Rahman and unleashed a reign of terror in East Pakistan. In due course, the political agitation of the East Pakistanis turned into a demand for an independent Bangladesh.

Indira Gandhi, then prime minister of India, raised her voice against the massive repression of people in East Pakistan and pledged India's support to the cause of Bangladesh. She also gave sanctuary to the thousands of refugees escaping into India. By November 1971, India was sheltering close to ten million refugees.

The U.S. mission in Dacca urged the U.S. administration to issue a strong statement against the human rights abuse in East Pakistan. Unfortunately, neither the White House nor the State Department was inclined to listen. Nixon, like many of his predecessors and successors, had a soft corner for Pakistani military rulers. He felt committed to Yahya Khan. The president's directives were conveyed in his own handwriting on a Kissinger memo: "To all hands. Don't squeeze Yahya at this time."

To draw attention to India's mounting burden of refugees and also to plead for a political solution in East Pakistan, Mrs. Gandhi took a three-week tour of Western capitals at the end of October 1971. She met with some sympathy in London and Paris, but was stonewalled in Washington.

Nixon, who nursed a disdain for India from his days as vice president, was mistrustful of Mrs. Gandhi. Her reference in a speech at the White House ceremonies on November 4, 1971, to the "man-made tragedy of vast proportions" of East Pakistan angered Nixon so much that he kept Mrs. Gandhi waiting for forty-five minutes before meeting her at the White House the next day.

This was an unprecedented breach of etiquette between two heads of government. As anticipated, the meeting was frosty. Not a word of sympathy came from Nixon or Kissinger for the hapless victims of Pakistani repression or the ten million Bangladeshi refugees in India.

On December 4, 1971, Pakistan declared war against India after a surprise attack on eight airfields in western India. The Indian army swung into action and engaged the Pakistani army in the east. In twelve days, by December 16, Pakistan had surrendered, with 93,000 soldiers taken as POWs. Bangladesh emerged into nationhood.

The rapid pace of events not only caught Nixon and Kissinger on the wrong foot but also prompted them to order a pointless display of American military power. The USS *Enterprise* was dispatched to the Bay of Bengal with the ostensible purpose of evacuating U.S. nationals in the region. Its unstated mission was to serve a warning to India and the Soviet Union to stay off Pakistan. It was also intended to demonstrate to the Chinese that the United States could be counted upon as a trusted ally.

The U.S. Navy, as it turned out, had no role to play in the crisis. To Bangladesh and India, the deployment was a demonstration of callous American indifference to the sufferings of millions of people struggling for nationhood. It was also symbolic of U.S. gunboat diplomacy in the late twentieth century.

The comments of the late Senator Moynihan are relevant. "Far from a diplomatic victory the whole affair proved an unnecessary and embarrassing diplomatic setback for the United States. Through their misreading of the crisis, and their pro-Pakistan bias, Richard Nixon and Henry Kissinger succeeded in needlessly transforming a regional dispute into one which threatened to become a great power showdown. The main consequences were severe and long lasting damage to U.S. relations with India and enhanced Soviet influence with New Delhi."[17]

Case study 4
1989: Super 301—The sledgehammer approach

Expressing concern about the chronic U.S. balance of payments deficits, the U.S. Congress passed the Omnibus Trade and Competitive Act in 1988. Section 301 of

---

17.   Daniel Patrick Moynihan in ibid., xxiii.

the act, popularly known as Super 301, authorized the president to take retaliatory action against countries that purportedly restricted U.S. exports.

Armed with Super 301, the administration of George H. W. Bush initiated proceedings in April 1990 against Japan, India, and Brazil.

The Office of the United States Trade Representative (USTR) was undoubtedly aware that trade surpluses and deficits were normal in a system of free international trade. It also knew that the correct recourse against alleged violations of free trade was to approach the General Agreement on Tariffs and Trade (GATT) and not inflict unilateral penalties against the parties concerned. The administration nevertheless opted for a muscular approach, which was administered by the soft-spoken and diminutive USTR, Mrs. Carla Hills. She made it clear that she would use Super 301 as a "crowbar" to crack open all the difficult markets in the world.

Faced with the threat of punishment, Japan and Brazil discreetly negotiated concessions with the USTR and were taken off the list. India remained defiant, threatening to take up the issue with GATT. India's total, two-way trade with the United States in 1989 was $5.8 billion, which included a surplus of $690 million in India's favor. Modest compared with Japan's surplus of $60 billion, it could hardly justify the American demands for immediate changes in India's foreign investment and patent laws.

It was largely due to the persuasive diplomacy of India's then ambassador, Abid Hussain, that the White House and the USTR finally cooled off, thereby averting an ugly diplomatic crisis. At a White House meeting with President Bush, Ambassador Hussain succeeded in shifting the focus from the minutia of trade disputes to the potential benefits of a wider strategic and economic cooperation between the two countries. The Indian economy was poised for dramatic growth and the United States would benefit from the opportunities opening up in trade and industry, especially in new sectors such as defense technology and civil aviation. Hussain also reminded the president that the world looked up to Washington for its global leadership in supporting democracy and free trade. Bush was sufficiently persuaded to call Hills during the meeting and urged her to give India a favorable hearing.

Indo-U.S. trade has expanded nearly five times since 1990, and India has continued to post a modest trade surplus every year—without facing the sledgehammer so far.

The Post–Cold War: From Strategic Irrelevance to Strategic Partnership

The fall of the Berlin Wall, the implosion of the Soviet Union, and the end of bipolarity had no immediate impact on Indo-U.S. relations. Two major irritants from the Cold War period—"the two Ps," Pakistan and proliferation—however, remained intractable.

Indians saw the U.S. offer to play the honest broker between India and Pakistan on Kashmir as an act of hypocrisy. After all, Pakistan was an American ally, generously aided and supplied with sophisticated weaponry that it actually used against India. Americans also failed to appreciate that Kashmir was integral to India's identity as a secular and democratic nation. As long as India perceived Washington to be tilted toward Islamabad, it could not accept an American mediatory role in resolving the Kashmir issue.

Nuclear proliferation was the other obdurate issue. Differences had been simmering since India refused to sign the NPT in 1968. India opposed the NPT as an iniquitous agreement that created a club of nuclear weapon superpowers from which the rest of the world was permanently excluded. As Strobe Talbott observed, "the NPT embodied for Indians 'the three Ds' of U.S. Nuclear Policy—dominance, discrimination and double standards."[18]

In 1995 the Clinton administration made a determined effort to "cap, roll back, and eliminate" India's nuclear program. A defiant India responded by conducting nuclear tests in 1998, declaring itself a nuclear weapon power. India regarded nuclear weapons as essential to its national security and big-power status.

On both the issues of Kashmir and nuclear proliferation, the United States underestimated the strength of Indian nationalist sentiment, its fierce pride in its civilizational status, and its desire to be treated with equality and respect by the other major powers. Noticeably absent from Indo-U.S. bilateral relations was the most important element that cements the friendship of nations—the element of trust.

Paradoxically, while the issue of nuclear testing plunged Indo-U.S. relations into crisis, it also set the stage for the adoption of a new American approach toward the relationship. The seeds of that new approach had been sown at the outset of the 1990s, when India's economic reforms created a new and powerful constituency within the United States: the American business community. From being regarded a "basket case" for five decades, India began to be seen as an emerging market and a rising global power. The high profile and political activism of the two million-strong Indian-American community reinforced this new image.

Notwithstanding his furious reaction to India's nuclear tests in June 1998, President Bill Clinton was the one who took the bold step of reaching out to India. In March 2000, on the eve of his landmark visit to India, Bill Clinton was presented with a brief prepared by the State Department under the title "Ten Reasons Why We Need to Engage India." These reasons were briefly

- to seek better ties with "an emerging global power and the world's largest nation in the making";
- to support shared democratic values;

---

18.   Strobe Talbott, *Engaging India: Diplomacy, Democracy and the Bomb* (New Delhi: Viking, 2004), 91.

- to maximize the U.S. partnership with one of the world's largest economies;
- to help move India toward the global nonproliferation mainstream;
- to enhance joint efforts on urgent global issues such as terrorism and narcotics;
- to work together to deal with challenges to regional stability;
- to protect the global environment;
- to join hands on global health issues such as polio and AIDS;
- to upgrade U.S. access to world-class Indian players in the vital area of information technology; and
- to enlarge links in education, culture, and people-to-people exchanges.[19]

New Delhi and Washington had reached a stage where they could no longer view each other as adversaries.

The Clinton visit to India in March 2000, the first visit by a U.S. president in twenty-two years, was a signal for India that the United States would hereafter display greater sensitivity to India's sense of self-respect and national aspirations.

Clinton reassured India on the two outstanding bilateral issues, Kashmir and nonproliferation. He brought to an end the pro-Pakistan tilt in U.S. foreign policy. On nonproliferation, he was willing to accept the reality of India's new nuclear status. Above all, after five decades of troubled relations, Clinton established a new relationship of trust.

The change of track from "coercive" to "persuasive" diplomacy is best illustrated in two case studies of recent negotiations between India and the United States.

Case study 5
1998–2000: A dialogue of civilized nations

In May 1998, when India conducted a series of nuclear tests and declared itself a nuclear-weapon power, an infuriated Bill Clinton slapped crippling sanctions against India and persuaded the major powers of the world to do likewise.

But in June 1998 he asked Strobe Talbott, his friend and deputy secretary of state, to initiate a dialogue with India. Over the next two years, Talbott and his counterpart Jaswant Singh, the Indian external affairs minister, met fourteen times in seven countries on three continents. It was the longest, highest-level, and most intense dialogue the two countries had ever undertaken. Reversing five decades of mutual hostility, the Talbott-Singh discussions paved the way for the new strategic partnership later announced by George W. Bush.

---

19. Cohen, *Emerging Power*, 4.

In terms of substance and style, Talbott deserves to be rated as one of the outstanding American negotiators in recent times. His approach was notable for the following features:

- Conscious of his lack of exposure to India, Talbott (a Russia specialist) undertook a crash course on India's history and culture. He absorbed the immense complexity of India with intense curiosity and diligence.
- He was a careful and patient listener, allowing his counterpart to speak extensively on India's approach to issues, especially on its nuclear policy, its relations with Pakistan, and the dispute over Kashmir.
- He and Singh agreed in the beginning to explore each other's positions as they went along without a predetermined road map. A Rajasthani proverb cited by Jaswant Singh became their motto and guideline: "Don't ask the way to the village if you don't want to get there." The rest of the dialogue became a joint voyage toward a common destination.
- Talbott was quick to admit responsibility in cases where the United States had crossed the line and offended India's sensibilities. One such instance was Clinton's initiative in asking China's Jiang Zemin to join the United States in applying pressure on India after the 1998 nuclear tests. Admitting this as a serious error, Talbott later wrote, "Our goal with the Indians was to change their policies and attitudes, not to insult, embarrass or frighten them."[20]

By July 1998, the second month of the dialogue, Talbott and Singh had reached the core issue of the negotiations: the differences over nuclear policy. Talbott recognized that India's proclaimed status as a nuclear-weapon power was nonnegotiable: "India had put the world on notice that it was now unambiguously, unapologetically and irrevocably a nuclear armed power."[21] His goal therefore was to circumscribe India's nuclear ambitions and bring them in line with the global nonproliferation architecture that the United States was upholding.

Soon the outline of a possible agreement began to emerge. The United States was prepared to withdraw the sanctions in place against India and offer its hand of friendship, if India agreed to

1. sign the Comprehensive Test Ban Treaty (CTBT);
2. negotiate a Fissile Material Cut-off Treaty (FMCT);
3. observe a strategic restraint regime; and
4. enforce stringent world-class controls over the export of dangerous materials and technologies.

---

20. Talbott, *Engaging India*, 19.
21. Ibid., 51.

These four benchmarks, described as the four legs of the elephant, became the main agenda for the rest of the dialogue.

The Talbott-Singh dialogue ended on an inconclusive note in September 2000. The Clinton presidency came to an end soon after.

With characteristic modesty, Talbott admits that "Jaswant Singh came closer to achieving his objective in the dialogue than I did in achieving mine."[22]

The dialogue was not about scoring points but about seeking a common path to the village. Together, Talbott and Singh succeeded in creating a rapprochement in Indo-U.S. relations after fifty years of mutual hostility.

Case study 6
2005–08: The Indo-U.S. nuclear deal

A bold move that turned conventional wisdom on its head, the Indo-U.S. nuclear understanding, was a brilliant stroke of diplomacy. The author of the idea of a strategic partnership with India was undoubtedly George W. Bush. However, credit for mentoring the nuclear deal, which is the linchpin of the strategic partnership, goes to Condoleezza Rice and her team of negotiators. Considering the complexity of the issues and the formidable opposition faced by the leaders on both sides, within and outside their administrations, the Indo-U.S. nuclear cooperation agreement stands out as a model of successful diplomacy.

George W. Bush and his senior advisers recognized the contradiction in accepting India as a strategic partner and yet treating it as a nuclear pariah. The problem was that under U.S. law, especially the Nuclear Non-Proliferation Act, the administration was prohibited from transferring dual-use technology to any nation that had not signed the NPT.

In March 2005, Rice, making her maiden trip abroad as secretary of state, met Prime Minister Manmohan Singh in New Delhi and unfolded President Bush's grand vision for the region and the central role he had reserved for India. The United States was prepared to make a one-time exception and amend its domestic laws to permit civilian nuclear cooperation with India. The United States would also liberalize the transfer of high military technology to India. Above all, the United States would assist India in becoming a global power. The Indian leadership was taken aback by the sheer boldness of the proposal.

Between the Rice visit in March and Manmohan Singh's trip to Washington in July, there were hectic high-level exchanges between officials on both sides. The nuclear issue was a tough nut to crack, considering the bitter legacy of hostility and suspicion of the preceding six decades.

---

22. Ibid., 5.

Even as the Indian prime minister arrived in Washington, a wide gap remained between the two sides. Not willing to give up, on July 17, 2005, Rice broke protocol and called on External Affairs Minister Natwar Singh at his hotel. A marathon negotiating session ensued, ending again in a deadlock. Rice said she would make one last effort and refer the difficult issues to President Bush.

On the morning of July 18, as they proceeded for their official talks, neither Bush nor Manmohan Singh could foresee if an agreement would be reached on civilian nuclear cooperation. The confirmation was flashed to them just as they headed for their meeting with the press. It was the beginning of a new chapter in Indo-U.S. relations.

It took almost three years of complex and intense negotiations for the nuclear deal to cross the formidable hurdles in its way. The Hyde Act, which was passed by the U.S. Congress in December 2006 with nearly 85 percent bipartisan support, enabled India to resume civilian nuclear cooperation with the United States. This was followed by the bilateral 123 Agreement in mid-2007 detailing the terms for such cooperation.

The government of Manmohan Singh faced fierce resistance at every step of the negotiations not only from the opposition Bharitya Janata Party but also from his coalition partners—the Communists and other leftist parties. This forced him to risk the future of his government by seeking a vote of confidence in Parliament, which he won by a paper-thin margin in July 2008.

In August 2008, India concluded a special Safeguards Protocol with the International Atomic Energy Agency. And finally, in early September 2008, after two stormy sessions, the forty-five-member Nuclear Suppliers Group granted a "clean waiver" that removed three decades of technological sanctions against India.

This would not have been possible without the heavy lifting done by the United States through personal interventions, especially at the levels of the national security adviser and the secretary of state. The last of the recalcitrant states opposing the waiver for India were finally brought around by President Bush picking up the phone and urging their leaders to drop the objections.

The bold attempt to think outside the box and restructure the global nonproliferation architecture by bringing India into it is a striking example of innovative American diplomacy.

2009 and Beyond: A Narrower Cultural Gap

The dramatic change in American negotiating behavior toward India from coercive to persuasive diplomacy during the past decade merits an explanation, especially as it seems at odds with the experience of other countries. Prior to the election of Barack Obama, the prevailing view in the world was that Americans after 9/11 had become more unilateralist, intolerant, and culturally insensitive in their relations with other nations, including their close allies. Why then was the Indian experience so different?

There are two broad explanations for this phenomenon. The first is that—as discussed above—in the post–Cold War period, New Delhi and Washington for the first time discovered a convergence of their strategic interests. A second and more important explanation is that, at the popular level, cultural understanding and appreciation between the two societies have steadily grown. By the turn of the twenty-first century, Americans were better informed about India. Indian food, music, dance, spirituality, and yoga have become a part of the American multiethnic mosaic, helped by a highly visible and active Indian-American community.

On the Indian side, perceptions about the United States also changed. To start with, the average Indian is much better informed about the United States, thanks to the greater reach of the American media and the popularity of Hollywood movies. There were no doubt strong negative images in the beginning. The conservative elements in Indian society disapproved of the promiscuity and hedonism depicted in American movies and magazines, while Indian intellectuals and liberals were disturbed by America's aggressive capitalism and its lack of concern for the poor and the disadvantaged. And Indians of all persuasions did not find it easy to accept racial prejudice and discrimination in a country that claimed to be the global leader in democracy and freedom. The revered Nobel laureate poet Tagore, a great admirer of the United States, hastily canceled his tour in 1929 after being insulted at the airport by an immigration official.

Indian diplomats were generally spared such experiences—but not always. Indian ambassador G. L. Mehta had a taste of it when he was thrown out of a restaurant in 1955 at the Houston airport, because it was reserved "For Whites Only." His successor, Justice M. C. Chagla, had to decline membership in Washington's prestigious Cosmopolitan Club when he discovered that his African colleagues were not entitled to join.

As American society grappled with the issue of racism and eventually removed the legal and constitutional stigma imposed on black Americans, the United States became a magnet for the brightest and best among Indian students and professionals. More than one hundred thousand Indian students are presently enrolled in American universities, forming the largest body of foreign students in the country. In the popular Indian mind, the United States is still seen as a land of enormous opportunity, freedom, and prosperity. Even in recent years, as the global approval rating of the United States plummeted, Indians retained their faith in the country. The Pew Global Attitude Survey, released in June 2008, shows a 66 percent favorable rating for the United States among Indians—one of the highest in the world.[23]

---

23.   Jaishankar, Dhruva, "America, Sunny Side Up," *Indian Express* (New Delhi), June 19, 2008.

The twin effects of the closing of the cultural gap between the two countries and the assertions of common values and strategic interests have led to greater sensitivity and mutual respect in dealing with each other. India, for its part, has also shed a lot of its earlier prickliness and has acquired a more confident and self-assured role in dealing with all major powers, including the United States.

It was a far cry from the coercive diplomacy of John Foster Dulles when, on March 2, 2006, George W. Bush and Manmohan Singh announced in New Delhi their satisfaction with "the great progress the United States and India have made in advancing our strategic partnership to meet the global challenges of the twenty-first century."[24]

U.S. negotiators and policymakers today understand more clearly than ever that the key to success in diplomacy with India is persuasion, not coercion. This new approach tallies with the statement made by James Glassman, the U.S. under secretary of state for public diplomacy, on June 15, 2008:

> Foreigners recognize that the United States is the world's most powerful nation and ultimately, we will do what is in our national interest, as we should. But they also believe, rightly or not, that we don't listen carefully to them, or act as a reliable partner or take their views into account. They want a more respectful hearing.[25]

That is exactly the kind of hearing that India now believes it is getting.

---

24. "India-US Joint Statement," March 2, 2006, http://pmindia.nic.in/India-US.pdf.
25. James K. Glassman, "The Animosity Does Not Run Deep," *New York Times*, June 15, 2008.

13

Negotiating Multilaterally: The Advantages and Disadvantages of the U.S. Approach

David Hannay

ultilateral diplomacy, that process of permanent negotiation in a whole string of international organizations—some global, some regional, some like the United Nations dealing with largely political issues, some like NATO dealing with international security, and many handling highly technical but still politically sensitive matters such as trade (World Trade Organization), finance (International Monetary Fund), or development (World Bank)—was really a child of the Second World War. There were of course some international organizations in existence before 1945, the most prominent being the ill-fated League of Nations, and multilateral diplomacy was practiced at many international conferences. But such international organizations as there were tended to be institutionally weak with little decision-making capability, and international conferences were more talking shops than effective instruments for managing international problems. Bilateral diplomacy still dominated the profession, leaving multilateral practitioners in the margins of decision making, with little influence over the shaping of national foreign policies. American diplomats had even less experience than others of practicing multilateral diplomacy, given the U.S. Congress' decision not to join the League of Nations. In any event, such multilateral diplomacy as there was foundered in the chaotic and desperate years before the Second World War when economic slump, protectionism, and the aggressive policies of the Axis Powers dominated the scene.

In 1945 all that changed as the victorious allies decided to set up a world body, the United Nations, with universal membership and an ambitious charter directed at achieving collective security, decolonization, and international development. The

Western allies also established a string of economic institutions (usually known as the Bretton Woods institutions) designed to put behind them the protectionism and competitive currency devaluations of the interwar period. Thereafter, many other international organizations were set up, including universal ones, such as agencies of the United Nations dealing with health, food, refugees, or nuclear energy, and regional ones, such as the European Union, often with extensive institutional structures and decision-making powers. This massive expansion of multilateral diplomacy, although partially crippled by Cold War rivalries, transformed the profession of diplomacy and the shaping and implementation of foreign policies. After the end of the Cold War in the late 1980s, many constraints on international cooperation resulting from that confrontation fell away.

This chapter takes a critical look at the way United States diplomacy and American diplomats responded to this major shift in the practice of diplomacy. How did they fare in this permanent process of negotiation? How well did the U.S. negotiating style and practice adapt? The viewpoint is, of course, that of an outsider—one whose working experience of U.S. multilateral diplomacy was mainly limited to trade negotiations in the 1970s and to the United Nations in the immediate aftermath of the Cold War.

The U.S. Strategic Approach to Multilateral Diplomacy

The United States was certainly not dragged unwillingly into this massive expansion of multilateral diplomacy and negotiation. It was indeed "present at the creation," to use Dean Acheson's phrase; it was the moving spirit behind many of the international organizations that were established, thanks to a conscious decision by Presidents Franklin D. Roosevelt and Harry S. Truman to serve the national interest of the United States by strengthening collective security in the widest sense. That decision was endorsed by Congress when it ratified the United Nations Charter and the establishment of NATO.

But the U.S. attitude toward international organizations, and in particular toward those that imposed binding legal constraints and obligations on U.S. policymaking, was, from the outset, distinctly ambivalent. Gradually a pattern of U.S. exceptionalism took shape, often driven by congressional acts and pressure, under which the United States held other members of these many organizations to tighter disciplines than they were prepared to submit to themselves. And successive U.S. administrations pursued very different policies toward the use of multilateral diplomacy: some, such as the early post–World War II presidents and President George H. W. Bush, put it at the center of their foreign policymaking; others, such as Presidents Ronald Reagan and George W. Bush, regarded it as, at best, an optional extra, and they frequently used organizations such as the United Nations as a whipping boy for their frustration when they encountered resistance to U.S. policy choices.

This pattern of U.S. exceptionalism and the sharp zigzags in different administrations' attitudes toward international organizations have imposed a severe handicap on those who have had to practice multilateral diplomacy day by day on behalf of the United States. Indeed, this self-imposed disadvantage has often more than outweighed the country's natural advantages as the predominant and, after the end of the Cold War, sole superpower and as the indispensable participant in, or supporter of, any action to be undertaken by the organizations in question.

The almost fortuitous—and certainly unexpected—emergence of the United States as the sole remaining superpower considerably complicated the U.S. conduct of multilateral diplomacy. During the Cold War much multilateral diplomacy was formulaic and static; large areas of policy and many regions of the world, where the two superpowers were in direct confrontation, were off-limits. With the lifting of those taboos a whole new range of problems forced their way onto the agenda of international organizations.

The United States alone had to decide on pretty well every one of them whether to back collective action or to prevent any collective response or to see it fail through neglect. These were choices faced, often not with much success, in Bosnia, Somalia, and Rwanda. Whereas other members of the international community could afford to pick and choose on which issues to focus their efforts—for example, Great Britain decided to stand aside completely from policymaking on Haiti and Somalia—the United States enjoyed no such luxury. These demands led to the overloading of the policymaking machine in Washington and also to the overload on the U.S. ambassador at the United Nations, where so much multilateral negotiating has to be handled at the top level.

In parallel with this widening of the gap between the punch weight of the United States and the rest came a widening gap in perceptions. As almost every other member of the international community became more convinced of the need for multilateral responses to the challenges facing the post–Cold War world—the European Union's embrace of "effective multilateralism" as a key objective of its 2003 security strategy being a case in point—the United States was tempted by the shortcut of unilateralism and "coalitions of the willing," and the chance to avoid all those tiresome delays and compromises inherent in the successful practice of multilateral diplomacy. The impact of these different factors does something to explain why the new world order proclaimed by President George H. W. Bush now more closely resembles a new world disorder.

U.S. Practice of Multilateral Diplomacy

Moving now from these general considerations to more specific, down-to-earth aspects of the daily practice of multilateral negotiation, let us consider some of the strengths and weaknesses of the U.S. performance. Foremost among the strengths of U.S. multilateral diplomacy is the existence of a worldwide network of diplomatic missions staffed with well-qualified professionals, present in almost every capital of the world except some "pariah" states. No other country can match that outreach. And it does count.

Multilateral negotiations may be conducted in a handful of places where the headquarters of international organizations are sited—New York, Geneva, Brussels, to mention the most obvious ones—but they more and more involve subject matter of the greatest political sensitivity that requires direct input from every national government involved. And the best way to influence that input is to not just focus exclusively on the place where the negotiations are conducted, where the practitioners may in any case be trying to turn a deaf ear to their instructions, but to also talk directly to national governments in their capitals. The U.S. advantage here is not purely quantitative. There are few capitals in the world where the U.S. ambassador will not have rapid and direct access to the highest level of government. The same is not true of many other diplomatic missions.

Does the United States make good use of this advantage? In my experience on the whole, they do. Again and again in Security Council negotiations, I have seen prima donnas of the New York diplomatic scene discomfited when U.S. influence was brought to bear in their capital, and they were either brought back into line or the line was changed. The United States does benefit too from the professionalism and integrity of its diplomats. You are a good deal less likely to be told an outright lie by a U.S. diplomat than by many others. Contrary to popular belief, diplomacy does not simply consist of groups of devious and untrustworthy people misleading one another. The art of negotiation—and it is an art not a science—requires a degree of trust and confidence between the practitioners that is incompatible with outright trickery and an inability to deliver on what you have offered.

One further advantage for Americans in multilateral negotiations (an advantage shared with other English-speaking countries) is that they work most of the time in their own native tongue and that the international agreements and texts upon which they are seeking to agree will almost all be set down (even if they are subsequently translated) in English. The predominance of the English language as the principal world medium for the conduct of business, science, and diplomacy so far remains unchallenged. But if English speakers are to capitalize fully on this advantage, they must speak and write simply and clearly and avoid the excessive use of slang expressions and complex vocabulary—above all, they must eschew sporting metaphors, particularly when the sports in question are not generally played elsewhere. Neither the Americans (nor the British for that matter) are immune from this practice. One wonders, for example, how much time was wasted and irritation caused by the need to understand and explain the term "slam dunk."

But the U.S. performance reveals plenty of weaknesses too, many of them a reflection of the complex and idiosyncratic nature of the American body politic.

Making political appointments to an ever-widening range of diplomatic posts is one such weakness. The practice of multilateral negotiation is becoming steadily more professionalized as the technical complexity of the subject matter increases. Most countries staff their multilateral negotiating teams with diplomats, many of whom have years of experience in such negotiations. The United States relies more heavily on political appointees. While not all political appointees under the U.S. system are at a disadvantage, lack of the relevant professional experience can be a real handicap.

Another weakness is the lack of focus on the part of some political appointees, who are only really part-time operators in the multilateral negotiations for which they are responsible. This problem is particularly acute with respect to the U.S. ambassador to the United Nations. Unlike the other UN ambassadors who work full time in New York, the U.S. ambassador is often a political appointee with a Washington as well as a New York agenda. Additionally, the practice by these political appointees of lambasting the United Nations in public speeches or statements may play well on Fox News or among conservative think tanks in Washington, but it tends to infuriate and antagonize those other ambassadors with whom the daily business of multilateral diplomacy must be transacted.

Enough has been said to demonstrate the increasing complexity of multilateral negotiations, with the negotiators on the ground in a continuous dialogue with a wide range of departments in their own capitals who have some connection to the subject matter under negotiation. This complexity poses formidable problems of interdepartmental coordination and also of ensuring a reasonable degree of coherence between positions adopted in one set of negotiations and those in another. Every government has had difficulty grappling with those problems. But certain governments, the Europeans, for example, and perhaps also the Chinese, are proving more adept at it than is the United States.

There seems to be a degree of cumbersomeness and slowness in the original formulation of a U.S. response to an emerging problem or crisis and of rigidity in responding to the developing positions of others that often leaves U.S. negotiators at a disadvantage and leads to opportunities being missed before negotiating positions are set in concrete. At the United Nations in New York, U.S. negotiators often receive instructions slowly and late and in the form of fully worked-out texts formulated in Washington that take more account of reconciling interdepartmental tensions there than of accommodating the views of others who are being asked to sign up to a particular policy. In nine out of ten cases, the Foreign Office in London sets the objectives to be pursued by the British mission in New York but does not seek to lay down the precise terms of a resolution, thus leaving a good deal of flexibility to the mission and its own legal adviser. Each iteration of a resolution or agreement is then checked and, if necessary, corrected overnight before the negotiation resumes the next day. The U.S. mission usually has no such flexibility.

It often seemed to me that the simple fact of being in the same time zone as their own capital was a handicap for the U.S. negotiators. At least some of the rigidities imposed on them and escaped by others seemed to be derived from that factor. It is not of course one than can be remedied!

Possible Remedies for U.S. Weaknesses

This analysis of the past performance of the United States in multilateral negotiations would seem to indicate a tendency to underperform and to have less influence than the inherent strengths of the U.S. international position would justify. That tendency should not be exaggerated. For many of those daily involved in transacting business multilaterally, the single inescapable reality of their lives is the indispensability of the United States and the futility in practical terms of trying to gang up against it. Even many of those who rail against this predominant American position spend much of their time seeking to persuade the United States to accommodate their views and are ready, in the last analysis, to go a long way toward meeting U.S. requirements in order to win American support for the eventual outcome.

So what are the prospects for a more effective American performance in multilateral negotiations? It is important not to set that bar unrealistically high. That will lead only to frustration and to further damage to the structure of the international organizations on which so much of the world's security and prosperity depends. No one who has studied American history and who has any knowledge of the complexities of the fashioning of U.S. foreign policy can seriously suppose that the United States is, in the foreseeable future, going to put all its eggs in the multilateral basket. There are plenty of other countries around the world who will not do that either. But a more consistently constructive approach to the potential of multilateral negotiations to secure the basic national interests of all the participants, a reduction in the sharp zigzags between U.S. administrations as they succeed each other, and a remedying of the weaknesses in past performance that have been identified—all these should be achievable.

Quite a few of the remedies are within the gift of the executive branch of the administration. The staffing of U.S. negotiating teams for multilateral negotiations and of U.S. diplomatic posts at the headquarters of international organizations could be much more rigorously professionalized. That does not mean avoiding all political appointments. But it does mean ensuring that anyone appointed should genuinely be equipped with the knowledge and experience required, particularly when it comes to choosing those to fill the top jobs. Ensuring that U.S. ambassadors to international organizations, and in particular U.S. ambassadors to the United Nations, devote themselves full time to the job in hand and are not distracted by a wider role in the formulation and communication of U.S. foreign policy should also be relatively straightforward. Calls to make the U.S. ambassador to the United Nations a member of the cabinet, which in any case hardly ever meets, should certainly and usefully be avoided. Making the system of interdepartmental coordination in Washington more responsive and more flexible in the handling of often fast-moving negotiations is also within the realm of the possible.

But much of the conduct of multilateral negotiations straddles the responsibilities of the U.S. executive and legislative branches, and here the challenge of bringing about change is clearly more formidable. Simply to assume at the outset that it is incapable of being achieved would be a counsel of despair and would in any case fly in the face of previous experience. For many years, it was assumed that the U.S. Congress would never accept the limitations on its freedom of action entailed in a mandatory international rules-based system for the settlement of trade policy disputes. And yet the successful conclusion of the Uruguay Round of trade negotiations required precisely that, and it was ratified by Congress.

Is it inconceivable that Congress could recognize the advantage to the United States of finally ratifying the UN Law of the Sea Convention, which has come into force and is accepted by all, including the United States, as representing customary international law, and in that way providing for U.S. membership in its institutions and enabling Americans to influence its future development? Might Congress not be persuaded that U.S. ratification of the Comprehensive Nuclear Test Ban Treaty is a necessary and indeed desirable component of any wider strategy designed to reverse the fraying of the nuclear nonproliferation regime? Is it not likely to prove the case that acceptance of mandatory internationally negotiated limits on U.S. carbon emissions will be an essential part of any effective successor to the Kyoto Protocol, particularly one designed to bring within its scope the main developing country polluters, such as China, India, and Brazil? Could not Congress be persuaded that, when the United States votes in the UN Security Council to set up an international peace operation, it should be committed to financing its share of the costs of that operation? If, as seems highly probable, future administrations are going to be extremely cautious about involving the United States in unilateral military interventions or even those mounted by coalitions of the willing and if it is not in the wider U.S. interest simply to turn its back on disorder and state failure, then the United States is going to need to give more wholehearted backing to the strengthening of international peacekeeping efforts, both by the United Nations and by regional organizations such as the African Union.

No one who has ever participated in a multilateral negotiation can suppose that successful outcomes are easily achievable or that they provide ideal solutions for all the participants. But, in an interdependent world where many global challenges require global responses if they are to be overcome at all, multilateral negotiations are a necessity, not an optional extra. The manner in which the United States handles such negotiations and its willingness to participate in good faith in agreed collective disciplines will often determine their success or failure.

14

Negotiating with Savoir Faire: Twelve Rules for Negotiating with the United States

Gilles Andreani

From 1986 to 2005, I spent two decades in the French Ministry of Foreign Affairs, dealing mostly with security policy. Upon joining the Quai d'Orsay, I first handled nuclear issues in the strategic affairs directorate and later became head of the disarmament bureau, a position I held from 1989 to 1993. Then I was at NATO, where I was deputy chief of the French mission until 1995. Finally, I served as head of the Centre d'analyse et de prévision, the functional equivalent of the U.S. policy planning staff, from 1995 to 1999, and again from 2002 to 2005, spending eighteen months in between doing research at the International Institute for Strategic Studies in London.

I spent quite some part of these twenty years interacting with Americans. In security policy, even at the time of the Cold War, much of the negotiation used to take place among allies, rather than with the other side. During the negotiations that led to the 1990 treaty on conventional forces in Europe (CFE), for instance, a NATO body in charge of coordinating allied positions saw discussions just as tense and decisive for the outcome of the process as those that were taking place with the Warsaw Pact in Vienna.

In addition, the United States is not just any other ally, and the Atlantic Alliance is not just any other multilateral forum. One may think of the European Union as a constellation with big and small stars, but NATO is more like a solar system, a web of bilateral relations centered on the United States. For an idea to take off in the organization, it must be endorsed by the United States. As a result, formal multilateral discussions among allies are held parallel with a lot of bilateral or small group negotiations aimed at reaching common positions between key allies and the United States.

With France often being at one end of the transatlantic debate and the United States at the other, Paris was more likely than many others to be a party to such parallel discussions. As a result, I had the opportunity to witness and participate in a series of interactions between American and French officials, ranging from behind-the-scenes coordination on the intermediate-range nuclear forces (INF) negotiation in the mid-1980s, to the 2003 bloodbath on the Iraq War. The issues at stake included, to name the most important among many others, conventional arms negotiations and the chemical weapons convention, command and control arrangements for the NATO operation in Bosnia, the development of a European defense identity, the reform of the NATO command structure, and the southern command issue (whether to devolve the southern regional command of NATO, a post held by an American admiral since the 1960s, to a European, as part of a process of "Europeanization" of NATO).

I have generally positive memories of these experiences and of the way American officials dealt with their French interlocutors: they listened, were bound to seek solutions rather than add to problems, and kept their side of bargains. All were candid in stating their country's objectives and determined to achieve them, but at the same time they sought to understand our positions and genuinely tried to explore possibilities for compromise. Some were unnecessarily suspicious of our motives and tried to read too much into our positions, consistent with a culture of suspicion of the other side that, it is fair to say, the French tend to share. Most were professional and personally easy to deal with. The few undiplomatic characters I met stood out as exceptions, and they were no less controversial among their fellow American diplomats than among their European counterparts.

Our relationship with America is enduring and friendly, if historically fraught with many small problems and a few serious difficulties. Most of these have been rooted in substantive policy differences, but some difficulties have stemmed from, or been exacerbated by, differences in negotiating styles. For instance, the French like to go from general principles to the particularities of an issue; they will never admit that their position has changed—only that circumstances or the positions of others have. The Americans will start with the specifics of an issue, cite previous or similar cases to support their position, and appeal only as a last resort to principles. They will not be ashamed about changing their mind or their position (or about defending inconsistent positions). Further, they will not hesitate to claim that a single case has invalidated or redefined past practice, whereas the French will re-gard such a case as an aberration or an exception.

Whether because of stylistic or substantive differences, the French-American record has certainly been mixed. But this mixed record has its positive side, not least the fact that the relationship is not hobbled by excessive expectations or blinded by emotional involvement. From the French standpoint, the relationship is neither adversarial nor subservient. And, at least in the security field where I worked, it was dense enough to allow habits and patterns to emerge. Altogether, I found it a good vantage point from which to observe American negotiating behavior.

Of course, France can hardly claim any superior knowledge of how to deal with the United States. In hindsight, during the years I saw French diplomacy interact with the United States, we made many mistakes (and so did the United States). These mistakes and resulting failures, no less than the numerous instances where our relationship proved successful and productive, have suggested to me a handful of lessons on how to approach negotiation with the Americans.

The Twelve Rules

I present these lessons here in the form of "rules for negotiators," in the manner of old treatises on diplomacy. My goal is to offer these lessons, which are the fruit of experience, while acknowledging the modesty of that experience and maintaining some analytic distance. Intuitive and personal in character, the recollections on which these lessons are based suffer from inherent limitations, which I want to recognize at the outset. Needless to say, my recollections and the lessons that I am offering do not reflect an accepted body of thought within the French Foreign Ministry. (At no point in their careers are French diplomats offered training in negotiation, let alone training in country-specific negotiations.) It is in this spirit that I present the following rules for those engaged in negotiation with the United States.

Rule 1: Start at the top

Getting a clear mandate to negotiate from the top is the best way to focus the U.S. diplomatic machinery and to make sure that whoever is in charge on the American side will have the authority to negotiate with you. In two instances, France and the United States seriously engaged each other on the issue of NATO reform and explored options to change France's relations with the military structure: in both cases what made the process possible at all was the commitment of the two presidents (François Mitterrand and George H. W. Bush at their May 1989 meeting in Kennebunkport, Bill Clinton and Jacques Chirac in Paris in December 1995).

Rule 2: Prioritize issues

You cannot disagree with the Americans on every issue or seek to engage them on everything. My own country has too often neglected to sort out, from among those issues where it disagreed with the United States, those that most deserve its energy and resources. It is best to pick a few and, having done that, to keep them separate and deal with each one on its merits: the tactic known as *junktim*, which consists of linking issues unrelated in substance to gain leverage on a partner, is ill-advised and should be avoided. It is sure to backfire with the Americans, who can usually come up with a number of issues more important to you than to them, which they can then hold hostage to the negotiation at hand.

During the period of worst tension with the United States, as France opposed the Iraq War in March 2003, the French government consciously sought to downplay every other possible disagreement (one might argue at the expense of either consistency or pride), going so far as to grant U.S. military aircraft generous overflight rights over French territory at the outset of the war. The Bush administration, on the other hand, suspended its cooperation with France on a number of unrelated issues. But there were limits to this strategy, known as "punish the French," as it met with resistance over time from within the U.S. system, especially from the State Department, and some of its excesses were reversed. I personally have no doubt that if France had not made every effort to circumscribe her disagreement with the United States, the adverse consequences for the relationship between the two countries would have been much worse.

Rule 3: Present your demands early and do not add new ones as you go

It is a pretty basic rule of all negotiations that late demands are unwelcome and difficult to sustain. They tend particularly to irk the Americans, whose decision-making process is slow and cumbersome, and whose ability to take into consideration the viewpoint of other countries is limited. They dislike surprises, especially if their consequence should be to reopen decisions painfully arrived at in Washington. Within the American system, those most opposed to your viewpoint in the first place can use the irritation provoked by your late demands to unwind the previously agreed U.S. position and engineer something worse for you. When France unexpectedly asked for the devolution of NATO's southern command to a European in the summer of 1996, those Americans who had most opposed the freshly agreed Berlin reform of NATO saw their chance and brought about a hardening of the U.S. position that pretty much interrupted the process.

Rule 4: Cover your back

Americans base their negotiating tactics to some degree on the presumption that some interlocutors in a given system are more favorably disposed to their country, or at least more open than others to hearing their views. They will decide on their démarches in capitals accordingly, and target those officials they perceive as more amenable to their position or whom they hold responsible for official policy positions. The French or the British take a more abstract view of the systems they interact with, attach less importance to the preferences of individuals, and will satisfy themselves that their positions have been conveyed to the appropriate level in the capital concerned.

When meeting resistance from foreign negotiators, the United States may test their credit at home, seek to circumvent them, or have them disavowed by higher authorities. In debates at NATO, real-time U.S. démarches in capitals to have a representative's position changed from above were not uncommon when I served there (and they were not always carried out in a gentlemanly way). As a rule, Americans will poke around in your home system to find the point of least resistance: it is best, then, to have firm support as you deal with U.S. representatives.

All along when speaking with American colleagues in Paris, I was struck by how important they considered the characterization of specific French officials as pro-American or anti-American. One of them once told me, "You are not nearly as anti-American as I was told in Washington," which incidentally shows how erroneous these characterizations could be—I was labeled an "Atlanticist" in the French system. Perhaps an American disbelief that people could genuinely oppose their views explains why Americans would seek to ascribe such opposition to an individual's presumed bias against their country.

Rule 5: Beware of bumper stickers

The ability to define the terms of the problem at hand is a good measure of a country's influence. A negotiation is more than half won when one has that ability. Soviet diplomacy understood that truth; it thus never yielded on the semantics of an issue, because it believed that words largely commanded substance. Whether American diplomacy consciously shares such a belief in the power of words, I do not know. I find the Americans to be very effective, however, at defining problems in self-serving terms, which, once established, inevitably restrict the freedom of their partners and the outcome of the negotiation. For instance, when France and a few others argued after the Cold War that new circumstances warranted a new balance of responsibilities between the European Community and the Atlantic Alliance, U.S. diplomacy coined the term "the Euro-Atlantic community" to designate the latter, a term which NATO then endorsed. The implication of this new semantic was that if all that was one and the same thing, the case for rebalancing had in fact no grounds. By the same token, in the context of the Israeli-Palestinian issue, a "performance-based" road map for peace carries implications very different from those of, say, a "justice-based," or a "balanced and fair" road map. Such an a priori semantic determination of issues should be resisted. At times, however, it is simply too hard to do so: who, after all, can object to a good alliance being labeled a community, or a road map to peace taking into account the performance of the parties? The virtue of being the only remaining superpower is to put on others the burden of proof: unless it is grossly manipulative, or deeply offensive to somebody, the American characterization of the issue will normally carry a great weight.

Rule 6: Keep your cards close to your chest

This is a sensitive issue on which one will want only to tread very lightly. The United States closely integrates diplomacy and intelligence. At times, the integration can become embarrassingly close—as when it appeared that an American agent had attempted to bribe an adviser to the prime minister into providing information on the French negotiating position at a critical juncture of the General Agreement on Tariffs and Trade (GATT) negotiations in 1994–95.[1] (By its magnitude and public character, this episode stands as an exceptional blunder.) While there is no way to tell how much intelligence will be brought to bear on a given negotiation, or how exceptional the practice is, past incidents show that there is a U.S. record in this field, one that partners of the United States should recognize. My own instinct is that the Americans derive very few benefits from such practices, assuming they are still in existence. French negotiating positions in trade negotiations are mostly public, open for all to see. There are very few instances when an inside glance at your partner's game will determine the outcome of the party.

Rule 7: Reach within the machine (but only at key points)

The innumerable difficulties the United States has in coordinating the branches of its government, and the various agencies within the executive, into a unified negotiating position present foreign governments with a special dilemma: how much should they try to sway the U.S. decision-making process and better make their case by influencing from within? There is no easy answer. In theory, you do not want to exonerate the U.S. government from its responsibility to present its partners with a single unified position. On the one hand, divisions within the U.S. system are a fact of life: American negotiators suffer from a situation that makes the views they defend contingent on the positions of contending bureaucracies. On the other hand, they tactically benefit from their home debate, which adds to the arguments they can use to oppose your demands. All in all, it is worth intervening within the U.S. system at key junctures, to help remove specific obstacles, but futile to seek to become an effective party to the U.S. interagency process.

Newly elected president Chirac chose to go to Washington and meet with the Republican leadership of Congress (Speaker of the House Newt Gingrich and Senator Bob Dole) on June 14, 1995, to plead for a UN-sponsored European rapid re-

---

1. Two persuasive accounts of the story were published in the *New York Times*: Craig R. Whitney, "5 Americans Are Called Spies and Asked to Leave," February, 23, 1995, and David E. Sanger and Tim Weiner, "Emerging Role for the CIA: Economic Spy," October 15, 1995.

action force able to stand up to the Bosnian Serbs in the context of the UN hostage crisis in Bosnia and Herzegovina. This move helped to remove Congress's opposition (stemming from the Republican majority's opposition in principle to new UN mandated peacekeeping forces) and allowed UN Security Council Resolution 998 to be adopted the next day and the force to be authorized. The dramatic character of the move ensured its success, but it is naturally bound to remain exceptional.

Rule 8: Be reassuring and determined

Americans are not much used to meeting opposition to their demands or positions markedly different from their own. They tend to view such resistance with a mixture of suspicion and disbelief. They are suspicious of its motives, which they attribute either to a general hostility toward their country or a specific desire for mischief. They doubt the solidity of such resistance and the resolve of the country whose opposition they meet, at least if it is a friend or ally. In a nutshell, they tend to read too much into it and to be unduly dismissive at the same time. Under these circumstances, foreign negotiators face the difficult task of conveying a message both of reassurance and of firmness. They must reassure the United States that their ultimate motives are benign, but they must also make clear that they have serious reasons behind their negotiating aims and will not be distracted from them.

There were many instances when France had trouble conveying either message. In the early 1990s, it was extremely hard for us to convince the United States that our plan to establish a Franco-German military unit—which later evolved into the Eurocorps—was motivated by the simple desire to foster European integration rather than by a nefarious desire to prove the irrelevance of NATO and weaken America's influence on the continent. After the 2003 crisis over Iraq, an American official told me that he had previously concluded that France, being a "realist" country and recognizing the cost of remaining in direct opposition to the United States, would yield in the end. Of these two requirements of reassurance and resolve, conveying the latter should be less problematic, because one's firmness, being a matter of fact, is easier to establish than one's good faith, which is a matter of trust. In reality, both are necessary and equally difficult.

Rule 9: Close ranks (but not too much)

In Europe, one hardly ever negotiates alone with the United States. For all the bilateral interaction, security policy nearly always brings a plurality of partners to any such discussion. And, of course, having others on your side is essential to the favorable outcome of any discussion with the Americans. Closing ranks, and not remaining alone, has been especially important for France, because our record of opposing the United States on a number of issues has, in turn, made the Americans eager to characterize transatlantic disagreements as mostly occurring between the French and them. Ascribing genuine differences of views with the Europeans to a compulsive French propensity for opposition has enabled the United States to minimize the scope and the political significance of these disagreements. But although finding allies is essential to any meaningful negotiation with the United States, experience shows that one should be discreet and low-key about the process. In the run-up to the June 1996 Berlin ministerial meeting, the Europeans had been uniquely united in demanding a more balanced distribution of military responsibilities within NATO in the face of extreme reluctance from the U.S. military. The experience left a mark (for a few months afterward, some in Washington characterized instances when Europeans were united in opposing U.S. positions in NATO as "the Berlinization of an issue"). It also paved the way for the backlash that ensued on the southern command issue (see rule 3).

Rule 10: Empathize

The elephant may be big, but it has feelings. The first feelings you must take care of are those of the U.S. negotiators themselves. They have often spent credit at home expressing your concerns, as they ask for some leeway in their negotiating position to accommodate them. What they come back with may be insufficient and at times minuscule to the point of looking offensive. But sometimes, blood has been spilled in Washington to get there. Therefore, you should first recognize the efforts of your counterpart, who may have paid a price for the concessions, before dismissing them as insufficient. At a more general level, while most American diplomats tend to be personally modest, their nation is infused by a collective pride that is second to none. However big the disagreement on the issue at hand, you should take care to frame it within a positive political context, within which your country displays a positive view of the United States and values its relation with it.

More than the substance of the case, I personally believe that what plagued the southern command negotiation in 1996–97 was that the Americans had rightly or wrongly concluded that Chirac did not care anymore about a substantive improvement of France's relations with the United States. Up to this day, by contrast, Nicolas Sarkozy has managed to make this very objective a general framework of his interaction with the Americans.

Rule 11: Do not lose them

For Americans, negotiating with another country is not a matter of course, like it is for Europeans who negotiate among themselves all year round on an incredible variety of issues. It is a serious affair, one whereby foreigners are allowed somehow to influence U.S. decisions. That is not natural for American democracy, which has historically been autarkic in character, or for the American people, whose nationalism can be as intense as it is unacknowledged. As a result, negotiation is not, in the United States, what it is for most people in other parts of the world—that is, a sensible thing to do to obtain something from another country. Rather, it is a privilege bestowed on deserving foreigners, as an exception to the normal course of affairs for Americans, which is to decide by themselves on issues of interest to them, including international ones.

Aside from the issue of tradition and national character, the solid fact of American power often makes negotiation just one of several options for the United States. These many factors combine to make negotiation a privilege that the United States can always suspend or revoke if it deems the results unsatisfactory or if the U.S. policy debate so decides. Other countries should remind themselves that the United States has a choice and that, rather than negotiate, it can resort to other options (consistent with a behavioral approach that holds that a proper mixture of incentives and punishments should be able to modify the course of action of other nations, even without speaking to them). The United States can ignore other nations, circumvent them, or steamroller them (the treatment France experienced at the time of the Iraq crisis being a combination of those three elements). It is important to keep this reality in mind when negotiating with the United States: negotiation should not be taken for granted, and one may conceivably lose the United States in the course of action.

At the end of George H. W. Bush's presidency, some in his administration had lost patience with us—after a long series of disagreements on NATO, European defense, and the Middle East—and simply chose to ignore us. This attitude was best illustrated by Secretary of State James Baker, who, in the course of a NATO ministerial meeting where a French representative had objected to a U.S. formula in the communiqué, distinctly said, "Let's give this guy a footnote and move on."

Rule 12: Take a long view

The elephant not only has feelings, but it also has a memory. Each country has a record within the U.S. foreign policy establishment, and it tends to go a long way. One's negotiation with the United States takes place against this background and will become part of it once it is over. As a result, there is more in determining one's negotiating position than the merits of a given issue. Defeat will be remembered and will come at a cost. So will victory, perhaps even more so. Never lose sight of the lasting impact of a negotiation, as it will become part of your country's record in Washington.

Conclusion

These lessons, and the observations they are based on, correspond to a relatively narrow experience in dealing with the Americans, mostly confined to security policy. I honestly cannot say if they would also apply to trade or other specialized fields.

Limited as they are, however, they seem to me to reflect not only the dominant position of the United States in the international system and the wealth of political and other resources it invests in foreign policy, but also cultural patterns that go beyond the unique position of the United States and tend to persist. These patterns include the contrast between the modesty of individuals and the arrogance of the system, a resistance to negotiation as it allows foreigners to have a say in American decisions, a tendency to attribute divergence of views to ill will or bias against the United States itself, and, once negotiations are engaged, a pragmatic desire for success coupled, if needed, with energy and at times brutality.

Is it more difficult to interact today with the United States than it was twenty years ago? It seems to me that these patterns in their positive and less positive aspects have not changed much—nor have American negotiators. The George W. Bush administration may have been unique in its lack of diplomacy, but the U.S. system has always produced people, including diplomats (albeit a small minority alongside a distinguished and open professional diplomatic corps), who sought to build their reputation at home by standing up to foreigners as much as by conducting diplomacy with them. The outside world dealt with John Bolton in the 2000s as it dealt with Richard Holbrooke in the 1990s and Jeane Kirkpatrick in the 1980s.

On the other hand, circumstances have changed. Ever since 9/11, the United States has been intractable on issues related to homeland security (but on other issues its negotiating attitude has not changed much). The main change for France and Europe, however, took place in the 1990s. It was not related to the United States itself but to the end of the Cold War. For all the asymmetry in power and influence, as long as there was a Soviet threat, the Americans needed to agree with the Europeans, at least on key security issues. Mutual dependency gave the Europeans leverage, as the Americans had to genuinely seek agreement with them. What has changed is that on most issues, transatlantic agreement and, as a result, negotiation itself has become for the United States more an option than a necessity. It is in the mid-1990s that this structural change, coupled with an unprecedented level of self-confidence on the part of the United States, modified the nature of Europe's interaction with America. It is distinctly harder to negotiate with a country that says, "Together if we can, alone if we must."[2]

---

2. A phrase often used to describe the outlook of the Clinton administration. See, for instance, Strobe Talbott, "Bush, Iraq, and the World," in *Encyclopædia Britannica* (2009), http://www.britannica.com/EBchecked/topic/1517806/Bush-Iraq-and-the-World.

The years ahead may witness change again. We will not return to the compelling alliance of the Cold War, but the necessity to act collectively and the readiness to pay a price for it and take into account the views of others have gained ground in the United States since 2004. The hubris of the 1990s is no longer there. At the end of the day, there will be an opportunity to engage the United States again and return to diplomacy. The important thing is not that negotiation with the United States will be easy or difficult; it is that it will be possible at all.

Part V

Conclusions

15

Conclusion:
Negotiating in a Transforming World

Strengths and Weaknesses in American Diplomacy

As noted at the outset of this volume, the goal of this study is to assess *how* American officials negotiate, not *how well* they negotiate. One can certainly point to instances in which individuals have helped to achieve America's negotiating objectives, but one can rarely, if ever, measure that contribution very accurately given the number and range of variables involved in any negotiation.

That said, and as the preceding eight chapters have amply demonstrated, foreign diplomats are not reluctant to comment on the effectiveness of their American counterparts. Sometimes, note foreign officials, American negotiators secure agreements on terms favorable to the United States not because of their adroit diplomacy but because they come to the table backed by the political and economic resources of a preponderant power with intimidating military and intelligence capabilities. "If the United States can dictate to its negotiating counterparts," observes Soviet arms control negotiator Yuri Nazarkin, "why should it look for compromises?"[1] American national power often overrides the need for the negotiating skills that diplomats of lesser powers must hone to serve their nation's interests.

But while the United States may today be preeminent as an international power, it is not omnipotent. There are numerous examples of the inability of the U.S. government to invoke its substantial resources in well-coordinated fashion to achieve desired ends. America's national power has its limits, and even (particularly?) small countries have shown themselves to be immune to, or capable of resisting, American negotiating pressure. The will of the U.S. government can seldom be simply imposed, and many objectives can be reached only through negotiation and compromise—as

---

1. Nazarkin, "Negotiating as a Rival," 249.

objectionable as that may be to the self-image of American officials and their desire to assert and promote deeply held interests and values. In such instances, the skills of the negotiator come into their own.

Those skills, as most of the foreign contributors to this volume make clear, are not inconsequential. David Hannay, for instance, has no doubts that the United States "does benefit . . . from the professionalism and integrity of its diplomats."[2] Gilles Andreani pays tribute to the American officials with whom he had dealt: "They listened, were bound to seek solutions rather than add to problems, and kept their side of bargains. All were candid in stating their country's objectives and determined to achieve them, but at the same time they sought to understand our positions and genuinely tried to explore possibilities for compromise."[3] John Wood echoes similar sentiments, applauding "the energy, creativity, and relative open-mindedness that mid-level U.S. officials were prepared to bring to the process of jointly examining formulas to produce programs of action."[4] Yuri Nazarkin, too, gives good marks to the Americans with whom he negotiated: "Regardless of the level of our personal relationship, all of them were very tough negotiators. They defended their positions with real skill and ingenuity. But when they saw that their proposal had no chance of being accepted by the Soviet side, they were equally skillful in looking for compromise solutions."[5] These positive assessments reflect the power and appeal of an American culture of optimism, openness, and "can-do" pragmatism.

The picture painted by foreign diplomats, however, is by no means entirely positive. Koji Watanabe, for example, offers this long-suffering appraisal: "Exhibiting high-handedness, self-centeredness, and impatience, American negotiators cite their own domestic constraints while ignoring the domestic difficulties of their negotiating counterparts."[6] Chan Heng Chee's judgment is equally unflattering: "Americans don't really negotiate and don't know how to negotiate very well. Americans often present their views at a forum and negotiating table using a very direct approach and expect the other party or parties to accept them or adjust to them."[7]

What are we to make of these contrasting assessments? Do they suggest that one or more of the four defining facets of American negotiating behavior identified in part II of this volume are negotiating assets while the others are impediments?

At first consideration, the businesslike and legalistic mind-sets might seem to qualify as negotiating advantages, whereas the moralistic and superpower attitudes

---

2. Hannay, "Negotiating Multilaterally," 274.

3. Andreani, "Negotiating with Savoir Faire," 280.

4. Wood, "Negotiating within Washington," 229.

5. Nazarkin, "Negotiating as a Rival," 241.

6. Watanabe, "Negotiating Trade," 205.

7. Chan, "Different Forums, Different Styles," 190.

are disadvantages. On further assessment, however, the evidence presented through-out this volume shows that each of the facets can be *either* an asset or a handicap depending on the specific context of a negotiation, or even *both* an asset and a handicap at the same time.[8] To take a few examples of elements within each:

- Businesslike mind-set
  - A transactional, results-oriented approach can get concrete results, but it tends to ignore and can damage relationship-building efforts.
  - The sense of urgency can help to push the other side to make a deal, but the other side can also use that impatience as leverage; the focus on short-term results produces concrete short-term gains but often at the expense of longer-term interests.
  - Straightforwardness reduces the dangers of ambiguity and misunder-standing, but bluntness increases the risk of offending the other side and provoking resistance or alienating an interlocutor accustomed to a more indirect or subtle form of communication.
  - Economic inducements can be effective but not always as effective as Americans imagine, especially when the counterpart's political and ideo-logical concerns take precedence over economic considerations

- Legalistic mind-set
  - Attention to preparation and precision helps reduce unwelcome surprises at the bargaining table, but a preoccupation with fine print and a prefer-ence for explicit statements can offend some negotiating partners.
  - Dispassionate professionalism prevents emotions from poisoning the ne-gotiating atmosphere and/or blinding American officials to the interests at stake, but a cold, formalistic, and aloof manner does little to build trust, empathy, and relationships.
  - Lawyerly drafting skills can help to produce textually watertight agree-ments, but lawyers often presume, wrongly, that a signed agreement will actually be implemented.[9]

- Superpower mind-set
  - A readiness to flex muscle can cause a counterpart to submit to U.S. de-mands, but it can also produce long-term resentment or hostility.
  - A sense of preponderance can support self-confidence, but it can also pro-duce a self-deluding sense of omnipotence.

---

8. This judgment was also reached by a group of highly experienced American diplomats who met to discuss American negotiating capacities at the United States Institute of Peace on April 17, 2009.

9. As one of the participants at the April 2009 meeting of seasoned diplomats commented, "And something that Americans, given their legalistic background, often don't appreciate, is that once you cut a deal it's only the start of the next phase, which is negotiating the implementation."

- A lack of concern about a counterpart's domestic political considerations can help push through a deal, but it may make that deal susceptible to public or political second-guessing if not renunciation or renegotiation.

- Moralistic mind-set
  - Expressions of high principle can boost domestic support for a negotiating stance and may impress foreign publics, too, generating "soft power," but it can also offend the sensibilities of foreign governments and publics, creating resistance to American demands.
  - A moralistic posture can contribute to a counterpart's respect for American commitment to its principles, but when that posture shifts to accommodate practical compromises, accusations of hypocrisy and double standards may follow.
  - A puritanical opposition to extravagance—and populist aversion to government spending—can help keep American negotiators focused on the substance and bottom line of a negotiation, but neglect of hospitality denies Americans an opportunity to impress counterparts and to build goodwill by reciprocating hospitality received.
  - Exceptionalism—married with preponderant power—can impel Americans to seek better terms than other actors, but it can fuel resentment, if not opposition.

Individually, each of the four facets can be a strength or weakness, depending on the context of a particular negotiation. Collectively, however, they have well served American interests. The historian Walter Russell Mead challenges critics of American foreign policy who decry "its naïve 'oscillation between idealism and isolationism'" and urge the embrace of "the mature, sophisticated, worldly approach of European statesmen." Such criticism, Mead observes, seems to overlook the fact that American diplomacy "has been remarkably successful. . . . The United States is not only the sole global power, its values inform a global consensus, and it dominates to an unprecedented degree the formation of the first truly global civilization our planet has known."[10]

Much the same could be said of American negotiating behavior. It can sometimes seem a blunt and unsophisticated instrument or a soapbox for parochial self-regard, but it has helped the United States become the world's preeminent power. Over the past fifty years, American negotiators have played their part in keeping war from America's shores, extending American ideas and influence, and enabling American industry and commerce to build and sustain the world's largest economy. The four-faceted negotiator has been able to shift gears as circumstances require,

---

10. Mead, *Special Providence*, 10.

emphasizing one or another facet according to the identity of a negotiating counterpart, the issue under discussion, the stakes involved, and the temperament of the president and the temper of the nation. At the same time, each of the facets has normally been present to some degree, upholding a valuable continuity in negotiating practice despite sometimes abrupt switches in policy.

The Changing World of International Negotiation

The four facets have served America well in the twentieth century, but will they be adequate to the negotiating challenges of the twenty-first?

This question is especially pertinent because American negotiators work today in a world that is changing rapidly and profoundly. Gone are the days in which almost all negotiations were bilateral and dealt with just one or two issues. Today, bilateral encounters are hardly uncommon,[11] but the United States also confronts a multiplicity of negotiating arenas, a diverse array of negotiating counterparts, and a slew of multi-issue, multi-stakeholder negotiations. From negotiations over peace in the Middle East, to talks on the nuclear ambitions of North Korea, to meetings addressing climate change and energy security, U.S. officials are likely to find themselves in conversations with representatives of numerous other governments and international organizations (IOs)—and often nongovernmental organizations (NGOs) as well. In addition to these subject-specific negotiations, American policymakers and diplomats also attend a series of crowded, annual international gatherings with equally crowded agendas: the G-20 (involving the world's twenty largest economies), the Summit of the Americas (featuring the leaders of the countries of North, Central, and South America and the Caribbean), the Asia-Pacific Economic Cooperation forum (involving twenty-one Pacific Rim countries), the summit of the Association of Southeast Asian Nations (ASEAN), and the UN General Assembly, among others.

This carousel of multilateral negotiation with its cavalcade of riders is driven by forces that are reshaping not just the field of negotiation but also the entire diplomatic landscape. Five of these forces are particularly powerful.

In the first place, many of the problems and dangers now confronting the world can be dealt with only by a collective response from the international community. As Henry Kissinger has observed, "Economic and financial globalization, environmental and energy imperatives, and the destructive power of modern weapons all impose a major effort at global cooperation."[12] Failed and fragile states, whose weakness opens the door to exploitation by terrorists and criminal gangs and whose

---

11.   Today, as in the past, most trade agreements that the United States signs are bilateral, not multilateral, and the United States enters into more such agreements than other varieties.

12.   Henry A. Kissinger, "The Three Revolutions," *Washington Post*, April 7, 2008.

instability can radiate far beyond their borders, are another common danger that demands a coordinated response from the international community. Despite the disappointment voiced, especially in the United States, with the performance of IOs such as the United Nations and an alphabet soup of regional defense and diplomatic organizations (the OAS, the AU, NATO, ASEAN, etc.), even the most stringent critics of such collective efforts have recognized the requirement of international cooperation to deal with shared concerns.[13]

Second, many of these growing problems require not just collective action but also nonmilitary—especially negotiated—solutions. The military remains an essential component of America's national security, but the military itself sees the need for a readjustment of its relationship with the civilian and diplomatic elements of the country's foreign affairs institutions. As Secretary of Defense Robert Gates asserted in the summer of 2008, "Broadly speaking, when it comes to America's engagement with the rest of the world, it is important that the military is—and is clearly seen to be—in a supporting role to civilian agencies."[14]

Third, the international environment is growing more complex as the Westphalian nation-state system weakens under the impact of the forces of globalization, the rise of politically activated mass publics, and the emergence of subnational and supranational groups empowered by new technologies.[15] Nonstate actors, whether terrorist organizations or humanitarian nongovernmental groups, now play significant roles and must be dealt with as foreign policy challenges or negotiating collaborators. In some instances—for example, the campaign to outlaw landmines—single-issue NGOs have led the way in setting the international agenda, and U.S. officials, unaccustomed to the need to negotiate or work with NGOs, have reacted slowly and have been playing catch-up.

Fourth, the number of civilian agencies involved in many negotiations is growing in response to the multifaceted complexity of the issues at play. When it comes to setting negotiating strategies and, in many cases, implementing them, State Department personnel are increasingly likely to be working alongside people from the Treasury, the Office of the U.S. Trade Representative, various intelligence agencies,

---

13.   See, for example, *American Interests and UN Reform: Report of the Task Force on the United Nations* (Washington, D.C.: United States Institute of Peace Press, 2005), vi.

14.   Quoted in Ann Scott Tyson, "Gates Warns of Militarized Policy," *Washington Post*, July 16, 2008.

15.   Many informed observers have noted that the bipolar twentieth-century world of the Cold War superpowers has given way to a complex international environment of strikingly contrasting modalities. Henry Kissinger, for instance, has identified three concurrent "revolutions" confronting any government seeking to advance its interests abroad: the rise of major states such as China and India operating on the classic nation-state, balance-of-power approach to the world; radical Islamist organizations that reject notions of state sovereignty in favor of a universal Islamic empire—a new caliphate; and a Europe struggling to define its future as a supranational union of societies. In addition, there are the multitude of subnational organizations—ranging from humanitarian assistance NGOs to drug cartels and terrorist organizations—increasingly influential in international affairs given the empowering effects of new communication technologies or the economic resources generated by narcotics trafficking. See Kissinger, "The Three Revolutions."

the Department of Energy, and so forth. Furthermore, issues such as global warming call for highly specialized expertise, and much of this has to be brought in from outside government in the form of technical experts recruited from academia, research organizations, and the business world.

Fifth, the global balance of power is shifting. American political and economic influence seems to be losing its preeminence, at least in relative terms, as new centers of power (primarily in Asia) grow stronger. Even if U.S. power is not waning in absolute terms, globalization and the multilateral complexity of the international system would require a reorientation of the American approach to international negotiation. Emerging realignments in economic and military power and cultural influence will shape America's ability to respond to changing global circumstances and will require American diplomacy to shoulder more of the burden of defending and advancing U.S. national interests throughout the world.

Enhancing America's Negotiating Capacities

In an increasingly globalized world, Americans will have to adjust to the reality that they cannot live apart from "foreign" problems, and that their national strengths do not obviate the need for effective diplomacy.

Inexorably, inescapably, negotiation is becoming more important as a tool of foreign policy, as the military—above all—has recognized. The American inclination to regard negotiation as—in the words of Gilles Andreani—"a privilege bestowed on deserving foreigners"[16] is a luxury America cannot afford. Nor can America merely cross its fingers and hope that the four-faceted negotiating style that has served the country well in the past will continue to do so in a rapidly evolving future. From Foggy Bottom to Capitol Hill, from the innermost sanctum of the White House to the farthest-flung of America's diplomatic outposts, presidents, policymakers, political appointees, senior diplomats, and mid-level Foreign Service officers (FSOs) all must ask themselves how the country can enhance its negotiating capacities to deal with new and emerging challenges.

Determine what can and cannot be changed

Before deciding what *should* be changed, it is first necessary to identify what *can* be changed and, just as importantly, what *cannot*. Negotiating practice that is deeply rooted in America's national culture and institutions cannot be modified easily or

---

16.   Andreani, "Negotiating with Savoir Faire," 287. Chan Heng Chee makes a similar observation in her chapter; Chan, "Different Forums, Different Styles," 189–190. Americans, of course, are not necessarily oblivious to this trait. Leslie Gelb, for example, echoes something of Andreani's and Chan's complaint in a 2009 article in *Foreign Affairs*: "Time and again, the demons of ideology, politics, and arrogance have come to dominate, or at least exercise disproportionate influence on, governmental and public debate about foreign policy." Leslie H. Gelb, "Necessity, Choice, and Common Sense," *Foreign Affairs* (May–June 2009): 56–72.

swiftly because the underlying culture itself changes only slowly and incrementally. Thus, it would make little sense for those charged with directing, and redirecting, American foreign policy to demand that officials suddenly abandon those negotiating styles that have characterized America's diplomacy for many years. None of the four facets of American negotiating behavior is about to disappear from the scene. Some shift in their relative prominence may occur—for instance, the superpower impulse may diminish as the world becomes more multipolar[17]—but such changes will be gradual and incremental.

More specific behavioral traits are likewise not going to vanish. For instance, there is no point in wishing away the American negotiator's pronounced sense of urgency, even though that impatience can trap the official into making compromises in the interest of reaching a timely deal. The Americans' relatively short-term perspectives on issues that may not be "ripe" for short-term solutions will continue to hinder strategies for dealing with long-term intractable conflicts (as in the Middle East, North Korea, and elsewhere). American officials are not about to transform from diplomatic sprinters into dawdlers. Nor are they likely to become masters of indirect communication, abandoning explicit language for the subtleties of unspoken messages, giving an ambiguous "Yes, I understand," when they mean "No," and paying more attention to the context than the content of a message.

Negotiating characteristics rooted in the nation's political and institutional systems are also resistant to change. For instance, that very American trait of "moving the goalposts" during a negotiation owes much to congressional second-guessing of diplomatic initiatives and to Congress's constitutionally mandated responsibility to review and approve treaties that the executive has negotiated with foreign powers. Reflecting widespread mistrust of diplomacy among their constituents, members of Congress have traditionally given only limited support to the work of the Department of State and other civilian agencies of the foreign affairs community. The role of Congress has tended to be one of critic, advocate of special interests, or (financial) constrainer of specific foreign policy programs and negotiations—and this role will not change easily.

Similarly, the president will continue to exert the greatest influence over American negotiating practice and the management of certain "high-context" negotiations. The president empowers negotiators, defines their objectives, and sets the tenor for negotiations. He can protect negotiators or expose them to political attack. In the case of political appointees, the president has a direct say in their appointment. If a negotiator enjoys the confidence and support of the president, he or she has perhaps the most valuable asset that a negotiator can bring to the

---

17. That, however, is by no means certain. Russian power is a shadow of what it was when the Soviet Union was extant, but old habits die hard and many Russian negotiators still behave in the imperious fashion characteristic of the tsarist and Soviet chapters of Russian history. See Schecter, *Russian Negotiating Behavior*, 11 and chapter 3.

table. A president's desire to leave a diplomatic legacy—a desire that grows more pronounced as the end of term approaches—can reanimate a stalled negotiation, but it can also lead to overhasty negotiating initiatives that complicate, rather than resolve, thorny disputes. Above all, the president establishes the character of the interagency process that a negotiator must work with. None of this will change fundamentally.

The interagency process is not immutable—indeed, its character always shifts to some degree from one administration to another—but dramatic change is highly unlikely. America's traditions encourage entrepreneurship and competition, and the U.S. governmental system is structured around competing centers of power and bureaucratic rivalries. In the diplomatic enterprise, this structure sets in motion the interagency byplay that captivates and bedevils both foreign and American diplomats alike. The competitive nature of the system is useful because it gives the president a broad range of ideas and options for negotiating objectives and strategies from which to select his preferred policy, and it can help reconcile complex interests at stake. But if interagency rivalries become too pronounced, they can distract an administration from its negotiating objectives, undermine its ability to implement a coherent and disciplined negotiating strategy, or even give domestic special interest groups and foreign negotiators and their lobbies an opportunity to exploit the administration's divisions.[18] According to Ambassador Ronald Neumann, "bureaucratic turf wars can completely immobilize a negotiation unless the issues rise to the importance that the president cuts the Gordian knot and adjudicates between departments." Furthermore, "the dysfunction of our interagency system is likely to exact a higher price as time goes on," because the issues being negotiated "cut across disciplines, across agency responsibilities."[19] Thus, presidential leadership will become yet more important to disciplining rivalries—and to encouraging and directing the strong and constructive American capacity for teamwork.

American negotiating traits that have deep cultural or constitutional roots are by no means always impediments to productive negotiation. They can be burdensome and restrictive, chaining hapless American officials who would otherwise be free to display fancy diplomatic footwork while crafting inventive agreements. But just as often—indeed, more often—they are assets, giving U.S. negotiators powerful leverage over their foreign counterparts, ensuring that American diplomacy resonates with the will of the American people, and allowing American officials to play to their strengths. Whether they are advantages or disadvantages, however, is largely moot in terms of deciding how to enhance the country's negotiating capacities.

---

18.   The influence of foreign government lobbies is spotlighted in John Newhouse, "Diplomacy, Inc.," *Foreign Affairs* (May–June 2009): 73–92. One consequence of the increasing use of retired political figures by domestic and foreign lobbying firms to influence negotiations through their contacts in the White House and Congress is the further circumvention of the role of the State Department as the lead agency in U.S. diplomacy.

19.   Ronald Neumann, e-mail to Richard H. Solomon, August 4, 2009.

If those traits can be changed at all, they can be modified only modestly and very gradually.

But other aspects of American negotiating behavior *are* amenable to alteration. In the remainder of this chapter, we offer some recommendations for changes that can and should be made so as to give the country's officials a better chance of rising to the negotiating challenges that lie ahead. Our proposals range from relatively minor bureaucratic reforms targeted at FSOs to more ambitious efforts to foster greater interagency collaboration.

Adapt the training of FSOs to twenty-first century requirements

Remarkably, few of the officials charged with negotiating for their country—whether FSOs or political appointees—have received explicit training in negotiating skills. The individual with a business or legal career may have had direct experience as a negotiator in the private sector, and the career FSO will have "learned by doing" the skills of his or her profession. But until recently, the U.S. Foreign Service has provided almost no focused training in negotiating techniques to its career officials. Advancement in the service is largely a mentoring process. FSOs who are successful in negotiating their way through the career system, who are recognized by their superiors as having "natural" negotiating talent, and who are assigned supporting roles in specific negotiations, are the ones who are promoted to senior positions and given responsibility for managing negotiations.

In the past few years, the State Department has begun to improve the training it offers its diplomats, including short courses in the theory and practice of negotiation and in cross-cultural communication. Different courses target different diplomatic levels, from junior FSOs to the rank of ambassador; even "national employees" (foreign staff recruited in-country) now receive at least a basic grounding in negotiation during their training.[20] These initiatives, however, need to be developed and expanded. At present, training programs are still very limited and focus largely on dealing with the media and working within Washington's interagency process. They need to give more attention to developing cross-cultural negotiating skills and negotiation-management strategies through simulations and gaming exercises such as "red teaming" (i.e., playing the part of the adversary to acquire a better understanding of its perspectives and options).

It could be argued that such training would be superfluous, because most FSOs spend little time actually negotiating and focus instead on the business of day-to-day diplomatic interaction. However, although noncareer political appointees may often lead negotiating teams, those officials rely on FSOs for critical operational support, and such support will be more useful if the professionals who deliver it are

---

20. Whiteside, interview, 9–13.

well versed in negotiating strategies, tactics, and processes—their own as well as those of counterpart governments.

Officials must also be educated in different diplomatic levels and tracks that are likely to bear complex negotiating traffic in the coming decades. The State Department, which has itself been slow to appreciate the value of working with nontraditional agents of international influence, such as humanitarian assistance NGOs, should encourage FSOs not only to see nonstate actors as potential negotiating partners but also to familiarize themselves with the organizational structures of NGOs, their modes of operation, cultures, needs, and concerns.

FSOs should be taught how to reach out yet further, beyond NGOs to the media and the mass publics they inform. The State Department does offer courses on dealing with the media, but these tend to focus on how to perform in front of a camera rather than how to develop and execute a public information strategy in support of a negotiating effort. Concepts and techniques of public diplomacy need to be redefined to the requirements of this new era of diverse forms of electronic communication (the Internet, blogging, Twittering, Facebook, satellite and cell-phone voice and video transmissions, and so forth). Officials should be monitoring—and trying to influence—the blogosphere, journalistic and propagandistic Web sites, and other media and forms of communication that shape the public context within which negotiations occur.

In an era of weak states threatened by ethnic and religious conflict, and equally weak IOs, the FSO must be prepared for the roles of development adviser and conflict manager. This requires training in skills needed to advise host governments, as well as the FSO's own, and in measures needed to prevent mass violence, rehabilitate flagging economies, promote internal political reform, and elicit cooperation on shared security interests. To be effective in such missions, the FSO will need not only appropriate conceptual and policy orientation and enhanced negotiating and mediation skills, but also intensive training in esoteric languages and cultures.[21] In short, FSOs will need nothing less than a redefined self-conception of the role of the diplomat. The traditional notion of the diplomat as the voice of presidential authority, reporter of local conditions, promoter of commercial interests, and influencer of elite opinion must be expanded to encompass the role of leader of collective action to prevent and manage conflicts.[22]

---

21.   Ironically, it has been the U.S. military, operating in foreign environments such as Iraq and Afghanistan, that has stressed the need for, and developed training programs in, foreign languages and cultures. Military units have also incorporated civilian talent—linguists and anthropologists—into their field operations.

22.   If the trend set by U.S. military personnel and the staff of international humanitarian agencies continues, FSOs may in the future find themselves conducting local-level negotiations with local governments, communities, and belligerents in efforts to stem violence and build stability. The U.S. (and Canadian) militaries have been significantly enhancing the training in negotiation that they provide to members of Provincial Reconstruction Teams deployed in Afghanistan; see Major Charles B. Ericson, "Winning Hearts and Minds Is Not for Amateurs: Preparing to Negotiate," research report (Air Command and Staff College, Air University, Maxwell Air Force Base, Alabama, April 2008). The kinds of negotiations conducted by members of UN agencies and NGOs in order

The professional training and intellectual development of FSOs must be adapted to the needs of contemporary foreign relations—but an understaffed and under-resourced State Department will not be able to achieve that goal. Until the Foreign Service has the resources needed to provide release time for professional training at various stages of an FSO's career (in much the same way that the U.S. military enhances the skills of its personnel through required periodic training programs) and to make career advancement dependent on field experience in negotiation, political development, and economic reconstruction, it will lack the human resources needed for effective diplomacy. Efforts to expand the size of the Foreign Service to enable such training, however, have in the past run afoul of congressional resistance to expanding the State Department's budget and personnel complement.[23]

Improve institutional memory

The pronounced urgency that characterizes American negotiating behavior makes it imperative to provide greater continuity of management on issues that are unlikely to be resolved in two-, four-, or eight-year timeframes. The most practicable way of accomplishing this is to bolster the Foreign Service's institutional memory of specific negotiations.[24] At present, the only assessments of high-profile negotiations are carried out by senior officials who write books for commercial publication after they leave office. And official documentary control of negotiating records is only beginning to be managed through electronic filing and retrieval systems. The

---

to persuade belligerents to allow the delivery of humanitarian assistance is discussed in Daniel Toole, "Humanitarian Negotiation: Observations from Recent Experience" (Harvard Program on Humanitarian Policy and Conflict Research, Harvard University, February 21, 2001).

23.   For instance, during the administration of George W. Bush, many FSOs were reassigned to Iraq, but Congress refused to increase State Department funding to allow it to recruit people to fill the vacated positions. Operations in Iraq and Afghanistan also spotlighted the dearth of linguists in the State Department who could speak the local languages.

A report issued in June 2007 by the Foreign Affairs Council noted that Congress had twice denied money for Secretary of State Condoleezza Rice's plan to adjust the geographic spread of diplomatic postings to suit post–Cold War realities. Foreign Affairs Council, Task Force, *Managing Secretary Rice's State Department: An Independent Assessment* (Washington, D.C.: Foreign Affairs Council, June 2007).

Toward the end of her tenure as secretary of state, Rice made a determined effort not only to reconfigure Foreign Service postings but also to increase the number of FSOs. As the *Federal Times* reported in March 2008, "about one-fifth of the State Department's midlevel Foreign Service positions are vacant, and the department says it needs Congress to approve long-overdue funding to fill them. . . . But [Congress has refused] to fund Foreign Service hiring since 2004. . . . State is asking Congress for enough money to hire about 700 Foreign Service officers in fiscal 2009. Secretary of State Condoleezza Rice is pushing hard for additional hiring as she briefs lawmakers on the proposed budget." Stephen Losey, "State Grapples with Vacancies in Midlevel Positions," *Federal Times. com*, March 25, 2008, http://www.federaltimes.com/index.php?S=3444490.

Rice's advocacy helped lay the groundwork for the significant funding increase approved by Congress in July 2009 (see below, pp. 309–10).

24.   Another advantage of improved institutional memory has been noted by Theodore Sorenson: "The [State] department's institutional memory, in-depth planning and orderly procedures can protect an eager president from his errors as well as his enemies." Sorenson, "The President and the Secretary of State," *Foreign Affairs* (Winter 1987–88): 238.

State Department had no centralized electronic system for managing its information services until October 1998.[25]

In 2006, in a significant move to enhance the sharing of knowledge within America's foreign affairs agencies, the Office of eDiplomacy created an online encyclopedia called Diplopedia. Access to Diplopedia, which contains "sensitive" but no classified material, is restricted to the staff of foreign affairs and intelligence agencies at home and abroad. "Anyone who can access Diplopedia is invited and encouraged to contribute his or her experience, knowledge and expertise in the form of articles, discussion or editing of material submitted by others," explains the State Department's website. "It is fast becoming a reference and starting point for all topics of interest to the Department and U.S. Government foreign affairs community."[26]

The State Department's assessment and recording process should be further strengthened in a variety of ways:

- The Foreign Service should emulate the U.S. military and institute after-action reporting and assessment procedures. A postnegotiation evaluation of lessons learned is an elemental resource for an official newly entrusted with a negotiating brief on some ongoing diplomatic process (such as the Middle East peace process or the Six Party Talks on North Korea). In an encouraging development, the House of Representatives attached to its appropriation of funds for the State Department in 2010 a requirement that the secretary of state establish a "Lessons Learned Center"—a requirement that Secretary Hillary Clinton supported. This center is intended to be the hub of a broad-ranging effort to collect, analyze, archive, and disseminate observations, best practices, and lessons learned by FSOs and support personnel in the Department of State and USAID.[27]

- The documentary record of negotiations across the boundary of different administrations can be remarkably patchy. The phenomenon of political appointees taking their personal records, and some nonpersonal ones, with them when they leave office needs to be addressed by ensuring, at a minimum, that the State Department creates and maintains a central database of electronic copies of all documents that record understandings, commitments, and other agreements, both explicit and implicit, made during a formal negotiating process.[28] Many documents related to high-level exchanges are dispersed across

25.   Steven W. Hook, "Domestic Obstacles to International Affairs: The State Department under Fire at Home," *PSOnline*, January 2003, 28 n. 3, http://journals.cambridge.org/download.php?file=%2FPSC%2FPSC36_01%2FS1049096503001641a.pdf&code=ad314416b92f6c000e7fa9d615b280fd (accessed August 13, 2009).

26.   See http://www.state.gov/m/irm/ediplomacy/115847.htm.

27.   When this book went to press, the Senate had yet to decide whether to support the House's recommendation. House Report 111–136, Foreign Relations Authorization Act, Fiscal Years 2010 and 2011, Sec. 303.

28.   See the discussion in chapter 5, "Americans Negotiating with Americans," 141.

the country in various institutions and archives. The libraries of thirteen presidents (including all presidents from Calvin Coolidge onward) make up the Presidential Library Network and are now searchable online. Many other libraries and archives, however, are not accessible in that fashion.

- Most institutional memory is located in the minds of individual diplomats, and thus greater efforts need to be made to assess and retain the expertise and experience of senior negotiators. (A key consideration in developing Diplopedia was to prevent the loss of knowledge that occurs whenever a diplomat is reassigned. As the head of the Office of eDiplomacy, Chris Bronk, rhetorically inquired, "Every diplomat moves every two or three years. . . . How do you pass their knowledge down?")[29] One managerial procedure that could be taken in this direction would be to overlap assignments so that an outgoing FSO has the time and opportunity to pass on his or her operational knowledge to the incoming FSO. More far-reaching measures could include pushing back the retirement age for senior diplomats; providing incentives for experienced negotiators to remain in the Foreign Service rather than having them "retire" to better-paid private-sector careers; and lengthening the terms of individual assignments so that diplomats involved in a specific negotiation can provide greater continuity of management as well as sustained interpersonal relationships with negotiating counterparts.

- A strategic planning mechanism should be constructed to compensate for the short-term focus of individual administrations. Such strategizing has tended to be done outside the State Department, in the foreign policy–oriented think tanks or university research centers that house retired officials or academic specialists. In theory, the State Department's Policy Planning staff could provide such support, but its work tends to be limited to the short-term needs of the secretary of state. Some promising moves have been taken to remedy this situation, however. Beginning in late 2007, the Department of State led Project Horizon, a fifteen-agency strategic planning exercise that looked ahead two decades.[30] This group developed five alternative futures in which the State Department and other government agencies would have to operate. In July 2009, the State Department announced that it would undertake a review of U.S. diplomatic and development objectives and priorities in a Quadrennial Diplomacy and Development Review (QDDR) akin to the Department of

29. See Micah L. Sifrey, "Diplopedia, State Department 2.0?" Personal Democracy Forum, August 5, 2006, http://personaldemocracy.com/content/diplopedia-state-department-20.

30. Harry W. Kopp and Charles A. Gillespie, *Career Diplomacy: Life and Work in the U.S. Foreign Service* (Washington, D.C.: Georgetown University Press, 2008), 187–188; Sid Kaplan, "Project Horizon: A New Approach to Interagency Planning," *Federal Times.com*, February 13, 2006, http://www.federaltimes.com/index.php?S=1527532.

Defense planning studies on Quadrennial Defense, which began in 1993. The QDDR team will engage with Congress and cabinet agencies and will seek input from nongovernment experts.[31]

Foster greater interagency collaboration

The challenges of international operations in the twenty-first century require heightened levels of interagency collaboration based on common strategies, policies, and operational plans. Such collaboration may seem a remote possibility at first blush, given the competition among agencies to persuade the president to embrace one or another negotiating strategy, but, as noted earlier in this chapter, the character of the interagency process is not immutable. American culture does value teamwork as well as competition, and the U.S. military provides an example of a tradition of intense rivalry that gave way—under congressional direction—to significant collaboration.

The Goldwater-Nichols Defense Reorganization Act of 1986 sought to control the fierce institutional rivalries among the services of the U.S military by weaving together their capabilities within the framework of joint operations.[32] The legislation centralized operational authority "through the Chairman of the Joint Chiefs [as opposed to the service chiefs] . . . [who] was designated as the principal military advisor to the president, National Security Council and secretary of defense. The act established the position of vice-chairman and streamlined the operational chain of command from the president to the secretary of defense to the unified commanders."[33] The legislation also introduced the concept of a "purple" (joint service) officer corps. The demands of contemporary foreign policy implementation require no less an effort at "purple" foreign affairs management.[34]

Development of heightened interagency coordination will, no doubt, generate considerable political and bureaucratic tensions and raise thorny management questions: Which is the "lead" agency for a particular mission, or for foreign policy in general? Is there a "super secretary of state" to coordinate and direct the activities of a dozen foreign affairs–relevant agencies of the U.S. government? What is the relationship between civilian and military operations? How are nongovernmental

31.   Gordon Adams, "Strategic Planning Comes to the State Department," *Bulletin of the Atomic Scientists*, July 30, 2009, http://www.thebulletin.org/web-edition/columnists/gordon-adams/strategic-planning-comes-to-the-state-department.

32.   Joel Bagnal, "Goldwater-Nichols for the Executive Branch: Achieving Unity of Effort," in Bert B. Tussing, ed., *Threats at Our Threshold* (Carlisle, Penn.: U.S. Army War College [2006]), 44, http://www.carlisle.army.mil/usacsl/publications/Threats%20at%20Our%20Threshold/Chap%202%20-%20G-N%20for%20the%20Executive%20Branch.pdf.

33.   National Defense Library Web site, http://www.ndu.edu/library/goldnich/goldnich.html.

34.   One recent practice has been for military officers to take over the work of diplomats. See Dana Priest, *The Mission: Waging War and Keeping Peace with America's Military* (New York: W.W. Norton, 2003).

humanitarian assistance organizations, the business world, and IOs to be involved in planning and operations? Such issues must be resolved, however, if the substantial resources of the United States are to be effectively mobilized and coordinated in support of "whole-of-government"[35] diplomacy and security programs.[36]

One consequence of interagency feuding is that U.S. negotiators tend to spend far more time discovering and responding to the agendas of their Washington colleagues than assessing and planning how to deal with the negotiating approach of their foreign counterparts at the bargaining table. One way to compensate for this preoccupation would be to make "red teaming" not only a regular feature of the training of FSOs (as proposed above) but also a regular practice during preparations for a negotiation. In other words, a well-informed governmental entity should "game out" a forthcoming negotiating encounter by playing the role of the foreign counterpart.

Increase funding of the State Department

Several of the above proposals to improve the training of FSOs and institutional memory require enhanced funding for the State Department. The secular trend is for congressional funding for the diplomatic enterprise to be about 6 percent of the budgetary support given the Department of Defense.[37] Rational appeals for greater support of the foreign affairs establishment have been voiced by secretaries of state going back decades, but they have lately been joined by none other than the secretary of defense. "America's civilian institutions of diplomacy and development," declared Secretary Gates in 2008, "have been chronically undermanned and un-

---

35. The "whole-of-government" concept (which has been discussed for a decade or more in various contexts) was formally embraced by the Pentagon in 2009. As the *Washington Post* reported, "Defense Secretary Robert M. Gates has formally adopted the concept that national security planning and budgeting cannot be done by the Pentagon alone, according to the Defense Department's ... Quadrennial Roles and Missions Review Report [released in January 2009]. 'The Department supports institutionalizing whole-of-government approaches to addressing national security challenges,' the document says, adding, 'The desired end state is for U.S. Government national security partners to develop plans and conduct operations from a shared perspective.'" Walter Pincus, "Pentagon Recommends 'Whole-of-Government' National Security Plans," *Washington Post*, February 2, 2009.

36. Some commentators argue strongly that the key to greater interagency collaboration is to be found in the NSC. David Rothkopf contents that "we need a high-functioning NSC with as broad a membership as possible to provide the fullest array of tools to the president.... Today [2005], with an ascendant Defense Department dominating a declining State Department, it will fall on the NSC and future presidents to strike a new balance, not just one between agencies but one that encompasses diplomatic, security, intelligence, political, developmental, trade, law enforcement, homeland security, global health, global environment, science and technology, international, bilateral, regional, public and private, permanent and ad hoc factors." David Rothkopf, *Running the World: The Inside Story of the National Security Council and the Architects of American Power* (New York: Public Affairs, 2005), 455–456.

37. "In the final Congressional appropriations for FY 2008, the ratio of funding for military forces versus non-military engagement was 16:1. Despite Secretary Gates' lament about this disparity, his defense budget for FY 2009 actually widens it to 18:1." For FY2009, the administration has asked for almost $550 billion for the Pentagon, while the amount requested for the State Department is less than $40 billion, one-fifth of which is earmarked for foreign military and security assistance. Institute for Policy Studies, *Report of the Task Force on a Unified Security Budget for the United States: FY 2009* (Washington, D.C.: Institute for Policy Studies, September 2008), 3, 9.

derfunded for far too long—relative to what we traditionally spend on the military, and more importantly, relative to the responsibilities and challenges our nation has around the world."[38] In addition to urging Congress to adequately fund the national diplomatic enterprise, Gates also took the unprecedented step of transferring Defense Department funds to the State Department (specifically to cover the costs of bringing in civilian expertise to help the U.S. military with its global reconstruction efforts).[39]

Such pleas for greater funding, however, run up against an enduring congressional suspicion that the State Department fails to promote American interests with sufficient vigor, a very limited congressional constituency for support of diplomacy and foreign aid, as well as the contrasting strong congressional backing for a robust military. (Like the American public as a whole, many members of Congress tend to see diplomacy and military force as separate or even contradictory elements of America's foreign relations, even though—as effective negotiators well know—they are in fact complementary and mutually reinforcing.) One of the arguments in favor of a "Goldwater-Nichols" approach to an integrated foreign affairs–national security enterprise process is that it would facilitate a more effective allocation of resources among the different government agencies involved in implementing foreign policy. Indeed, one of the more far-reaching proposals for budgetary reform advanced in recent years is the creation of a consolidated foreign affairs budget.[40]

Diplomacy may be viewed warily by many members of Congress, but the State Department is not without its champions on Capitol Hill. In 2008, for instance, Senator Richard Lugar, ranking member of the Senate Committee on Foreign Relations, recommended "increasing the capacity of civilian agencies and integrating them with our military power" and urged that the State Department and USAID be given "the resources to carry out what are clearly civilian missions. . . . The foreign affairs budget is roughly equivalent to what the Pentagon spends on health care alone. We must adjust our civilian foreign policy capabilities to deal with a dynamic world where national security threats are increasingly based on non-military factors."[41]

One sign that Lugar's remarks may not have fallen on deaf ears occurred in July 2009, when the U.S. House of Representatives approved a $48.8 billion foreign

---

38. Tyson, "Gates Warns of Militarized Policy."

39. See Gerry J. Gilmore, "Gates, Rice Support Extension of Security-Assistance Legislation," U.S. Department of Defense, Armed Forces Press Service, April 18, 2008, http://www.defenselink.mil/news/newsarticle. aspx?id=49584.

40. The idea is not new; it was, for instance, advanced back in the mid-1990s by Lawrence Eagleburger and Robert Barry in "Dollars and Sense Diplomacy: A Better Foreign Policy for Less," *Foreign Affairs* (July–August 1996). It has, however, recently enjoyed a surge of renewed interest. The year 2008 marked the first time that USAID and the Department of State submitted a joint budget request—but today there are nearly two dozen government agencies that operate in international affairs.

41. Senate Committee on Foreign Relations, *Implementing Smart Power: Setting an Agenda for National Security Policy*, April 24, 2008; Senator Lugar's opening remarks are available online at http://foreign.senate.gov/ testimony/2008/LugarStatement080424a.pdf.

affairs budget for fiscal year 2010 that will fund the hiring of more than 1,300 Foreign Service officers for duty—mainly in Afghanistan and Pakistan. It remains to be seen whether this step signals the beginning of a congressional reevaluation of the role and importance of diplomacy or whether it is a onetime measure driven chiefly by concern to help secure a victory over the Taliban.[42]

Add a fifth negotiating facet?

Among the many challenges facing America's negotiating machinery in the coming decades, we have noted the need to expand the conception of the role of the diplomat, orchestrate interagency efforts, draw on technical expertise, work with unfamiliar foreign cultures and languages, build and maintain multilateral coalitions, and devote more effort to nurturing relationships (with foreign publics as well as officials in foreign governments). When viewed collectively, these challenges suggest that the future success of American diplomacy may hinge on the cultivation of a fifth facet or professional orientation to complement the four that have characterized American negotiating behavior in the past. This fifth facet might be termed "political," in the sense that it embodies the mind-set of an elected American official.[43]

Not only are political negotiators themselves unconstrained by traditional notions of the role of professional diplomats, they are also adept at operating in environments with multiple actors and elements and are particularly expert at navigating through Washington's complex political and institutional systems. One of their greatest strengths is their ability to reach out to all stakeholders or power centers whose interests are affected by a negotiator and to develop relationships with them; to understand the other side's need to reach a deal it can sell to its constituents; and to craft elaborate compromises and workable political deals. Furthermore, they are likely to have a practiced ease with the media, a gift for communicating with publics both at home and abroad, and the ability to mobilize support via their political connections.

If this political mind-set is, indeed, highly appropriate to the kinds of negotiations that may dominate the American diplomatic agenda this century, then it is fortunate—but probably not coincidental—that the phenomenon of the political negotiator, while hardly unknown in past practice, is becoming more common. In recent years, a number of retired or serving elected officials have come to play major negotiating roles. Senator George Mitchell, for instance, played a leading part

---

42. As reported in "Area Votes in Congress," *Philadelphia Inquirer*, July 12, 2009, http://www.philly.com/inquirer/local/20090712_Area_Votes_in_Congress.html.

43. The idea of a fifth facet emerged during a discussion among veteran American diplomats at the United States Institute of Peace in April 2009. We are particularly indebted to Ambassador Samuel Lewis for articulating key elements of the idea.

in the negotiations between Republicans and Loyalists in Northern Ireland that led to the signing of the Good Friday Agreement in 1998. In 2009, Mitchell was brought back into the negotiator's realm when President Obama appointed him special envoy for the Middle East. Congressman Bill Richardson was recruited by President Clinton for a number of diplomatic missions, including negotiations with North Korea, Sudan, and Iraq, and was subsequently appointed U.S. ambassador to the United Nations. Senator Hillary Clinton became secretary of state in 2009, the first elected official to occupy the position since Edward Muskie in 1980.

Former presidents have also come to play major negotiating roles. Bill Clinton was appointed UN special envoy to Haiti (see below) in May 2009, and in August of the same year he flew to North Korea to negotiate the release of two American journalists who had been sentenced by the North Korean government to twelve years of hard labor for "hostile acts." According to the *New York Times*, during his visit to Pyongyang, Clinton "won the freedom of two American journalists, opened a diplomatic channel to North Korea's reclusive government and dined with the North's ailing leader, Kim Jong-il."[44] Jimmy Carter has been very active as a negotiator since he left the White House, having been involved in highly sensitive negotiations involving countries such as North Korea, Haiti, Israel and the Palestinian Authority, Colombia, and Ecuador.

One invaluable asset that the political negotiator possesses is the ability to engage with other Americans. Senior political operatives such as Clinton, Mitchell, and Richardson are highly experienced in reaching out to the American public through the media. They also have the contacts, credentials, and know-how to reach deep inside the American political and institutional systems. Sure-footed on the politically precarious heights of Capitol Hill, and familiar with the corridors of power within and between government agencies, political negotiators are more adept than most officials at building consensus among disputatious departments and more likely to gain the senior-level political support from Congress and the White House needed to achieve diplomatic breakthroughs.[45]

The political negotiator's ability to mobilize support via their public stature can be an asset not only with the American public but also with foreign constituencies. This attribute was certainly part of UN secretary-general Ban Ki-moon's calculation in May 2009, when he asked Bill Clinton to serve as the United Nations'

---

44.   Mark Landler and Peter Baker, "In Release of Journalists, Both Clintons Had Key Roles," *New York Times*, August 4, 2009, http://www.nytimes.com/2009/08/05/world/asia/05korea.html.

45.   The State Department is not alone in seeking politically savvy negotiators. According to a report in the *Washington Post*, the Department of Defense replaced General McKiernan as head of U.S. forces in Afghanistan with General McChrystal at least in part because McKiernan was seen by the secretary of defense as "too languid, too old-school and too removed from Washington. He lacked the charisma and political savvy that Gen. David H. Petraeus brought to the Iraq war." The decision "reflects a view among senior Pentagon officials that top generals need to be as adept at working Washington as they are the battlefield, that the conflict in Afghanistan requires a leader who can also win the confidence of Congress and the American public." Rajiv Chandrasekaran, "Pentagon Worries Led to Command Change," *Washington Post*, August 17, 2009.

special envoy to Haiti. The former president's standing in that country has remained high since 1994, when he threatened the use of U.S. military force to persuade the military junta in Port-au-Prince to relinquish power, and the Clinton Foundation is active in Haiti in the areas of health care, AIDS, the environment, and economic development.[46] The appointment was welcomed in the United States by the secretary of state. Without mentioning their marriage, Hillary Clinton "praised the appointment of such 'a high-profile envoy. . . . It's the kind of partnership we are looking for across the board,' she told reporters at the White House, explaining that she had already been preparing a team to help Haiti. 'This is going to be an added bit of leverage and focus for us.'"[47]

Enlisting and deploying high-level political negotiators can be a risky gambit, however, for secretaries of state and presidents. Accustomed to giving rather than taking orders, mindful of their carefully crafted public images, and associated in the minds of audiences both at home and abroad with particular policies and principles, political negotiators may be reluctant to conform to the objectives and style of the administration that seeks to use them. For instance, as noted in chapter 4, the Clinton administration felt that Jimmy Carter exceeded his authority when acting as an intermediary in dealing with North Korea in 1994. The use of such talent from "outside the system" also tends to degrade the standing and effectiveness as negotiators of career Foreign Service officers, who are seen as less influential than a special envoy appointed by the president or secretary of state.

Know yourself

American negotiators are well aware of the advantages of understanding the interests, motivations, and ambitions at work on the *other* side of the bargaining table. Indeed, one of the hallmarks of American negotiating behavior is careful preparation, which involves mining intelligence reports and a wide variety of print and online sources to build a reliable picture of the negotiating counterpart. Given this trait, American negotiators may fairly be regarded as diligent disciples of Chinese strategist Sun Tzu's injunction, quoted at the outset of this volume, to "know your adversary." But what of the other part of Sun Tzu's tenet: "Know yourself"?

Like Americans in general, perhaps, American diplomats tend to be more outward-looking than introspective, more extroverted than introverted. They do look inward from time to time, but they are more interested in what goes on around them; they are keener to look to the future than to the past; and they are more interested in discovering (and then adjusting) the clockwork of the world than in examining what makes themselves tick.

---

46.   "Clinton Named UN Envoy to Haiti," *CBCnews.com*, May 19, 2009, http://www.cbc.ca/world/story/2009/05/19/clinton-un-envoy-haiti364.html.

47.   "Clinton Named as UN Envoy to Haiti," Associated Press, May 19, 2009.

This predisposition has many benefits for a negotiator: a readiness to engage with a problem, a refusal to let the weight of history deflate hopes for a better future, and an appetite for crafting inventive and carefully calibrated solutions. Yet it has its drawbacks. A lack of introspection denies one the opportunity to see oneself as others do—hence, for instance, the disbelief of so many American negotiators at being tagged as "hegemonic" by so many of their foreign counterparts. A dearth of self-awareness makes it hard to recognize one's vulnerabilities (impatience, for example), hard to see how one's strengths can sometimes become weaknesses (how legalistic precision, say, can sometimes seem pedantic and mistrustful), and hard to know how to correct, mask, or compensate for those deficiencies. And an inadequate understanding of how one's own culture influences what one says and does virtually ensures that one will mishear, misunderstand, or simply miss the subtle inflections in the behavior of one's foreign counterpart.

Sun Tzu's advice may be twenty-five hundred years old, intended for kings and generals, and written when China's seven nations were constantly warring for control of their country, but it is no less relevant for contemporary American negotiators, who must navigate between almost two hundred countries continually vying for diplomatic advantage. No matter how the diplomatic world shifts in the coming decades, self-awareness will remain one of the keys to effective negotiating performance. If this volume—inspired by China's great strategist—leads to heightened self-reflection among its American readers, it will have done its job.

Appendix

Analytical Categories Used in the Cross-Cultural Negotiation Project

A long-term goal of the United States Institute of Peace's Cross-Cultural Negotiation Project is to create a database that not only captures details of the negotiating behavior of specific countries but also can be used to draw cross-cultural comparisons and reveal patterns in negotiating behavior that transcend national differences.[1] To facilitate the creation of such a database, the CCN country-specific studies have been informed by a common set of analytical categories. Within the context of an individual study, these categories help an author determine research parameters—in other words, they help an author decide what questions to ask and issues to explore in the given case. Within the context of the CCN project as a whole, the analytical categories indicate the kinds of subjects for which data is available on multiple cases.

The categories—some of which inevitably overlap—are the following:

Overall Attitude toward Negotiation

- **Nature of negotiation** (e.g., does the negotiator tend to regard negotiations in general as a zero-sum or a win-win proposition, as an opportunity to

---

1. As of this writing (the summer of 2009), development of a highly interactive cross-cultural database is under way. Once completed, the database will allow practitioners and policymakers—as well as scholars and other researchers—to explore negotiations comparatively from a wide variety of perspectives (e.g., specific countries, issues under negotiation, particular negotiating tactics or traits); to switch instantly from one perspective to another; to see the relationships between issues, individuals, and negotiating approaches; to access the texts of many negotiated agreements and accounts of specific negotiations; and to monitor continuously updated press or diplomatic reports of significant developments in ongoing negotiations. The database will be accessible online, thereby allowing negotiators to consult it at any time and from any location.

trade concessions to mutual advantage, or as an occasion to wrest unilateral advantage?)

- **Purpose of negotiation** (e.g., does the negotiator tend to regard negotiations in general as an opportunity to build relationships, to trade/wrest concessions, to air or remedy grievances, to project a specific public image? is negotiating viewed as a positive process of problem solving or as a reactive way of fending off pressures from the counterpart, buying time, or misleading the counterpart government?)
- **Expectation of success** (e.g., does the negotiator approach negotiations in general in a positive or negative frame of mind, enthusiastically or reluctantly, optimistically or pessimistically?)
- **Tenor** (e.g., is the overall tone of the negotiator's approach businesslike or imperious, apprehensive, legalistic, bullying, etc.? is it formal or relaxed, cordial or aggressive, cooperative or obstructive?)

Domestic Context

- **Historical context** (e.g., what is the country's history of negotiation both in general and in relation to the specific counterpart and issue at hand? is the country's past negotiating record seen as strong or weak, as generating valuable benefits or as creating or exposing vulnerabilities?)
- **Bureaucratic context** (e.g., what is the structure of the bureaucracy within which the negotiator operates? how are decisions made? how does the bureaucracy determine negotiating goals and strategies [reached by consensus, set by dominant agency, etc.]? how does the bureaucracy train, assign, instruct, monitor, and manage the negotiator before and during a negotiation?)
- **Political context** (e.g., which actors within the political system have authority over a negotiation? how does the political system interact with the bureaucracy to influence negotiating goals and strategies? to what extent and how do shifts in the constellation of political forces influence ongoing negotiations? to what extent and how does the political system of the negotiator's country influence the negotiator's behavior during a negotiation?)
- **Public context** (e.g., to what extent does public opinion influence the goals and conduct of a negotiation? how is public opinion factored into political and bureaucratic decisions regarding negotiating goals and strategies? to what extent and how do shifts in public opinion influence ongoing negotiations?)
- **Negotiator's interaction with his or her domestic systems** (e.g., to what extent and how can the negotiator shape the bureaucratic, political, and public context before and during a negotiation?)

Process of Negotiation

- **Negotiation as a process** (e.g., does the negotiator regard a negotiation as a linear series of fairly discrete stages, possessing a starting point and an endpoint, or is negotiation viewed as a cyclical or unstructured process wherein certain arguments, issues, and interactions are repeated until they are resolved or abandoned, or is there no sense of process?)
- **Phases of negotiation** (e.g., how many and what kinds of phases does the negotiator expect a negotiation to involve—prenegotiations, opening phase, middle game, endgame, implementation? which of those phases does the negotiator regard as most important and which as least important?)
- **Preparation and management**
  - **Research and study** (e.g., does the negotiator prepare carefully for a negotiation? does the negotiator know the history of the issue as well as the current status? does the negotiator study the record of past negotiations with the counterpart? does the negotiator draw on intelligence, as well as other sources, about the counterpart's interests, capacities, constraints, and members of the negotiating team?)
  - **Developing strategies and tactics** (e.g., to what extent does the negotiator plan and strategize? to what extent does the negotiator develop tactics in advance of a negotiation? to what extent is the negotiator able to adjust the negotiating approach to the strategy and tactics of the counterpart?)
  - **Countertactics** (e.g., to what extent does the negotiator seek to counter the counterpart's own traits and tactics? is the negotiator generally unconcerned to do so [and if so, why] or does the negotiator devote considerable attention to devising countertactics? which traits and tactics does the negotiator seek to counter? how does the negotiator counter [by mirroring the counterpart's behavior, by protesting it, by emphasizing one or more of the negotiator's own traits or tactics, etc.]?)
- **Endpoint of negotiation** (e.g., does the negotiator envision a negotiation as ending with the signed final agreement, as continuing through implementation, or as an unending process of continual renegotiation?)
- **Implementation** (e.g., does the negotiator faithfully implement agreements and follow through on promises and commitments? or does the negotiator seek to evade commitments, to observe the letter but not the spirit of an agreement, or to continually renegotiate the terms of an agreement?)

Negotiating Traits and Tactics

- **Negotiating as an individual or team effort** (e.g., how is the negotiating team, and its leader, appointed? are negotiating teams typically small or large?

are they usually restricted to diplomats or do they also feature technical experts, lawyers, etc.? how much authority does the team leader have over the team and within the political/bureaucratic system? is a team usually kept on a short and tight leash by the government or allowed some latitude and flexibility to explore options during the negotiations? what degree of internal discipline and unity does a team typically display?)

- **Sense and use of time**
  - **Attitudes toward the past, the present, and the future** (e.g., is the negotiator forward-looking or backward-looking? does history figure prominently in the negotiator's calculations and outlook? is the negotiator focused chiefly on redressing past wrongs or on creating a brighter future?)
  - **Temporal purview** (e.g., does the negotiator display a long- or short-term outlook? is the negotiator chiefly interested in long-term, mid-term, or short-term interests and gains?)
  - **Sense of urgency** (e.g., is the negotiator eager to forge ahead in a negotiation or content to let a negotiation proceed at its own pace? does the negotiator move more quickly through some phases of a negotiation than others?)
  - **Deadlines** (e.g., is the negotiator conscious of and/or responsive to deadlines? are deadlines imposed on the negotiator by the negotiator's own team, bureaucracy, or government? does the negotiator seek to impose deadlines on the negotiating counterpart?)
  - **Stalling** (e.g., does the negotiator seek to stall or slow down a negotiation? if so, how does the negotiator do so?)
- **Use of language**
  - **Degree of precision** (e.g., does the negotiator use explicit or implicit language? is language legalistic or impressionistic, precise or ambiguous? is language used in so blunt a fashion that it can offend negotiating counterparts? is language used in so elliptical a fashion that it can exasperate or confuse negotiating counterparts? is there a marked difference between the language used in the terms of written agreements and the language employed in verbal exchanges?)
  - **Degree of credibility** (e.g., does the negotiator lie, and if so, often or occasionally? alternatively, does the negotiator have a reputation for honesty and trustworthiness? does the negotiator take pains to maintain credibility for the accuracy of the negotiator's statements?)
  - **Bluster** (e.g., does the negotiator bluster and use emotionally charged language? or does the negotiator maintain a calm, restrained, soft-spoken demeanor?)
  - **Rhetoric** (e.g., does the negotiator employ formalistic or formulaic presentations? if so, what kinds of rhetorical formulations or stylized presentations are used, and at which points in a negotiation?)

- **Body language** (e.g., how, if at all, does the negotiator use body language or contextual factors to communicate? is the negotiator attentive to and responsive to nonverbal clues and cues?)
- **Preferred and foreign languages** (e.g., in what language is negotiation usually conducted? is the negotiator comfortable in negotiations involving foreign languages? what degree of fluency does the negotiator have in the counterpart's language? does the negotiator use interpreters, and if so, how are they trained and recruited?)

- **Argumentation**
  - **Use of logic** (e.g., does the negotiator argue logically for his or her case and seek to explain the philosophical basis of that case? does the negotiator argue deductively or inductively? is logic used at some phases or in relation to some issues but not others?)
  - **Factual argumentation** (e.g., does the negotiator cite numerous facts and figures? does the negotiator tend to give more weight to facts and figures than to emotions, relationships, and other intangible factors?)
  - **Moralistic arguments** (e.g., does the negotiator base his or her arguments on moral or ethical principles? does the negotiator appeal to a universal set of principles or to his or her own particular moral code? does the negotiator sermonize or proselytize?)
  - **Assertion** (e.g., does the negotiator tend simply to assert and reassert his or her position and demands rather than to argue?)
  - **Compromise** (e.g., is the negotiator prepared to compromise—and if so, on what? or is the negotiator fundamentally inflexible? does the negotiator pocket compromises made by the counterpart or reciprocate with his or her own concessions? is the negotiator's opening position near or far from his or her final position?)

- **Pressure tactics**
  - **Linkages** (e.g., does the negotiator link the issue[s] being negotiated to other issues not, at first, under consideration? if so, how does the negotiator establish and press these linkages?)
  - **Deadlines and stalling** (e.g., does the negotiator use deadlines to increase pressure on the counterpart? to what extent are those deadlines "real"? to what extent are they flexible? alternatively, does the negotiator stall to impose pressure on the counterpart? if so, how does he or she stall?)
  - **Escalation of demands** (e.g., to what extent does the negotiator "move the goalposts," seeking additional concessions once the counterpart has agreed to some concessions? what factors encourage a negotiator to up the ante? at what point and why does the negotiator decide to stop escalating demands?)
  - **Threats** (e.g., does the negotiator use threats? if so, what kinds [to disengage from negotiations, to penalize or punish, to use military force, etc.]?

do threats tend to escalate? does the negotiator make good on threats or do threats lack credibility? how does the negotiator give threats credibility?)

- **Hostility and intimidation** (e.g., does the negotiator seek to intimidate the counterpart? does the negotiator use aggressive language and/or gestures to cow the counterpart? what contextual factors can be manipulated to heighten pressure, to intimidate?)

- **Enticements**
  - **Appeals to friendship** (e.g., does the negotiator appeal to ties of friendship, personal or national?)
  - **Quids pro quo** (e.g., is the negotiator prepared to compromise, to trade one kind of concession for a concession of a similar kind?)
  - **Bartering** (e.g., what kinds of enticements does the negotiator barter to secure his or her goals? does the negotiator seek to buy off the counterpart with financial enticements, political recognition, prestige-enhancing opportunities [such as state visits], etc.?)
- **Hospitality** (e.g., does the negotiator use hospitality as a negotiating tool? if so, does the negotiator seek to create a cordial atmosphere, to flatter the counterpart, or to overawe the counterpart? what kinds of hospitality does the negotiator provide? alternatively, does the negotiator provide deliberately meager or purely functional hospitality?)

Communications

- **Back channels** (e.g., does the negotiator use back channels never, rarely, sometimes, or often? are back channels more likely to be used when negotiating particular issues or with particular counterparts? what kinds of back channels does the negotiator use? are back channels kept confidential?)
- **Use of media** (e.g., does the negotiator seek to use the media to shape the goals, agenda, and/or course of a negotiation? which media does the negotiator target—domestic or international, elite or mass, press or television, etc.? which kinds of audiences is the negotiator seeking to reach via the media—the negotiator's own government, bureaucracy, colleagues, or public; the counterpart's? how does the negotiator use the media [planting stories, leaking, orchestrating domestic constituencies, appealing to the counterpart's public, etc.]?)

Selected Bibliography

Acheson, Dean. *Present at the Creation: My Years in the State Department.* New York: W. W. Norton, 1969.

Adair, W. L., J. M. Brett, and T. Okumura. "Negotiation Behavior When Cultures Collide: The United States and Japan." *Journal of Applied Psychology* 80, no. 3 (2001).

Adamishin, Anatoly, and Richard Schifter. *Human Rights, Perestroika, and the End of the Cold War.* Washington, D.C.: United States Institute of Peace Press, 2009.

Adler, Nancy. *International Dimensions of Organizational Behavior.* 4th ed. Cincinnati: South-Western College Publishing, 2002.

Adler, Nancy J., and John L. Graham. "Cross-Cultural Interaction: The International Comparison Fallacy?" *Journal of International Business Studies* 20 (1989).

Albright, Madeleine K. *Madam Secretary: A Memoir.* New York: Hyperion, 2003.

———. *The Mighty and the Almighty: Reflections on America, God, and World Affairs.* New York: HarperCollins, 2006.

Anonymous. "Negotiating with the Americans." *Contract Management* (1983).

Armstrong, D. *The Rise of the International Organization: A Short History.* New York: St. Martin's, 1982.

Art, Robert J., and Patrick M. Cronin, eds. *The United States and Coercive Diplomacy.* Washington, D.C.: United States Institute of Peace Press, 2003.

Association for Diplomatic Studies and Training. *Frontline Diplomacy: The U.S. Foreign Affairs Oral History Collection.* CD-ROM. Arlington, Va.: Association for Diplomatic Studies and Training, 2000.

Avruch, Kevin. *Culture and Conflict Resolution.* Washington, D.C.: United States Institute of Peace Press, 2004.

Bacevich, A. J. *American Empire: The Realities and Consequences of U.S. Diplomacy.* Cambridge, Mass.: Harvard University Press, 2002.

———. *The Limits of Power: The End of American Exceptionalism.* New York: Metropolitan, 2008.

Bagnal, Joel. "Goldwater-Nichols for the Executive Branch: Achieving Unity of Effort." In *Threats at Our Threshold,* edited by Bert B. Tussing. Carlisle, Penn.: U.S. Army War College, 2006.

Baker, James A., III, "The Big Ten: The Case for Pragmatic Idealism." *National Interest* (August 29, 2007).

———. *The Politics of Diplomacy: Revolution, War, and Peace, 1989–1992.* New York: Putnam's Sons, 1995.

Baker, James A., III, and Steve Fiffer. *Work Hard, Study . . . and Keep Out of Politics! Adventures and Lessons from an Unexpected Public Life.* 2nd ed. Evanston, Ill.: Northwestern University Press, 2008.

Baritz, Loren. *Backfire: A History of How American Culture Led Us into Vietnam and Made Us Fight the Way We Did.* New York: Morrow, 1985.

Barnes, William, and John Heath Morgan. *The Foreign Service of the United States: Origins, Development, and Functions.* Washington, D.C.: U.S. Department of State, Historical Office, 1961.

Barthe, Sébastien, and Charles-Philippe David. "Kosovo 1999: Clinton, Coercive Diplomacy, and the Use of Analogies in Decision Making." *Whitehead Journal of Diplomacy and International Relations* 8, no. 2 (2007).

Beisner, Robert L. *Dean Acheson: A Life in the Cold War.* New York: Oxford University Press, 2006.

Bendahmane, D., and J. W. McDonald, Jr., eds. *Perspectives on Negotiation.* Washington, D.C.: Foreign Service Institute, 1986.

Benedick, Richard Elliot. *Ozone Diplomacy: New Directions in Safeguarding the Planet.* Enlarged edition. Cambridge, Mass.: Harvard University Press, 1998.

Berlin, Isaiah, and Henry Hardy. *The Soviet Mind.* Washington, D.C.: Brookings Institution Press, 2004.

Berridge, G. R., *Diplomacy: Theory and Practice.* 3rd ed. Basingstoke, England, and New York: Palgrave Macmillan, 2005.

Berridge, G. R., and Alan James. *A Dictionary of Diplomacy.* 2nd ed. Basingstoke, England: Palgrave Macmillan, 2003.

Berton, P., H. Kimura, and I. W. Zartman, eds. *International Negotiation: Actors, Structure/Process, Values.* New York: St. Martin's, 1999.

Bilder, Richard, "The Office of the Legal Advisor." *American Journal of International Law* 54 (1962).

Black, P. W., and Kevin Avruch. "Culture, Power, and International Negotiations: Understanding Palau-U.S. Status Negotiations." *Millennium: Journal of International Studies* 22, no. 3 (1993).

Blacker, C. D. *Reluctant Warriors: The United States, the Soviet Union, and Arms Control.* New York: Freeman, 1987.

Blaker, Michael, Paul Giarra, and Ezra F. Vogel. *Case Studies in Japanese Negotiating Behavior.* Washington, D.C.: United States Institute of Peace Press, 2002.

Bohlen, Charles. *Witness to History, 1929–1969.* New York: Norton, 1973.

Brett, J. M. "Culture and Negotiation." *International Journal of Psychology* 35, no. 2 (2000).

Brinkley, D., ed. *The Reagan Diaries.* New York: HarperCollins, 2007.

Brofenbrenner, U. "The Mirror-Image in Soviet-American Relations." *Journal of Social Issues* 16 (1961).

Brzezinski, Zbigniew. *Second Chance: Three Presidents and the Crisis of American Superpower.* New York: Basic, 2007.

Bull, Hedley. *The Anarchical Society: A Study of Order in World Politics.* 3rd ed. New York: Columbia University Press, 1977.

Bundy, McGeorge, et al. *The Dimensions of Diplomacy.* Baltimore: Johns Hopkins University Press, 1964.

Burns, R. D., ed. *Guide to American Foreign Relations since 1700.* Santa Barbara, Calif.: ABC-CLIO for the Society of Historians of American Foreign Relations, 1983.

Bush, George Herbert Walker. *All the Best: My Life in Letters and Other Writings.* New York: Scribner, 1999.

Bush, George W. "Address to a Joint Session of Congress and the American People." United States Capitol, September 20, 2001. http://www.whitehouse.gov/news/releases/2001/09/20010920-8.html.

Calleo, David P. *Beyond American Hegemony: The Future of the Western Alliance.* New York: Basic; Washington, D.C.: New America, 1987.

Carbaugh, Donal. "Some Distinctive Features of U.S. American Conversation." In *The Changing Conversation in America: Lectures from the Smithsonian.* Edited by William F. Eadie and Paul E. Nelson. Thousand Oaks, Calif.: Sage, 2002.

Carothers, T. H. *In the Name of Democracy: United States Policy toward Latin America in the Reagan Years.* Berkeley: University of California Press, 1991.

Carroll, Holbert N. *The House of Representatives and Foreign Affairs.* Rev. ed. Boston: Little Brown, 1966.

Carter, Jimmy. *Negotiation: The Alternative to Hostility.* Carl Vinson Memorial Lecture Series. Macon, Ga.: Mercer University Press, 2003.

———. *Our Endangered Values: America's Moral Crisis.* New York: Simon and Schuster, 2005.

———. *Why Not the Best? The First Fifty Years.* New York: Simon and Schuster, 1996.

Chehabi, H. E. "Sport Diplomacy between the United States and Iran." *Diplomacy and Statecraft* 12, no. 1 (2001).

Cheng, Joseph Y. S., and King-Lun Ngok. "The 2001 'Spy Plane' Incident Revisited: The Chinese Perspective." *Journal of Chinese Political Science* 9, no. 1 (2004).

Chollet, Derek, and James Goldgeier. *America between the Wars: From 11/9 to 9/11.* New York: Public Affairs, 2008.

Clifford, Clark. *Counsel to the President: A Memoir.* New York: Random House, 1991.

Cogan, Charles. *French Negotiating Behavior: Dealing with La Grande Nation.* Washington, D.C.: United States Institute of Peace Press, 1999.

Cohen, Raymond. *Negotiating across Cultures: International Communication in an Interdependent World.* Rev. ed. Washington, D.C.: United States Institute of Peace Press, 1997.

Cortright, David, and George A. Lopez. "Bombs, Carrots, and Sticks: The Use of Incentives and Sanctions." *Arms Control Today* 35 (March 2005). http://www.armscontrol.org/act/2005_03/Cortright.

Costigliola, F. *Awkward Dominion: American Political, Economic, and Cultural Relations with Europe, 1919–1933.* Ithaca: Cornell University Press, 1984.

Crocker, Chester A. "The Art of Peace: Bringing Diplomacy Back to Washington." *Foreign Affairs* 86, no. 4 (July–August 2007).

———. *High Noon in Southern Africa: Making Peace in a Rough Neighborhood.* New York: W. W. Norton, 1992.

Crocker, Chester A., Fen Osler Hampson, and Pamela Aall, eds. *Leasing the Dogs of War: Conflict Management in a Divided World.* Washington, D.C.: United States Institute of Peace Press, 2007.

———. *Taming Intractable Conflicts: Mediation in the Hardest Cases.* Washington, D.C.: United States Institute of Peace Press, 2005.

Dahl, Robert. *Congress and Foreign Policy.* New York: Harcourt Brace, 1950.

Dallek, Robert. *Franklin D. Roosevelt and American Foreign Policy, 1932–1945.* Oxford: Oxford University Press, 1979.

———. *Nixon and Kissinger: Partners in Power.* New York: HarperCollins, 2007.

Dam, Kenneth W. *The Rules of the Global Game: A New Look at U.S. International Economic Policymaking.* Chicago: University of Chicago Press, 2001.

De Santis, H. *The Diplomacy of Silence: The American Foreign Service, the Soviet Union, and the Cold War, 1933–1947.* Chicago: University of Chicago Press, 1983.

De Tocqueville, Alexis. *Democracy in America.* Garden City, N.Y.: Doubleday, 1969.

Dizard, Wilson, Jr. *Digital Diplomacy: U.S. Foreign Policy in the Information Age.* Washington, D.C.: Center for Strategic and International Studies, 2001.

———. *Inventing Public Diplomacy: The Story of the U.S. Information Agency.* Boulder, Colo.: Lynne Rienner, 2004.

Dobrynin, Anatoly. *In Confidence: Moscow's Ambassador to America's Six Cold War Presidents.* New York: Times Books, Random House, 1995.

Druckman, Daniel. "Stages, Turning Points, and Crises: Negotiating Military Base Rights, Spain and the United States." *Journal of Conflict Resolution* 30, no. 2 (1986).

Druckman, Daniel, et al. "Cultural Differences in Bargaining Behavior: India, Argentina, and the U.S." *Journal of Conflict Resolution* 20, no. 3 (1976).

Dueck, C. "Ideas and Alternatives in American Grand Strategy, 2000–2004." *Review of International Studies* 30, no. 4 (2004).

Dutta-Bergman, M. J. "U.S. Public Diplomacy in the Middle East: A Critical Cultural Approach." *Journal of Communication Inquiry* 30, no. 2 (2006).

Eagleburger, Lawrence, and Robert Barry. "Dollars and Sense Diplomacy: A Better Foreign Policy for Less." *Foreign Affairs* 75, no. 4 (July–August 1996).

Eisenhower, Dwight D. *Mandate for Change, 1953–1956.* Garden City, N.Y.: Doubleday, 1963.

———. *Waging Peace: The White House Years, 1956–61.* Garden City, N.Y.: Doubleday, 1963.

Elgstroem, Ole. "The Role of Culture." In *Negotiation Eclectics: Essays in Memory of Jeffrey Z. Rubin.* Edited by Deborah Kolb. Cambridge, Mass.: PON Books, 1999.

Engel, Jeffry, and George H. W. Bush. *The China Diary of George H. W. Bush: The Making of a Global President.* Princeton: Princeton University Press, 2008.

Ericson, Charles B. "Winning Hearts and Minds Is Not for Amateurs: Preparing to Negotiate." Research report. Air Command and Staff College, Air University, Maxwell Air Force Base, Alabama, April 2008.

Faure, Guy Oliver, and Jeffrey Z. Rubin, eds. *Culture and Negotiation.* Thousand Oaks, Calif.: Sage, 1993.

Feith, Douglas J. *War and Decision: Inside the Pentagon at the Dawn of the War on Terrorism.* New York: Harper, 2008.

Ferrell, R. H. *American Diplomacy: A History.* 3rd ed. New York: Norton, 1975.

Fisher, Glen. *International Negotiation: A Cross-Cultural Perspective.* Yarmouth, Maine: Intercultural Press, 1980.

Fisher, R., and W. Ury. *Getting to Yes: Negotiating Agreement without Giving In.* New York: Penguin, 1991.

Foreign Affairs Council, Task Force. *Managing Secretary Rice's State Department: An Independent Assessment.* Report. Washington, D.C.: Foreign Affairs Council, June 2007.

Freeman, Chas. W., Jr. *Arts of Power: Statecraft and Diplomacy.* Washington, D.C.: United States Institute of Peace Press, 1997.

———. *The Diplomat's Dictionary.* Rev. ed. Washington, D.C.: United States Institute of Peace Press, 1997.

Fulbright, William. *The Arrogance of Power.* New York: Random House, 1966.

Gaddis, John Lewis. *The Cold War: A New History.* New York: Penguin, 2005.

————. *Strategies of Containment: A Critical Appraisal of Postwar American National Security Policy*. New York: Oxford University Press, 2005.

————. *The United States and the Origins of the Cold War, 1941–1947*. New York: Columbia University Press, 1972.

Gates, Robert. "Landon Lecture." Speech presented at Kansas State University, Manhattan, Kansas, November 26, 2007. Department of Defense, Defenselink: http://www.defenselink.mil/speeches/speech.aspx?speechid=1199.

Gelb, Leslie H. "Necessity, Choice, and Common Sense." *Foreign Affairs* 88, no. 3 (May–June 2009).

————. *Power Rules: How Common Sense Can Rescue American Foreign Policy*. New York: HarperCollins, 2009.

Gingrich, Newt. "Rogue State Department." *Foreign Policy* 137 (July–August 2003).

————. "Transforming the State Department: The Next Challenge for the Bush Administration." Speech presented at the American Enterprise Institute, Washington, D.C., April 22, 2003.

Goldblat, Jozef. *Arms Control: The New Guide to Negotiations and Agreements*. 2nd ed. Thousand Oaks, Calif.: Sage, 2002.

Goodwin, Doris Kearns. *Lyndon Johnson and the American Dream*. New York: Harper and Row, 1976.

Graham, John. "The Japanese Negotiation Stye: Characteristics of a Distinct Approach." *Negotiation Journal* 9, no. 2 (March 1989).

Greene, A. S. "U.S. Diplomacy in the Age of the Internet." Ph.D diss., Old Dominion University, 2003.

Grove, Brandon. *Behind Embassy Walls: The Life and Times of an American Diplomat*. Columbia: University of Missouri Press, 2005.

Gutman, R. *Banana Diplomacy: The Making of American Policy in Nicaragua, 1981–1987*. New York: Simon and Schuster, 1988.

Haass, Richard N. "Sanctioning Madness." *Foreign Affairs* 76, no. 6 (November–December 1997).

Haig, Alexander M., and Charles McCarry. *Inner Circles: How America Changed the World*. New York: Warner, 1992.

Halberstam, David. *The Best and the Brightest*. New York: Random House, 1992.

Hall, E. T., and M. R. Hall. *Understanding Cultural Differences: Germans, French and Americans*. Yarmouth, Maine: Intercultural Press, 1990.

Herken, Gregg. *Counsels of War*. Rev. ed. New York: Oxford University Press, 1987.

Hermann, M. G., and N. Kogan. "Effects of Negotiators' Personalities on Negotiating Behavior." In *Negotiations: Social-Psychological Perspectives*, edited by D. Druckman. Thousand Oaks, Calif.: Sage, 1977.

Herring, George C. *From Colony to Superpower: U.S. Foreign Relations since 1776*. New York: Oxford University Press, 2008.

Hersh, Seymour M. *The Price of Power: Kissinger in the Nixon White House*. New York: Summit, 1983.

Hodgson, G. *The Myth of American Exceptionalism*. New Haven: Yale University Press, 2009.

Hoff-Wilson, J. *Ideology and Economics: U.S. Relations with the Soviet Union, 1918–1933*. Columbia: University of Missouri Press, 1974.

Hofstede, Geert. *Culture's Consequences: Comparing Values, Behaviors, Institutions, and Organizations across Nations*. Thousand Oaks, Calif.: Sage, 2001.

Holbrooke, Richard. *To End a War*. New York: Random House, 1998.

Huang, X., and E. Van de Vliert. "A Multilevel Approach to Investigating Cross-National Differences in Negotiation Processes." *International Negotiation* 9, no. 3 (2004).

Hufbauer, Gary Clyde, et al. *Economic Sanctions Reconsidered*. 3rd ed. Washington, D.C.: Peterson Institute for International Economics, 2008.

Hunt, M. *Ideology and U.S. Foreign Policy*. New Haven: Yale University Press, 1987.

Immerman, R. H., ed. *John Foster Dulles and the Diplomacy of the Cold War*. Princeton: Princeton University Press, 1989.

Indyk, Martin. *Innocent Abroad: An Intimate Account of American Peacemaking in the Middle East*. New York: Simon and Schuster, 2009.

Institute for Policy Studies. *Report of the Task Force on a Unified Security Budget for the United States: FY 2009*. Washington, D.C.: Institute for Policy Studies, September 2008.

Jenks, C. W. *The Prospects of International Relations: The Law of International Institutions*. Dobb's Ferry, N.Y.: Oceana, 1964.

Johnson, Lyndon Baines. *The Vantage Point: Perspectives of the Presidency, 1963–1969*. New York: Holt, Rinehart and Winston, 1971.

Johnson, M. R., ed. *Unofficial Diplomats*. New York: Columbia University Press, 1977.

Kagan, Robert. "The September 12 Paradigm." *Foreign Affairs* 87, no. 5 (September–October 2008).

Kahn, E. J. *The China Hands*. New York: Viking, 1972.

Kazin, Michael. "The Right's Unsung Prophet." *Nation*, no. 248 (February 20, 1989).

Kennan, George F. *American Diplomacy, 1900–1950*. Chicago: University of Chicago Press, 1951.

———. *Memoirs, 1925–1950*. Boston: Little Brown, 1967.

———. *Memoirs, 1950–1963*. Boston: Little Brown, 1972.

Keohane, Robert. *Transnational Relations and World Politics*. Cambridge, Mass.: Harvard University Press, 1972.

Kissinger, Henry. *Diplomacy*. New York: Simon and Schuster, 1994.

———. "Reflections on American Diplomacy." *Foreign Affairs* (October 1956).

———. "The Three Revolutions." *Washington Post*, April 7, 2008.

————. *White House Years*. Boston: Little Brown, 1979.

————. *Years of Renewal*. Boston: Little Brown, 1999.

————. *Years of Upheaval*. Boston: Little Brown, 1982.

Kissinger, Henry, and J. A. Billington. *Does America Need a Foreign Policy?* New York: Simon and Schuster, 2002.

Kimball, Warren. *Forged in War: Roosevelt, Churchill, and the Second World War*. Chicago: Ivan Dee, 1997.

————. *The Juggler: Franklin Roosevelt as Wartime Statesman*. Princeton: Princeton University Press, 1991.

Kluckhohn, Clyde. "The Study of Culture." In *The Policy Sciences*. Edited by D. Lerner and H. D. Lasswell. Stanford: Stanford University Press, 1951.

Knock, Thomas. *To End All Wars: Woodrow Wilson and the Quest for a New World Order*. New York: Oxford University Press, 1992.

Koh, Tommy. "The United States and Southeast Asia." In *America's Role in Asia: Asian and American Views, 2008*. San Francisco: Asia Foundation, 2008.

Kolko, Gabriel. *The Politics of War: The World and United States Foreign Policy*. Rev. ed. New York: Pantheon, 1990.

Kopp, Harry W. *Commercial Diplomacy and the National Interest*. Washington, D.C.: American Academy of Diplomacy; New York: Business Council for International Understanding, 2004.

Kopp, Harry W., and Charles A. Gillespie. *Career Diplomacy: Life and Work in the U.S. Foreign Service*. Washington, D.C.: Georgetown University Press, 2008.

Kremenyuk, Victor, ed. *International Negotiation: Analysis, Approaches, Issues*. 2nd ed. San Francisco: Jossey-Bass, 2002.

Kurtzer, Daniel C., and Scott B. Lasensky. *Negotiating Arab-Israeli Peace: American Leadership in the Middle East*. Washington, D.C.: United States Institute of Peace Press, 2008.

Kux, Dennis, ed. *India-Pakistan Negotiations: Is Past Still Prologue?* Washington, D.C.: United States Institute of Peace Press, 2006.

Lang, Winfried. "A Professional's View." In *Culture and Negotiation*. Edited by Guy Oliver Faure and Jeffrey Z. Rubin. Thousand Oaks, Calif.: Sage, 1993.

Langholtz, Harvey J., and Lawrence S. Eagleburger. *Psychology and Peacekeeping*. Praeger, 1989.

Layne, Christopher. *The Peace of Illusions: American Grand Strategy from 1940 to the Present*. Ithaca: Cornell University Press, 2006.

LeBaron, Michelle. "Culture-Based Negotiation Styles." Beyond Intractability Knowledge Base Project. Edited by Guy Burgess and Heidi Burgess. Conflict Research Consortium, University of Colorado, Boulder, July 2003. http://www.beyondintractability.org/essay/culture_negotiation/?nid=1187.

Leffler, Melvyn P. *For the Soul of Mankind: The United States, the Soviet Union, and the Cold War*. New York: Hill and Wang, 2007.

Li, Chien-pin. "Trade Negotiations between the United States and Taiwan." *Asian Survey* 34, no. 8 (August 1994).

Limbert, John. *Negotiating with Iran: Wrestling with the Ghosts of History.* Washington, D.C.: United States Institute of Peace Press, 2009.

Lindsay, James M. "Congress and Foreign Policy: Why the Hill Matters." *Political Science Quarterly* 107, no. 4 (Winter 1992–93).

Linke, D. J. "The Life and Times of George F. Kennan, 1904–2005: A Centennial Retrospective." *Princeton University Library Chronicle* 66, no. 2 (2005).

Lipset, Seymour Martin. *American Exceptionalism: A Double-Edged Sword.* New York: W. W. Norton, 1996.

Liu, Henry C. K. "US Unilateralism: Nonproliferation and Unilateral Proliferation." *Global Research*, August 29, 2006. http://www.globalresearch.ca/index.php?context=viewArticle&code=LIU20060701&articleId=3089.

Madsen, D. L. *American Exceptionalism.* Edinburgh: Edinburgh University Press, 1998.

Mandelbaum, Michael. *The Case for Goliath: How America Acts as the World's Government in the Twenty-first Century.* New York: Public Affairs, 2005.

———. *The Fate of Nations: The Search for National Security in the Nineteenth and Twentieth Centuries.* Cambridge: Cambridge University Press, 1988.

Mandelbaum, Michael, and Strobe Talbott. *Reagan and Gorbachev.* New York: Vintage, 1987.

Mandell, Brian. "The Limits of Mediation: Lessons from the Syrian-Israeli Experience, 1974–1994." In *Resolving International Conflicts.* Edited by Jacob Bercovitch. Boulder, Colo.: Lynne Reinner, 1995.

Mann, James. *The Rebellion of Ronald Reagan: A History of the End of the Cold War.* New York: Viking Penguin, 2009.

McCormick, Thomas J. *America's Half-Century: United States Foreign Policy in the Cold War.* Baltimore: Johns Hopkins University Press, 1989.

McNeill, John H. "U.S.-USSR Nuclear Arms Negotiations: The Process and the Lawyer." *American Journal of International Law* 79, no. 1 (January 1985).

Mead, Walter Russell. *Special Providence: American Foreign Policy and How It Changed the World.* New York: Knopf, 2001.

Mearsheimer, John. *The Tragedy of Great Power Politics.* New York: W. W. Norton, 2001.

Mecham, J. L. *The United States and Inter-American Security, 1889–1960.* Austin: University of Texas Press, 1961.

Mee, Charles L., Jr. *The Marshall Plan: The Launching of the Pax Americana.* New York: Simon and Schuster, 1984.

Metcalf, Lynn E., et al. "Cultural Influences in Negotiations." *International Journal of Cross Cultural Management* 7, no. 2 (2007).

Michishita, N. "Coercing to Reconcile: North Korea's Reponse to US 'Hegemony.'" *Journal of Strategic Studies* 29, no. 6 (2006).

Miller, Aaron David. *The Much Too Promised Land: America's Elusive Search for Arab-Israeli Peace.* New York: Bantam, 2008.

Monaghan, A. "'Calming Critical': Evolving Russian Views of US Hegemony." *Journal of Strategic Studies* 29, no. 6 (2006).

Morgan, William, and Charles Stuart Kennedy, eds. *American Diplomats: The Foreign Service at Work.* Lincoln, Neb.: iUniverse, 2004.

Morgenthau, Hans. *Politics among Nations.* New York: Knopf, 1948.

Newhouse, John. "Diplomacy, Inc." *Foreign Affairs* 88, no. 3 (May–June 2009).

Newsom, David D. *Diplomacy and the American Democracy.* Bloomington: Indiana University Press, 1988.

———. *The Public Dimension of Foreign Policy.* Bloomington: Indiana University Press, 1996.

Nicholson, Harold. *Diplomacy.* New York: Harcourt Brace, 1969.

Nincic, Miroslav. *Renegade Regimes: Confronting Deviant Behavior in World Politics.* New York: Columbia University Press, 2006.

Nixon, Richard. *The Memoirs of Richard Nixon.* New York: Grosset and Dunlap, 1978.

Nye, Joseph. "Public Diplomacy in the 21st Century." Excerpt from Nye's *Soft Power: The Means to Success in World Politics. The Globalist,* May 9, 2000. http://www.theglobalist.com/StoryId.aspx?StoryId=3885.

———. *Soft Power: The Means to Success in World Politics.* New York: Public Affairs, 2004.

Perkins, Dexter. "The Department of State and American Public Opinion." In *The Diplomats: 1919–1939.* Vol. 1: *The Twenties.* Edited by Gordon A. Craig and Felix Gilbert. New York: Atheneum, 1963.

Powell, Colin L., and Joseph E. Persico. *My American Journey.* New York: Random House, 1996.

Pruitt, Dean G. *Negotiation Behavior.* New York: Academic, 1981.

Quandt, William B. *Camp David: Peacemaking and Politics.* Washington, D.C.: Brookings Institution Press, 1986.

Rabie, M. *U.S.-PLO Dialogue: Secret Diplomacy and Conflict Resolution.* Gainesville: University Press of Florida, 1995.

Reiselbach, Leroy N. *The Roots of Isolationism: Congressional Voting and Presidential Leadership in Foreign Policy.* Indianapolis: Bobbs-Merrill, 1966.

Rice, Condoleezza. "Remarks at Town Hall Meeting." Transcript released by U.S. State Department, Dean Acheson Auditorium, Washington, D.C., January 30, 2001. http://merln.ndu.edu/archivepdf/nss/state/41414.pdf.

Ross, Christopher. "Public Diplomacy Comes of Age." *Washington Quarterly* 25, no. 2 (Spring 2002).

Ross, Dennis. *The Missing Peace: The Inside Story of the Fight for Middle East Peace*. New York: Farrar, Straus, and Giroux, 2004.

————. *Statecraft: And How to Restore America's Standing in the World*. New York: Farrar, Straus, and Giroux, 2007.

Rothkopf, David. *Running the World: The Inside Story of the National Security Council and the Architects of American Power*. New York: Public Affairs, 2005.

Rubin, B. M. *Paved with Good Intentions: The American Experience in Iran*. Harmondsworth, England: Penguin, 1980.

Rubin, J. P. "Stumbling Into War." *Foreign Affairs* 82, no. 5 (2003).

Saccone, Richard. "A Substantive Grounded Theory of Cross-Cultural Negotiation between North Korea and the United States." Ph.D diss., University of Pittsburgh, 2002.

Salacuse, Jeswald W. "Implications for Practitioners." In *Culture and Negotiation*. Edited by Guy Oliver Faure and Jeffrey Z. Rubin. Thousand Oaks, Calif.: Sage, 1993.

Schaller, M. *The United States and China in the Twentieth Century*. 2nd ed. New York: Oxford University Press, 1990.

Schechter, Jerrold L. *Russian Negotiating Behavior: Continuity and Transition*. Washington, D.C.: United States Institute of Peace Press, 1994.

Schechter, Jerrold L., and Leona Schecter. *Sacred Secrets: How Soviet Intelligence Operations Changed American History*. Washington, D.C.: Brassey's, 2002.

Schlesinger, Arthur M., Jr. *The Cycles of American History*. New York: Houghton Mifflin, 1999.

Schulzinger, Robert D. *American Diplomacy in the Twentieth Century*. 3rd ed. New York: Oxford University Press, 1994.

Senate Committee on Foreign Relations. *Implementing Smart Power: Setting an Agenda for National Security Policy*, April 24, 2008.

Shultz, George P. "Sustaining Our Resolve." *Policy Review* 137 (August–September 2006).

————. *Turmoil and Triumph*. New York: Scribner, 1993.

Sigal, Leon. *Disarming Strangers: Nuclear Diplomacy with North Korea*. Princeton: Princeton University Press, 1998.

Simon, William E., and John M. Caher. *A Time for Reflection: An Autobiography*. Washington, D.C.: Regnery, 2004.

Slavin, Barbara. *Bitter Friends, Bosom Enemies: Iran, the U.S., and the Twisted Path to Confrontation*. New York: St. Martin's, 2007.

Smith, G. *Morality, Reason, and Power: American Diplomacy in the Carter Years*. New York: Hill and Wang, 1986.

Smith, Gaddis. *American Diplomacy during the Second World War, 1941–1945*. 2nd ed. New York: Knopf, 1985.

Smyser, W. R. *How Germans Negotiate: Logical Goals, Practical Solutions.* Washington, D.C.: United States Institute of Peace Press, 1998.

———. *Kennedy and the Berlin Wall.* Lanham, Md.: Rowman and Littlefield, 2009.

Snow, N., and P. M. Taylor. "The Revival of the Propaganda State: US Propaganda at Home and Abroad since 9/11." *International Communication Gazette* 68, nos. 5–6 (2006).

Snyder, Scott. *Negotiating on the Edge: North Korean Negotiating Behavior.* Washington, D.C.: United States Institute of Peace Press, 1999.

Solomon, Richard H. *Chinese Negotiating Behavior: Pursuing Interests through "Old Friends."* Santa Monica, Calif.: RAND, 1995; rev. ed., Washington, D.C.: United States Institute of Peace Press, 1999.

Sorenson, Theodore. "The President and the Secretary of State." *Foreign Affairs* 66, no. 2 (Winter 1987–88).

Spanos, W. J. *American Exceptionalism in the Age of Globalization: The Specter of Vietnam.* Albany: State University of New York Press, 2008.

Stearns, Monteagle. *Talking to Strangers: Improving American Diplomacy at Home and Abroad.* Princeton: Princeton University Press, 1996.

Strobel, Warren P. *Late-Breaking Foreign Policy: The News Media's Influence on Peace Operations.* Washington, D.C.: United States Institute of Peace Press, 1997.

Stueck, W. W. *The Road to Confrontation: American Policy toward China and Korea, 1947–1950.* Chapel Hill: University of North Carolina Press, 1981.

Swisher, Claton E. *The Truth about Camp David: The Untold Story about the Collapse of the Middle East Peace Process.* New York: Nation Books, 2004.

Talbott, Strobe. *Deadly Gambits: The Reagan Administration and the Stalemate in Nuclear Arms Control.* New York: Knopf, 1984; distributed by Random House.

———. *Endgame: The Inside Story of SALT II.* New York: Harper and Row, 1979.

———. *Engaging India: Diplomacy, Democracy, and the Bomb.* Rev. ed. Washington, D.C.; Brookings Institution Press, 2004.

———. "Globalization and Diplomacy: A Practitioner's Perspective." *Foreign Policy* 108 (Fall 1997).

———. *The Russia Hand: A Memoir of Presidential Diplomacy.* New York: Random House, 2002.

Task Force on the United Nations. *American Interests and UN Reform: Report of the Task Force on the United Nations.* Washington, D.C.: United States Institute of Peace Press, 2005.

Taulbee, J. L. "NGO Mediation: The Carter Center." *International Peacekeeping* 10, no. 1 (2003).

Toole, Daniel T. "Humanitarian Negotiation: Observations from Recent Experience." Harvard Program on Humanitarian Policy and Conflict Research, Harvard University, February 21, 2001.

Toros, Harmonie. "'We Don't Negotiate with Terrorists!': Legitimacy and Complexity in Terrorist Conflicts." *Security Dialog* 39, no. 4 (July 2004).

Trask, David. *A Short History of the U.S. Department of State, 1781–1981.* Washington, D.C.: Government Printing Office, 1981.

Voorhees, James. *Dialogue Sustained: The Multilevel Peace Process and the Dartmouth Conference.* Washington, D.C: United States Institute of Peace Press; Dayton, Ohio: Charles F. Kettering Foundation, 2002.

Waltz, N. "Globalization and American Power." *National Interest* (Spring 2000).

Wanis-St. John, Anthony. "Back-Channel Negotiation: International Bargaining in the Shadows." *Negotiation Journal* 22, no. 2 (April 2006).

Wank, S., ed. *Doves and Diplomats: Foreign Offices and Peace Movements in Europe and America in the Twentieth Century.* Westport, Conn.: Greenwood, 1978.

Whitehead, John C. *A Life in Leadership: From D-Day to Ground Zero.* New York: Basic; Washington, D.C.: New America, 2005.

Wiseman, Geoffrey. "Pax Americana: Bumping into Diplomatic Culture." *International Studies Perspectives* 6 (2005).

Wisner, Frank, et al. *New Priorities in South Asia.* New York: Council on Foreign Relations, 2003.

Witkowsky, Anne, project director; George L. Argyros, Marc Grossman, Feliz G. Rohatyn, project cochairs. *The Embassy of the Future.* Washington, D.C.: Center for Strategic and International Studies, 2007.

Wittes, Tamara Cofman, ed. *How Palestinians and Israelis Negotiate: A Cross-Cultural Analysis of the Oslo Peace Process.* Washington, D.C.: United States Institute of Peace Press, 2005.

Zakaria, F. "The Wrong American Exceptionalism." *Newsweek*, October 22, 2007.

Zartman, I. William. "A Skeptic's View." In *Culture and Negotiation.* Edited by Guy Oliver Faure and Jeffrey Z. Rubin. Thousand Oaks, Calif.: Sage, 1993.

Zeng, K. *Trade Threats, Trade Wars: Bargaining, Retaliation, and American Coercive Diplomacy.* Ann Arbor: University of Michigan Press, 2004.

Index

United States Institute of Peace Press

Since its inception, the United States Institute of Peace Press has published over 150 books on the prevention, management, and peaceful resolution of international conflicts—among them such venerable titles as Raymond Cohen's *Negotiating Across Cultures*; *Herding Cats* and *Leashing the Dogs of War* by Chester A. Crocker, Fen Osler Hampson, and Pamela Aall; and I. William Zartman's *Peacemaking and International Conflict*. All our books arise from research and fieldwork sponsored by the Institute's many programs. In keeping with the best traditions of scholarly publishing, each volume undergoes both thorough internal review and blind peer review by external subject experts to ensure that the research, scholarship, and conclusions are balanced, relevant, and sound. As the Institute prepares to move to its new headquarters on the National Mall in Washington, D.C., the Press is committed to extending the reach of the Institute's work by continuing to publish significant and sustainable works for practitioners, scholars, diplomats, and students.

Valerie Norville
Director

About the
United States Institute of Peace

The United States Institute of Peace is an independent, nonpartisan institution established and funded by Congress. The Institute provides analysis, training, and tools to help prevent, manage, and end violent international conflicts, promote stability, and professionalize the field of peacebuilding.

Chairman of the Board: J. Robinson West
Vice Chairman: George E. Moose
President: Richard H. Solomon
Executive Vice President: Tara Sonenshine
Chief Financial Officer: Michael Graham